Long

ISLAND

AN ENVIRONMENT FOR SUCCESS

PHOTO BY ROB AMATO, BRUCE BENNETT STUDIOS.
COVER PHOTO BY ROB AMATO, BRUCE BENNETT STUDIOS.

Produced in cooperation with the Long Island Association.

LIBRARY OF CONGRESS CATALOGING-IN-PUBLICATION DATA

Barohn, Ellen Sterling, 1944-
    Long Island: an environment for success / by Ellen Sterling Barohn;
corporate profiles by Doris Meadows; featuring the photography of
Bruce Bennett Studios. - 1st ed.
    p. cm.
    "Produced in cooperation with the Long Island Association."
    ISBN 1-58192-035-0
    1. Long Island (N.Y.)-Civilization. 2. Long Island (N.Y.)-Pictorial works.
3. Long Island (N.Y.)-Economic conditions. 4. Business enterprises-New York (State)-Long
Island. I. Title.
    F127.L8 B24 2002
    974.7'21-dc21   2001001800

Long
ISLAND

AN ENVIRONMENT FOR SUCCESS

By Ellen Sterling Barohn
Corporate Profiles by Doris Meadows
Featuring the Photography of Bruce Bennett Studios

The Long Island Association and Community Communications, Inc., would like to express our gratitude to the following companies for their leadership in the development of this book.

BAE SYSTEMS

HSBC

KEYSPAN

Long
ISLAND
AN ENVIRONMENT FOR SUCCESS

By Ellen Sterling Barohn
Corporate Profiles by Doris Meadows and
Michele Marrinan
Featuring the photography of
Bruce Bennett Studios

Produced in cooperation with
the Long Island Association

Staff for *Long Island: An Environment for Success*

Project Director	Linda Frank
Acquisitions	Henry S. Beers
Editor in Chief	Wendi L. Lewis
Managing Editors	Wendi L. Lewis and Kurt Niland
Profile Editor	Mary Catherine Richardson
Design Director	Scott Phillips
Designer	Matt Johnson
Photo Editors	Wendi L. Lewis, Kurt Niland, and Matt Johnson
Production Manager	Jarrod Stiff
Editorial Assistants	Eleanor Planer and Krewe Maynard
Proofreading	Heather Ann Edwards
National Sales Manager	Bob Sadoski
Sales Assistant	Sandra Akers
Accounting Services	Stephanie Perez
Pre-Press Production	DCR Graphics

CCI

Community Communications, Inc.
Montgomery, Alabama

Chief Executive Officer	David M. Williamson
President	Ronald P. Beers
Chief Operating Officer	W. David Brown

TABLE OF CONTENTS

Chapter One

THE TIME BEFORE 1775, PAGE 18

Before animals or people, there were the glaciers, masses of ice that shaped today's rich environment. Native Americans welcomed the Europeans who, in turn, brought their own sensibilities to Long Island, along with their innovations, their politics, and their religion. By the late eighteenth century, the Dutch had left and the English— divided into Patriots and Loyalists—were poised for revolution.

Chapter Two

1775 TO 1800, PAGE 74

Long Island was still comprised of today's Brooklyn, Queens, and Suffolk Counties. The people at the western end tended to be Tories, favoring the crown. The east enders, with their close ties to New England, favored independence. Though Long Island saw little action aside from the Battle of Brooklyn, the British did occupy several communities and an active Long Island spy ring helped General Washington immensely. The end of the war left the Long Islanders who were still here to clean up from the occupation and to rebuild their lives.

Chapter Three

1800 TO 1876, PAGE 86

With the Revolution ended, there was peace and, even, prosperity. A hard-working farmer could keep his family comfortable and well fed. A whaling industry began to grow on Long Island in Sag Harbor, Greenport, and Cold Spring Harbor. The War of 1812, fought mostly on the water by privateers, briefly interrupted the flow of life, but Long Island continued to grow. Roads were built, the railroad began to operate, and great ships were built in local yards. But, as part of the larger nation, Long Island was deeply touched by the Civil War and by the slavery issue. War's end brought boom times. Better transport and communications meant less isolation. Long Island was becoming part of a larger world.

PHOTO BY ROB AMATO,
BRUCE BENNETT STUDIOS.

Chapter Four

1876 TO 1918, PAGE 118

The nation celebrated its centennial in a new machine age in which wonders abounded. Long Islanders began expanding their horizons, raising ducks imported from China, building hotels and resorts, and, early in the twentieth century, giving the nation a president. The geography of Long Island was changing, too. Queens County was divided in two, with the eastern part becoming the new Nassau County. There were automobiles, electric lights, trolleys, and airplanes. It was a glorious time to be an American and an especially glorious time to be a Long Islander.

Chapter Five

1918 TO 1945, PAGE 196

It was an era of stark contrast. After World War I, the Jazz Age was in full swing, aviation was taking off in earnest, and Long Island was the epicenter of all the activity. The Gold Coast and the Hempstead Plains hosted the wealthy, the adventurous, and, even, the Prince of Wales. But the good times ended with the 1929 Stock Market crash. Out of the ashes rose much of modern Long Island, including the Grumman Corporation and the public works projects of Robert Moses. Long Island was not immune to darker forces—the Ku Klux Klan and the American Nazi Party— whose hatred was tearing apart civilization. World War II defense plants brought prosperity in the form of a thriving industry that would be the basis of the regional economy for years to follow.

Chapter Six

1945 TO 1959, PAGE 248

The post-war years began the real boom times on Long Island. When the modern suburb was born in Levittown, life on Long Island and in America changed forever. The population of Nassau and Suffolk Counties began to swell, bringing the need for a range of services. All of a sudden, Long Island had new school districts, shopping malls, and new politics. But, still, there was a feeling that Long Island was a bedroom for Manhattan.

Chapter Seven

1959 TO 1976, PAGE 290

In 1960, life couldn't be better. A new president promised to land a man on the moon by the end of the decade, and Grumman Corporation would play a key role in that undertaking and in the local economy. Large national corporations were beginning to see Long Island as an excellent home and the business community began to grow rapidly, with significant technology being developed in some of those businesses. The war in Vietnam and concern about the environment were deeply felt on the Island. For the first time, however, the population of Nassau County was declining and more young people than ever were leaving to live elsewhere.

Chapter Eight

1976 TO 1989, PAGE 348

It was a changing world; a changing Long Island. The baby boomers were growing up and their parents' values no longer seemed to sustain them. The plan to build a nuclear power plant in Shoreham brought protests at first. Then, along with Hurricane Gloria, Shoreham brought down the Long Island Lighting Company. Baby Jane Doe made national headlines, as did the Islip Garbage Barge. Long Island's aerospace industry began to die. At the same time, significant achievements in new technology were just over the horizon and Long Islanders were beginning to be a real community, very distinct from its neighbor to the west. Arts began to flourish and portents of the future could be seen in EAB Plaza and the Long Island High Technology Incubator.

Chapter Nine

1989 AND BEYOND, PAGE 384

The marriage of entrepreneurship and technology led to an economic renaissance on Long Island. A thriving research engine promises more of the same to come. Perhaps more significant is the hard evidence that Long Islanders—diverse in background, education, and a host of other qualities—are a community that responds as one when tragedy strikes. Statisticians and prognosticators see a prosperous future for the region, and some Long Island leaders tell us what they believe the future holds.

PHOTO BY LISA MEYER,
BRUCE BENNETT STUDIOS.

PREFACE

While often a mirror of national history, Long Island's history is uniquely our own.

Writing this book has taken me on a wonderful journey through that history. Along the way, I learned about the events and about the real people we honor today with their names on buildings and street signs.

I learned that in every generation of Long Islanders there were people whose dreams shaped the destiny of this place and of its people. Some—like Robert Moses and Leroy Grumman—we know a great deal about. Others—most notably my newest hero, Hal B. Fullerton—are less known, but had a tremendous impact on Long Island.

I am grateful I had the opportunity to tell the story and I want to thank the people who helped me do so. In particular I am indebted to Barbara Kelly of the Long Island Studies Institute and Wally Broege of the Suffolk County Historical Society, as well as Wendi Lewis of Community Communications and Gary Wojtas of the Long Island Association.

I hope you will enjoy visiting the past and looking into the future with this book. We live in an amazing place, in an amazing time. We are fortunate, indeed, to be Long Islanders.

Ellen Barohn
Author

FOREWORD

Long Island is a special place, unique in its ambiance, rich in its history, and rooted in tradition. From the quaint village shops sprinkled along local Main Streets, to the hi-tech research and medical centers and world-class educational institutions, Long Island has created a distinctive blending of the past with the future.

Whether it was building the lunar module that landed men on the moon or legendary fighter planes during World War II, Islanders have already left their mark on history. With exciting new projects like the Millennium Centers for Convergent Technologies on the horizon, that involvement is destined to continue.

The region, a familiar setting for many authors, artists, and filmmakers, also has lent itself and its resources to many renowned projects in the arts. Walt Whitman, Jackson Pollack, Billy Joel, and too many others to name have found inspiration from the people and places that make up Long Island. Still today, we continue to prosper and benefit from all that Long Island has to offer; we continue to make history. By building on its past successes, Long Islanders continue to be at the forefront of the new millennium.

In addition to its many resources, Long Island always will have its beauty. Completely surrounded by water, it is perhaps one of the most picturesque places to visit in the United States. Its renowned vineyards and beaches, historical museums, parks, and amusement centers draw millions each year. We have tried to offer you a small glimpse into life on Long Island in *Long Island: An Environment for Success* and hope you enjoy the Long Island experience as much as we do.

Matthew T. Crosson
President
Long Island Association

THE TIME BEFORE 1775

If environment is destiny, then, from the beginning, the people inhabiting Long Island have been destined for success.

It was twenty-one thousand years ago that the last Wisconsin glacier of the Pleistocene period covered the 120-mile stretch of land that became Long Island. Three thousand years later, as the glacier began to melt and withdraw from south to north, it left behind tundra, a vast expanse of frozen soil. Over the next six thousand years the temperature warmed and life began.

The glacier left in its wake a climate unique to the northeast coast with softer, steadier breezes that endow the Island with an extremely long growing season. Glaciers also left five rivers, a multitude of brooks, deep-water harbors, open prairies, pine barrens, groves of strong trees, and rocky north shore beaches, balanced on the south shore by stretches of pristine sand dunes.

Historians put the arrival of the first people at six thousand years ago. By the time Europeans began to arrive, there were thirteen "tribes" of the woodland Algonquian nation spread across the island from Brooklyn to Montauk. Though more alike than not, each group had its own *sachem*, the leader who served as judge when required and presided at tribal councils. Because they were relatively isolated from any but the others who lived on Long Island, the early Native Americans shared language, customs, and values.

From the beginning, this was a fertile land. The tribes grew simple crops, fished, and whaled. By the time the European settlers arrived, there were sixty-five hundred Native Americans on Long Island.

They dressed in loose skins, with aprons worn both front and rear. In cold weather they added skin or hemp robes. Men and women wore moccasins, leggings, and belts. With no pockets, pouches suspended by thongs from around their necks served to transport small valuables. Wampum, their medium of exchange, was worn as necklaces, was stitched to garments, or made into bracelets and earrings.

Wampum was made of clam and periwinkle shells polished into white and blue beads, the blue being the most valuable. Long Island wampum—especially that made by south shore tribes—was considered to be of the best quality. In fact, it was so desirable that one of the Dutch names for Long Island was *seawanhackey* or, "place of shell beads." Ultimately, wampum was the victim of inflation, as tools brought by the Europeans led to overproduction of the beads and they lost their value altogether.

The first recorded sighting of Long Island by a European is in dispute. The account alleges that, in 1524, Giovanni da Verrazano, a Spaniard sailing under the French flag for King Francis I, sailed into New York Harbor and, eventually, for a distance along the south shore of Long Island. But mystery surrounds the Verrazano tale. We do know for sure that more than eighty years would pass after Verrazano sailed before Henry Hudson on his ship the *Half Moon*, sailed into New York harbor on behalf of the Dutch in 1609.

Hudson, who happened on North America during his search for a passage to the Orient, was followed by Adrian Block, an entrepreneurial Dutch attorney who

THE GLACIER THAT ONCE COVERED LONG ISLAND CARVED OUT A LANDSCAPE FEATURING FIVE RIVERS, A MULTITUDE OF BROOKS, DEEP-WATER HARBORS, OPEN PRAIRIES, PINE BARRENS, GROVES OF STRONG TREES, AND ROCKY NORTH SHORE BEACHES. PHOTO BY J. GIAMUNDO, BRUCE BENNETT STUDIOS.

believed a lot of money was to be made by trapping the abundant New World wildlife and selling the fur back home.

Block succeeded in trapping enough pelts to fill his ship. With this precious cargo in the hold, Block was anchored off what is today the tip of Manhattan Island when his ship, the *Tiger*, was destroyed by fire. Stranded over the winter, Block and his crew managed to build another ship, christened the *Restless*, and in springtime sailed it eastward through the Sound, around Montauk Point and westward along the south shore. Block noted that the landmass east of where the *Tiger* had burned was an island, rather than an extension of the mainland.

He drew a map of his journey and called that landmass "T Lange Eilandt." The name remains today in its English translation.

European settlement followed quickly. In 1621, the Dutch West India Company was chartered by the government of Holland to oversee settlement of the New World for purposes of commerce. One of those settlements, named New Netherland in honor of the mother country, was at the southern tip of Manhattan Island where Block had originally anchored. The principal city of the settlement was named New Amsterdam.

Other Dutch homesteaded on the southwestern tip of Long Island in what is today Brooklyn. There they founded Vlackte-Bosch (Flatbush), Boswijck (Bushwick), Nieuw Amersfoord (Flatlands), Bruecklen (Brooklyn), and Nieuw Utrecht.

As the Dutch settlers pushed east, English who were dissatisfied with the Puritan colonies came south from

PHOTO BY BRIAN WINKLER,
BRUCE BENNETT STUDIOS.

THE WATERS SURROUNDING LONG ISLAND WERE FIRST AN AVENUE FOR EARNING A LIVELIHOOD THROUGH FISHING, WHALING, AND SHIPBUILDING; TODAY THESE WATERS ALSO ARE A SOURCE OF PLEASURE FOR SAILORS AND SPORTSMEN. PHOTO BY J. GIAMUNDO, BRUCE BENNETT STUDIOS.

Connecticut and Massachusetts. The Towns of Southold and Southampton were chartered in 1640; East Hampton in 1648. English settlements were quickly established across Long Island. Huntington (1653), Setauket (1655), Northport (1656), Stony Brook (1660), Smithtown (1665), and Wading River (1670) were stretched along the north shore. The English also settled the southern part of Huntington—which is today Babylon Township—during the late 1650s.

The line between Dutch and English settlements was drawn at Oyster Bay. In 1650, a formal boundary line—somewhat to the west of today's Nassau-Suffolk border—was established to separate the New Amsterdam and New England claims through the Treaty of Hartford, although border disputes continued and the British government never officially recognized the agreement.

Although the story is told today of the English settlers seeking religious tolerance in a New World, and of the Dutch as being tolerant, each settlement had problems rooted in fear and ignorance.

In East Hampton the death of Elizabeth Gardiner Howell, daughter of Lion Gardiner, was blamed on one Goodwife Elizabeth Garlick. A deathbed accusation caused Goody Garlick—a shrewish woman given freely to criticism of others—to be indicted for witchcraft and sent to Hartford for trial in May 1657.

She was acquitted and returned to East Hampton, a feared woman. It was Lion Gardiner who finally gave her and her husband a cottage away from the more populous town on Gardiner's Island. They lived into their 90s.

Long Island's other witchcraft trial arose from the 1664 death of George Wood of Setauket and, shortly after, the death of his baby son. Mary and Ralph Hall, the Woods' neighbors, were accused of witchcraft in these deaths. They were acquitted after a 1665 trial that was the only witchcraft trial ever in New York State. They returned briefly to Setauket, sold everything they owned, and moved to the settlement in the west.

Meanwhile, in New Amsterdam, Governor Peter Stuyvesant waged battle with John Bowne, a wealthy Quaker settler in Flushing. The Quaker settlers who had come in search of religious freedom were treated abominably wherever they went. Stuyvesant made it

LONG ISLAND BOASTS A VARIETY OF LANDSCAPES, FROM WOODLAND PATHS AND TREE-LINED STREETS TO MARSHY FIELDS AND SANDY BEACHES. PHOTOS BY R. AMATO (TOP), AND DEBBIE ROSS (BOTTOM), BRUCE BENNETT STUDIOS.

against the law to give a Quaker shelter. In other places they were branded and mutilated in other ways. Finally, in 1657, the Flushing Quaker settlement explained their views in a document called the "Flushing Remonstrance."

> "We desire...not to judge lest we be judged,
> neither to condemn lest we be condemned,
> but rather let every man stand and fall by
> his own Master."

Stuyvesant likely would have continued the persecution, but the Dutch West India Company was more practical. They needed to enrich their New Netherlands settlement by attracting immigrants. Ill-treated immigrants did not invite their friends and families to join them. Thus, Stuyvesant was ordered to treat people of all religions well and the early Dutch settlers became known in popular history as a tolerant group.

Through all this, the Native Americans had been inexorably pushed aside, their land and hunting rights sold to the Europeans. The Dutch and English gave them coats, blankets, tools, trinkets, and rum in payment for the land. In 1653, the Massapequa tribe was eliminated in a battle with the English that was begun in retaliation of the defeat of a New Jersey tribe by the Dutch. Although that was the only major battle between settlers and Native Americans, each group had little or no understanding of the other.

The English wanted to encourage people to pull up stakes and move to the New World. Toward this end, they engaged Daniel Denton, who served first as Town Clerk of Hempstead and, later, Jamaica, to write *A Brief Description of New-York: Formerly Called New-Netherlands* in 1670, the first description of Long Island written in English.

To reassure the people back home that the Native Americans should not be a source of concern, Denton wrote, "It hath been generally observed, that where the English come to settle, a Divine Hand makes way for them; by removing or cutting off the Indians, either by Wars one with the other, or by some raging mortal Disease."

In 1660, following the Restoration, England's King Charles II made plans to take over the Dutch New Netherland, which included Long Island, and give it to his brother, James, the Duke of York. Thus, in 1664, a British expeditionary force of five hundred soldiers in four warships landed in New Amsterdam. The force was headed by Colonel Richard Nicolls, later the first English governor of New York, who successfully demanded the Dutch turn over control of their colony to the English.

The city was swiftly renamed New York, in honor of the Duke, while the name of the entire colony—including Long Island—was changed to Yorkshire Province, after the Duke's seat, Yorkshire, England. It has stayed thus with the exception of a brief time in 1673 when the Dutch again held the settlement and named it New Orange. The English ultimately prevailed when, a year later, the colony was passed back to England in exchange for the South American territory of Suriname.

GENERATIONS HAVE MADE THEIR HOMES AND RAISED THEIR FAMILIES ON LONG ISLAND. PHOTO BY ROB AMATO, BRUCE BENNETT STUDIOS.

A SURE SIGN OF FALL—A HARVEST OF HEALTHY ORANGE PUMPKINS RIPE FOR CARVING. PHOTO BY M. LEIDER, BRUCE BENNETT STUDIOS.

Geographical lines were drawn and redrawn by the English until they divided the colony into twelve shires, or counties. "Shire" is an English word derived from the Anglo-Saxon word for "division." Because shires in England were governed by counts or earls, they were informally called "counties."

Three of those counties—Kings, Queens, and Suffolk—made up Long Island. Whereas Suffolk County's boundaries remain much the same today as in the seventeenth century and Kings County is today's borough of Brooklyn, Queens County included both today's borough of Queens and today's Nassau County.

Suffolk County, named after an English maritime district, was formed in 1683 with six towns: Southold, Southampton (settled in 1640), East Hampton (1648), Huntington (1653), Brookhaven (1655), and Smithtown, then called "Smithfield," (1665).

In 1720, Islip, which had been settled in 1660, became the seventh town. Shelter Island, which had been settled in 1653, was made distinct from Southold in 1730. Residents in the western part of Southold decided to form their own town, naming it Riverhead in 1792. Eighty years later, in 1872, residents of the area called South Huntington decided to secede from Huntington and formed the Town of Babylon.

When, finally, in 1674, the Dutch left North America, they left a legacy that included the Dutch Reformed Church, the distinct Dutch colonial architecture, the myth of Santa Claus, and slavery.

After they failed to convince the Native Americans to work with them to build their empire, the Dutch

attempted to convince the East India Company to send them indentured servants. That request was denied, but the company suggested the Dutch imitate the Virginia colonists and use slaves from Africa for heavy labor.

The first slaves were brought to New Amsterdam in 1626. It is believed that the first slaves in today's Suffolk County were brought by Nathaniel Sylvester when he bought Shelter Island and moved there from Barbados in 1654. That began the local practice of importing slaves from both Africa and the Caribbean. By 1698, the 588 blacks in the county represented more than 21 percent of Suffolk's population.

There is evidence, too, that the settlers enslaved Native Americans. A property inventory from 1688 in Southampton lists "an Indian girle a slave." Other records show "Indian servants" being willed by a wealthy landowner to his sons. The black and Native American population often intermarried and, if the mother were a slave, any children would also be enslaved.

The 1730 census showed 15 percent of New York's population were slaves—a larger number than in Virginia.

By the 1790 census, blacks represented eight percent of the total New York State population. That census enumerated 56,949 people in Kings, Queens (including present day Nassau) and Suffolk Counties. Of these, 30,130 were white; 6,819 were black. Of the blacks, 1,980 were free; 4,839 were enslaved.

In 1790, more than 25 percent of New York State's black people lived on Long Island. Blacks made up one-fifth of the population in Queens County. By 1790, Suffolk was the only county in New York State in which free blacks outnumbered slaves. In Kings County, only three percent of blacks were free.

A LAYER OF WHITE SPARKLES IN THE LONG ISLAND WINTER SUNSHINE AND PROVIDES THE PERFECT SETTING FOR RECREATION SUCH AS CROSS-COUNTRY SKIING. PHOTOS BY BRUCE BENNETT (TOP) AND DEBBIE ROSS (BOTTOM), BRUCE BENNETT STUDIOS.

In 1657, the Flushing Quaker settlement explained their views in a document called the Flushing Remonstrance: "We desire...not to judge lest we be judged, neither to condemn lest we be condemned, but rather let every man stand and fall by his own Master."
Photo by Rob Amato, Bruce Bennett Studios.

Long Island's slaves were found mostly in the western communities. Slave ownership was spread among all occupations, from farmers to clergy to merchants. For awhile, ownership of slaves was a status symbol and, always, the evidence that exists tell us slaves were treated as chattel. Like any valuable property, slaves for the most part were protected and cared for. The slaves, however, did not take enslavement passively. There are records of runaways, of tool sabotage, and of other forms of resistance.

Slavery on Long Island reached its peak in the mid- to late-eighteenth century when the Quaker campaign to end slavery took hold. New York State officially outlawed slavery in 1827, although it is believed seamen in the Fire Island area kept slaves until the Civil War.

Life on Long Island was, like elsewhere in the New World, bone-crushingly difficult for most settlers. They built their communities where Native Americans had settled centuries before. Every family and every community had to be self-sufficient and every family member was expected to contribute. Life was focused on survival and all else was secondary.

Long Islanders were more fortunate than most settlers because of their environment. There was abundant wildlife—large and small game, wild fowl, fish, and shellfish. In 1700 it was reported that seven whales were found on the beach during a walk between East Hampton and Bridgehampton.

The 60,000-acre Hempstead Plains were public land, the only prairie east of the Mississippi River. It was here that herds of sheep, cattle, and hogs were carefully tended to provide wool, leather, and meat. Grains, vegetables, and orchards were also cultivated there.

At first, the demand for labor led to earlier marriage and more children until, in the mid-eighteenth century, land subdivision among families was causing land shortages. Thus, like their European forbears, the settlers once again married later and had fewer children.

Mills were built near water to process grain and lumber. On the East End, windmills were built to take advantage of the power harnessed by the ocean breezes to grind grain.

In addition, craftspeople and artisans opened for business. Blacksmiths, furniture makers, tavern keepers, and shoemakers were plentiful on Long Island by the eighteenth century. Food and products were exported across the Long Island Sound to Connecticut, Massachusetts, and Rhode Island. Natural harbors led to the rise of the shipbuilding, sailmaking, and whaling industries.

The wealthy built manor houses and operated tenant farms. Early in the 1700s, the Floyds of Mastic, the Lloyds of Horse Neck in Huntington, the Sylvesters in Shelter Island and, of course, the Gardiners on their own island, all had sizeable property and fortunes.

The wealthier people tended to retain English customs, religion, and loyalty to the monarchy, while those not as blessed by wealth or land tended to desire democracy and the religious freedom their families had left England to obtain.

But these differences did not interfere too much with life on Long Island until 1775. ■

BEFORE THE BROWNS OF WINTER, FALL LENDS BREATHTAKING COLOR TO THE LANDSCAPE AS LEAVES TURN CRIMSON AND GOLD. PHOTO BY ROB AMATO, BRUCE BENNETT STUDIOS.

(ABOVE) THE SOUTH SHORE IS MARKED BY
STRETCHES OF PRISTINE SAND DUNES. PHOTO
BY J. MCISAAC, BRUCE BENNETT STUDIOS.
(LEFT) LONG ISLAND IS ENDOWED WITH SOFT,
STEADY BREEZES AND AN EXTREMELY LONG
GROWING SEASON. PHOTO BY ROB AMATO,
BRUCE BENNETT STUDIOS.

LONG ISLAND'S 13 TRIBES

It was until recently believed that Native American place names on Long Island represented distinct tribes. Historians today, however, believe that the names traditionally used to describe separate "tribes" are perhaps most accurately reflective of place names, not of the people living there.

John A. Strong, in his book, *The Algonquian Peoples of Long Island from Earliest Times to 1700*, says that Native American communities were linked by lineage and clan membership. Borders between them were loosely drawn and there were no disparate tribes as was formerly believed.

The Algonquian language is mostly extinct today, but the lore of Native American place names and their alleged meanings live on. Below, a list compiled by former Suffolk County Historian Paul Bailey in the 1960s.

- Canarsies (meaning "at the fenced place")—Brooklyn and parts of Jamaica;
- Rockoways ("sandy land")—parts of Queens and the southern part of today's Town of Hempstead;
- Merrikokes, or Merrics ("plains country")—Baldwin to Seaford and possibly, part of the Hempstead Plains;

- Massapequas—("great waterland") Seaford to Copaigue;
- Matinecocks—("at the hilly land") north shore from Queens to the Nissequogue River in Smithtown
- Setaukets—("land at the mouth of the river") Stony Brook to Wading River
- Corchaugs—("principal place") Wading River to Orient Point
- Manhansets—("island sheltered by islands") Shelter, Ram, and Hog Islands
- Secatogues—("black, or colored, land") Islip to Patchogue
- Unkechaugs ("land beyond the hill") and Poosepatucks—Bayport to Eastport; Poosepatucks were a branch of the Unkechaugs
- Shinnecocks—("at the level land") Eastport to Bridgehampton
- Montauketts—("at the fortified place") Bridgehampton to Montauk Point and Gardiner's Island

By the time Europeans began to arrive on Long Island, there were thirteen "tribes" of the woodland Algonquian nation spread across the island from Brooklyn to Montauk. Because they were relatively isolated from any but the others who lived on Long Island, the early Native Americans shared language, customs, and values. Photos on facing page by J. McIsaac; photos this page by Bruce Bennett (top) and J. McIsaac (bottom), Bruce Bennett Studios.

LONG ISLAND WAMPUM—CLAM AND PERIWINKLE SHELLS POLISHED INTO WHITE AND BLUE BEADS—
WAS CONSIDERED TO BE OF THE BEST QUALITY. IN FACT, IT WAS SO DESIRABLE THAT ONE OF THE DUTCH
NAMES FOR LONG ISLAND WAS "SEAWANHACKEY" OR, "PLACE OF SHELL BEADS." PHOTO BY ROB AMATO,
BRUCE BENNETT STUDIOS.

HENRY HUDSON SAILED INTO NEW YORK HARBOR ON BEHALF OF THE DUTCH IN 1609. IN 1621, THE
DUTCH WEST INDIA COMPANY WAS CHARTERED BY THE GOVERNMENT OF HOLLAND TO OVERSEE SETTLEMENT
OF THE NEW WORLD FOR PURPOSES OF COMMERCE. HOPING TO ATTRACT IMMIGRANTS AND ENRICH THEIR
NEW NETHERLANDS SETTLEMENT, THE DUTCH WEST INDIA COMPANY ORDERED THAT PEOPLE OF ALL
RELIGIONS BE TREATED WELL. THUS, THE EARLY DUTCH SETTLERS BECAME KNOWN IN POPULAR HISTORY
AS A TOLERANT GROUP. PHOTO BY LISA MEYER, BRUCE BENNETT STUDIOS.

LONG ISLAND'S LONG HISTORY IS REVEALED
IN MANY OF ITS HOMES, SHOPS, AND VILLAGE
MARKERS, MANY OF WHICH HAVE ENDURED IN
ORIGINAL OR RESTORED STATES. PHOTOS BY
ROB AMATO (TOP THIS PAGE AND OPPOSITE)
DEBBIE ROSS (BOTTOM), AND SCOTT LEVY
(OPPOSITE BOTTOM) BRUCE BENNETT STUDIOS.

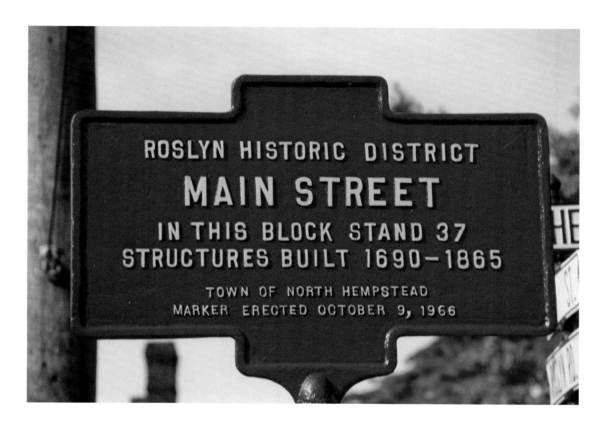

VISITORS TO AND RESIDENTS OF LONG ISLAND CAN VISIT A VARIETY OF HISTORIC SITES DATING BACK TO THE ISLAND'S EARLIEST DAYS. PRESERVATION EFFORTS HAVE ENSURED THAT THESE PLACES WILL REMAIN LIVING HISTORY LESSONS FOR GENERATIONS TO COME. PHOTO BY ROB AMATO, BRUCE BENNETT STUDIOS.

PHOTO BY ROB AMATO, BRUCE BENNETT STUDIOS.

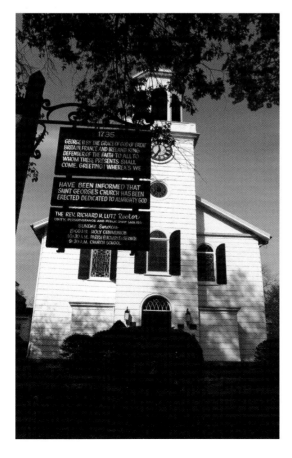

PHOTO BY DEBBIE ROSS (LEFT) AND ROB AMATO (RIGHT), BRUCE BENNETT STUDIOS.

THE GARDINER FAMILY BURYING GROUND ON GARDINER'S ISLAND. PHOTO COURTESY OF THE NASSAU COUNTY DIVISION OF MUSEUM SERVICES/LONG ISLAND STUDIES INSTITUTE/HOFSTRA UNIVERSITY.

SHAPING THE FACE OF TODAY'S LONG ISLAND

In 1635, an English engineer and builder of forts named Lion Gardiner agreed to come to the New World to lend his expertise to English hopes for expansion of their empire. Gardiner stayed for a short while in Massachusetts Bay. He traveled then to the mouth of the Connecticut River to build a defense against the Dutch and the Pequot tribe who were, according to contemporary accounts, all doing their best to keep English settlements in the area from being built.

Small skirmishes with the Pequots escalated into a major war in which the English, joined by other Native Americans, defeated the Pequots, almost eliminating the entire tribe in 1637. Shortly after the war, Wyandanch, the sachem of the Montaukett tribe of Long Island, approached Gardiner to ask that his people be permitted to trade with the English.

In exchange for the right to trade, Wyandanch transferred to Gardiner the tribute payments he had been giving to the Pequots in exchange for his people's safety. Gardiner assented and he and Wyandanch began both to trade and to develop a firm, long-lasting friendship.

In 1639, when the terms of contract for his services to the English settlement were complete, Gardiner bought a 3,500-acre island from Wyandanch. He named it the Isle of Wight, although we know it today as Gardiner's Island.

The close friendship between the Englishman and the Native American was cemented when Gardiner lent Wyandanch his negotiating expertise in 1653, to help win the freedom of Wyandanch's daughter when the Niantic tribe from Rhode Island kidnaped her.

The two remained friends until death. In 1659, Gardiner bought approximately 10 square miles of land from Wyandanch. He later sold it to Richard Smith, who founded today's Smithtown on that property. Wyandanch was also involved in selling or trading land to the English that includes parts of today's Montauk, Huntington, Hempstead and North Hempstead.

Wyandanch died in 1660. In his will he named Gardiner guardian of his son and gave Gardiner "a small tract of land." In fact, that land totaled 30,000 acres. Gardiner wrote of his own loss at his friend's death and, without any additional details, mentioned that his friend was poisoned.

Gardiner moved with his wife to East Hampton in the early 1650s, leaving his island to his son. He was buried in his red English army uniform in the Old Cemetery in East Hampton. His epitaph reads, in part, "Venerated and honoured and under many trying circumstances in peace and war, brave discrete and true."

Lion Gardiner named the 3,500-acre island he bought from Wyandanch the "Isle of Wight." Today, we know it as Gardiner's Island. Photo by Rob Amato, Bruce Bennett Studios.

GARDINER'S ISLAND, AERIAL VIEW. PHOTO BY ROB AMATO, BRUCE BENNETT STUDIOS.

THE SADDLE ROCK GRIST MILL, SHOWN CA. 1900, BUILT AROUND 1700 WAS A "TIDAL" MILL, OPERATING ONLY WITH THE EBB AND FLOW OF THE TIDE. TODAY IT LOOKS AS IT DID WHEN BUILT. PHOTO COURTESY OF THE NASSAU COUNTY DIVISION OF MUSEUM SERVICES/LONG ISLAND STUDIES INSTITUTE/HOFSTRA UNIVERSITY.

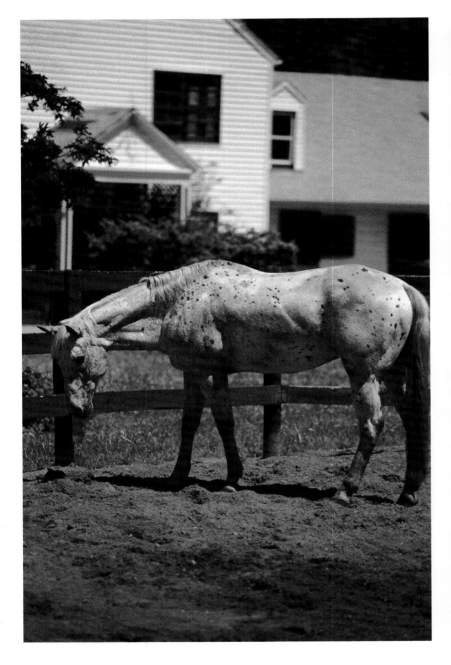

LONG ISLANDERS WERE MORE FORTUNATE THAN MOST SETTLERS BECAUSE OF THEIR ENVIRONMENT. THERE WAS ABUNDANT WILDLIFE—LARGE AND SMALL GAME, WILD FOWL, FISH, AND SHELLFISH. ON THE HEMPSTEAD PLAIN, HERDS OF SHEEP, CATTLE, AND HOGS WERE CAREFULLY TENDED TO PROVIDE WOOL, LEATHER, AND MEAT. GRAINS, VEGETABLES, AND ORCHARDS WERE CULTIVATED THERE BY FARMERS. PHOTOS BY JOE ROGATE (LEFT), GARY FOX (TOP RIGHT) AND J. GIAMUNDO (BOTTOM RIGHT), BRUCE BENNETT STUDIOS.

PHOTO BY M. LEIDER, BRUCE BENNETT STUDIOS.

PHOTOS BY GARY FOX (LEFT) AND SCOTT LEVY (RIGHT), BRUCE BENNETT STUDIOS.

TODAY, THE WATERS SURROUNDING LONG ISLAND
ARE STILL AN INTEGRAL PART OF LIFE. RESIDENTS
ENJOY FISHING FOR PLEASURE AND PROFIT, AS
WELL AS RECREATION. PHOTOS BY DEBORAH ROSS
(ABOVE) AND ROB AMATO (RIGHT),
BRUCE BENNETT STUDIOS.

(ABOVE) THE GARDINER WINDMILL STILL STANDS TODAY IN EAST HAMPTON BY THE VILLAGE POND. PHOTO BY SAMUEL H. GOTTSCHO CA. 1930. PHOTO COURTESY OF THE NASSAU COUNTY DIVISION OF MUSEUM SERVICES/LONG ISLAND STUDIES INSTITUTE/HOFSTRA UNIVERSITY. (BELOW) ON THE EAST END, WINDMILLS WERE BUILT TO TAKE ADVANTAGE OF THE POWER AVAILABLE VIA THE OCEAN BREEZES TO GRIND GRAIN. PHOTO BY ROB AMATO, BRUCE BENNETT STUDIOS.

PHOTO BY SCOTT LEVY, BRUCE BENNETT STUDIOS.

BAE SYSTEMS

BAE SYSTEMS was born in November 1999 out of the merger with British Aerospace and Marconi Electronic Systems. The Advanced Systems is headquartered in Greenlawn, New York, where the facility previously earned its renowned reputation as Hazeltine. BAE SYSTEMS offers an outstanding performance as a prime contractor in all of the main defense sectors and the civilian market. The 550 employees in Greenlawn help engineer and manufacture products that focus on communications, electronic identification, displays, and antenna design. Current products include IFF, airborne displays, stealth technology, visual guidance systems, and a tornado warning system. The company has one basic goal: to be the benchmark aerospace and defense systems company worldwide and works toward this goal by maximizing the value of its existing business and capabilities, as well as by business growth and leading the global consolidation of the aerospace and defense systems industry.

PHOTO BY F. ABADIE, BRUCE BENNETT STUDIOS.

PHOTO BY ROB AMATO, BRUCE BENNETT STUDIOS.

BRIARCLIFFE COLLEGE

On the leading edge of technology education, Briarcliffe College maintains a commitment to academic excellence, while offering a wide range of programs and degree levels to its growing student body. Briarcliffe's strong ties to the business community are exemplified by the college's establishment of an on-site high-tech incubator, which in collaboration with the Long Island Software and Technology Network (LISTnet), provides services to start-up technology-based companies on Briarcliffe's main campus.

"With a focus on professional preparation, students' educational goals at Briarcliffe are primarily career entry, career advancement, and career change," stated Briarcliffe President C. Ronald Kimberling, Ph.D. "This is consistent with our mission statement of providing specialized academic programs that integrate theory and practice, utilize advanced technologies, and incorporate liberal arts course offerings."

BROOKHAVEN NATIONAL LABORATORY

While providing scientific leadership for the nation, Brookhaven strives to be a good neighbor to Long Islanders. Sunday tours for the general public during the summer months attract thousands of visitors, and a children's science museum welcomes 25,000 students per year. Brookhaven opens its facilities to students from kindergarten to postgraduate levels. Programs range from an annual elementary school fair to summer research programs for high school and college students, and postdoctoral fellowships for students from universities around the world. Brookhaven also gives back economically to the local community. The laboratory is the fourth largest high-tech employer on Long Island, and it spends tens of millions of dollars per year on goods and services in the area.

PHOTOS BY ROB AMATO (TOP) AND DEBORAH ROSS (BOTTOM), BRUCE BENNETT STUDIOS.

PHOTOS BY BRUCE BENNETT (TOP) AND SCOTT LEVY (BOTTOM), BRUCE BENNETT STUDIOS.

CATHOLIC HEALTH SERVICES OF LONG ISLAND

Catholic Health Services of Long Island (CHS) is a dynamic, geographically diverse, service-rich organization that stands as a leader in providing high-quality, compassionate care to hundreds of thousands of Long Islanders each year. Founded in 1997, CHS has created a single universe of care, one which includes some of Long Island's finest health and human services agencies and related organizations, including five hospitals, three nursing homes, a hospice and home care network, a community-based agency for persons with special needs, and an ambulance service.

CHS has encouraged each of the member organizations embraced under its umbrella to retain their link to history, their distinctive personality, and the service specialties which have positioned each member to effectively serve their communities.

COMPUTER ASSOCIATES (CA)

Computer Associates (CA) delivers the software that manages eBusiness. CA's world-leading solutions address all aspects of eBusiness process management, information management, and infrastructure management, enabling customers and partners to gain and sustain competitive advantages. CA's field-proven and critically acclaimed eBusiness software portfolio is focused on six solution areas: enterprise management, security, storage, eBusiness transformation and integration, portal and knowledge management, and predictive analysis and visualization. CA's 25 years of continuous innovation and unwavering commitment to quality makes CA the technology partner-of-choice for the next generation of eBusiness. Whether you're a client, a strategic partner, an investor, a potential employee, or just someone who is interested in learning more about CA, visit http://ca.com to explore the extensive information available on CA's web site—and discover how CA is changing the face of eBusiness.

PHOTOS BY ROB AMATO (TOP) AND BRIAN WINKLER (BOTTOM), BRUCE BENNETT STUDIOS.

CREATIVE BATH PRODUCTS, INC.

Creative Bath Products designs and produces more than 4,000 different bath and houseware accessory items which are supplied to retailers all across the nation and to 50 foreign countries. Items manufactured by Creative Bath are found at a vast spectrum of retailers—from Fortunoff to Wal-Mart, with Bloomingdale's; Bed, Bath and Beyond; Sears; Linens 'N Things; and JCPenney included among its valued customer base of department stores, linen specialty shops, national chains, and mass merchants. Essential to its success, and especially to its enviable reputation in the bath accessories industry, are its creative functions. President and CEO Mathais Meinzinger stressed: "Creativity is the lifeblood of our company. This is the single most important factor—our ability to design new, innovative, and decorative merchandise for the bath."

PHOTO BY JIM MCISAAC, BRUCE BENNETT STUDIOS.

EAB

EAB's Chairman and Chief Executive Officer, Edward Travaglianti, explains the company's winning strategy: "To keep ourselves current in a fast-paced and increasingly competitive marketplace, each year we at EAB develop business and community strategies that address our organization's fundamental mission: meeting our customers' financial needs. We believe that we are differentiated in the marketplace by our people and our personal service." The bank's President and COO, Brendan J. Dugan, added, "At EAB, corporate and personal involvement in community activities is not optional. It is essential to achieve our mission." Corporate support from EAB thus means far more than funding for a much-needed community project— it frequently means the personal involvement of EAB employees will impact the lives of many in the surrounding area.

PHOTOS BY SCOTT LEVY (LEFT) AND BRUCE
BENNETT (RIGHT), BRUCE BENNETT STUDIOS

EDO CORPORATION

EDO's potential for bringing new business to
Long Island is greater than ever. The company
remains dedicated to the defense and aerospace
industries while actively seeking new commercial markets.

EDO will continue to invest in new technologies applicable to the defense and space
industries, and provide critical aircraft and ship
platforms for both the domestic and international
defense communities. EDO is dedicated to
future growth through both internal research
and development investments, and external
acquisitions of companies with complementary
product lines.

As EDO grows, the facilities here will also
continue to grow, maintaining the presence of a
major defense supplier on Long Island.

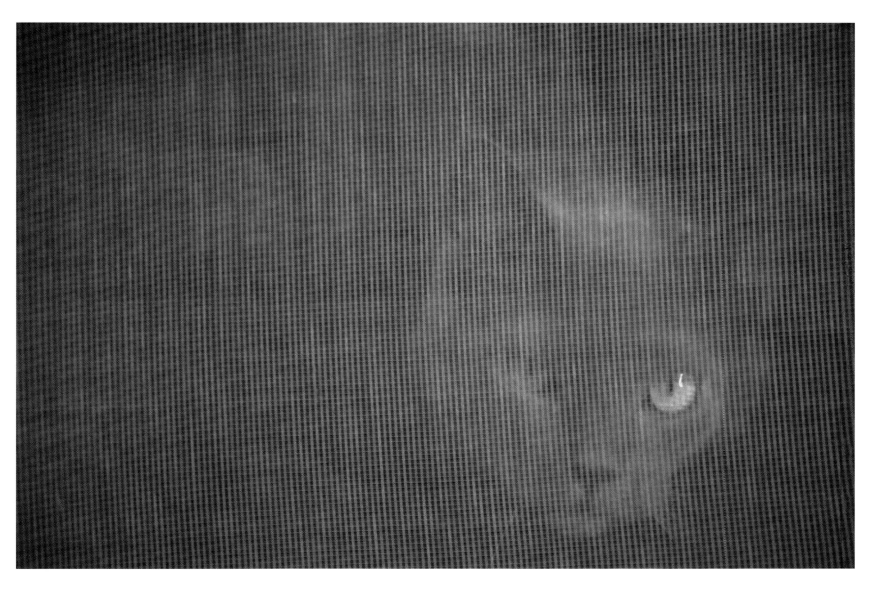

E.W. HOWELL CO., INC.

Established on Long Island in 1891, E.W. Howell Co., Inc. concentrated on building palatial homes for some of Long Island's most prestigious families but gradually expanded into commercial construction. The company performs most of its work on Long Island but also does work in the surrounding tri-state area. E.W. Howell has also expanded into the Atlanta and Chicago areas, where it has offices, though, according to Howard Rowland, president and C.O.O., "our focus remains in New York City and on Long Island." When Elmer Howell established the company 110 years ago, he insisted that quality be placed ahead of profit. That philosophy remains very much intact today, and that same spirit can be seen in its many charitable contributions.

PHOTOS BY ROB AMATO (TOP) AND JIM MCISAAC (RIGHT), BRUCE BENNETT STUDIOS.

PHOTO BY JIM MCISAAC, BRUCE BENNETT
STUDIOS.

HSBC BANK USA

HSBC Bank USA is a leading financial services
organization with combined assets of the bank
and its U.S. holding company, HSBC USA Inc., of
$83 billion. The organization is the third largest
depository institution and has the most extensive
branch network in New York State. In addition
to having more than 430 branches throughout
New York, the institution has seven branches in
Florida, two in Pennsylvania, three in California
and 11 in Panama. HSBC USA Inc. is the 11th
largest U.S. holding company in total assets and
is an indirectly-held, wholly-owned subsidiary of
HSBC Holdings plc (NYSE: HBC), which is headquartered in London. For more information about
HSBC Bank USA and its products and services
visit www.us.hsbc.com.

LONG ISLAND COMMERCIAL BANK

The corporate mission for Long Island Commercial Bank has always been to provide superior levels of service and response to the niche market that it had set out to serve. Said Douglas Manditch, the bank's president and CEO: "We serve primarily privately-owned businesses and professional practices, and also accommodate the businesspeople we work with by handling their private banking needs. The bank seeks to treat every request we receive with a sense of urgency and provide superior personal service to our customers." Responding to customer inquiries, "with a sense of urgency," is ingrained in the bank's corporate culture. With superior service and urgency established company bywords, Manditch said "we're best known for our ability to provide quick decisions to our customers."

PHOTOS BY ROB AMATO (TOP) AND JOE ROGATE (BOTTOM), BRUCE BENNETT STUDIOS.

PHOTOS BY ROB AMATO, BRUCE BENNETT
STUDIOS.

LONG ISLAND POWER AUTHORITY

Beyond the average islandwide rate cut of 20 percent it implemented in May, 1998, the Long Island Power Authority opened its market to retail competition in August, 1999.

While deregulation is being implemented statewide by the State's Public Service Commission, LIPA is introducing competition on Long Island under its LIChoice Program.

In 1999, LIPA launched Phase I of LIChoice, which opened the Long Island market to electric retail competition for the first time. Eventually, all electric consumers on Long Island will have the ability to select an Energy Service Company (ESCO) based on competitive retail prices when LIChoice is fully implemented by May 2003.

Under the LIChoice Program, the cost of electricity will get cheaper as competition gets keener, which is LIPA's primary goal.

LONG ISLAND UNIVERSITY

The nation's eighth-largest independent university, Long Island University concentrates on personalized teaching. Its activities range from award-winning honors programs where the academic challenges rival those at the nation's most elite colleges, to a large Higher Education Opportunity Program assisting academically and economically disadvantaged students, to library and pharmacy schools and dozens of Master's and doctoral-level offerings and continuing education classes. The University operates Tilles Center for the Performing Arts and Long Island's Public Radio Network.

The University's distinctive place in higher education, said President David J. Steinberg, stems from its dual roles. It not only attracts "outstanding, nationally-competitive students who seek a nurturing learning environment" but also is "determined to offer that same supportive environment to highly motivated students whose potential has yet to be realized."

PHOTOS BY ROB AMATO (TOP) AND DEBORAH ROSS (BOTTOM), BRUCE BENNETT STUDIOS.

MSC Industrial Direct

For more than 60 years, MSC has offered the highest level of service to its customers. These customers can get everything from cordless drill kits and sanders to utility pumps and manifolds. "Because we don't manufacture anything, our entire focus is on servicing and delighting our customers by providing real value to them. Our ultimate goal is to help our customers by addressing their specific needs while driving cost out of their overall procurement process." says Mitchell Jacobson. MSC defines its success through a company culture that revolves around four key groups of people: Associates, customers, owners, and suppliers. A fine balance of these key groups enables MSC to maintain high standards while developing the company for the future.

PHOTOS BY ROB AMATO (TOP) AND DEBORAH ROSS (BOTTOM), BRUCE BENNETT STUDIOS.

NEW YORK INSTITUTE OF TECHNOLOGY

NYIT's technology-infused curriculum incorporates the vital elements that give every student a competitive edge in the 21st century business world: familiarity with and understanding of computers and their applications; oral and written communication skills; problem-solving abilities; and a team-oriented work ethic. These elements combine with a solid foundation in liberal arts and sciences—including history, literature, math, and sciences—and a choice of comprehensive preprofessional courses within each academic program to prepare students for the rewards and challenges of a successful career. The college's ongoing mission to provide career-focused education, access to opportunity, and applications-oriented research will continue to position the college as a leader in higher education, preparing students for the future in an environment that fosters knowledge, personal growth, and success.

PHOTOS BY DEBORAH ROSS (TOP) AND ROB AMATO (BOTTOM), BRUCE BENNETT STUDIOS.

PHOTO BY ROB AMATO, BRUCE BENNETT STUDIOS.

POLYTECHNIC UNIVERSITY

Founded in 1854, Polytechnic University, the nation's second oldest private science and engineering school, has been an education leader on Long Island for four decades.

Since the aerospace era, Polytechnic University has been Long Island's principal provider of high-quality graduate education in engineering, science, and management. Over the past 10 years, close to 900 students on Long Island have graduated from Polytechnic's graduate programs and more than 1,600 students have taken courses. Among the university's graduates are more than 200 top executives of Long Island firms. Today, in the Information Age, Polytechnic's commitment to serve the professional-development needs of Long Island industry continues and expands through the University's Long Island Graduate Center for Professional Studies.

PHOTO BY SCOTT LEVY, BRUCE BENNETT STUDIOS.

RUTTURA & SONS
CONSTRUCTION CO., INC.

Ruttura & Sons performs demolition, excavation, storm drainage, sanitary systems, water service work, as well as all phases of cast-in-place concrete, and the company is well known in the construction industry. Recent and past projects include work for Korean Airlines at JFK International Airport, a residence hall at Fordham University, a parking garage and day care center at Computer Associates in Islandia, N.Y., Stabile Hall at Pratt Institute, the Asian center at SUNY Stony Brook, and much more. Although Ruttura & Sons takes on projects in Queens, Brooklyn, the Bronx, Manhattan, and New Jersey, the bulk of its work remains on Long Island. The company takes great pride in its workforce. Richard Pearsall, Ruttura & Sons' assistant vice president, has referred to its employees as "the greatest workforce in greater New York."

PHOTOS BY DEBORAH ROSS (TOP AND BOTTOM LEFT) AND SCOTT LEVY (ABOVE AND BOTTOM RIGHT), BRUCE BENNETT STUDIOS.

SOUTH NASSAU COMMUNITIES HOSPITAL

South Nassau Communities Hospital, a 429-bed, full-service acute care facility located in Oceanside, provides advanced medical technology and services designed with one person in mind—the patient. Expanding and adding services such as new, dedicated state-of-the-art centers for Outpatient Dialysis and Physical Rehabilitation and Sports Medicine, expanded Pediatric and Ambulatory Service Units, and recruiting top physicians and nurses are just a few examples of South Nassau's commitment to meet the diverse health care needs of the patients it serves. These innovations, and the many others that are sure to follow, enable South Nassau to stand as a model of excellence that other health care facilities strive to emulate.

STONY BROOK UNIVERSITY

Daring, aggressive, and intellectually first-rate, Stony Brook University is fulfilling the vision of University President Shirley Strum Kenny: "To be a great national university, you must first be a great local university." The University has been in the forefront of the national effort to bring the resources of research universities into the lives and education of undergraduates. Stony Brook's faculty, known for thinking unconventionally and creatively, are breaking barriers to scientific discoveries, medical cures, and technological innovations. A major center for learning and research, Stony Brook is a source of new ideas that fuel economic growth, advance science, improve health care, and strengthen government, but its primary commitment is to help bright, motivated young men and women from a diverse array of backgrounds and cultures realize their dreams.

PHOTOS BY ROB AMATO, BRUCE BENNETT STUDIOS.

SUTTON & EDWARDS INC.

The name Sutton & Edwards Inc. is synonymous in the Long Island business community with quality, excellence, service, and value. It has fashioned its position as a service-oriented commercial real estate provider by leveraging innovative solutions, attention to detail, and a commitment to technology to create value for its clients. The working relationships the firm fosters, enables it to serve as an integral role in real estate planning and a facilitator during the implementation process.

"Providing traditional real estate services is only part of the equation. If you want to differentiate yourself, you need to do more." said President Alan H. Rosenberg. "In our case, doing more involves strategic planning, process management, and coordinated service delivery—all with a global scope," concluded Chief Executive Officer Herbert S. Agin.

PHOTO BY ROB AMATO, BRUCE BENNETT STUDIOS.

THE UNIVERSITY HOSPITAL AND MEDICAL CENTER AT STONY BROOK

A center for scientific discovery. An institution of higher learning. A hallmark of outstanding health care, and a beacon for broad-reaching community service programs. University Hospital and Medical Center at Stony Brook provides the most sophisticated and compassionate medical care available today, and is actively bringing research to life to improve the quality of life for everyone on Long Island.

Conceived in the early 1970s as an academic medical center that could deliver the highest level of tertiary health care to Suffolk County's then 1.3 million residents, University Hospital and Medical Center has since exploded into a diverse, forward-looking institution that succeeds at providing a broad range of tertiary, urgent, and primary care services to all Long Islanders in need of them.

PHOTOS BY SCOTT LEVY (TOP) AND JIM MCISAAC
(BOTTOM), BRUCE BENNETT STUDIOS.

VERIZON COMMUNICATIONS

While Verizon now has a presence around the globe and ranks among the country's largest corporations, it is basically a company that has grown up on Long Island. For more than 100 years, it has served Long Islanders from Cold Spring Harbor to Great South Bay, from Kings Point to the Montauk Lighthouse. Be it resorts or wineries, dotcoms, or farms, high tech firms or single-family homes, no communications company understands Long Island's needs like Verizon.

Verizon and its customers on Long Island have been partners in the transformation and growth of the new economy on Long Island—the "Silicon Island" miracle. Nassau and Suffolk counties have made what has sometimes been a bumpy transition from an economy based on the defense industry to today's booming economy based on high tech industries.

WIEDERSUM ASSOCIATES, P.C. ARCHITECTS

Wiedersum Associates is a family-owned and operated architectural firm responsible for the design of a great many of Long Island and the metropolitan area's public buildings, many of which are schools, hospitals, and museums, along with area prisons, therefore making a contribution to the welfare of the community at the same time as doing quality work. Wiedersum Associates built its reputation, and continues to maintain it, by designing functional structures for Long Island and its surrounding areas through its superior design abilities and long-standing commitment to remain with its projects through to successful conclusion and beyond. As President Richard C. Wiedersum said: "We never leave the job." He explained that once the construction process begins "we're out on the project sites, administering the development of the projects, sometimes acting as the project's construction manager."

PHOTOS BY SCOTT LEVY, BRUCE BENNETT STUDIOS.

CHAPTER TWO

1775 TO 1800

The shots fired on Lexington Green in Massachusetts at dawn on April 19, 1775 reverberated swiftly on Long Island.

The thirty thousand people living in the places we today call Brooklyn, Queens, Nassau, and Suffolk Counties were very self-sufficient, with the majority of their toil devoted to farm and family. While farming remained the basic way of life, some farmers did have other businesses. There were smiths, coopers, shoemakers, and carpenters. Barring disaster, each generation was usually able to add a bit more to the family property and wealth. Society, however, was not classless, nor was it a democracy as we think of it today.

The wealthiest families—the Gardiners, the Nicolls, and the Floyds, for instance—were scattered across the landscape in elegant manor houses surrounded by a great deal of land. From the beginning, history tells us that those few at the top controlled an amount of wealth far out of proportion to their numbers.

These were the men who ran the business of government on Long Island, much as did the landed gentry in England. They also tended to belong to the Anglican Church and be loyal to the crown. Their children often intermarried, so that, for example, members of the Nicoll and Floyd families each married members of the other family in succeeding generations.

The question of independence also tended to divide Long Island geographically.

Although the English government never ratified the 1650 Hartford Treaty, there was still a dividing line in mid-Long Island. While not a literal line, it was common to find the crown loyalists, or Tories, living nearest Manhattan. Sentiments on the eastern end of Long Island, where English settlers from Connecticut and Massachusetts had followed Lion Gardiner to the area, leaned toward independence. These East End patriots, or Whigs, would work diligently for freedom from the crown.

FOR THE 1995 COLUMBUS DAY PARADE IN HUNTINGTON, THE REVOLUTIONARY HUNTINGTON MILITIA WAS REENACTED. ©1995 *NEWSDAY*.

THE DECLARATION OF INDEPENDENCE WAS ADOPTED ON JULY 4, 1776, AND READ ALOUD ON LONG ISLAND
SHORTLY AFTER. BY THE END OF THE NEXT MONTH THE BATTLE OF LONG ISLAND WAS UNDERWAY.
PHOTO BY ROB AMATO, BRUCE BENNETT STUDIOS.

As in other parts of the land, outrage grew on Long Island with each new indignity pressed onto the colonies by the crown. In the 1750s and 1760s laws were passed limiting the colonies' right to conduct their own business with other countries. Taxes were levied on a variety of items, including tea. The 1764 act imposing a duty on molasses and sugar, and the 1765 Stamp Act forcing colonists to put stamps on every document, led to the formation of the Sons of Liberty, the first group overtly pushing for independence.

Strenuous objections by New York and other colonies did lead to the repeal of some of those acts but the unrest continued. In December 1773, the Boston Tea Party took place and, three-and-one-half months later, the British closed Boston Harbor.

To many on Long Island, the time was ripe for revolution. Following the Boston Tea Party, East Hampton, Huntington, and Smithtown agreed to cease trading with

the British. On June 21, 1774, the Town of Huntington passed a Declaration of Rights and, in place of the Union Jack, hoisted a banner known as the Long Island flag.

The Huntington document said, "Every freeman's property is absolutely his own, and no man has a right to take it from him without his consent, expressed either by himself or his representatives.

"That, therefore, all taxes and duties imposed on His Majesty's subjects in the American colonies by the authority of Parliament are wholly unconstitutional and a plain violation of the most essential right of British subjects."

That same year, the First Continental Congress met in Philadelphia. Twelve of the thirteen colonies—Georgia was not represented—sent a total of fifty-six delegates to the First Continental Congress. Out of that meeting came the Association of 1774, which urged all colonists to avoid using British goods, and to form committees to

VISITORS TO LONG ISLAND'S OLD BETHPAGE VILLAGE TAKE HOME A SENSE OF THE HARD WORK THE
EARLY SETTLERS UNDERTOOK ON A DAILY BASIS TO CARVE A HOME OUT OF THE NEW COUNTRY.
PHOTO BY M. LEIDER, BRUCE BENNETT STUDIOS.

enforce this ban. The Second Continental Congress convened the next year. George Washington was named Commander-in-Chief, a navy was created, and the search for foreign aid for the war was begun. The colonies were directed by the Congress to write constitutions and otherwise act to dissolve their ties to England.

Of course, some Long Islanders believed that remaining part of the British Empire would bring the most benefit to the colonies. The issue was so divisive that citizens of the north end of Hempstead Town seceded from the south end after a vote to give the town's allegiance to King George III was passed at an April 1775 town meeting. North and South Hempstead remain separate to this day.

When war finally came, Long Islanders discovered they lived in a region that was desired by both Loyalists and Patriots. The English held New York, and from Brooklyn to Brookhaven, the British army and their Hessian mercenaries were quartered on Long Island.

The Declaration of Independence was adopted on July 4, 1776 and read aloud on Long Island shortly after. By the end of the next month the Battle of Long Island was underway.

Strategically, Long Island's natural resources and access to shipping made the region critical. If the British could hold New York, they could render New England ineffective because they could then isolate it from the rest of the colonies.

Recognizing their importance, some residents of East Hampton wrote to Connecticut's Revolutionary War Governor Jonathan Trumbull in September 1776 to request protection. They said in their "present distressed and perplexed situation, they hope they may not be as a torch on fire at both ends."

They were reacting to news about the Battle of Long Island.

On August 22, 1776, the British commander, General Lord William Howe, attacked with one-third of his army—fifteen thousand men—and eighty-eight frigates. Howe's troops were able to capture strategic positions. The Patriots lost more than a thousand men. But General Howe did not immediately take advantage of his superior position.

Howe's plan was to complete the rout of New York with a naval bombardment of Brooklyn Heights from the East River. However, rain and a stiff north wind and outgoing tide prevented the deployment of his ships in the river.

During the night of August 29, 1776, the foul weather enabled General Washington to ferry his ten thousand troops, along with their equipment and supplies, across the East River to safety Manhattan. When the weather cleared and the British were able to get behind Patriot lines, they discovered the Patriot enemy had retreated into Manhattan and were there unreachable.

While large-scale battle never again came that close to Long Island, the people were still deeply involved on both sides of the war. One out of six Long Islanders fled for the duration—Patriots fled to Connecticut for safety, Tories, upstate.

Sporadic fighting took place in Sag Harbor when the Patriots attacked the British fort there by boat from Connecticut and in Mastic, when the Patriots were able to capture Fort St. George. The Patriots were also successful in their attack on Fort Slongo (today's Fort Salonga in Smithtown), named for its builder George Slongo.

Major Benjamin Tallmadge, a Setauket native who was later the Continental Army's Chief of Intelligence, led these guerilla raids throughout the occupation. Launched from Connecticut, this "whaleboat warfare" proved helpful in derailing the British.

With the British living among them, the Long Island Patriots, led by Tallmadge, were able to make a singular and important contribution to the war by building a network of spies to pass information to Washington's troops. It was Tallmadge who saw through the disguise of British Major John Andre and detained him for questioning. This led to the exposure of Benedict Arnold's plan to turn over West Point to the British.

In 1778, after accepting Washington's invitation to head the Secret Service, Tallmadge formed a spy ring that would report to him in Connecticut. The group included Tallmadge's Setauket neighbors Austin Roe, a tavernkeeper, the courier who rode fifty-five miles from Setauket to Manhattan at least once each week; Abraham Woodhull, a farmer; Caleb Brewster, a whaler; and Anna Smith Strong, who was called Nancy, a Strong's Neck neighbor of Tallmadge's.

When it became obvious that Woodhull's absences from Setauket to do the business of spying in Manhattan were being noticed, he recruited Oyster Bay merchant Robert Townsend—who also happened to be a volunteer journalist for a Loyalist newspaper—to take his place.

They were known as the Setauket, or Culper, Spy Ring. Woodhull's code name was Samuel Culper, Sr., Townsend's, Samuel Culper, Jr., and Brewster was Agent 725.

Operating out of a New York City tavern frequented by British soldiers, Woodhull and Townsend gathered information about troop movements and transmitted it to Roe either orally or on paper with invisible ink.

Roe took the information to Setauket, passed it to Brewster who, in turn, carried it by whaleboat across the Sound to Tallmadge in Connecticut. Tallmadge then relayed the information to George Washington.

Anna Strong, whose husband Judge Selah Strong was taken prisoner by the British for his Patriot activities, was the go-between. It was she who was designated to tell Roe that Brewster was waiting in a nearby cove. Roe would then give Brewster information to bring to Tallmadge in Connecticut. To alert Roe, she hung a black petticoat on her wash line. The location of the cove at which Roe could find Brewster was revealed by the number of white handkerchiefs Strong hung next to the petticoat. The number of handkerchiefs would correspond to the number assigned to each of six coves.

As the end of the war neared, thousands of Tories left New York and Long Island to settle in Canada in the spring and fall of 1783. The war officially ended by treaty with the British on September 3, 1783. On December 4, all of the British were finally gone from Long Island.

If the land was not devastated by wartime cannon, then it certainly was by wartime neglect. Houses in which the British stayed were often ruined. Farmers who fled were forced to let their land lie fallow and become overgrown. Long Island's forests had been stripped to provide hardwood for building and burning, and livestock supplies were badly depleted.

With the war finally over, and the monumental task of rebuilding their lives and livelihoods still being confronted, Long Islanders received a slap in the face from the New York State Legislature.

In addition to canceling all debts in the state that Patriots might owe to Loyalists, and disbarring Loyalist lawyers, the legislature fined Long Island $100,000, "as compensation to other parts of the state for not having been in a condition to take an active part in the war against the enemy." ∎

THIS PRESERVED CARRIAGE HOUSE LOOKS AS IF ITS RESIDENT WILL RETURN ANY MOMENT TO HITCH A HORSE TO THE BUGGY OR SELECT A TOOL FOR A JOB AT HAND. PHOTOS BY ROB AMATO, BRUCE BENNETT STUDIOS.

(LEFT) TODAY, LONG ISLAND RESIDENTS PROUDLY FLY THE SYMBOL OF FREEDOM—THE AMERICAN FLAG. PHOTO BY DEBORAH ROSS, BRUCE BENNETT STUDIOS. (RIGHT) BORN IN CONNECTICUT BUT FOREVER TIED BY HISTORY TO LONG ISLAND, NATHAN HALE WAS HANGED BY THE BRITISH AS A SPY AT THE AGE OF 21 AND LEFT GROTESQUELY SUSPENDED FROM THE GALLOWS FOR THREE DAYS AS A LESSON TO THE HATED REBELS. WHEN HE WAS CUT DOWN, HE WAS CAST INTO AN UNMARKED GRAVE SOMEWHERE ON MANHATTAN ISLAND. THIS MONUMENT, ERECTED IN 1894, COMMEMORATES THE PATRIOT'S HEROISM AS HE FOUGHT FOR HIS COUNTRY'S FREEDOM. PHOTO BY ROB AMATO, BRUCE BENNETT STUDIOS.

KEEPING THE HEAT ON IN HUNTINGTON

As it became clear that the British would not succeed and the war began to slow down, there was one bit of nastiness left for the people in Huntington.

It came in the form of Benjamin Thompson, a Woburn Massachusetts native who is said to have possessed high intelligence, biting wit and, as a result of the latter trait, few friends. At age 19 he found himself in Rumford, Massachusetts, which is today's Concord, New Hampshire where he married a wealthy widow.

But, since he said, "She married me, not I her." it apparently surprised none of his contemporaries that he was not faithful. This was proven in 1775, when Isaiah Thomas, printer of pro-independence *Massachusetts Spy*, sued his wife for divorce and named Thompson as corespondent.

Based on his reputation in Boston, he was denied a commission in the Patriot army. He immediately turned around and signed on with the crown. Thompson went to London in 1776 at age 23, and stayed until 1781, when he returned as an officer. He saw some action in the southern colonies and was then ordered to bring his troops to winter in Huntington. There he embarked on a building project unmatched in its mean-spiritedness in the entire history of the war.

Thompson called his building project Fort Golgotha, the Hebrew name for Calvary, the mount on which Jesus was crucified. He built it on what today is the intersection of Nassau Road and Main Street and what was then the town cemetery.

In his 1845 History of Long Island, Nathaniel S. Prime quoted eyewitness accounts of tombstones being used for ovens and of bread coming out of those ovens imprinted with the epitaphs of those who were supposed to be resting in peace in that cemetery.

The irony of this oven building would become clear as Thompson found his place in the history of science building stoves of a type still used today called "Rumford" stoves. After the war, he returned to Europe and spent much of the remainder of his career working in Bavaria, where the government created him Lord Rumford, Count of the Holy Roman Empire.

(LEFT) WHEN GEORGE WASHINGTON VISITED LONG ISLAND, HE MADE PAPER AT THE ONDERDONK MILL IN ROSLYN. IN 1927 THAT VISIT WAS COMMEMORATED BY THE HISTORICAL COMMITTEE OF THE LONG ISLAND ASSOCIATION WHEN ITS MEMBERS RETRACED WASHINGTON'S 1790 STEPS. WASHINGTON WROTE OF THAT VISIT, "...WE WERE KINDLY RECEIVED AND WELL ENTERTAINED." PHOTO COURTESY OF THE NASSAU COUNTY DIVISION OF MUSEUM SERVICES/LONG ISLAND STUDIES INSTITUTE/HOFSTRA UNIVERSITY. (RIGHT) TODAY, MANY HISTORIC HOMES AND BUILDINGS ON LONG ISLAND BEAR SIGNS BOASTING "GEORGE WASHINGTON SLEPT HERE." PHOTO BY DEBORAH ROSS, BRUCE BENNETT STUDIOS.

A PRESIDENTIAL VISIT

That tourism is big business on Long Island today is only a natural extension of a trend started in 1790, when the brand new country's new president paid a call.

With his deep interest in farming, George Washington's surviving comments reflect his concerns about land use. He also recorded details of where he stayed and what he ate.

In 1790, the United States had a population of 3,750,000. Washington came to a Long Island that the first United States Census in 1790 tells had a population of 36,949 people—4,495 in Kings County; 16,014 in Queens (including today's Nassau); and 16,440 in Suffolk—who were for the most part engaged in farming.

Beginning his trip on April 20 (following a rain delay) in New Utrecht in a coach drawn by four horses, Washington traveled east to Jamaica, where he pronounced a local tavern "a pretty good and [decent] house."

He stopped to care for his horses in Hempstead and continued east to the Ketcham House in Copaigue and slept that night in West Bay Shore at Sagtikos Manor, the home of Isaac Thompson that had been occupied by the British during the war.

Washington continued his journey east to West Sayville, then to Patchogue, where he dined at Hart's Tavern. From there he headed north to Setauket, home of his chief spy Benjamin Tallmadge and the very effective Setauket Spy Ring.

Although he made no mention of his old allies, the President did note that Austin Roe's Tavern in Setauket "is tolerably [decent] with obliging people in it."

Having gone as far east as he would get, Washington headed back west along the north shore, stopping at the Widow Blydenburgh's house in Smithtown, then on to Huntington. There his journey was like a tour of Revolutionary War sites—taking him near Nathan Hale's landing spot and the Old Burying Ground destroyed by Benjamin Thompson. In Oyster Bay the President stayed in a home now owned by Charles Wang of Computer Associates that was then owned by Loyalist Daniel Youngs. He finished his journey on April 24, back in Brooklyn to the ferry that took him home to Manhattan.

On this trip, Washington noted the "impoverished soil, inherited from colonial times..." and the use of manure as fertilizer. He was interested in the use of "braided" trees to make "very indifferent" fences... it exhibits an evidence that very good fences may be made in this manner either of White Oak or dogwood, which from this mode of treatment grows thickest and most stubborn. This, however, would be no defense against Hogs."

(LEFT) SUFFOLK COUNTY NATIVE WILLIAM FLOYD REPRESENTED NEW YORK IN THE CONTINENTAL CONGRESS. AN AVID SEPARATIST, HE WAS A SIGNER OF THE DECLARATION OF INDEPENDENCE AND SERVED ONE TERM IN THE UNITED STATES CONGRESS. (RIGHT) THE FIRST UNITED STATES CUSTOM HOUSE IN NEW YORK STATE WAS IN SAG HARBOR. COMMEMORATING THAT EVENT IN 1950, LOCAL RESIDENTS DRESSED IN THEIR BEST EIGHTEENTH-CENTURY FINERY. PHOTOS COURTESY OF THE NASSAU COUNTY DIVISION OF MUSEUM SERVICES/LONG ISLAND STUDIES INSTITUTE/HOFSTRA UNIVERSITY.

TWO SIGNERS

The two Long Island "signers" of the Declaration of Independence had, in their day, little in common other than their very presence in Philadelphia. Oddly, each is remembered today with a secondary school and street named in his honor.

One Signature from Suffolk

Contemporary accounts noted that William Floyd did not fit in with New York's other delegates—who included John Jay and Alexander Hamilton—to the Continental Congress.

Born in 1734 in Brookhaven into a successful, wealthy family who had emigrated to America from Wales in mid-seventeenth century, Floyd was decidedly rural, most at home on his farm in Mastic and in conversation about hunting.

Like his father and grandfather, Floyd was very successful. There is even speculation that one of the prime reasons he was sent to Philadelphia was that he was one of the few who could afford to go. He inherited his family estate when he was 18 and, by the time he went to Congress, was the largest slave owner in Suffolk County, with fourteen slaves.

While others in Congress were promoting accord with the English, Floyd became close to delegates from New England whose pro-independence views matched his own. When the British held Long Island, Floyd and his family fled to Connecticut.

However, the delegates from New York spent many months awaiting instructions from the state government in Albany about how to vote on independence. John Jay wrote that Floyd's conduct "gained him much respect in Congress," noting that he "always appeared to judge for himself" any issue that required a vote and did not fall under the purview of Albany.

In May, 1776, while others in New York talked of reconciling with the English, Floyd said, "...we have little or no hopes [for that]....therefore we ought to be in a position to preserve our liberties another way."

Floyd's words were heeded only at the very last minute, when the Albany government relented and allowed its delegates to sign the Declaration of Independence.

After the war, Floyd served in the first United States Congress and, after losing re-election, in the

(continued)

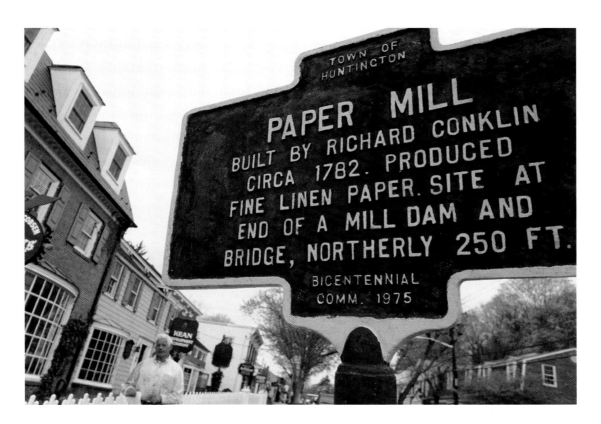

ALTHOUGH THE MAJORITY OF LONG ISLANDERS WERE ENGAGED IN FARMING IN THE EARLY PART OF THE CENTURY, INDUSTRY WAS GROWING AND INCLUDED PAPER MILLS, POTTERY WORKS, WOOLEN FACTORIES, PRINTING AND PUBLISHING, AND EVEN THE MANUFACTURE OF DRUMHEADS AND BANJO TOPS BEFORE THE CIVIL WAR. PHOTO BY SCOTT LEVY, BRUCE BENNETT STUDIOS.

New York State Senate. Widowed in 1781, Floyd remarried three years later.

In 1803 he deeded his Mastic estate to his son and moved to property he had bought upstate on the bank of the Mohawk River. He died in 1821.

A Second from Queens

If William Floyd was deeply rooted in the soil of Suffolk County, Francis Lewis was his polar opposite.

Born in Wales in 1713, Lewis was orphaned at age five. When, at 21, he inherited some property, he sold it and invested the profits. He was twice shipwrecked off the coast of Ireland before, at age 25, he emigrated to New York and went into business with an established merchant.

The two held a contract to supply clothing to the British army during the French and Indian War. This business led to Lewis' capture by the French, who sent him to imprisonment in France.

Although it is believed that he was rewarded for his service to the British with a tract of land in present-day Whitestone on which he built a farm, as a merchant, Lewis rapidly became angry at the trade restrictions the British put on their colonies. In protest of the Stamp Act, he joined the Sons of Liberty.

In forming the new nation men with Lewis' business expertise were highly prized and he was chosen to represent New York in the Continental Congress. In direct retaliation for signing the Declaration of Independence, the British ransacked his farm and took his wife prisoner. Although her release was negotiated by General Washington after six months, her health was broken and she died in 1778.

After the war Lewis retired to New York City and died there at 89 in 1803. He left behind an estate of $15,000 and a controversy about his business practices unsettled to this day.

While some hold Francis Lewis in high esteem for the money he gave to finance the revolution, others say he was shady, taking advantage of British soldiers by charging exorbitant prices for basic goods during the French and Indian War.

TODAY, LONG ISLAND IS A MIX OF THE PAST, PRESENT, AND FUTURE. HISTORIC HOMES AND BUILDINGS ARE CAREFULLY PRESERVED AND MARKED AS REMINDERS OF THE JOURNEY TO TODAY'S FREEDOMS, WHILE GENERATIONS OF LONG ISLANDERS RAISE THEIR OWN CHILDREN IN THIS UNIQUE PLACE. PHOTOS BY ROB AMATO (TOP LEFT AND RIGHT) AND BRUCE BENNETT, BRUCE BENNETT STUDIOS.

THE CHASE MANHATTAN BANK

The Chase Manhattan Bank is one of the world's premier financial services firms with more than $400 billion in assets and operations in more than 45 countries. Chase combines the best of commercial and investment banking, offers world-class information and transaction processing services, and has a leading U.S. consumer franchise. All of these businesses are bolstered by formidable technology to support the needs of Chase's broad customer base.

Historically, Chase has played a fundamental role in industry and trade since its founding in 1799—first in the United States and then internationally—and has maintained an unwavering commitment to the diverse communities it serves.

In the Long Island marketplace Chase is the leading bank for business by far, dedicating more Relationship Managers than any other bank to serving the financial needs of thousands of companies doing business here. Traditional banking services are at the heart of the bank's commercial banking. Yet Long Island's sophisticated business community needs more than "plain vanilla" banking. For this reason, Chase provides a full range of creative financial solutions designed to meet a company's unique needs. From credit and cash management to investment banking and corporate finance; from insurance to personal investments and private banking for the company's principals and senior executives—Chase's products and services focus on what businesses need to succeed.

Chase is rapidly adapting to the challenges and opportunities of the New Economy, driven by technology, entrepreneurship, business innovation, and structural change. The New Economy is revolutionizing how companies interact with consumers and with each other. Chase is at the forefront of the convergence of "bricks and mortar" with Internet start-ups, leveraging the power of its brand, leadership positions, and financial strengths. Through Chase.com (www.chase.com), Chase is successfully creating new business models for the New Economy to meet the needs of its broad customer base across the consumer and wholesale markets.

The bank is dedicated to good corporate citizenship in the neighborhoods where we live and work. That is nowhere more true than here on Long Island. Chase supports the arts, social services, education, sports, and other local organizations that enhance the quality of life for all. And as the leading bank for business on Long Island, Chase provides financial products and services that local companies need...and helps companies' owners, executives, managers, employees, customers, and suppliers meet their personal financial goals as well.

According to Joe Purcell, Division Executive of Chase's commercial banking on Long Island, "Our roots go deep here. We're proud to be a part of this special place, and proud to work with the people and businesses of Long Island." ■

CHASE MANHATTAN'S LONG ISLAND DIVISION EXECUTIVE STAFF. FRONT ROW (LEFT TO RIGHT) RAYMOND T. DOWNEY, SVP/SUFFOLK REGION; JOSEPH F. PURCELL, SVP/LONG ISLAND DIVISION EXECUTIVE; AND JOSEPH CALTAGIRONE, JR. VP/CHIEF OF STAFF. SECOND ROW (LEFT TO RIGHT) ROBERT RIKER, VP/ADMINISTRATIVE DEPUTY; WILLIAM G. FLISTER, SVP/NASSAU REGION; GLENN S. ALBERT, SVP/DIVISION CREDIT EXECUTIVE; AND ANDREW ACKERMAN, SVP/CORPORATE FINANCE REGION.

"Y ou can scarcely go into any quarter of this country, without finding those who were natives of this island, or who proudly claim descent from those that were. With all such, it has long been a maxim, that 'even a Long Island dog is a welcome guest.'"

So wrote Long Island historian Nathaniel S. Prime in 1845. He chronicled the first half of the nineteenth century, a time that brought enormous change to life on Long Island and to the lives of Long Islanders.

The 1800 census counted 42,167 people living on Long Island, the largest number of them in Suffolk. This was the first census showing a population shift away from outlying areas and into New York City, which, for the first time, had a population—60,489 people—greater than Long Island.

At the start of the century most people were farmers. They raised livestock and subsistance crops. But, as George Washington noted on his 1790 tour, the soil,

which was at best very sandy, was tired. Although the use of manure as fertilizer was known, and some farmers rotated crops, it was difficult to earn a good living as a farmer here.

But Ezra L'Hommedieu, a Southold farmer who was Suffolk County Clerk, constantly experimented to find soil-enrichment methods. He had tried, in addition to manure, sea plants and shells. Finally, he used an inedible fish, the menhaden, or "mossbunker." This worked so well that an entire industry grew around it and Long Island furnished the East Coast with a primary fertilizer for decades.

It was easy to catch menhaden; a lot more difficult to catch whales. But, the location of Long Island made whaling another natural industry.

Whales had proven useful to humans for centuries. Long Island's Native Americans used canoes to hunt whales by chasing them into shallow water where,

PHOTO BY ROB AMATO, BRUCE BENNETT STUDIOS.

inevitably, the huge mammal would become beached. The early colonists followed suit and also chased the whales onto the beach. They used blubber for lubricating and protecting their weapons and tools. They later used other parts of the whale for candle- and corset-making.

The colonists soon developed more sophisticated whaling methods.

Whale watchtowers were built along the south shore so that the animal or, more realistically, its spout, could be seen and then hunted. Sag Harbor, the first deepwater port in the country, soon had a thriving industry in whaling and merchant shipping of goods to and from the south Atlantic. The town was so successful, in fact, that it rivaled Manhattan as a port of entry.

The whaling industry prospered through much of the nineteenth century, at its height employing tens of thousands of sailors, shipbuilders, and others whose work supported whaling. The largest fleet was in Sag Harbor, but the Cold Spring Whaling Company in Cold Spring Harbor had nine ships and there was a small fleet sailing out of Greenport.

Port Jefferson, another deepwater harbor, became a boomtown in which 327 ships were built in 25 ship-building yards in between the late 1700s and late 1800s.

The seafaring life was a dangerous one, with one of the greatest dangers being impressment by the British navy. This pirating of sailors became such a danger that, in 1812, the United States declared war on Great Britain.

With a very small federal navy, the war was fought mostly by privateers—ship owners and crews who were paid to fight on behalf of one country or the other. Although the British fleet did anchor off Montauk and Oyster Pond Point (today's Orient), New York's Governor Tompkins decreed that no man from eastern Long Island was to be drafted, as the men were needed to protect the waters at home. Three forts were built in Sag Harbor and, instead of going off to fight elsewhere, Sag Harbor citizens formed a "home militia."

FOR GENERATIONS, LONG ISLANDERS HAVE MADE A LIVING FROM THE SEA. FISHERMEN WERE INVOLVED IN WHALING IN THE ISLAND'S EARLY DAYS, AND TODAY BRING IN A WIDE VARIETY OF FISH AND SHELLFISH. PHOTOS BY ROB AMATO (ABOVE) AND DEBORAH ROSS (LEFT), BRUCE BENNETT STUDIOS.

Sag Harbor's women and children were several times hustled into the woods to hide from the enemy. Historian Jacqueline Overton wrote, "It is said for six weeks one summer the women and children never undressed but lay down at night with their clothes on, fearful of the foe in the bay."

The British were particularly hated by a Sag Harbor man named Joshua Penny, keeper of the lighthouse at Cedar Island. Penny claimed to have survived a fifteen-year impressment in the British Royal Navy. During the War of 1812 he sailed around Gardiner's Bay in a primitive torpedo boat whose reputation exceeded its abilities. But the British commander was worried enough that he mounted an expedition that captured Penny, not at sea, but in the night in his own bed.

PHOTOS BY ROB AMATO, BRUCE BENNETT STUDIOS.

The tale is told that Penny claimed until the day he died that a Sag Harbor man betrayed him to the British for two hundred pounds sterling. He would say the man "sold his country for a Penny."

After the War of 1812, Long Island began to grow, becoming more a part of the larger world. This growth was owed in large measure to improvements in transportation.

Ferry routes ran along the coasts, in the Long Island Sound on the north shore; in the Great South Bay on the south. Ferries ran frequently and were used for business and for pleasure excursions. Travelers could go by ferry from Brooklyn to New York City; from New York City to all ports on Long Island, then on to Connecticut and Boston. Stagecoach companies traversed roads often so primitive that it could take three days to travel from Brooklyn to Montauk.

Long Island's original roads tended to follow the old Native American trails or to go through a settlement and then stop, as most people saw no need to travel very far.

The earliest main roads were North Road, Middle Road, and South Road, each still used today as North Country, Middle Country, and South Country Roads.

In 1801, the first turnpike was opened. Built by private companies, turnpikes featured strategically placed tollgates. There was a fee structure that took into account a full range of contingencies—number of passengers, horses, type and weight of freight, and so on. The nineteenth century was still young when a network of toll roads, with Jamaica as their hub, enabled travelers to criss-cross Long Island from west to east, north to south, and back again.

Coaches and travelers were serviced by a network of inns along the routes, but travel was not easy. Nathaniel S. Prime informed his readers in 1845, "...to one who has never travelled such a region of country [as Suffolk County], it is impossible to convey an adequate idea of the inconvenience and *obstruction* to locomotion which are here presented."

Prime went on to discuss the deplorable condition of Suffolk's roads in both wet and dry weather, for they were in turn too muddy or too sandy. Roads in western Long Island came in for high praise. Prime wrote, "The entire counties of King's and Queen's, in their public roads and numerous turnpikes, present as pleasant journeying for man, and as comfortable travelling for beast, in every direction and at all seasons of the year."

Although the majority of Long Islanders were engaged in farming in the early part of the century, industry was growing. When George Washington visited in 1790, he made paper at one of Henry Onderdonk's mills in Roslyn. In Cold Spring Harbor, Brown Brothers Pottery works and the Jones Woolen Factory in Huntington Harbor thrived for many years and there the Van Velsor family began to manufacture drumheads and banjo tops in before the Civil War. In 1791, David Frothingham published the Long Island's first newspaper, *The Long Island Herald*, in Sag Harbor and the same year began to publish books. His first was *An Oration on the Rights of Animals*.

New York was growing wildly. By 1835, Brooklyn became an incorporated city and, by 1845, it had a population of almost 68,691 people. Within twenty years the villages of Williamsburg and Bushwick were folded into the City of Brooklyn.

Still, compared to Manhattan, Brooklyn in the nineteenth century retained the feeling of being in the country and, because that was desirable—and because transportation made travel to Manhattan easily accessible—Brooklyn became the first true suburb in the United States.

With the growth of trade in New York, better transport was sought to export goods to other parts of the country. In 1834, in an effort to move products more quickly to anxious buyers in Boston, investors began to build the Long Island Rail Road.

The plan was to ferry people and goods from South Ferry at the tip of Manhattan to Brooklyn, then by train east across the center of Long Island to Greenport. From there, passengers and products would be ferried to Stonington, Connecticut, thence by train to Boston. When the railroad was begun, the tip from Brooklyn to Greenport alone took three days. The intention was to whittle the travel time to Boston down to eleven hours.

It took ten years to build the 96-mile line. When completed the railroad boasted eleven locomotives, twenty-two passenger cars and sixty-three freight cars. The locomotives, which were later differentiated by numbers, were given names. A contemporary report said the one called "Fanny" was said to be particularly fast "on the level." The fare from Brooklyn to Greenport was $2.25.

PHOTOS BY SCOTT LEVY,
BRUCE BENNETT STUDIOS.

Today, Long Island's sandy beaches draw vacationers as well as being a source to the sea's livelihood. Photo by Deborah Ross, Bruce Bennett Studios.

Historian Prime wrote of the railroad in 1845, "...it was a tedious journey of *three days* to travel by stage from Easthampton or Oysterponds to Brooklyn. But now the inhabitants of either of these towns may dine at home, and take tea in New York; then breakfast in New York and dine at home."

The inaugural trip took place amid a great deal of fanfare on July 27, 1844. The line was an immediate success but two years later was bankrupt because a direct New York to Boston rail connection was established by others.

The nineteenth century's great thinkers had a new society to ponder. The beginnings of the Industrial Revolution, the continued growth of already-large cities and the imperatives imposed on individuals by governments, gave birth to a philosophical movement that valued the individual above all.

Josiah Warren, who lived from 1798-1874, was a leading exponent of individual sovereignty. He wrote, "the forming of societies or any other artificial combinations IS the first, greatest, and most fatal mistake ever committed by legislators and by reformers." He believed that maximum human freedom and happiness could be attained by abolishing not just the state, but all other involuntary relationships and organizations as well.

Thus, in 1851, Warren and Stephen Pearl Andrews founded Modern Times, a utopian community in Suffolk County. Like-minded people came to this brave new world where nothing would be sold for more than it cost and labor was used as money. The outside world was scandalized by tales of divorce and free love in Modern Times.

Ultimately, the residents were unable to sustain their community economically. After a dozen years they renamed their settlement "Brentwood" and disbanded.

LONG ISLAND'S EARLIEST MAIN ROADS WERE NORTH ROAD, MIDDLE ROAD, AND SOUTH ROAD, EACH STILL USED TODAY AS NORTH COUNTRY, MIDDLE COUNTRY, AND SOUTH COUNTRY ROADS. PICTURED ABOVE, TRAFFIC FLOWS INTO ROSLYN, ONE OF LONG ISLAND'S OLDEST TOWNS. PHOTO BY SCOTT LEVY, BRUCE BENNETT STUDIOS.

Although slavery had been outlawed in New York State for decades, the topic of abolition was a hot one. Brooklyn minister Henry Ward Beecher—whose father had left his pulpit in East Hampton when refused a raise by his congregation in 1806—preached abolition was both "immoral and un-Christian."

In the 1860 election, Lincoln and his platform of abolition carried Suffolk County, but were soundly defeated in Brooklyn, where Democrats campaigned against freeing the slaves.

When the Civil War began there was no draft. States were assessed a number of soldiers they were expected to send into the Union army. During the first year, Long Island sent almost fifteen thousand men into battle and, in 1862, when Lincoln sent a call for three hundred thousand more Union soldiers, many more Long Islanders responded.

War was felt in almost every part of Long Island. Fundraising events were a constant, capped by the 1864 Sanitary Fair at the Brooklyn Academy of Music that, in three weeks, raised more than $400,000 for the Union effort to care for sick and wounded soldiers.

The end of the Civil War brought a period of unparalleled growth. A bridge connecting Brooklyn and Manhattan was begun and a tide of immigration brought a surge of people to New York.

As the nation celebrated its centennial at the Philadelphia Exposition in 1876, the possibilities for Long Island—as for the rest of the country—seemed limitless. ■

THE HAMLET OF HICKSVILLE BOASTS A NUMBER OF HISTORIC LANDMARKS, SOME VERY LOCAL IN NATURE. PICTURED, A HAND-PAINTED SIGN ALERTS VISITORS THAT THIS WAS THE RESIDENCE OF W.P. OVERTON, M.D., FROM 1875-1907. PHOTO BY ROB AMATO, BRUCE BENNETT STUDIOS.

AFTER THE WAR OF 1812, LONG ISLAND BEGAN TO GROW, BECOMING MORE A PART OF THE LARGER WORLD. FERRY ROUTES RAN ALONG THE COASTS, IN LONG ISLAND SOUND ON THE NORTH SHORE; IN THE GREAT SOUTH BAY ON THE SOUTH. FERRIES RAN FREQUENTLY AND WERE USED FOR BUSINESS AND PLEASURE EXCURSIONS. TRAVELERS COULD GO BY FERRY FROM BROOKLYN TO NEW YORK CITY; FROM NEW YORK CITY TO ALL PORTS ON LONG ISLAND, THEN ON TO CONNECTICUT AND BOSTON. THE PORT JEFFERSON FERRY SERVICE (SHOWN ABOVE) CONNECTS THAT CITY TO BRIDGEPORT, CONNECTICUT, PROVIDING A VITAL LINK BETWEEN THE TWO STATES FOR THOUSANDS OF STUDENTS, BUSINESS PEOPLE, AND TRAVELERS. PHOTO BY JIM MCISSAC, BRUCE BENNETT STUDIOS.

Surrounded by water on all sides, Long Island today stays connected to the mainland largely by ferry transportation, which still provides an important way of commuting for business people and students. Pictured are the Shelter Island Ferry (top), Fire Island Ferry (bottom left), and Cold Spring Harbor Station (bottom right). Photos by Jim McIsaac (top), J. Giamundo (bottom left) and Rob Amato (bottom right), Bruce Bennett Studios.

DANIEL WEBSTER CALLED THE LONG ISLAND
SOUND "THE MEDITERRANEAN OF THE WESTERN
HEMISPHERE," BUT A NINETEENTH CENTURY SEA
CAPTAIN WITH EXPERIENCE SAILING IN WATERS FROM
THE GREAT LAKES TO THE CHINA COAST CALLED IT
"ONE OF THE TOUGHEST RUNS IN THE WORLD."
THUS, BEGINNING IN 1797, THERE WERE TWENTY-
THREE LIGHTHOUSES BUILT AROUND LONG ISLAND.
PHOTOS BY F. ABADIE (LEFT) AND J. MCISAAC
(ABOVE), BRUCE BENNETT STUDIOS.

THE LONG ISLAND RAIL ROAD, PART OF THE METROPOLITAN TRANSPORTATION AUTHORITY, CONNECTS
MONTAUK AND GREENPORT ON THE EAST SIDE OF THE ISLAND WITH MANHATTAN AND BEYOND. THE
ISLAND-WIDE SERVICE IS AN IMPORTANT VEHICLE FOR MOVING PEOPLE EN MASSE ON A DAILY BASIS.
PHOTOS BY ROB AMATO (TOP), SCOTT LEVY (BOTTOM LEFT) AND BRUCE BENNETT (BOTTOM RIGHT),
BRUCE BENNETT STUDIOS.

(ABOVE) NATURE BATTLES PROGRESS, AS ILLUSTRATED BY THIS 1906 PHOTO OF LONG ISLAND RAIL ROAD WORKERS FIGHTING A "CATERPILLAR WAR" TO CLEAR THE TRACKS IN MONTAUK. ALTHOUGH THE RAILROAD'S ROLE WANED NATIONALLY OVER TIME, IT HAS ALWAYS REMAINED AN IMPORTANT MODE OF TRANSPORTATION IN LONG ISLAND. PHOTO FROM THE FULLERTON COLLECTION, COURTESY OF THE SUFFOLK COUNTY HISTORICAL SOCIETY. (BELOW) BY THE LATE NINETEENTH CENTURY, THE LONG ISLAND RAIL ROAD USED LOCOMOTIVES AND PASSENGER CARS LIKE THE ONE SHOWN HERE IN 1874. PHOTOS COURTESY OF THE NASSAU COUNTY DIVISION OF MUSEUM SERVICES/LONG ISLAND STUDIES INSTITUTE/HOFSTRA UNIVERSITY.

LONG ISLAND ARTS AND LETTERS, PART ONE

Walt Whitman

Had such honors been bestowed in the nineteenth century, Walt Whitman would have been this nation's poet laureate.

Born in 1819 in West Hills, Huntington Town, Long Island, Whitman's sole education was five years in the public schools of Brooklyn. At age 12, Whitman was apprenticed as a printer on the *Long Island Patriot* and, later, on Alden Spooner's pioneering newspaper the *Long Island Star.* When he couldn't find a job in printing, Whitman took posts he detested as schoolmaster at several schools in Suffolk County. He founded *The Long Islander*, a weekly newspaper still published in Huntington today, when he was 19. Whitman moved on to edit the *Brooklyn Daily Eagle* at 26.

During the 1840s Whitman's politics took shape, tending toward the Free Soil Movement, espousing the belief that slavery should not be extended to any new United States territorial acquisitions. These views cost him his Eagle job.

He developed an appreciation of Italian opera and his poetry came to reflect the style of the operatic libretto—long lines of irregular length.

In 1855, Whitman self-published *Leaves of Grass*, a title he would use again and again in succeeding editions. To promote his book, the poet reviewed it himself and published the reviews anonymously and, much as authors do today for book jacket blurbs, he sent copies to established figures for their responses. Ralph Waldo Emerson and Bronson Alcott responded favorably; Abraham Lincoln biographer Carl Sandberg reported that the young lawyer in Illinois was very fond of the book. John Greenleaf Whittier is alleged to have thrown his copy in the fire.

Whitman won fame, but continued to engender controversy throughout his life. Near the end, he was supported by public subscription. Walt Whitman died in Camden, New Jersey, on March 26, 1892, at the age of 72.

His roots on Long Island informed all of Whitman's poetry. Using its Native American name, he marveled at Long Island's beauty in "Fish-Shape Paumanok":

> *Starting from fish-shape Paumanok where I*
> *   was born,*
> *Well-begotten, and rais'd by perfect mother-*
> *O to go back to the place where I was born,*
> *To hear the birds sing once more,*
> *To ramble about the house and barn and over*
> *   the fields once more....*

In "Song of Myself" he paid tribute to his home:

> *My tongue, every atom of my blood, form'd from*
> *   this soil, this air,*
> *Born here of parents, born here from parents,*
> *   the same, and their parents the same...*

Whitman wrote of the view "From Montauk Point":

> *I stand a on some mighty eagle's beak,*
> *Eastward the sea absorbing, viewing (nothing*
> *   but sea and sky,)*
> *The tossing waves, the foam, the ships in the*
> *   distance,*
> *The wild unrest, the snowy, curling caps -that*
> *   inbound urge and urge of waves,*
> *Seeking the shores forever.*

Even in death Whitman was controversial. D.H. Lawrence called him "awful." Ezra Pound said, "He is America." Today, his birthplace at 246 Old Walt Whitman Road is an historic site open to the public.

William Cullen Bryant

William Cullen Bryant was a successful poet and editor of the *Evening Post.* He was also one of, if not *the* first commuter from Long Island to New York City.

In 1843, at the age of 49, Bryant bought Cedermere, forty acres in Hempstead harbor. Within the next year he added almost two hundred more acres, ponds, a mill and several buildings to his property.

The author of the poems *Thanatopsis* and *To A Waterfowl*, Bryant took to country life with passion. He ultimately spent half his time on Long Island, traveling by stage to the train station in Mineola, then by rail to New York City.

Bryant became a major benefactor of his adopted town and is even believed to have suggested changing the name of Hempstead Harbor to Roslyn.

James Fenimore Cooper

The author of the *Leatherstocking Tales*—those books that today define eighteenth century life on the upstate New York frontier—spent a great deal of time on Long Island.

Born in New Jersey on September 15, 1789, Cooper was the eleventh of twelve children born to William and Elizabeth Cooper. When he was a year old the family moved to upstate New York, establishing the settlement of Cooperstown.

(continued)

THIS MARCH 1997 VIEW OF FISH-SHAPE PAUMANOK TAKEN BY NASA CLEARLY ILLUSTRATES WHITMAN'S POEM. NASA PHOTO COURTESY OF *NEWSDAY*.

(LEFT) POET WALT WHITMAN, PICTURED HERE IN AN 1881 PHOTO, WROTE OF AMERICA, HIMSELF AND OF HIS NATIVE LONG ISLAND. PHOTO COURTESY OF THE WALT WHITMAN BIRTHPLACE STATE HISTORIC SITE. (RIGHT) THE POET, JOURNALIST, AND EDITOR WILLIAM CULLEN BRYANT (HERE CA. 1830) LIVED IN ROSLYN. HE WAS SO INFLUENTIAL THAT SOME SUGGESTED THAT THE NEW COUNTY CARVED OUT OF QUEENS IN 1899 BE NAMED IN HIS HONOR. PHOTO COURTESY OF THE NASSAU COUNTY DIVISION OF MUSEUM SERVICES/LONG ISLAND STUDIES INSTITUTE/HOFSTRA UNIVERSITY.

(LEFT) LIKE HIS BROTHER, WILLIAM SIDNEY, SETAUKET ARTIST SHEPARD ALONZO MOUNT WAS A WELL-KNOWN PORTRAITIST. HIS MOST FAMOUS WORK IS THIS PAINTING OF HIS DAUGHTER CALLED *THE ROSE OF SHARON*, PAINTED IN 1850. PHOTOS COURTESY LONG ISLAND MUSEUM OF AMERICAN ART, HISTORY & CARRIAGES. (RIGHT) SETAUKET ARTIST WILLIAM SIDNEY MOUNT PAINTED EVERYDAY SCENES OF EVERYDAY PEOPLE. *DANCE OF THE HAYMAKERS* OR, *MUSIC IS CONTAGIOUS*, WAS PAINTED IN 1845.

Cooper attended a private preparatory school and was admitted to Yale in 1803. He was expelled before he could complete his Yale education and signed onto the *Sterling*, as a merchant seaman. He loved the adventure of sea life so much that he entered the Naval Academy in 1808 but, as he had found at Yale, the level of discipline there was not to his liking. Marrying Susan De Lancy in 1811, Cooper left the Navy.

His wife came from a prosperous family with deep roots in New York State. Among her relatives were the Derings of Sag Harbor, the Nicolls of Shelter Island and the Floyds of Mastic. Visiting Shelter Island, he was reading a contemporary English novel. Throwing it down in disgust, he announced that he could write a better tale. His wife challenged him to do so and he produced his first novel, *Precaution*.

Eventually, Cooper wrote several novels about the sea, whaling, and sailors, setting them in the waters around Long Island.

Cooper died at Cooperstown on September 14, 1851, the day before he turned 62.

William Sidney Mount

If Walt Whitman gave voice to the common man of Long Island, William Sidney Mount painted his picture.

Born in Setauket in 1807, Mount, indeed, painted what he knew. Almost reportorial, or photographic, in their faithfulness to detail, Mount captured the daily life of Long Island. An accomplished violinist, Mount was always torn between the two arts he loved and he painted many scenes involving music and dance.

Mount traveled about the countryside in a specially built wagon containing all his artist's materials, and when he died in 1868 his local travels had yielded a snapshot of Long Island and its people caught in great detail going about the business of daily life. He painted men and women, people at work and at leisure. He painted African American and white people; people at rest and in the middle of a dance step.

Mount's paintings were so popular that some were engraved on contemporary currency. Copies were reprinted in the United States and Europe, giving Europeans one of their first glimpses of life in America.

Mount was very much an artist of his time, involved in the life of his community and the politics of his country. Today, his paintings can be seen in the Long Island Museum of American Art, History and Carriages in Stony Brook, where there is even a replica of his "studio on wheels."

(TOP) WALT WHITMAN'S BIRTHPLACE. PHOTO BY M. LEIDER, BRUCE BENNETT STUDIOS. (BELOW) PHOTO BY SCOTT LEVY, BRUCE BENNETT STUDIOS.

PHOTOS BY SCOTT LEVY, BRUCE BENNETT STUDIOS.

FUN AND GAMES

In a hard colonial life, recreation for the pure joy of just doing nothing but having fun was almost unknown. But, whenever the opportunity arose, Long Islanders would do their best to have a good time. Toward that end, they developed unique celebrations around two chores that farmers had to do each year.

Sheep were pastured communally on the Hempstead Plain and in Montauk. Hired "grazers," or herders tended the Montauk herds. In Hempstead, however, branded sheep were put into the communal flock and were allowed to roam the plain.

Then, on Election Day, the last Monday in October, it was time for "sheep parting."

On this day, the owners joined together to shepherd the sheep into a central holding pen located near what is now Westbury. Once there, owners chose those who bore their brands—usually on the ear—and put them into individual pens. All unclaimed sheep were auctioned.

At first, sheep parting was akin to a business meeting. Owners got their sheep, probably talked a bit with each other, then went home. Over the years, however, everyone who was able to travel came. They wold bring picnics, and peddlers with an assortment of wondrous goods would be there. Politicians would speak and impromptu horse races would be held.

While sheep roamed the plain, cattle were fed on the farm. A favored cattle feed was the plentiful salt grass, or sedge, that grew in the Hempstead marshes. Thus, on the second Tuesday in September, farmers would go en masse to "marsh."

They would arrive early and stake a claim to a section of the marsh by standing a farm implement upright in the sedge. The actual cutting, or marshing,

would begin at daylight. The cut grass was immediately taken by boat to dry land where it was spread out to dry. Then, the marshers would either use it for their own cattle or sell it.

Because marshing could take several days, participants lived in temporary huts and feasted on fresh bounty from the sea.

Much to the chagrin of the clergy, horse racing flourished on Long Island beginning in the seventeenth century.

In 1670, Daniel Denton wrote: "Towards the middle of Long-Island lyeth a plain sixteen miles long and four broad, upon which plain grows very fine grass, that makes exceeding good Hay, and is very good pasture for sheep or other Cattel; where you shall find neither stick nor stone to hinder the Horse heels, or endanger them in their Races, and once a year the best Horses in the Island are brought hither to try their swiftness, and the swiftest rewarded with a silver Cup, two being Annually procured for that purpose."

The first track was founded by Governor Richard Nicolls in 1665. He called the site, located near Hempstead, Salisbury Plain, and called the course New Market, naming both after their counterparts in England.

The Union Course in Jamaica was the site of an 1823 race between horses representing the north and south. Contemporary accounts estimated a gate of 60,000 people and, 22 years later, that was topped by attendance of 70,000 to watch another race.

By the time of the American centennial in 1876, there were tracks scattered across Long Island and, shortly thereafter, the region would begin to play a larger role in the nation's racing history.

PHOTO BY JOE ROGATE, BRUCE BENNETT STUDIOS.

SEA TALES: LIVES LOST, LIVES SAVED

Daniel Webster called the Long Island Sound "the Mediterranean of the Western Hemisphere," but a nineteenth century sea captain with experience sailing in waters from the Great Lakes to the China coast called it "one of the toughest runs in the world."

Thus, beginning in 1797, there were twenty-three lighthouses built around Long Island. They would stand sentry not only on the north shore's Sound waters, but on the south shore and East End as well. Lighthouses were also built to guide boats between the forks in Gardiner's Bay.

The Montauk Light was the first built in New York State, the fifth in a series of lights built by the federal government along the east coast.

In addition, lifesaving stations were built in the mid-nineteenth century on Long Island. Originally staffed by volunteers, the Life-Saving Service merged with the Revenue Cutter Service in 1915. The latter, originally called the Revenue Marines, was established by Treasury Secretary Alexander Hamilton in 1790 to ensure that inbound cargo that would be taxed while coming through an official port of entry. Until that time, ships would offload cargo outside these ports to avoid import tariffs.

Together, the Life-Saving and Revenue Cutter Services formed the United States Coast Guard.

Lighthouses, the Life-Saving Service, and the Coast Guard saved untold hundreds of lives in the last two hundred years. Some lives, however, were lost in shipwrecks off Long Island.

The most famous was the wreck of the *Lexington*, a ship that caught fire off Eaton's Neck in minus-ten-degree weather in January 1840. Only four people survived. One hundred thirty-nine were lost.

Remembering Disaster

Using historical material gathered for the *Suffolk Sun* newspaper, Barbara Marhoefer told Long Island stories to children in her book, *Witches, Whales, Petticoats & Sails.*

A survivor of another disaster at sea told her story in 1898, when she was 84 years old.

"The wind howled through the darkness...The vessel pitched and rolled," Maria Sayre recalled the 1827 voyage of the *David Porter* in the *Sag Harbor Express.*

Thirteen-year-old Maria was traveling to Manhattan with her aunt and uncle, Mr. and Mrs. Samuel L'Hommedieu. Their ship left Sag Harbor and, shortly after, it began to rain. Mrs. Sayre recalled feeling seasick in the storm and going below to rest. The storm continued through the night.

When morning came the *David Porter* was off Eaton's Neck and passengers urged the captain to bring the ship into harbor. When waves began to hit the ship broadside, Mrs. Sayre said, "Fearing I would be washed overboard, my uncle tied me up in the shrouds as high as he could reach. The captain called to him, advising him to take me down, for if the vessel foundered, I would go down with it."

(continued)

WHALING BOATS LIKE THIS ONE THAT SAILED OUT OF SAG HARBOR SO CAPTIVATED THE IMAGINATION OF JAMES FENIMORE COOPER THAT HE WROTE SEVERAL TALES OF WHALING SET IN AND AROUND LONG ISLAND. PHOTO COURTESY OF THE NASSAU COUNTY DIVISION OF MUSEUM SERVICES/LONG ISLAND STUDIES INSTITUTE/HOFSTRA UNIVERSITY.

Her uncle tied the child to a pump. The ship struck the shore and broke in two. The child was thrown into shallow water and was able to get to shore.

No one was lost in the sinking, but Mrs. Sayre did report her pink and lavender-striped dress was ruined. The *David Porter* broke apart. Mr. and Mrs. L'Hommedieu and their niece completed their journey into New York by coach.

Gold Rush Fever

Long Islanders were not immune to the lure of gold in California. Young—and not so young—men were leaving to seek fortune in the west and, because of this and the competition from whalers in New England, it was becoming more and more difficult to earn a living as a whaler.

Thus, in January 1849, nineteen Sag Harbor and East Hampton whaling captains joined with forty-one other men to form the Southampton and California Mining and Trading Company. They bought a whaling ship, the *Sabine*, and filled her hold with supplies they intended to sell to other miners. The nineteen seamen drew lots to

determine which shipboard responsibility each would assume. They left on February 7 and, after six months, managed to reach San Francisco harbor.

Albert Jagger of Southampton wrote his wife, describing the city. "Inhabitants seem to be coming and going all the time, and every nook and corner is full...[gold and silver] are almost as plenty as sand is with you."

Finding too much competition in San Francisco, they sailed up the Sacramento River and opened their ship store for business. Jagger, realizing the better money was to be made in selling supplies, stayed behind. Winter, however, brought almost no business and, ultimately, Jagger went prospecting. Shareholders sold the *Sabina* and her cargo, each making $350.

Captain Harry Green of Southampton bought the *Sabina* for $1,150 from the other investors (who had paid $8,000 for the ship back east) and sailed it back to San Francisco.

Jagger returned to Southampton in 1851. The *Sabina* was abandoned in San Francisco harbor. She broke apart and was buried in the landfill that extended the city.

HSBC BANK USA

HSBC Bank USA may be a fairly new banking brand name to New Yorkers, but the bank has a proud history in the region dating back to 1850 when it was founded as the Marine Trust Company in Buffalo for the purpose of financing the new shipping trade along the Great Lakes. As the bank expanded its services into the central areas, or midland, of New York, it assumed the name of Marine Midland Bank.

The name change to HSBC Bank USA from Marine Midland in 1999 was a result of a unified branding campaign designed to increase customer awareness about the bank's affiliation with HSBC Holdings plc, the bank's London-based parent company. HSBC Holdings plc is one of the world's largest financial service organizations with more than 6,500 offices in 79 countries and territories operating in Europe, the Asia-Pacific region, the Americas, the Middle East, and Africa.

The same year the bank adopted its new name, HSBC completed one of the most important events in the bank's history: the acquisition of Republic National Bank of New York, making HSBC the third largest depository institution with the largest branch network in New York State. Through the acquisition, the bank added branches in Florida and California. On Long Island, HSBC gained 12 additional branches, increasing the number of branches to 46.

By combining Republic with HSBC, the bank doubled its private banking, extended its domestic, personal, and commercial banking business, and enhanced its global markets business in treasury and foreign exchange. The bank also acquired world-leading banknotes and bullion trading operations, making it a world leader in banknotes

PORT WASHINGTON BRANCH LOCATED AT SOUNDVIEW MARKETPLACE/SHORE ROAD.

and bullion trading and the fifth largest factoring service in the U.S. The bank has also been named as the top bank in U.S. insurance sales in 1999 by the Financial Institutions Insurance Association.

HSBC Bank USA offers its retail customers a wide variety of banking services designed to meet consumers' investment goals, ranging from traditional products such as savings and checking accounts and certificates of deposit; to investment products and services including brokerage, insurance, estate planning, and portfolio management. As a major consumerlender, the bank issues home mortgages, home equity loans, auto and education lending, and other types of consumer loans. HSBC also issues its own credit cards.

HSBC draws upon its expert private bankers and investment professionals to help domestic and international private banking clients grow and preserve their capital. Among the vehicles employed are such services as tax andinheritance planning, portfolio management, trust and estate services, estate planning services, securities custody services, and foreign exchange.

As a leading Small Business Administration and commercial lender, HSBC offers its business customers the full range of deposit, cash management, and employee benefit trust services, and through the parent HSBC Group, access to a broad array of trade services in the U.S. and internationally.

HSBC also competes nationally in commercial finance and is a leading mortgage originator among commercial banks. Its commercial finance business includes secured lending through relationship managers. In its mortgage business, HSBC acts as a warehouse lender and services its own mortgages as well as those of other investors.

In addition to serving the business needs of customers, HSBC nurtures the communities in which it conducts business by supporting local organizations.

NEWLY DESIGNED INVESTMENT CENTER.

One Long Island community, which has benefited from HSBC outreach, is Bellport/East Patchogue which recently honored the bank for its assistance to the Bellport Hagerman East Patchogue Alliance, a group which strives to improve neighborhood conditions and the quality of life of community members through social service and housing programs, and also home ownership assistance for low- to moderate-income households.

HSBC is especially interested in helping people of modest means attain the goal of home ownership. As a result, it undertakes the development of programs which will serve to make home ownership affordable. The bank participates in Federal Home Loan Bank programs, which enable lower income families to obtain matching grants for down payments and closing costs. Recently, HSBC's association with the Federal Home Loan Bank of New York resulted in a $450,000 grant which subsidized mortgage payments for buyers of units in Woodcrest Estates, an affordable housing community for senior citizens located in Port Jefferson Station.

The bank has also worked with the Long Island Development Corporation, a not-for-profit corporation that provides financial and technical assistance to small businesses on Long Island. HSBC has contributed funds annually to a lending and assistance program which provides a source of procurement contracts to firms that would not otherwise be able to obtain government or private sector contracts.

Education is another focus of HSBC's community outreach. Manhasset's Institute for Student Achievement received an HSBC grant to support its programs for low-performing students at risk of failure. And students at SUNY-Old Westbury who plan to study abroad were helped to realize their goals through an HSBC sponsorship program.

As HSBC evolves it continues to dedicate itself to serving its customers and its customers' communities through its extensive branch network, through its commitments to community development, and through the international reach it offers all customers. ■

POLYTECHNIC UNIVERSITY

Founded in 1854, Polytechnic University, the nation's second oldest science and engineering school, has been an education leader on Long Island for four decades.

Today, Polytechnic is undergoing an extraordinary transformation on Long Island. It has strengthened and expanded its graduate programs by creating a Graduate Center for Professional Studies. The center, conducting programs in strategic locations, offers trend-setting courses and degrees in cutting-edge disciplines, including wireless, e-commerce, telecommunications, computer science, software engineering, and management of technology. For the first time, the university is offering three executive-format master's programs on Long Island: the Master of Engineering in Wireless, the Master of Science in Management of Technology, and the Master of Science in Telecommunications Information Management. These three masters programs provide exceptional opportunities for mid-career professionals who prefer to continue working full-time and attend school part-time on a concentrated and accelerated basis on weekends.

Long Island is a technology-based economy and society, said Dr. Ivan T. Frisch, Polytechnic's provost, executive vice president, and director of the university's new Graduate Center. "We all face the challenge of upgrading our knowledge and skills, adapting to new markets and leading innovations for the rest of the country," he said. "The keystone to meeting this challenge is education, reeducation and continuing education. That is our mission on Long Island."

Over the past 10 years, close to 900 students on Long Island have graduated from Polytechnic's graduate programs in engineering, science, and technology, and more than 1,600 students have taken courses. Among the university's graduates are more than 200 top executives

POLYTECHNIC PRODUCES LEADERS: JAMES M. SMITH, LEFT, PRESIDENT AND CHIEF OPERATING OFFICER OF AIL SYSTEMS INC. IN DEER PARK, CREDITS MUCH OF HIS SUCCESS TO A POLYTECHNIC MASTER'S DEGREE IN ELECTRICAL ENGINEERING, WHICH HE EARNED PART TIME. DAVID E. FOWLER, AN ENGINEER AT AIL, EARNED HIS B.S. IN MECHANICAL ENGINEERING FROM POLYTECHNIC AND IS PURSUING A MASTER'S DEGREE AT THE SCHOOL WHILE WORKING FULL TIME.

of Long Island firms. One executive, James M. Smith, president and chief operating officer of AIL Systems Inc., a defense, electronics, and aerospace company based in Deer Park, Long Island, took evening classes at Polytechnic's Long Island campus to earn a master's degree in electrical engineering in 1971. "Polytechnic gave me a first-class engineering education," said Smith. "The strong fundamentals I got at Polytechnic helped me and countless others on Long Island solidify our careers in engineering and other technical fields."

EXPERT TEACHERS: GRADUATE FACULTY AT POLYTECHNIC UNIVERSITY ON LONG ISLAND HAVE REAL-WORLD PROFESSIONAL EXPERIENCE AND HAVE WON PRESTIGIOUS PROFESSIONAL AND ACADEMIC PRIZES.

HIGH-TECH FACILITIES: STUDENTS AT
POLYTECHNIC UNIVERSITY'S GRADUATE CENTER
FOR PROFESSIONAL STUDIES ON LONG ISLAND
HAVE ACCESS TO STATE-OF-THE-ART LABORATORIES
AND PROGRAMS IN WIRELESS, E-COMMERCE,
TELECOMMUNICATIONS, COMPUTER SCIENCE,
SOFTWARE ENGINEERING, AND MANAGEMENT
OF TECHNOLOGY.

Polytechnic's enduring relationships with business and industry were a unique draw for Smith. "Polytechnic has a big influence on Long Island's technical preeminence," he said. "Continuing my career while earning a graduate degree was possible only because of that relationship."

Polytechnic's transformation is made possible by the university's $275 million Campaign for Polytechnic— *Fulfilling the American Dream*, including a $175 million bequest from the estates of Donald F. Othmer, a long-time Polytechnic professor of chemical engineering, and his wife, Mildred Topp Othmer. Their bequest is the largest private cash gift ever to an American university.

To guide the transformation, the university, led by President David C. Chang, has completed *Strategic Planning 2000*, a bold plan to expand graduate studies on Long Island while consolidating all undergraduate programs at a new world-class campus at MetroTech Center in Brooklyn. The transformation is well under way. The Graduate Center for Professional Studies has been established on Long Island, and more than $100 million is being invested in capital and intellectual improvements on the MetroTech campus.

One of the most important improvements at MetroTech is a $41 million, 16-story, 400-bed residence hall, a facility that allows Polytechnic to attract top students not only from Long Island but also nationally, and to increase its undergraduate enrollment from 1,800 to 2,800. This enlarged pool of skilled and motivated students are a major source of talent for industry on Long Island.

Under *Strategic Planning 2000*, the university is building upon its stellar history as a leader in research and education and is the metropolitan area's preeminent resource in science and technology. Polytechnic's roster of historic figures include Dr. Herman F. Mark, the father of polymer science, who established the Polymer Research Institute at the university in 1942, and Dr. Ernst Weber, former president of Polytechnic and a pioneer in microwave technology.

Today, the Polytechnic faculty continues to garner honors and acclaim: six faculty members, including Frisch, are members of the prestigious National Academy of Engineering. Three are among the 11 winners of the Heinrich Hertz Award, initiated in 1989 by the Institute of Electrical and Electronic Engineers (IEEE) to recognize outstanding achievements in Hertizian (radio waves), and 11 are IEEE Fellows, an honor limited to one-tenth of one percent of the organization's membership.

Polytechnic boasts three Nobel Prize winners: two alumni, Dr. Martin L. Perl, who won the Prize in physics in 1955, and Dr. Gertrude Elion, who won the Prize in medicine in 1988, and a former faculty member, Professor Rudolph Marcus, who won the Prize in chemistry in 1992. "The direction Polytechnic is taking in this new century is impressive," said Smith, "and should guarantee its standing as a first-rate school for a long time to come." ∎

FRONTIERS OF RESEARCH: POLYTECHNIC
UNIVERSITY HAS INCREASED ITS COMMITMENT
TO PROVIDE PART-TIME CUTTING-EDGE GRADU-
ATE COURSES ON LONG ISLAND TO ALLOW
PROFESSIONALS TO ADVANCE THEIR CAREERS
WHILE WORKING FULL TIME.

ROSLYN SAVINGS BANK

Founded in 1876 as "a conservative institution in the interest of the people of Long Island," Roslyn Savings Bank is one of the largest and most successful savings banks in New York State. Now operating a large full-service branch network throughout Nassau/Suffolk, Brooklyn, and Queens, Roslyn Savings Bank holds almost $8 billion in assets and is among the largest publicly held thrift institutions in New York. Through its wide-ranging branch network, the bank continues to fulfill an important aspect of its founding mission, "to assist people to build or purchase their homes."

SEPTEMBER 1, 1932, COMPLETED NEW BANK BUILDING. ROSLYN SAVINGS BANK STILL OPERATES A BRANCH OFFICE IN THE SAME BUILDING AT 1400 OLD NORTHERN BOULEVARD.

Roslyn Savings Bank, Long Island's first financial institution, acquired TR Financial in 1999, the parent company of Roosevelt Savings Bank which was founded in 1895.

Strong throughout its history and never having missed a dividend payment, Roslyn Savings Bank changed from a mutual savings bank to a public corporation in 1997. One hundred percent of its initial public stock offering was purchased by the bank's depositors; for many, this represented their first purchase of stock in any company. Additionally, the bank has paid a special dividend to its depositors each year for more than a decade, a record unparalleled in the banking industry.

As the dominant bank in each of the neighborhoods in which it does business, Roslyn Savings Bank has acquired a very loyal customer base. Bank leadership has also been highly stable: Chairman and CEO Joseph L. Mancino has been with the bank for more than 40 years, beginning his career as a safe deposit vault attendant. President and COO John R. Bransfield, Jr. is well-known and highly regarded in the financial community and has been the financial backbone of many commercial and residential construction projects throughout Long Island.

Executive Vice President and Retail Banking Officer Daniel L. Murphy began his banking career at Roslyn as a teller more than 20 years ago. Other senior managers and employees have similarly enjoyed long careers at Roslyn, living in the community, and becoming intimately involved in the community as they moved up in the bank's hierarchy. The result is that they know the customers of Roslyn Savings Bank, and have established a tradition and reputation for highly personal customer service.

Roslyn offers its customers a full range of banking services. Particularly notable among these services is its policy of offering free checking accounts with no minimum balances. Online banking and bill paying are also free to Roslyn depositors. Use of the Roslyn Bankcard offers free access at any Roslyn ATM and debit card purchases at retail Visa locations.

While the expansion of online banking services has added new layers of banking convenience for customers, offering them the opportunity to initiate and follow through on many banking functions from anywhere, at any time of the day or night, the emphasis at Roslyn Savings Bank remains its professionally staffed, full-service branches where employees are available to serve customers who prefer personal assistance. Each Roslyn Savings Bank branch has an on-premises specialist in alternative investments such as variable annuities. Many employees within the branch network are New York State licensed investment representatives and are thus able to prepare customized financial plans using a wide variety of mutual funds, annuities, and life insurance products to help customers meet their retirement or other long-term financial goals. Roslyn's customers also appreciate the bank's policy of extended hours. For the convenience of its depositors, bank hours extend until 8 pm on Mondays, and from 9 am to 1 pm on Saturdays.

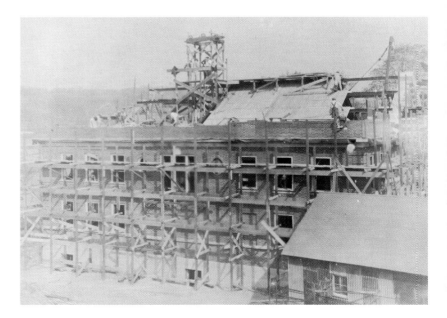

MAY 1, 1932, 1400 OLD NORTHERN BOULEVARD, ROSLYN, NEW YORK.

BANK FLOOR CIRCA 1940, 1400 OLD NORTHERN BOULEVARD.

For after-hours banking, Roslyn maintains a 24-hour, 7-day-a-week telephone banking service through which customers may arrange loans as well as completing other transactions. Last year Roslyn added mortgage origination to its many Internet-based services.

Roslyn Savings Bank has been a leader in helping generations of Long Islanders to achieve home ownership.

SITE OF A NEW MAIN BUILDING FINISHED IN SEPTEMBER OF 1932.

It has likely issued more home mortgages than any other bank serving the Long Island community. As a result, the bank also has developed strong relationships with the builder and development communities and has funded extensive commercial real estate as well. The Hamlet is among the highly visible communities it has funded on Long Island. Last year, as a natural extension of its activities in commercial lending, Roslyn entered the business banking and financial services market. This new activity allows business owners to consolidate their business and personal banking under one roof. Though its BusinesSuite product offerings Roslyn assists business owners in creating a customized package of services allowing them to address both their short- and long-term goals.

Roslyn Savings Bank's involvement in community programs is among the most extensive of such commitments among Long Island corporations. When it became a public company, Roslyn established a special charitable foundation with an allocation of approximately $22 million worth of stock. The bank has a particular commitment to supporting programs that provide food and shelter to the homeless, help needy children in the community, and preserve and revitalize Long Island's neighborhoods. Numerous community service organizations have benefited from the foundation's generosity, among them Interfaith Nutrition Network, Food Care, Community Development Corp. of Long Island, St. Christopher Ottlie Services for Families and Children, Tilles Center for the Performing Arts, Neighborhood Housing Services of New York City, and many others. ■

THE GARDEN CITY HOTEL

While the fuel that drives Long Island's economic success has changed over the past 125 years, one constant has remained on the region's business landscape—The Garden City Hotel and its commitment to meeting the needs of its corporate and social clients. Whether it was a meeting in 1904 between William Vanderbilt and his business associates, or a state-of-the-art videoconference in the year 2001 for a multi-site organization such as Canon USA, Inc., the luxurious, independent hotel centered in the historic Village of Garden City has served as Long Island's address for business success since the first hotel debuted on this site in 1874.

"The Garden City Hotel has a unique appeal that dates back more than a century," said president and general manager Cathy Nelkin Miller. "Like our predecessors, our commitment to superior quality and service has earned this hotel its reputation as being among the finest hotels in the world."

GARDEN CITY HOTEL'S GUEST ROOMS ARE APPOINTED WITH THE SAME HANDSOME FURNISHINGS ONE MIGHT FIND IN AN ELEGANT HOME.

The Address for Business Success

With 16 meeting rooms, which can accommodate groups from six to 600 people, the hotel also serves as the site of choice for meeting and travel planners throughout the metropolitan New York area.

"What separates us from other hotels is our intense interest in our clients, and our unparalleled knowledge of their industries," said Jennifer Pettas, Conference Services Manager. "This level of caring and 'going the extra mile' for a client is ultimately what makes for success. In our minds, the only truly successful business event is a flaw-less business event—and that begins with asking the right questions. It ensures that no detail is overlooked."

Each corporate client of the Garden City Hotel receives the attention of a dedicated member of the hotel's Conference Services team, who is then responsible for answering to the needs of that client and his or her event. These professionals work on all aspects of event planning, including scheduling events; identifying and securing needed technologies; and creating individualized menus for each conference.

"The success of a corporate function depends on creating the right atmosphere to achieve the goals of the event," added Allison Mitchell, Director of Sales. "Whether it is a luxurious ballroom to host an annual stockholders' meeting or the launch of a new product, or a quiet meeting room needed for thoughtful discussion, this hotel offers the complete spectrum of facilities and amenities for every business function."

THE GARDEN CITY HOTEL IS THE MOST PROMINENT LANDMARK IN THE LOVELY VILLAGE OF GARDEN CITY.

THE GRACIOUS BOARD ROOM OF THE GARDEN CITY HOTEL IS THE SITE FOR MANY IMPORTANT BUSINESS MEETINGS.

Fully equipped for Internet access, the Garden City Hotel utilizes state-of-the-art T-1 services to meet the interactive needs of corporations today. From streaming hotel-based events onto the World Wide Web to video-conferencing between sites around the world, the hotel's technical staff regularly works with corporations to identify and fulfill their communications needs according to each specific circumstance.

The Business Traveler's Choice

While offering all the Old World charm of its predecessors, the contemporary Garden City Hotel also provides the finest in modern amenities. The GCH Business Support Center offers a complete array of services, including faxing, photocopying, laser and color printing, computer workstation rentals, typing services, and Internet access.

The hotel's 280 exquisitely appointed guestrooms include nine executive suites with features and services geared strictly to the business traveler. Additionally, the hotel offers three grand suites and four penthouse suites, complete with fireplaces and terraces overlooking the historic Village of Garden City.

Because of its central location and rich history, the Garden City Hotel also serves as a favored gathering spot for governmental and business leaders and is the site for the "most powerful" of power breakfasts and lunches in the region. Whether they are dining in the hotel's premier restaurant, The Polo Grill, or enjoying a catered affair, the leaders and decision-makers who visit the Garden City Hotel enjoy culinary creations unmatched by other hotels in the region.

A Rich History

Perhaps the most notable event associated with the Garden City Hotel occurred on May 20, 1927, when Charles Lindbergh spent the night before his historic flight dining with friends and family as a guest of the hotel. However, with the Great Depression, the Gatsby-era excesses of the Garden City Hotel faded, as they did for the entire nation. It wasn't until after World War II that the community around the hotel began to grow and flourish as a residential suburban village.

All the while, the hotel continued to serve as land-mark lodging for the Long Island community, attracting vacationer and businessman alike. From a visit in 1959 by presidential-hopeful John F. Kennedy and his wife, Jacqueline, to the recent stays of First Lady Hillary Clinton and former Prime Minister Margaret Thatcher, the Garden City Hotel remains the hotel of choice for leaders from the worlds of business, government, entertainment, and society as they visit the New York area.

"The Garden City Hotel name has been associated with excellence in service and accommodations for more than a century," said Nelkin Miller, the hotel's president and general manager. "While the times have changed and the hotel industry has evolved, our goal today is to uphold that legacy and continue to offer world-class service for all who visit. It's that effort that has stood the test of time, and we will continue to ensure our guests receive the best hotel experience in this community." ■

A GRAND SUITE AT THE GARDEN CITY HOTEL INCLUDES A GENEROUS AREA FOR PRIVATE DINING.

LONG ISLAND RAIL ROAD

The oldest railroad in the United States still operating under its original name, the Long Island Rail Road (LIRR) has a proud history dating back to its founding in 1834. Today, the LIRR is the busiest commuter railroad in the country—during 2000 the railroad carried 85.3 million passengers, the highest number since 1949 and a continuation of an eight-year increase in ridership. Each weekday, the LIRR's 740 daily trains carry almost 300,000 passengers. With about 1,000 passengers passing through the western terminus, Penn Station, every 90 seconds, LIRR services more people than Kennedy and LaGuardia airports combined.

Penn Station, the most heavily used railroad facility in the United States, is unique in that it is shared by three railroads: Amtrak, New Jersey Transit, and the LIRR. More than 50 percent of the trains at Penn Station are operated by the LIRR.

An integral and essential part of the region's economy, the railroad's history and development are intimately tied to the history and development of Long Island. Over its long history, the LIRR has continually adapted itself to meet the changing transportation needs of Long Islanders. In the earliest years of the last century, the LIRR was a founder of the Long Island Association (LIA), the Island's first and still its most important chamber of commerce. The first office of the LIA was in Penn Station.

Speeding the way from Brooklyn to Boston

The Main Line of the LIRR was completed in 1844, long before the concept of a suburb had been envisioned. It was designed, in fact, to be a new and faster way of traveling to Boston from Brooklyn. The new railroad terminated in Greenport, where travelers boarded a

"ALL ABOARD!" LIRR CONDUCTOR SIGNALS DEPARTURE TIME.

steamboat to cross Long Island Sound, and then another train for the rest of the trip to Boston. The total time for this new express route north was 11 and a half hours.

During the railroad-building era that followed, there were several competing railroads on the Island, like the South Side Railroad, and the Flushing Railroad. There were fare wars, bankruptcies, and foreclosures until the railroad was finally unified in the early 1880s. Station locations were established as land was donated by local communities. The dream of service into Manhattan finally became a reality in 1910, when the Pennsylvania Railroad constructed a tunnel under the East River. Completion of this link, and nearly simultaneous electrification, spurred the development of real estate along the branches of the railroad, in turn leading to the LIRR's role as a commuter railroad.

In the 1950s, New York State took the first steps toward government ownership of the railroad. In 1968, the Metropolitan Transportation Authority was created, and today, the LIRR is an MTA agency.

Improving service for passengers

With driving on Long Island, particularly during rush hours, no less than a nightmare, part of the LIRR's ongoing mission has been to contribute to the economic well-being of Long Island, and to its quality of life, by offering a convenient, economical alternative to driving.

The LIRR is continually at work on projects to significantly improve its service. One major project, the $190-million renovation of the Penn Station terminal, resulted in riders now enjoying climate-controlled, well-lighted waiting areas. Electronic sign boards, located throughout the station, make it easy to find trains. A new entrance from 34th Street, as well as new stairways, escalators, and many other amenities, have similarly received high marks from riders.

ONE OF THE LIRR'S NEW DIESEL TRAINS TRAVELS EAST ACROSS THE SHINNECOCK CANAL BRIDGE. THE NEW BI-LEVEL COACHES WERE DESIGNED IN PART BY CUSTOMERS.

MAINTAINING THE FLEET IS ESSENTIAL FOR RELIABILITY. LIRR EMPLOYEES AT THE RAILROAD'S HILLSIDE MAINTENANCE FACILITY WORK TO KEEP COMPONENTS IN TIP-TOP SHAPE.

The LIRR has involved its passengers in another major improvement: replacement of its aging diesel fleet. During 1999, the railroad took delivery of 134 new bi-level coaches with interiors designed with commuter input. These new coaches feature wider aisles, more comfortable seats, and better lighting.

The company's initiatives have meant that the majority of riders need no longer change trains to arrive in Manhattan. Most of the LIRR service area now enjoys one-train service into Penn Station, with the exception of Eastern Long Island and a small portion of the North Shore; ridership in these areas was enhanced in 1999 with the addition of a new fleet of 46 diesel and dual-mode locomotives.

Current LIRR initiatives involve the long-awaited AirTrain and East Side Access. By 2003, through a Port Authority of NY and NJ/LIRR collaboration, Long Islanders traveling to Kennedy Airport will have a fast and convenient option as AirTrain links Kennedy's terminals with the LIRR's Jamaica Station where 10 of the railroad's 11 branches merge. The LIRR's East Side Access project will use an existing East River tunnel at 63rd Street and connect with a subway line running into Grand Central Station. By providing direct East Side access, the LIRR expects to reduce travel time for some 53 percent of its daily commuters in the future.

Although daily commuters constitute the largest portion of the LIRR's ridership, programs are in place to encourage use of the railroad for leisure-time and reverse-peak travel. Among the incentives developed are special family fares, reduced ticket prices to New York City attractions, and the coordination of train and bus schedules on Long Island. The LIRR also promotes tourism by running trips to Long Island's magnificent beaches, vineyards, museums, and its famed homes and gardens. ■

TRANSPORTATION OLD AND NEW. AN LIRR ELECTRIC TRAIN OPERATES THROUGH SCENIC PLANDOME ALONGSIDE A HORSEBACK RIDING TRAIL.

CHAPTER FOUR

1876 TO 1918

MONTAUK LIGHTHOUSE.
PHOTO BY ROB AMATO, BRUCE BENNETT STUDIOS.

The late nineteenth century was, indeed, an exciting time in which to live. A new age was heralded by Machinery Hall, the highlight of the 1876 Centennial Exposition in Philadelphia. Visitors there marveled at working models of steam engines and dynamos. For the first time, America was flexing its muscles as an industrial nation and Americans believed that nothing was out of reach; that machines were wonderful inventions that would only bring good things to humanity.

Long Island was looking at the sixth year of the thirteen it would take to construct the Brooklyn Bridge, coal mines and railroads had created a wealthy upper class who would soon begin to spend a lot of their money on Long Island. And, before the end of the century, a two-county Long Island as we know it today would take shape.

The 1870 census showed 31,134 people living in the Towns of Hempstead, North Hempstead and Oyster Bay, today's Nassau County. By 1880, the total population there would grow to 37,647. Suffolk's 1870 population of 46,924 would grow to 53,888 by 1880.

Long Island's farmers were growing potatoes, cabbages, strawberries, rye, peas, and cucumbers. Blue Point oysters made that south shore community famous. Abundant shellfish were harvested for home use and for the finest restaurants in New York. Mechanical dredges depleted the supply of home-grown oysters, so that seed beds—most notably using oysters from Connecticut— were planted. In 1873, Pekin Ducks were imported from China and duck farming became a major industry, most notably in Moriches, Eastport, and Speonk. Eventually, Long Island-raised ducks accounted for 60 percent of all duck dinners in the United States.

With no need to provide transit to New England, Long Island Rail Road officials began to look on Long Island for their business. They transported people and goods into and out of New York City. As Long Island grew they shaped what would ultimately become the largest commuter railroad in the United States.

The railroad was cobbled together out of several smaller lines—the South Shore line, the Flushing line, and the North Side Railroad. In addition, the railroad

ORIGINALLY BUILT AS A STEAM MILL WHEN IT WAS BUILT IN 1865, THIS BUILDING ON THE NORTH SIDE OF PRIME'S POND IN HUNTINGTON WAS USED AS A THIMBLE FACTORY AFTER 1871. IT IS SHOWN HERE IN 1895. COURTESY OF THE NASSAU COUNTY DIVISION OF MUSEUM SERVICES/LONG ISLAND STUDIES INSTITUTE/HOFSTRA UNIVERSITY.

SADDLE ROCK GRIST MILL IN GREAT NECK. PHOTO BY ROB AMATO, BRUCE BENNETT STUDIOS.

opened more routes on its own so that, by 1896, there were almost four hundred miles of track in the system and hundreds of thousands of commuters were using the line each weekday. By the end of the century, the Montauk and Port Washington lines were complete.

In addition to commuter services, the railroad began an intensive campaign to publicize the joys of vacationing, and living, on Long Island. A late-century brochure claimed that since the railroad had been built "towns and villages have sprung up, the highways graded and a wonderful growth of seaside resorts developed. There are no more fortunate people than those who have established permanent residence on Long Island."

From the middle of the eighteenth century, ships were used for passenger and cargo transport between Long Island and New York City. Until Robert Fulton's 1814 invention of the steam engine, some ships were even powered by horses on treadmills turning paddlewheels.

By 1835, the combination of steamboats and rail made the trip from New York to Boston—which only a few years before had taken the better part of a week— a journey of only fourteen hours.

Steamboats began operating into and out of Long Island ports early on. Port Jefferson was the busiest of shipbuilding towns, with twelve of Long Island's twenty-five yards located there. The first ship built in Port Jefferson was completed in 1796. The *Nonowontuc*, the first of P.T. Barnum's fleet, was built there. There were also yards in Huntington, Oyster Bay, and Greenport.

Long Island's seaside towns sported a variety of guesthouses and hotels, ranging from the very simple to Babylon's Argyle Hotel, which boasted 350 rooms and fourteen guest cottages. Built in 1882, the Argyle was never more than one-third occupied. It was demolished in 1904, having never fulfilled its promise as a premier resort.

THIS GROCERY STORE ON THE CORNER OF MAIN AND FRONT STREETS IN HEMPSTEAD WAS TYPICAL OF THE MID-1880S. COURTESY OF THE NASSAU COUNTY DIVISION OF MUSEUM SERVICES/LONG ISLAND STUDIES INSTITUTE/HOFSTRA UNIVERSITY.

Elsewhere, however, tourism flourished and attracted all manner of entrepreneurs. Of these, the most noted was likely Bridgeport, Connecticut, resident P.T. Barnum. With his friend Captain Charles E. Tooker and twenty-five other stockholders, Barnum formed the Bridgeport & Port Jefferson Steamboat Company.

Early ferry travelers were mostly Long Island farmers accompanying their crops to Bridgeport for sale and salesmen from Bridgeport with business on Long Island. There was also a brisk cargo trade. The company is still ferrying and now brings passengers year-round to Long Island and transports Long Islanders who wish to travel to New England. Today, the only reminders of Barnum's influence in Port Jefferson are two streets: Barnum Avenue and Caroline Avenue, the latter named for Barnum's daughter.

In 1906, the entrepreneurial spirit took hold in Long Beach, when developer William Reynolds began to see the possibilities there.

After the successful development of Bedford-Stuyvesant, Bensonhurst, and Coney Island's Dreamland Park, Reynolds decided to create Long Beach as the "Riviera of the East." He followed others who were unsuccessful in their development efforts. Reynolds had the grandest vision, establishing building codes so that all homes there would look like Spanish villas and restrictive covenants so that only white Anglo-Saxon Protestants could buy the homes. He also dredged a channel—today's Reynold's Channel—so that excursion boats could reach Long Beach. A master of publicity, Reynolds had some of his Coney Island elephants brought to Long Beach to, he said, help build the boardwalk there.

Reynolds' company failed in 1918. The restrictive covenants were lifted and the City of Long Beach—so designated by the State Legislature in 1922—became a strong community of people of all backgrounds. Cab Calloway, James Cagney, Humphrey Bogart, and John Barrymore lived there at various times.

Of course, Long Island was not growing in a vacuum. In fact, any population or mercantile growth on Long Island would pale next to that experienced by her western neighbors, Brooklyn and Queens.

The entire region was becoming more and more cosmopolitan. Immigrants were flooding New York Harbor, bringing new cultures and religions to America's shores. The first synagogue on Long Island was dedicated in Sag Harbor in 1898—the same town where, in 1829, the first Catholic mass was said.

Of all the places on Long Island, by the mid-nineteenth century Brooklyn was the fastest growing. Established as one of the original towns in Kings County, by the end of the century it resembled a series of nesting dolls, with the Village of Brooklyn incorporated within the Town of Brooklyn; the Village of Williamsburg incorporated within the Town of Bushwick; the Town of Brooklyn—which included the Village of Brooklyn—becoming the City of Brooklyn,

HEFFLEY'S DRUG STORE IN BABYLON, SHOWN HERE IN 1910, SOLD A VARIETY OF NECESSITIES, SMALL LUX-
URY ITEMS AND BOASTED A FULLY STOCKED SODA FOUNTAIN. COURTESY OF THE NASSAU COUNTY DIVISION
OF MUSEUM SERVICES/LONG ISLAND STUDIES INSTITUTE/HOFSTRA UNIVERSITY.

and so on. Finally, in 1896, seeing its commercial interests best served by doing so, Brooklyn became part of New York City under the legislative act that created Greater New York.

Meanwhile residents of eastern Queens had been feuding with those in the west. Ostensibly, the argument had begun in the 1830s over the proposed location for a new Queens County courthouse. The original court, built in today's Garden City Park 150 years before, needed to be replaced and, of course, those in the east wanted the replacement to be near the original; western residents wanted it moved west so they could reach it more quickly.

In addition, the Democrats in the west had deep political and philosophical differences with the newly formed Republican Party in the east. The Civil War exacerbated those differences.

After the Civil War, the first attempt was made in the state legislature to divide Queens in half. Early proposals for the new county included the Town of Huntington, of which today's Town of Babylon was then a part. Huntington voters defeated that step in 1877.

When the state legislature voted to build the new courthouse in Long Island City, the secessionists had the ammunition they needed.

On January 22, 1898, at a meeting in Allen's Hotel in Mineola, representatives of the Towns of Hempstead, North Hempstead, and Oyster Bay met to discuss formation of a new county.

"Resolved that it is the sense of this meeting that the towns of Hempstead, North Hempstead and Oyster Bay withdraw from the county of Queens, and that a new county to include the said towns be formed."

THE BROOKLYN BRIDGE AS IT APPEARED IN A
1900 PHOTO. PHOTO COURTESY OF THE
BROOKLYN HISTORICAL SOCIETY.

One attendee at the meeting, Edward N. Townsend of Hempstead, firmly stated his opinion that "the county would be an inexpensive one to govern."

North Hempstead resident Benjamin D. Hicks, a leader of the secessionist movement, was elected chair of the meeting which, further, requested the towns' supervisors *"to obtain authority...to expend a sum, not exceeding $250 for each town in defraying expenses [for] drafting and preparation of such bills as may be necessary to carry into effect the desire of the people to have a county free from entangling alliance with the great city of New York."*

Although the debate continued, with the Queens County Board of Supervisors lobbying against the secession, Republican Governor Frank S. Black signed the law creating a new county. The founders considered many names, including "Bryant." "Nassau" was chosen and celebrated its birth on New Year's Day, 1899. A new county courthouse was thereafter built in Mineola.

Originally much of today's Five Towns area was left in Queens—but outside of the consolidated New York City. That error was rectified shortly after Nassau was formed when Lawrence, Cedarhurst, Elmont, and Bellrose were added to Nassau County.

Ground for the new courthouse was broken in ceremony led by New York's Governor Theodore Roosevelt, not far from the former site of Camp Black, where troops were mobilized for the Spanish American War of 1898.

At the beginning of the War, Assistant Secretary of the Navy Roosevelt made a name for himself when he raised a mounted regiment, the Rough Riders, which achieved fame in the Battle of San Juan Hill. When the brief war ended, Roosevelt's troops came to Camp Wycoff in Montauk's Fort Pond Bay for demobilization and, with the others soldiers who had fought in Cuba, to recover from the yellow fever that attacked them.

Montauk was distant enough from any population center that might be harmed by the disease. Out of twenty-five thousand men cared for in Montauk, only 126 were lost. Roosevelt wrote, "On the whole, however, the month we spent on Montauk before we disbanded was very pleasant."

Roosevelt was as good a publicist as he was a leader and obtained immense newspaper exposure as he recreated the charge up San Juan Hill on the plains of Montauk—the very site of the nation's first horse farm. After that, Roosevelt's rise was rapid. He became Governor of the State of New York a few months later. In 1900 he was elected William McKinley's vice-president. In September 1901 McKinley was assassinated and, at age 42, Theodore Roosevelt became President of the United States.

He served two terms, during which he became the first American ever to win a Nobel Prize for the peace he negotiated to end the war between Russia and Japan. He became the first president to visit overseas, when he went to Panama.

Throughout Theodore Roosevelt's life, his home of choice was the one he lived in on Long Island's Cove Neck. The home, Sagamore Hill, still stands today as a monument to Roosevelt the adventurer, the president, the teacher, and the student. His love of place and of learning are evident in the vast number of collections displayed there. Among the last words of his life— uttered the day before his death on January 6, 1919, at age 60—were to his second wife Edith: "I wonder if you will ever know how I love Sagamore Hill."

AS THE OYSTER BOAT RUDOLF H. HAFFMANN DEMONSTRATES, THE OYSTER CATCH OFF LONG ISLAND WAS STILL PLENTIFUL IN THE EARLY 1940S. PHOTO COURTESY OF THE NASSAU COUNTY DIVISION OF MUSEUM SERVICES/LONG ISLAND STUDIES INSTITUTE/HOFSTRA UNIVERSITY.

BY THE EARLY 1880S, LONG ISLAND'S SHELLFISHING INDUSTRY WAS FIRMLY ENTRENCHED. BLUE POINT OYSTERS MADE THAT SOUTH SHORE COMMUNITY FAMOUS. ABUNDANT SHELLFISH WERE HARVESTED FOR HOME USE AND FOR THE FINEST RESTAURANTS IN NEW YORK. MECHANICAL DREDGING DEPLETED THE SUPPLY OF HOME-GROWN OYSTERS SO THAT SEA BEDS—CREATED WITH OYSTERS FROM CONNECTICUT—WERE PLANTED. (ABOVE) CLAM DIGGING IN MECOX BAY AT WATER MILL IN 1898 WAS BOTH A FAMILY BUSINESS AND PLEASURE. PHOTO FROM THE FULLERTON COLLECTION, COURTESY OF THE SUFFOLK COUNTY HISTORICAL SOCIETY. (BELOW) OYSTERS FRESH OFF THE BOAT ON A GREAT SOUTH BAY BEACH, CA. 1900. PHOTO FROM THE FULLERTON COLLECTION, COURTESY OF THE SUFFOLK COUNTY HISTORICAL SOCIETY.

In the more populous city to the west, the problem of caring for the mentally ill was growing. New York City did not have space to care properly for these people and city officials looked outside city limits for places to send them. With the goals of providing mentally ill people with fresh air, rest, and some occupational therapy, their sights fell on Long Island.

Kings County built the first hospital, the Kings County Farm in the area we now know as Kings Park, in 1885. Two years later, New York City bought 1,000 acres in Central Islip for its hospital. These two hospitals were sufficient until 1928, when a third, Pilgrim State Hospital, was added in Brentwood.

In the 1950s, the three hospitals served a combined population of more than thirty-four thousand and, after that, housed fewer and fewer patients as new therapies evolved to more effectively treat mental illness and new laws about treatment of the mentally ill mandated other types of housing for them. Kings Park and Central Islip closed in 1996. Pilgrim today treats approximately twelve hundred patients.

THE SEA IS A WAY OF LIFE FOR MANY LONG ISLANDERS, EVEN TODAY. AND NO TOWN IN LONG ISLAND IS WITHOUT A SEAFOOD MARKET. PHOTO BY SCOTT LEVY, BRUCE BENNETT STUDIOS.

Each hospital was a self-contained community— Kings Park had 150 buildings—and each gave birth to a new outside community as workers moved to Long Island for jobs in the hospitals.

Suffolk County became the county as we know it today in 1873, when the communities in South Huntington seceded and formed the Township of Babylon out of today's Villages of Lindenhurst, Amityville, and Babylon.

PHOTO FROM THE FULLERTON COLLECTION, COURTESY OF THE SUFFOLK COUNTY HISTORICAL SOCIETY.

At the dawn of the twentieth century there were 55,428 people in Nassau County; 77,582 in Suffolk. Just ten years later, there were 83,930 in Nassau and 96,138 in Suffolk.

The new century also brought the completion of Long Island's physical links to New York City with the completion of the Brooklyn Bridge in 1883; the Williamsburg Bridge in 1903; the Queensboro—or 59th Street—and the Manhattan Bridges in 1909. Rail service, too, fostered the concept of suburban commutation and, on Long Island, a network of trolley lines eased local travel.

To underscore the arrival of a new era, naturalist Robert Cushman Murphy later noted that 1900 was the year the last rattlesnake was found on Long Island. The snake was killed by a Long Island Rail Road train on the tracks in Yaphank.

The Long Island Lighting Company got its official start in 1911 with the consolidation of four small electric companies. Just a few years later, consumers began to complain about the company's management salaries and rates. These complaints prompted government investigations.

It didn't take very long for Americans to fall in love with travel. The automobile culture was in its infancy and, right on the Hempstead Plain, a travel revolution was taking place.

The same flat land that had been a superb site for cattle and sheep grazing was inviting to aviators. Conveniently located, with few trees to impede take-off and landing, the Hempstead Plain after the Wright Brothers 1903 Kitty Hawk took title as the world's "Cradle of Aviation."

"OLD MAN" HAGGERTY WAS A NEIGHBOR OF THE FULLERTONS' IN HUNTINGTON. IN 1902 HE POSED BY HIS CIDER MILL. PHOTO FROM THE FULLERTON COLLECTION, COURTESY OF THE SUFFOLK COUNTY HISTORICAL SOCIETY.

After the Spanish-American War, Camp Black was used by aviators, and a National Guard Base was opened in Mineola in 1916. One year later, when the United States joined World War I, the base became Hazelhurst Field, used for training fighter pilots. In 1907, under the auspices of the Signal Corps, an aeronautical division had been formed there to build airplanes and train pilots. It was the forerunner of today's Air Force. Hazelhurst Field became Roosevelt Field in honor of Quentin Roosevelt, Theodore's son, a pilot killed in World War I action.

Pilots were also trained at Mitchel Field, which, in turn, was adjacent to Mills Field, where Douglas MacArthur led the training of national guardsmen from across the United States. These were the first infantry soldiers sent overseas during the war.

While the Hempstead Plains were crowded with the thirty thousand soldiers who passed through in training, Yaphank, in the middle of Suffolk County, was the site of Camp Upton. In a time when that part of Long Island was as remote and unsettled as it was two hundred years before, the building of the base was accomplished by housing workers at the site. ■

PHOTO BY ROB AMATO, BRUCE BENNETT STUDIOS.

(ABOVE) EARLY TRAINS, LIKE THIS MODEL BUILT PRIOR TO 1820, DID NOT USE RAILS AT ALL. INSTEAD, EMPLOYING A METHOD IN USE SINCE ROMAN TIMES, THESE STEAM WAGONS WITH FLAT-RIMMED WHEELS TRAVELED ALONG DEEP RUTS IN THE ROADBED. THE ENGINEER STEERED FROM A FLAT PLATFORM AND CARRIAGES WERE PULLED IN THIS MANNER. COURTESY OF THE NASSAU COUNTY DIVISION OF MUSEUM SERVICES/LONG ISLAND STUDIES INSTITUTE/HOFSTRA UNIVERSITY. (BELOW) ITALIAN WORKERS WERE BROUGHT TO SUFFOLK COUNTY TO WORK AT FULLERTON'S EXPERIMENTAL STATIONS—FARMS—IN WADING RIVER AND MEDFORD, AS WELL AS ON THE RAILROAD. HERE, SHOWING THAT THE RAILROAD WAS AN IDEAL WAY TO SHIP PRODUCE, THEY PREPARE TO MOVE THEIR GOODS FROM FARM TO MARKET. PROVING THE RAILROAD VIABLE FOR COMMERCE WAS PARTICULARLY IMPORTANT WHEN, IN 1910, A DIRECT RAIL LINK BETWEEN MEDFORD AND PENNSYLVANIA STATION WAS OPENED. PHOTO FROM THE FULLERTON COLLECTION, COURTESY OF THE SUFFOLK COUNTY HISTORICAL SOCIETY.

THE EVOLUTION OF THE RAILROAD IN LONG ISLAND LAID THE FOUNDATION FOR ITS IMPORTANCE TODAY AS A
VEHICLE FOR COMMUTERS TO AND FROM NEW YORK CITY, CONNECTICUT, AND SURROUNDING CITIES AND
TOWNS FOR WORK, SHOPPING, AND PLEASURE. PHOTO BY JOE ROGATE, BRUCE BENNETT STUDIOS.

CYCLISTS COMPETE IN A MOTOR TANDEM BIKE RACE IN 1899. PHOTO FROM THE FULLERTON COLLECTION, COURTESY OF THE SUFFOLK COUNTY HISTORICAL SOCIETY.

THIS BUCOLIC BICYCLE PATH IN SELDEN IN 1899 IS GONE TODAY. PHOTO FROM THE FULLERTON COLLECTION, COURTESY OF THE SUFFOLK COUNTY HISTORICAL SOCIETY.

TODAY, CYCLING ENTHUSIASTS PURSUE THIS PASTIME FOR BOTH FUN AND FITNESS. PHOTOS ABOVE AND OPPOSITE PAGE BY ROB AMATO, BRUCE BENNETT STUDIOS.

LONG ISLAND LEISURE, PART TWO

By the end of the nineteenth century, cycling was all the rage. Never a place to refuse an invitation to have fun, Long Island joined the cycling movement heart and soul. The Long Island Rail Road ran special cycling excursions and published a brochure about Long Island called *Cyclists' Paradise*.

The line even constructed a special one-mile wood runway next to the Farmingdale railroad track to test the claim of cyclist Charles Murphy that he could pedal at 60 miles per hour by racing beside a timed train. "Mile-A-Minute" Murphy made it in just 57.8 seconds.

While cycling soon retreated to a less prominent place in the list of leisure sports, automobiles jumped into first place and there are those that would argue that they remain in that position today.

William K. Vanderbilt, Jr. was an auto racing enthusiast of the first magnitude. He raced his Mercedes frequently and with much passion, and greatly desired to make auto racing a popular sport.

Toward that end, he announced a 300-mile international race between Lake Success on the Nassau-Queens border, and Jericho, in mid-Nassau. The race would be held on public roads and the winner would receive the Vanderbilt Cup, a sterling silver trophy designed by Louis Comfort Tiffany.

In 1906, the third year of the race, so many spectators jammed the roadway that one was killed. The Automobile Club withdrew its support of racing on public roads, so Vanderbilt decided to build his own road. It would be a toll road used by the public, and it would be used for races and to test automotive innovations.

The Vanderbilt Motor Parkway, constructed in 1908, ultimately stretched from near Bayside in eastern Queens to Hauppauge in central Suffolk. It included overpasses and bridges built to avoid intersecting traffic. It did not, however, ensure safer races.

The 1910 Vanderbilt Cup Race was the last, as the public outcry against the four deaths and twenty injuries incurred in the race demanded a halt.

Vanderbilt's Motor Parkway lived on for awhile, succeeding as a tourist destination for picnickers and as a comparatively fast way to traverse Long Island. Tolls gradually lowered until, in 1933, it had gone to 40 cents from its opening high of two dollars.

The opening of the Northern State Parkway finally put the Vanderbilt road out of business. Today, a 13-mile stretch of pleasant, hilly Vanderbilt Motor Parkway remains. It's a nice way to get from Commack to Ronkonkoma.

(continued)

LIKE THE BICYCLE, MOTORING CAPTURED THE FANCY OF LONG ISLAND AND THE NATION AT THE TURN OF THE CENTURY. THIS PROMOTIONAL EXHIBIT FOR CONTINENTAL TIRES WAS SET UP AT RIVERHEAD TOWN FAIR. CAR RACING WAS JUST ONE EXPRESSION OF LONG ISLAND'S ENJOYMENT OF SPORTS. POLO, HUNTING, CYCLING, YACHTING, AND GOLFING WERE A FEW OF THE OTHERS POPULAR AT THE TURN OF THE CENTURY. PHOTO FROM THE FULLERTON COLLECTION, COURTESY OF THE SUFFOLK COUNTY HISTORICAL SOCIETY.

While Vanderbilt was racing cars, some of his peers were racing horses. In 1905, August Belmont, Jr. and William C. Whitney opened Belmont Park Racetrack on 650 acres in Elmont on the Queens-Nassau border. Site of the Belmont Stakes, the third leg of the Triple Crown, Belmont Park ensured that Long Island would have a permanent place in the history of thoroughbred racing.

In addition, the track served as the northern terminal of the first New York to Washington, DC, airmail service in 1919.

The gentlemen who came to Long Island in the Gilded Age brought with them British-style manor houses and the British game of polo. They played their exclusive game at exclusive clubs, The Meadow Brook in Old Westbury and the Rockaway Hunting Club in Cedarhurst. Fox hunting, too, was pursued in these places. Like the fortunes that spawned them, however, these sports all but disappeared with the Depression.

There were also several "sportsmen's" clubs which were designed to ensure a good day of duck or bird hunting for their members. The first was formed in the early nineteenth century. In 1858 August Belmont formed the Suffolk Club on

the Carmen's River and, in 1865, William K. Vanderbilt, W. Bayard Cutting, and Pierre Lorrilard formed the Southside Sportsmen's Club on the Connetquot River.

Yacht clubs sprang up along Long Island shores that, today, are filled with both public and private marinas and, in 1892, Shinnecock Hills was the first golf club in the nation.

Samuel Parrish, a founder of Shinnecock Hills, later wrote: "In the beginning, so quietly and unobtrusively was golf introduced into this country that it was some time after the Shinnecock Club house had been built and the game was being played in the 'Hills' in all its red-coated, white collared and monogrammed brass-buttoned splendor (a picturesque but for many years past an abandoned feature of the early days of golf, I still have the buttons; the moths the coat) before the game became sufficiently well-known to attract the slightest notice from the newspapers.

"From 1893 on," Parrish continued, "...a veritable craze swept over the country, and the Shinnecock club became the Mecca for golfing pilgrims from all sections of the country, seeking information before trying to construct their own links."

THE RIVERHEAD RACEWAY IS CROWDED WITH FANS AS AN EXCITING STOCK CAR RACE GETS UNDERWAY.
PHOTOS BY JIM MCISAAC, BRUCE BENNETT STUDIOS.

(ABOVE) BELMONT PARK RACETRACK WAS OPENED IN 1905 BY AUGUST BELMONT, JR. AND WILLIAM C. WHITNEY. THE TRACK WAS CROWDED WITH SPECTATORS THE DAY THIS PHOTO WAS TAKEN IN 1909. PHOTO FROM RUTHER'S *LONG ISLAND TODAY*. COURTESY OF THE NASSAU COUNTY DIVISION OF MUSEUM SERVICES/LONG ISLAND STUDIES INSTITUTE/HOFSTRA UNIVERSITY. (BELOW) MANY HORSE FARMS, SUCH AS THE RED BARN HORSE FARM, ARE OFFSPINS OF THE HORSE RACING INDUSTRY, WHICH TO THIS DAY DRAWS THOUSAND OF SPECTATORS TO LONG ISLAND.

THE BELMONT PARK RACETRACK IS STILL ONE OF THE TOP VENUES FOR HORSE RACING. PHOTOS BY DEBORAH ROSS, BRUCE BENNETT STUDIOS.

SHINNECOCK HILLS IN SOUTHAMPTON WAS THE NATION'S FIRST GOLF CLUB. THE STANFORD WHITE BUILDING
STILL STANDS TODAY. IN 1901, WIVES OF THE MEMBERS POSED ON THE LAWN OUTSIDE THE CLUBHOUSE.
PHOTO FROM THE FULLERTON COLLECTION, COURTESY OF THE SUFFOLK COUNTY HISTORICAL SOCIETY.

WHEATLEY HILLS GOLF CLUB. PHOTOS BY
RON AMATO, BRUCE BENNETT STUDIOS.

(ABOVE, LEFT) THE GARDEN CITY HOTEL CA. 1880. BUILT IN 1871, IT FEATURED 101 ROOMS OPEN FOR PUBLIC USE. THE REST OF THE BUILDING WAS USED AS THE RESIDENCE OF MRS. A.T. STEWART. IT BURNED IN 1889 AND WAS LATER REBUILT. PHOTO COURTESY OF THE NASSAU COUNTY DIVISION OF MUSEUM SERVICES/LONG ISLAND STUDIES INSTITUTE/HOFSTRA UNIVERSITY. (ABOVE, RIGHT) IN 1973, THE 78-YEAR-OLD GARDEN CITY HOTEL WAS DEMOLISHED TO MAKE WAY FOR A MORE MODERN BUILDING. PHOTO © 1973 *NEWSDAY*. PHOTO BELOW BY BRUCE BENNETT STUDIOS.

(LEFT) SERGEANT IRVING BERLIN, ALREADY A FAMOUS SONGWRITER, USED HIS EXPERIENCE WHILE STATIONED AT CAMP UPTON TO WRITE *YIP, YIP YAPHANK*. HERE, HE PERFORMS THE SONG *OH, HOW I HATE TO GET UP IN THE MORNING*, IN THE 1918 NEW YORK CITY PRODUCTION OF THE SHOW. PHOTO COURTESY OF BROOKHAVEN NATIONAL LABORATORY. (RIGHT) WHEN *YIP, YIP YAPHANK* WAS PRODUCED ON BROADWAY, ITS CAST WAS MADE UP OF SOLDIERS FROM CAMP UPTON. MANY OF THEM, INCLUDING IRVING BERLIN (CENTER) APPEARED IN DRAG. PHOTOS COURTESY OF BROOKHAVEN NATIONAL LABORATORY.

HOW THE OTHER HALF LIVED

Today, even the estates that remain as public places and have been restored, are frozen in their time, stripped of the people and the life that made them the vivid exemplars of their times. They were built in the Gilded Age—the last time in America when pre-income tax money existed—and the Jazz Age, the decade after World War I that was a time of unprecedented prosperity. Today, they allow us to imagine what life was like when Long Island's fabled Gold Coast was born.

As New York City grew, and the wealthiest Americans looked for playgrounds that were both spacious and more convenient to business than Newport, Long Island became a choice location. In the last decade of the nineteenth century and the three decades of the twentieth century, astonishing wealth was poured into real estate on Long Island.

Stanford White was truly a man of this time. Born in 1853, he was the preeminent architect of the Gilded Age and his reputation was further shaped by the way he chose to live his life.

Among his designs are Pennsylvania Station, the Morningside Heights campus of Columbia University, the Boston Public Library, the Washington Square Arch and, twice—since his first incarnation burned down—redesigned the 1871 Garden City Hotel. He also designed a number of private homes and churches. Many of these were on Long Island and many survive today.

A partner in the firm of McKim, Mead and White, he blended neo-classicism with the eclectic architecture style of the nineteenth century.

Among White's more spectacular designs was Harbor Hill, the six million dollar 1899 home built by Clarence Mackay in Roslyn. This French chateau was built on more than six hundred acres. In the 1920s Harbor Hill would be the site of what is reputed the grandest party ever—a 1924 reception welcoming the Prince of Wales. Harbor Hill was demolished after World War II.

The footnote always appended to Clarence Mackay's story is that, in 1926, his daughter Ellin married songwriter Irving Berlin. Mackay never forgave her for marrying a Jewish man and never spoke to her again.

White's roots on Long Island came through his wife, Bessie Springs Smith, a descendent of the fabled founder of Smithtown, Richard "Bull" Smith.

(continued)

(ABOVE) LUXURY COTTAGES, SHOWN HERE
IN A 1905 PHOTO, WERE BUILT ON THE BEACH AT
LONG BEACH. THEY BURNED DOWN IN 1907.
PHOTO COURTESY OF THE NASSAU COUNTY
DIVISION OF MUSEUM SERVICES/LONG ISLAND
STUDIES INSTITUTE/HOFSTRA UNIVERSITY.
(LEFT) TODAY, THE LONG ISLAND SHORE IS
STILL DESIRABLE REAL ESTATE, AND MANY HOMES
AND VACATION COTTAGES ARE BUILT ALONG THE
WATER'S EDGE. PHOTO BY ROB AMATO, BRUCE
BENNETT STUDIOS.

Because his wife preferred not to live in New York City, White rented, and later bought, Box Hill, a farmhouse in the St. James area.

Box Hill became White's perpetual work-in-progress. He added gables and other exterior details that made the house truly distinctive. The interior, too, employed specially commissioned materials. The Wetherill House, standing above Stony Brook Harbor, is a unique octagon shape.

His work in St. James includes a schoolhouse and Penney's, a garage and filling station on Route 25A in St. James that is still in use today. He designed the clubhouse for the nation's first golf club, Shinnecock Hills, in Southampton and homes on the South Fork, including an enclave of shingled seaside homes in Montauk of which five remain today. White's last design was Wardenclyffe, Nikola Tesla's laboratory.

In June, 1906, while attending the opening of a show on Madison Square Garden's roof in the building he had designed, White was shot and killed by Harry Thaw, the jealous husband of

White's lover, former chorus girl Evelyn Nesbit.

Stanford White is buried in the graveyard of St. James Episcopal Church in St. James.

One of the most interesting private homes from that time that has come into public use today is Planting Fields.

William Robertson Coe bought an existing estate in Oyster Bay in 1913. Coe chose the location because the nearby Vanderbilt Motor Parkway enabled him to drive to his Wall Street office in just thirty minutes, thus giving him the best of both worlds. Five years later, the estate burned and Coe took the opportunity to build another home on the site. This one was fireproof.

Born in England, Coe commissioned architects Walker and Gillette to build an ancestral home for his family; a Tudor home on 409 acres that, built in sections, would look as if it had stood and evolved for generations.

When completed in 1921, the 76-room Coe estate featured stained glass brought over from Hever

(continued)

ONE OF THE MOST INTERESTING PRIVATE HOMES THAT HAS COME INTO PUBLIC USE TODAY IS PLANTING FIELDS. THE NAME OF THE ESTATE CAME FROM ITS NATIVE AMERICAN HISTORY AND THE GARDENS THAT WERE DESIGNED BY THE OLMSTEAD BROTHERS. THESE GARDENS REMAIN TODAY AS THE CENTERPIECE OF THE PLANTING FIELDS ARBORETUM, SITE OF A RENOWNED SUMMER CONCERT SERIES AND AN OUTSTANDING BOTANICAL COLLECTION. PHOTOS BY ROB AMATO (LEFT) AND DEBORAH ROSS (RIGHT), BRUCE BENNETT STUDIOS.

Castle, the ancestral home of Anne Boleyn, and other stained glass from sixteenth century France. The only room that is not in the English style is the Louis XVI reception room, done in pale green.

Curious details abound in the home: at one side of the second floor landing is a carving of a rooster facing east into the sunrise; the other side features a carved owl facing west in sunset. There is an archway frieze of laborers and carvings representing the crops Native Americans tilled on the land and the ships that brought Coe his fortune. Coe's love of the west is proved in his purchase of Buffalo Bill Cody's Wyoming ranch and in Robert Chandler's paintings in the Buffalo Room at Planting Fields.

The name of the estate came from both its Native American history and the gardens that were designed by the Olmstead Brothers. These gardens remain today as the centerpiece of the Planting Fields Arboretum, site of a renowned summer concert series and an outstanding botanical collection.

John Phillip Sousa, the "March King," bought his Sands Point estate, Wildbank, in 1914. He wrote, "The North Shore is so near Paradise that I have no idea of ever renting or selling my place."

Eagle's Nest, the estate of William K. Vanderbilt, II, is today the Suffolk County Vanderbilt Museum and Planetarium. The E.F. Hutton-Marjorie Merriweather Post estate houses the campus of C. W. Post College of Long Island University. Idle Hour, the 1878 mansion of William K. Vanderbilt, is now the administration building at Dowling College. Caumsett State Park in Huntington was the estate of Marshall Field III. This list goes on. The names of the owners of Gold Coast estates are a roll call of the richest, most powerful, most influential of this nation's citizens in the fifty years between 1875 and 1925.

Few, if any, of the grand mansions that survive are privately owned and occupied. Most have been given over to public use. Many, unfortunately, exist only in memory and old photos.

(ABOVE) THE SEASHORE DRAWS VISITORS FROM THROUGHOUT THE REGION, AS WELL AS INSPIRING OTHERS TO MAKE THEIR HOME ON LONG ISLAND. PHOTO BY ROB AMATO, BRUCE BENNETT STUDIOS. (BELOW) THE MONTAUK LIGHTHOUSE SHOWN HERE IN A 1910 POSTCARD IS STILL STANDING. IT HAS BEEN RECENTLY REFURBISHED AND THE RAVAGES OF EROSION CORRECTED. COURTESY OF THE NASSAU COUNTY DIVISION OF MUSEUM SERVICES/LONG ISLAND STUDIES INSTITUTE/HOFSTRA UNIVERSITY.

(ABOVE) TO PUBLICIZE HIS NEW "RIVIERA OF THE EAST," WILLIAM REYNOLDS BROUGHT ELEPHANTS FROM HIS DREAMLAND PARK IN CONEY ISLAND TO HELP BUILD THE LONG BEACH BOARDWALK IN 1906. PHOTO COURTESY OF THE NASSAU COUNTY DIVISION OF MUSEUM SERVICES/LONG ISLAND STUDIES INSTITUTE/HOFSTRA UNIVERSITY. (BELOW) TODAY, OTHER SPECTACLES DRAW THE ATTENTION OF BEACH VISITORS. PHOTO BY ROB AMATO, BRUCE BENNETT STUDIOS.

(ABOVE) CASTLE-BY-THE-SEA WAS A SUPPER CLUB OPERATED ON THE BOARDWALK IN LONG BEACH FROM 1912 TO 1929 BY THE WORLD-FAMOUS DANCE TEAM OF VERNON AND IRENE CASTLE. PHOTO COURTESY OF THE NASSAU COUNTY DIVISION OF MUSEUM SERVICES/LONG ISLAND STUDIES INSTITUTE/HOFSTRA UNIVERSITY. (LEFT) TODAY, THE BOARDWALKS OF LONG ISLAND ARE THE PATHWAY TO THE BEACHES, AS WELL AS A PLATFORM FOR FUN. PHOTO BY BRUCE BENNETT, BRUCE BENNETT STUDIOS.

PHOTO BY ROB AMATO, BRUCE BENNETT STUDIOS.

LONG ISLAND ARTS AND LETTERS, PART TWO

It wasn't any easier being an artist in the late nineteenth century than it is today. Art collectors seemed to prefer buying their collections overseas. With this tight market, established American artists protected their turf with all their might and newer, struggling, artists had to seek work in other fields.

Luckily, magazines were beginning to use illustrators and cartoonists and the new Art Students League, established in 1875, needed teachers. In addition, consumer tastes had spawned the Aesthetic Movement in which the decorative arts displayed by European nations at the 1876 Centennial Exposition created a demand for similar objects by Americans.

Scorning this turn of events, one artist said, "...decorative mania had fallen like a destructive angel upon the most flourishing cities in America, turning orderly homes into bristling and impenetrable curiosity-shops."

Some artists, however, desiring to eat, joined the aesthetic movement, albeit on their own terms.

Some turned exclusively to decorative arts; others formed "clubs" with their peers in which they could work and commiserate together.

Thus, painter Louis Comfort Tiffany joined others in Associated Artists, an interior design firm. Tiffany ultimately was able to open his own studio in which he developed, patented, and produced his unique stained glass paintings.

Tiffany's Cold Spring Harbor estate, Laurelton Hall, was a showplace for Tiffany. It burned to the ground in 1957 and all that was within was destroyed. In 1989, stained glass Tiffany windows in St. Mark's Episcopal Church in Islip were damaged by fire. Careful salvage of the pieces and expert restoration ensured their restoration and, today, they grace the rebuilt church on Main Street.

One group of artists, including the painter Winslow Homer, formed a fraternal organization. They debated about which type of decorative art they wanted to produce and, finally, settled on painted ceramic tiles.

(continued)

PHOTOS BY DEBORAH ROSS, BRUCE BENNETT STUDIOS.

In addition to Homer, the "Tile Club" included Francis Millet, William Merritt Chase, and Walter Paris. Architect Stanford White was a late inductee. The members gave each other nicknames, cultivated a mystique about their group, and took "field trips" together, painting side by side. They traveled to eastern Long Island in 1876, 1880, and 1881, staying at various times in East Hampton, Bridgehampton, Montauk—where they met with David Pharoah, the great Montaukett chief who denied them permission to paint his portrait—Greenport and, on their last trip, Port Jefferson.

Tile Clubber William Mackay Laffan said of Port Jefferson, "It is rich in historical interest...its people are...as sincere as if it had never known a summer boarder and New York were a thousand miles away." It was also, he noted, "a place of peace and cheapness."

In Port Jefferson they held clambakes, played instruments, and paid homage to William Sidney Mount by visiting his homestead.

The Tile Club was an important step in the development of eastern Long Island as a hospitable environment for artists.

Popular magazines, like *Scribner's Monthly* and *Harper's Weekly,* printed illustrations done by Tilers and chronicled the Club's exploits. The members proved to be excellent publicists for themselves. The Tile Club disbanded in the 1880s.

(ABOVE) LONG ISLAND BEACHES WERE THE KEY TO LEISURE IN THE EARLY TWENTIETH CENTURY AS THEY ARE NOW. IN 1902, THE ROCKAWAY HOTEL WAS A POPULAR WATERFRONT TOURIST MAGNET. PHOTO FROM THE FULLERTON COLLECTION, COURTESY OF THE SUFFOLK COUNTY HISTORICAL SOCIETY. (BELOW) EVEN CHILDREN COULD FIND PEACE AND RESPITE IN CENTERPORT'S LOWER HARBOR IN 1901. PHOTO FROM THE FULLERTON COLLECTION, COURTESY OF THE SUFFOLK COUNTY HISTORICAL SOCIETY.

(ABOVE) EDITH LORING FULLERTON AND DAUGHTER, HOPE, AT A ROADSIDE WELL IN WEST HILLS, HUNTINGTON, 1903. PHOTO FROM THE FULLERTON COLLECTION, COURTESY OF THE SUFFOLK COUNTY HISTORICAL SOCIETY. (BELOW) IN 1903, FULLERTON PHOTOGRAPHED HOPE ON THE BEACH AT COLD SPRING HARBOR. PHOTO FROM THE FULLERTON COLLECTION, COURTESY OF THE SUFFOLK COUNTY HISTORICAL SOCIETY.

SCENE STEALERS

The movie industry was born in New York City and, before it moved way out west, it spent some time out east, here on Long Island.

As early as 1911 *The Stuff Heroes Are Made Of* was filmed for Vitagraph by director D.W. Griffith in Lynbrook. A few years later, a Vitagraph studio was opened in Bay Shore. The sand dunes of Montauk served as the sand dunes of the Sahara for Rudolph Valentino in *The Sheik*. Valentino's contemporaries, Vernon and Irene Castle, were filmed in 1914 dancing on the Long Beach Boardwalk, a site Woody Allen used seventy years later in *Zelig*.

When location shooting away from the studios began in earnest, Long Island was ready with spectacular scenery.

Gold Coast mansions that are today public spaces have been used as backdrops for some memorable characters and action. The exterior of Charles Foster Kane's mansion in *Citizen Kane* is the exterior Oheka Castle, for example.

Old Wesbury Gardens served as the setting for *North By Northwest, Love Story, Wolf, Cruel Intentions*, and Martin Scorsese's *Age of Innocence*. It's neighbor, the Knole Estate, was used in *Arthur* and as the Von Bulow estate in *Reversal of Fortune*.

Oddly, a very typical Tennessee Williams saga of a decadent Southern family, *Cat On A Hot Tin Roof*, starring Elizabeth Taylor, Paul Newman, and Burl Ives, was filmed at the Coleman estate in Muttontown.

Both versions of *Sabrina* were filmed in Glen Cove, albeit at different mansions. And the singular pink mansion on the cliff in Belle Terre was home to Meryl Streep in *She-Devil*.

Sands Point hosted *Malcolm X, Scent of A Woman*, and the recent re-make of *Great Expectations*. In 1961's *Splendor in the Grass*, Bellport stood in for Kansas.

As Sonny Corleone in *The Godfather*, James Caan was executed at Mitchel Field. *The Godfather* series also used a Mill Neck mansion as Diane Keaton's home and the infamous horse's head scene was filmed at Falaise, the Guggenheim estate in Sands Point.

The entire Village of East Hampton was the setting of the 1986 Alan Alda film, *Sweet Liberty* and the Village of Northport doubled for small-town Indiana in *In & Out*.

A number of *Seinfeld* episodes took place in Nassau and on the East End and in *The Nanny*, poor Fran always longed for a "house in Great Neck." On *Everybody Loves Raymond*, Ray is a *Newsday* sportswriter. For the first two years, his opening voice-over talked about living "in" Long Island, a correct usage for the rest of the country, apparently, but not for those who live "on" Long Island.

On the other hand, films that are clearly set on Long Island often are not filmed here. For example, none of the versions of *The Great Gatsby*—two for theaters; one for television—was filmed on Long Island. The independent hit *Love and Death on Long Island* was filmed in Canada.

One film, a Steven Seagall version of the John Westermann mystery *Exit Wounds*, was not only filmed in Toronto instead of the Long Island locale of the novel, but the setting itself was changed from suburban Nassau to very urban Detroit.

Long Island's home-grown independent film-makers, however, often stay close to their roots. Hal Hartley's films have been shot at his relatives' homes in several local communities. Edward Burns' first commercial success, *The Brothers McMullen*, used his parents' Valley Stream home as the McMullen home in the film.

(ABOVE) GOLD COAST LIVING WAS EXEMPLIFIED BY CASTLEGOULD, BUILT IN 1902 BY HOWARD GOULD ON WHAT IS TODAY PART OF THE SANDS POINT PRESERVE. MODELED ON IRELAND'S KILKENNY CASTLE, IT WAS ORIGINALLY DESIGNED AS AN EQUESTRIAN PARADE STABLE AND CARRIAGE HOUSE. PHOTOS COURTESY OF THE NASSAU COUNTY DIVISION OF MUSEUM SERVICES/LONG ISLAND STUDIES INSTITUTE/HOFSTRA UNIVERSITY. (LEFT AND BELOW) MANY OF LONG ISLAND'S HOMES TODAY SERVE AS SETTING FOR MOVIES. HOMES HAVE BEEN SEEN IN SUCH FILMS AS *CITIZEN KANE, CAT ON A HOT TIN ROOF, LOVE STORY, AGE OF INNOCENCE, GREAT EXPECTATIONS* AND, PERHAPS MOST NOTABLE, *THE GODFATHER* SERIES. PHOTOS BY LISA MEYER, BRUCE BENNETT STUDIOS.

NASSAU COUNTY celebrated its birth on
New Year's Day, 1899, and a new county
courthouse was built in Mineola. Photos by
Rob Amato, Bruce Bennett Studios.

(ABOVE) IN 1898 *LESLIE'S WEEKLY*, A POPULAR MAGAZINE, FEATURED A PHOTO ESSAY ON THE SPANISH-AMERICAN WAR. ONE PHOTO SHOWED THE CHANGING OF THE GUARD AT CAMP BLACK IN GARDEN CITY. PHOTO COURTESY OF THE NASSAU COUNTY DIVISION OF MUSEUM SERVICES/LONG ISLAND STUDIES INSTITUTE/HOFSTRA UNIVERSITY.

AT THE BEGINNING OF THE SPANISH AMERICAN WAR, ASSISTANT SECRETARY OF THE NAVY THEODORE ROOSEVELT MADE A NAME FOR HIMSELF WHEN HE RAISED A MOUNTED REGIMENT, THE ROUGH RIDERS, WHICH ACHIEVED FAME IN THE BATTLE OF SAN JUAN HILL. WHEN THE BRIEF WAR ENDED, ROOSEVELT'S TROOPS CAME TO WYCOFF IN MONTAUK'S FORT POND BAY FOR DEMOBILIZATION. PHOTO FROM THE FULLERTON COLLECTION, COURTESY OF THE SUFFOLK COUNTY HISTORICAL SOCIETY.

(ABOVE) DURING THE PRESIDENCY OF THEODORE ROOSEVELT, HIS FAMILY HOME IN OYSTER BAY— SAGAMORE HILL—SERVED AS THE SUMMER WHITE HOUSE. HERE HE POSES WITH HIS FAMILY ON THE LAWN CA. 1906. PHOTO COURTESY OF THE NASSAU COUNTY DIVISION OF MUSEUM SERVICES/LONG ISLAND STUDIES INSTITUTE/HOFSTRA UNIVERSITY. (BELOW AND FACING PAGE) TODAY, SCORES OF VISITORS COME TO SEE THE BELOVED ROOSEVELT HOME. PHOTO BELOW BY DEBORAH ROSS, BRUCE BENNETT STUDIOS.

PHOTOS BY ROB AMATO, BRUCE BENNETT STUDIOS.

(ABOVE) A CONTEMPORARY POSTCARD SHOWS A BAYONET DRILL AT CAMP MILLS CA. 1918. (BELOW)
DURING WORLD WAR I, GUESTS CALLED AT THIS GUESTHOUSE FOR SOLDIERS STATIONED AT CAMP MILLS IN
GARDEN CITY. THE ROAD IN FRONT OF THE BUILDING IS CLINTON ROAD. PHOTOS COURTESY OF THE
NASSAU COUNTY DIVISION OF MUSEUM SERVICES/LONG ISLAND STUDIES INSTITUTE/HOFSTRA UNIVERSITY.

(ABOVE) LONG ISLAND'S BAYPORT AERODROME SOCIETY PRESERVES THE PAST THROUGH MAINTENANCE OF HISTORIC AIRCRAFT, WHICH THEY STILL FLY. PICTURED ARE TWO PLANES OVER LONG ISLAND SOUND. PHOTO BY T. ABADIE, BRUCE BENNETT STUDIOS. (BELOW) A FOREST IN THE MID-SUFFOLK VILLAGE OF YAPHANK WAS TURNED INTO CAMP UPTON—NAMED FOR A CIVIL WAR MAJOR GENERAL—IN 1917. *TRENCH & CAMP*, ITS NEWSPAPER, TELLS OF LIFE IN WHAT AMOUNTED TO A SMALL CITY, COMPLETE WITH THEATERS (SHOWN), RELIGIOUS SERVICES FOR THREE MAJOR DENOMINATIONS, STORES, WEDDINGS, AND TOURISTS. PHOTO COURTESY OF BROOKHAVEN NATIONAL LABORATORY.

CATHOLIC HEALTH SERVICES OF LONG ISLAND

Catholic Health Services of Long Island (CHS) is a single universe of care that includes some of the region's finest health and human services agencies and organizations. CHS is comprised of five hospitals with 1,700 beds, three nursing homes, a regional hospice and home care network, a community-based agency for persons with special needs, and an ambulance service. More than 13,500 staff and 2,700 medical professionals are employed within the CHS system, which generates annual revenues exceeding $1 billion. CHS is governed by a board of directors which guides activities and sets policy; its diverse membership is drawn from among

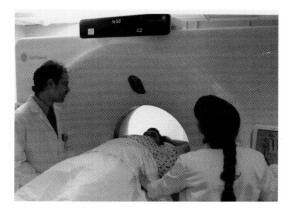

MERCY MEDICAL CENTER'S GE LIGHTSPEED CT SCANNER IS ABLE TO SCAN SIX TIMES FASTER THAN CONVENTIONAL CT SCANNERS AND WITH MUCH MORE DETAIL. IT PRODUCES THREE-DIMENSIONAL RENDERINGS, A FEATURE THAT IS PARTICULARLY IMPORTANT IN CARDIOLOGY AND FOR EARLY SCREENING OF LUNG CANCER IN HIGH-RISK PATIENTS.

healthcare professionals, clergy, businesspeople, and community leaders. Under the leadership of this board, CHS has made significant strides toward its objective of transforming Long Island's Catholic hospitals and related organizations into an effective, community-focused delivery system. At the same time, CHS has encouraged each of the member organizations embraced under its umbrella to retain their link to history, their distinctive personality, and the service specialities which have positioned each member to effectively serve their communities.

Founded in 1997 to oversee the Diocese of Rockville Centre's healthcare organizations, CHS serves hundreds of thousands of Long Islanders each year, providing care that extends from birth through to helping people live their final years in comfort, grace, and dignity.

The Diocese of Rockville Centre's healthcare ministry, organized under CHS, is focused on bringing health and healing to the people it serves. Since 1913, Catholic healthcare on Long Island has built a distinguished tradition of operating community hospitals and human service organizations. These services have become widely valued for the high quality of their compassionate care for people from all walks of life and of every religious belief and ethnic group.

Within the CHS system, member organizations offer virtually every medical speciality and clinical service, and share a dedication to continuously upgrading the scope, quality, and accessibility of care. CHS and its members are taking the vital steps necessary to enhance their ability to be more competitive, provide high-quality, more compassionate care, and to expand their continuum of healthcare and human services.

Serving the Underserved

In keeping with its mission of service to those people and communities whose social condition puts them at the margins of society, CHS provides nearly $25 million a year in care for the poor, the uninsured, and underserved. While much of this service was provided in emergency rooms and clinics, CHS also provides hundreds of free or reduced-fee outreach programs to improve individual and community health. Among programs targeted to low-income communities, seniors, women, children, and others with special needs, are health education screenings, support groups, counseling services, immunization programs, nutrition, transportation, patient education, advocacy for the poor, and blood drives.

Through the Bishop John R. McGann Mission of Caring Fund, CHS provides grants to community health and human services programs for underserved populations. A primary objective for the Mission of Caring Fund is expansion and support of the number of cooperative ventures between CHS, the parishes, schools, human service agencies, and other Apostolates of the Diocese of Rockville Centre. As a result, the fund supports

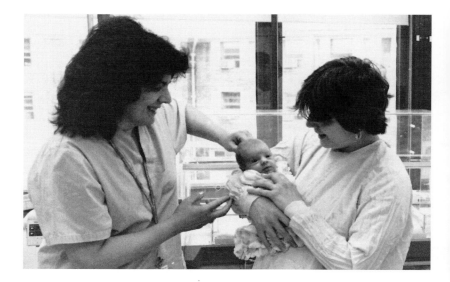

MERCY MEDICAL CENTER HAS A TRADITION OF EXCELLENCE IN MATERNITY SERVICES. MERCY HAS A PROUD HERITAGE AS THE BIRTHING CENTER FOR LONG ISLAND'S ORIGINAL "BABY BOOM." TODAY THE LEGACY CONTINUES WITH MODERN STATE-OF-THE-ART FACILITIES AND EQUIPMENT, AND A DEDICATED MOTHER/BABY STAFF PROVIDING EXPERT, COMPASSIONATE CARE.

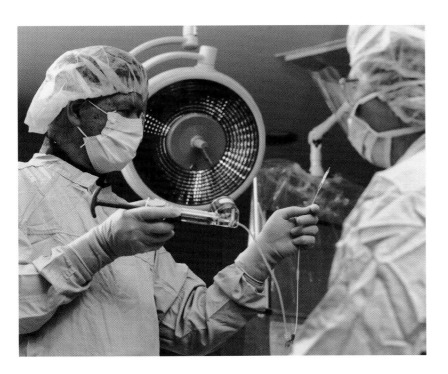

PHYSICIANS PREPARE A STENT DEPLOYMENT DEVICE.

collaborative programs between community organizations and Catholic-sponsored groups.

CHS is a dynamic, geographically diverse, service-rich organization that stands as a leader in providing high-quality, compassionate care.

Good Samaritan Hospital Medical Center

A 431-bed community medical center located in West Islip, on Suffolk County's south shore, Good Samaritan Hospital Medical Center was founded in 1959 and has since expanded its facility six times. Good Sam, as it is familiarly known, opened the area's first pediatric intensive care unit in 1997. Each year, this unit provides care for more than 17,000 children. Following the inauguration of the pediatric intensive care unit, the hospital expanded its Center for Pediatric Speciality Care, a multispeciality pediatric center with treatment specialities including cardiology, neurology, gastroenterology, endocrinology, and pulmonology.

Good Sam's Radiation Oncology Center serves cancer patients in Suffolk County with cutting-edge technology including two Varian 2100C Radiotherapy Linear Accelerators. Among treatment options at the center are external beam radiation therapy, brachytherapy (seed implants), and stereotactic radiosurgery. The hospital's Mammography & Breast Diagnostic Suite, the first comprehensive breast care center on Long Island, was also the first such facility on Long Island to be accredited by the American College of Radiology for excellence in performance of all types of stereotactic and ultrasound-guided biopsies. These advanced biopsy techniques have served to dramatically lower surgery rates for benign conditions, and to provide for superior outcomes when patients require surgical treatment for breast cancer.

The hospital's Vascular Suite boasts state-of-the-art equipment which enables radiologists to capture exceptionally high resolution, digitally-enhanced images of even the smallest abnormalities in the human vascular (blood vessel) system. In 2000, Good Sam performed its first endovascular grafting procedure, a recently approved minimally-invasive technique.

Cardiac care services at Good Sam are provided within the comprehensive facilities of the hospital's Coronary Care and Special Care unit. Additionally, Good Sam maintains a dedicated Cardiac Catheterization Laboratory where high-tech equipment assists physicians to evaluate patients with coronary heart disease and determine appropriate treatment modalities.

The Ambulatory Care Center includes a pre-surgical testing area with centralized facilities for physical examinations, necessary blood work, chest x-rays, and other required tests. Facilities have been expanded for physical therapy and for patients with chronic kidney disease. The hospital also has a 25-station Chronic Dialysis Center in Bay Shore and a 10-station center in Lindenhurst.

The hospital's other outreach services to the elderly include the Good Samaritan Nursing Home which offers skilled nursing care for 100 patient/residents, and a certified Home Health Care Agency which provides a wide variety of comprehensive healthcare and support services to elderly and other patients in their own homes.

One of Good Samaritan Hospital Medical Center's newest initiatives is the state-of-the-art Emergency Services department that opened during 2001.

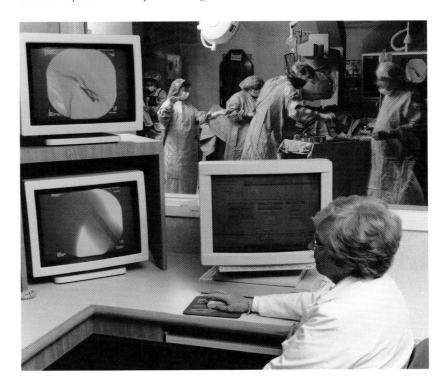

FLUOROSCOPIC IMAGES OF BLOOD VESSELS ARE MONITORED DURING A PROCEDURE IN GOOD SAMARITAN HOSPITAL MEDICAL CENTER'S VASCULAR SUITE.

THE BREAST HEALTH CENTER AT GOOD SAMARITAN
WAS CREATED IN RESPONSE TO COMMUNITY CON-
CERNS INDICATING A NEED FOR A COMPREHENSIVE
PROGRAM OF EARLY DETECTION AND DIAGNOSIS,
POSITIVE REINFORCEMENT THROUGH COUNSELING
AND SUPPORT, AND EFFECTIVE TREATMENT
UTILIZING THE LATEST EQUIPMENT IN THE BATTLE
AGAINST BREAST DISEASE.

Mercy Medical Center

One of Long Island's oldest medical institutions,
Mercy Medical Center was founded in 1913 by the
Congregation of the Infant Jesus. Mercy is a 387-bed
general community hospital and Level II Trauma Center
which is located in Nassau County's south shore, in
Rockville Centre. The 500-member attending physician
staff provides the south shore region with a wide
variety of medical and surgical specialities, particularly
maternal and child health, oncology, physical medicine
and rehabilitation, orthopedics, behavioral health care
services, and ophthalmology. Each year Mercy has
more than 15,000 admissions and provides more than
102,000 days of patient care which include almost
2,100 births and 9,200 operating room procedures. The
hospital's emergency room records more than 35,000
visits each year. Its ambulatory care unit performs almost
5,000 endoscopy procedures a year. A leader in maternity
services, during Long Island's baby boom years following
World War II, Mercy was the fourth hospital nationwide
in the number of births recorded annually. Today, its
state-of-the-art Labor, Delivery, and Recovery suites
and Neonatal Intensive Care Unit continue to keep the
hospital at the forefront of maternal and infant care.

Regional firsts for Mercy Medical Center include its
pioneering work with cochlear ear implant surgery for
the profoundly deaf, its acquisition of the Harmonic
Scalpel for performing virtually bloodless surgery,
and the use of the GE Lightspeed CatScan for faster
whole body imaging. In recent years, Mercy has added
innovative programs, among them a Pain Management
Service, a Sleep Disorders Center, a Bone Densitometry

program, and the Joint Endeavor Program which promotes faster recoveries and better outcomes in joint
replacement surgery.

In 1996, Mercy entered into an agreement with
the world-renowned Memorial Sloan-Kettering Cancer
Center of New York City. The result, the MSK Cancer
Center at Mercy's Bishop McGann Center, provides
world-class protocols and diagnosis to Long Island's
oncology patients.

Among the hospital's latest initiatives is the construction of an Endoscopy Suite and Ambulatory Surgery
Suite. Another advance for the community was realized
with the opening of the Women's Imaging Center.

Maryhaven Center of Hope

An important source of services to Suffolk County's
physically and mentally challenged population,
Maryhaven Center of Hope in Port Jefferson Station
serves almost 2,000 clients ranging in age from five to
80, and employs more than 950 people in programs
operating across the county. The agency's history dates
back to 1928 when a donation by William J. Wharton
provided for the construction of a building. The new
facility was dedicated to the support, care, education,
and medical and surgical treatment of a population that
was then called "blind, crippled, and defective children."
Its history reflects a proactive approach in assessing the
needs and potential of individuals with disabilities. In
1961, the organization changed its name to Maryhaven
School for Exceptional Children. It then existed as a
haven for handicapped children unable to be cared for
in their own homes in the community.

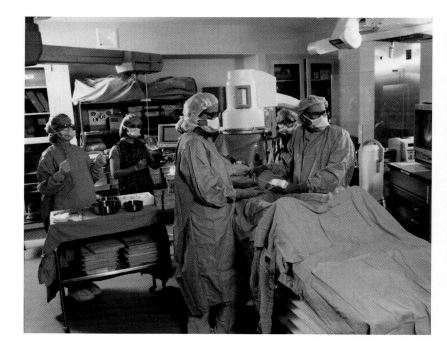

THE NATION'S FIRST MYELOSCOPY—A PROCEDURE
UTILIZING A LASER FOR LOW BACK PAIN—
WAS PERFORMED AT GOOD SAMARITAN HOSPITAL
MEDICAL CENTER.

FROM HOME CARE, TO SENIOR SERVICES, TO HOSPICES, CATHOLIC HEALTH SERVICES OF LONG ISLAND PROVIDES HOPE AND COMPASSION TO THE INDIVIDUALS IT IS PRIVILEGED TO SERVE.

As public awareness grew and attitudes toward the handicapped became more enlightened during the 1960s, Maryhaven's administrators recognized the necessity of addressing the establishment of a program to teach vocational skills to adults, and so the agency broadened its mission of service and became Maryhaven Center of Hope.

Maryhaven has since created a succession of programs which have allowed the agency to grow and expand to become one of the largest multiservice agencies on Long Island. During the 1970s, Maryhaven opened a Community Residence program, a Day Treatment program, and a Community Support Services program, and also relocated its vocational programs to Yaphank. These years also saw a curriculum revision which enabled Maryhaven to serve a more severely handicapped/multiply-involved population. In 1977, at the urging of New York State's Office of Mental Health (OMH), Maryhaven added community-based vocational services for adult psychiatric patients being discharged from hospitals.

Maryhaven evolved even further during the 1980s and '90s, introducing initiatives for consumer independence, inclusion, individuality, and productivity. The agency also opened the Children's Residential Project to meet the needs of children diagnosed as being both developmentally disabled and emotionally disturbed. It was during this time that Maryhaven established its first classrooms for autistic children, and for adults began a Day Habilitation program and its own transportation fleet. Other new programs, including Continuing Day Treatment and Intensive Psychiatric Rehabilitation Treatment, were developed to assist individuals diagnosed with psychiatric disabilities. In 2000, Maryhaven received approval to develop Wisdom Gardens, a 40-unit apartment complex that will be New York's first subsidized housing complex aimed at providing affordable housing to both senior citizens and individuals with developmental disabilities, enabling them to reside as neighbors.

Although the means and methods of caring for a special needs population have expanded significantly over the decades since its founding, the mission of Maryhaven Center of Hope remains consistent. Then as now, Maryhaven strives to make a positive difference in the lives of people with special needs, creating opportunities that foster independence, integration, and productivity, while valuing personal commitment, sharing of ideas, and respect for the dignity of the individual.

CHS Home Care & Hospice
Nursing Sisters Home Care

A certified home healthcare agency, Nursing Sisters Home Care provides registered nurses; home health aides; physical, occupational, and speech therapy; medical social work; and specialized services in pediatric care, rehabilitation, diabetes management, psychiatric care, and infusion therapy from offices in Brooklyn, and in Nassau and Suffolk counties. Other services provided by Nursing Sisters include an Interfaith Pastoral Care Program and Caring Voice, a personal emergency response system.

The roots of Nursing Sisters Home Care lay in The Nursing Sisters of the Sick Poor, founded in Brooklyn in 1905 by Sister Marie Antoinette, a French nun who, along with two other sisters, tended to the sick and poor throughout Brooklyn. As they learned Brooklyn's needs, they changed their mission to center on the delivery of home-based care. Though the non-profit agency's work has expanded greatly since those early days its mission remains the same. All of its income

CATHOLIC HEALTH SERVICES OF LONG ISLAND IS COMMITTED TO OFFERING A CONTINUUM OF WORLD-CLASS CARE AND SPIRITUAL SUPPORT TO EVERY MEMBER OF EVERY COMMUNITY.

from governmental and private grants, and as a Medicare provider, is reinvested to build more programs and assist patients who cannot pay for home care. Nursing Sisters has never turned a patient away because of inability to pay.

In addition, Nursing Sisters manages the following subsidiary corporations:

CHS Home Support Services

This consolidation of the system's respiratory, oxygen, infusion, pharmacy, and home medical equipment divisions has enabled CHS to provide a complete range of home care services in an efficient, customer-responsive manner to individuals living across Long Island.

CHS at Home

This licensed home care service agency provides home health aides and personal care attendants throughout Nassau and Suffolk counties.

Catholic Health Services Hospice

Compassionate end-of-life care is provided throughout Nassau and Suffolk counties by Catholic Health Services Hospice. The mission of Hospice is to provide comfort and anticipatory guidance during the dying process, and to affirm life by enabling individuals to make their transition to death in peace and with dignity. Hospice provides a wide range of medical and support services including home health aides, weekly registered nurse visits for pain and symptom management, medical supplies and equipment, bereavement care services, and social work and pastoral care visits. Depending upon individual need, Hospice care is given in private homes, skilled nursing facilities, or inpatient units at CHS hospitals. CHS Home Care and Hospice services are easily reached by calling 1-877-CARING-1.

Our Lady of Consolation

Founded in 1894 by the Sisters of St. Dominic, Our Lady of Consolation provides quality care and services for frail, ill, and elderly individuals. Originally called Saint Catherine's Infirmary, it was a convalescent home in Amityville. In 1975, Our Lady of Consolation was relocated to West Islip where it operated as a 250-bed geriatric nursing home until 1997 when dramatic growth resulted in an 80,000-square-foot, 200-bed addition to the existing facility and the adoption of its present name— Our Lady of Consolation Nursing and Rehabilitative Care Center, a designation which more accurately reflects its many and diverse services.

ST. FRANCIS HOSPITAL—THE HEART CENTER— REACHES OUT TO CARE FOR THE UNDERSERVED IN THE COMMUNITY AND ASSISTS CHILDREN FROM THROUGHOUT THE WORLD WITH PRO BONO HEART SURGERY.

Today, as a 450-bed long- and short-term nursing and rehabilitative care center, Our Lady of Consolation provides compassionate care for residents and patients aged 16 and older who are in need of geriatric care, restorative rehabilitative care, respiratory care, medically complex care, and specialized dementia disease care. In addition, the organization continues to offer a wide array of coordinated plans of healthcare and supportive services for home care patients enrolled in its Long-Term Home Health Care Program.

With a long history of enriching the lives of the elderly whose skilled nursing care needs can no longer be met at home or in the community, Our Lady of Consolation respects the rights and individuality of each resident, and strives to help each achieve his or her highest level of independent functioning. Its Geriatric Center offers skilled medical services; care in nutrition, hospice, and dementia; religious services; and recreational therapy activities. Through its Long Term Home Healthcare Program, individuals are afforded the opportunity to receive a nursing home level of care in their own homes. The guiding philosophy of the Home Health program is to provide each participant the individualized care which allows a person to remain in, or return to the family environment. Our Lady of Consolation's Short Term Care Program is designed for patients who are medically stable but whose rehabilitative or complex medical needs necessitate short term, multidisciplinary care to facilitate recovery, optimize functioning, and increase independence.

Our Lady of Consolation plays an integral role in the healthcare delivery system of the Diocese of Rockville Centre and offers expertise in the field of long-term care and subacute care.

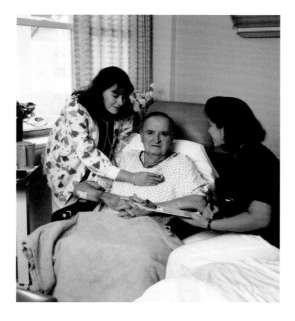

99 PERCENT OF PATIENTS SAY THEY WOULD RECOMMEND ST. FRANCIS HOSPITAL TO A FRIEND, AN ACHIEVEMENT THAT REFLECTS EXCEPTIONAL PATIENT CARE.

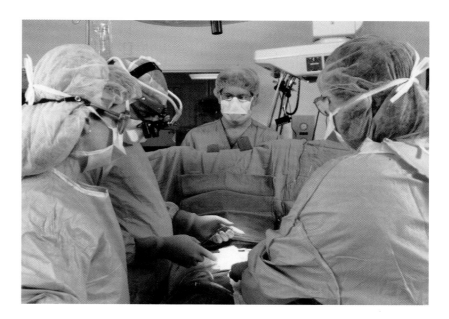

ST. FRANCIS HOSPITAL'S HIGH SURVIVAL RATE FOR CORONARY ARTERY BYPASS AND INNOVATIVE TECHNIQUES, AFFIRMS ITS EXCELLENCE IN OPEN HEART SURGERY.

St. Catherine of Siena Medical Center

A focus of medical care for the Smithtown region since 1966 when it was founded as St. John's Episcopal Hospital by the Episcopal Diocese of Long Island, St. Catherine of Siena Medical Center has long provided quality healthcare to residents of the surrounding communities. Purchased in 2000 by Catholic Health Services and renamed St. Catherine of Siena Medical Center, the organization is located on a 110-acre campus. It consists of St. Catherine of Siena Hospital, a 310-bed acute care facility; St. Catherine of Siena Nursing Home, a 240-bed facility; Siena Village, a 298-unit senior housing complex; and a medical office building.

Medical speciality areas at St. Catherine of Siena Medical Center span a full range of medical/surgical, pediatric, maternity, psychiatric, oncology, emergency, radiology, cardiac care, orthopedic, physical therapy, intensive care, and dialysis services, as well as assistance with alcohol and chemical dependencies. Its 13-bed coronary care unit and step-down telemetry area provides cardiac patients with a continuity of care. Complementing these units are diagnostic services including cardiac catheterization, stress testing, ecocardiography, nuclear cardiology, electrophysiology, and cardiac ablation. Up-to-date radiology diagnosis is accomplished through the use of MRI, CatScan, and Dex-Scan bone density testing. Operative services at St. Catherine of Siena Medical Center are delivered in eight operating rooms, and an Ambulatory Surgery Unit (ASU) which provides surgical and diagnostic patient treatment. Various procedures performed in the ASU, a facility which eliminates the need for two-to-three day hospital stays, include colonoscopies, blood transfusions, removal of growths, breast biopsies, and arthroscopies.

OUR LADY OF CONSOLATION OFFERS A WIDE
ARRAY OF NURSING AND REHABILITATIVE CARE
SERVICES, SOME OF WHICH INCLUDE PHYSICAL
THERAPY, OCCUPATIONAL THERAPY, TOTAL JOINT
REPLACEMENT REHABILITATION, AND GENERAL
ORTHOPEDIC REHABILITATION.

The hospital's Woman Child Care Center (WCCC) offers inviting birth rooms which combine the labor through recovery process. Midwife services are available as a patient option. WCCC is also the site for community services such as Lamaze training, Vaginal Birth after Caesarean support, health and fitness, and grief support.

Along with medical services based at the hospital, St. Catherine of Siena Nursing Home offers geriatric care for people with Alzheimer's disease, hemodialysis care, subacute care, respiratory care, and terminal care. Siena Village is a 298-unit seniors apartment complex which offers residents access to transportation, social workers, and case managers.

Outreach programs at St. Catherine of Siena Medical Center include a yearly community health fair and hosting support groups open to the community.

St. Charles Hospital and Rehabilitation Center

Through its network of sites throughout Long Island, Port Jefferson's St. Charles Hospital and Rehabilitation Center is an important regional provider of rehabilitative services. The institution was originally founded in 1907 as the Brooklyn Home for Blind, Crippled, and Defective Children by the Daughters of Wisdom. Several years later, already caring for more than 250 children, it had come to be known as St. Charles Hospital and had founded the first outpatient clinic on Long Island. During the years of the polio epidemic St. Charles achieved nationwide renown as a research and treatment center. By 1949 St. Charles was treating more than 600 children afflicted with polio. The hospital played a role in the development of serum treatment protocol for infantile paralysis, and also established its expertise in rehabilitating polio survivors.

By the mid-1960s, St. Charles had expanded to include inpatient and outpatient rehabilitation programs, as well as maternity services. By the late 1970s, St. Charles, in conjunction with Eastern Suffolk BOCES, was working closely with area schools in providing educational services to children with disabilities.

St. Charles completed a major modernization project in 1997 which expanded and upgraded its maternity service and neonatal intensive care unit. The expanded hospital also includes a full service pediatrics unit; a Critical Care Pavilion encompassing an emergency room, radiology, ICU/CCU, and operating rooms; new orthopedics and rehabilitation pavilions; a dedicated Pediatric Rehabilitation Unit including Long Island's only dedicated traumatic brain injury unit; and 31 diagnostic treatment clinics for children and adults with disabilities. In its most recent expansion of services, St. Charles opened a telemetry unit featuring central monitoring adjacent to its cardio-pulmonary rehabilitation unit.

The St. Charles Rehabilitation Network brings outpatient physical, occupational, and speech therapy services closer to children and adults in need of comprehensive rehabilitation. This network maintains 24 rehabilitation sites throughout Long Island and the New York metropolitan area. Two of the sites, Centereach and Ronkonkoma, specialize in women's services.

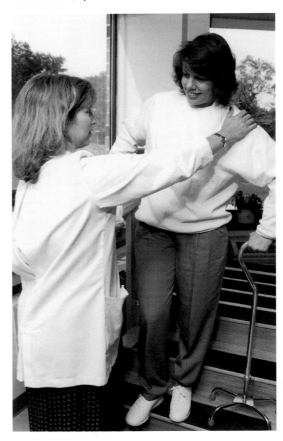

OUR LADY OF CONSOLATION PROVIDES BOTH LONG
AND SHORT TERM NURSING AND REHABILITATIVE
CARE FOR RESIDENTS AND PATIENTS WHO ARE 16
YEARS OLD AND OLDER.

Complementing its extensive rehabilitative services, St. Charles has also expanded its educational programs and now has Educational and Therapeutic Centers in Port Jefferson, Southampton, Aquebogue, and Huntington. These centers, which focus on the needs of children aged six weeks to six years, include day care centers, on-site kindergartens, early intervention programs for developmentally delayed or physically disabled children, and preschool programs for children with disabilities. More than 500 children are served on a daily basis at these regional centers.

St. Francis Hospital-The Heart Center

Throughout its history, Roslyn's St. Francis Hospital has maintained a place on the leading edge of technology and technique. Founded by the Franciscan Missionaries of Mary in 1922 as a summer camp, and later as a sanatorium for children with rheumatic fever, St. Francis was established in the spirit of high-quality, compassionate care. Developments in the field of cardiology and in related areas continue to shape its practice of medicine and surgery. Today, St. Francis Hospital is New York state's only specialty cardiac center and ranks among the nation's largest cardiac centers.

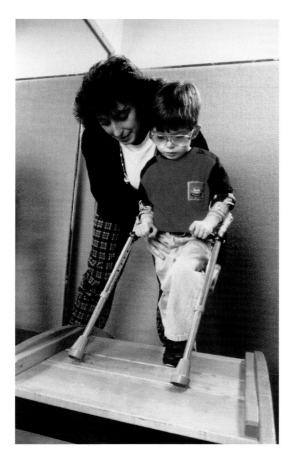

ST. CHARLES HOSPITAL IS A RECOGNIZED LEADER IN REHABILITATION. THE HOSPITAL'S FACILITIES INCORPORATE THE LATEST EQUIPMENT WITH THE FINEST TRAINED PROFESSIONALS TO PROVIDE SUPERIOR PATIENT CARE.

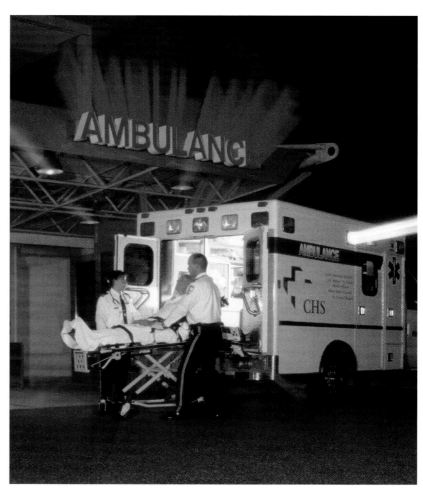

CHS AMBULANCE SERVICES PROVIDES PATIENTS WITH THE BENEFIT OF STATE-OF-THE-ART MEDICAL TRANSPORTATION SERVICES AND THE EXPERTISE OF HIGHLY TRAINED PROFESSIONALS.

Following the tradition of its founders, St. Francis Hospital nurtures its mission of reaching out to those in need through free screening programs and provides care to children from around the world who need heart surgery. The hospital leads the Northeast as a regional referral center for tertiary cardiac care and also provides additional medical and surgical services.

St. Francis Hospital-The Heart Center fights heart disease with comprehensive programs for diagnosis, treatment, clinical research, and public education. It maintains the nation's busiest Arrhythmia and Pacemaker Center and is the choice of thousands of patients who seek state-of-the-art specialized care. St. Francis Hospital performs the most bypass surgeries in the state and is one of just four New York medical facilities with a risk-adjusted mortality rate significantly below the statewide average for coronary bypass surgery for the most recent three-year period analyzed by the New York State Department of Health.

Over the past decades, St. Francis Hospital has built upon its experience in cardiac care to offer new diagnostic and treatment options. Significant advances in

ALMOST 2,000 BABIES ARE DELIVERED EACH YEAR AT ST. CATHERINE OF SIENA HOSPITAL.

minimally invasive open-heart surgery have revolutionized cardiac surgery. St. Francis Hospital was the site of the first Port-Access™ minimally invasive cardiac surgery performed on Long Island and continues to explore similar options offering greater benefits. The Heart Center also builds upon its successful program in balloon angioplasty, the most common form of treatment for atherosclerosis, and has incorporated the use of coronary artery stents, new medications, and beta radiation therapy to avoid the return of plaque. Recently, St. Francis Hospital introduced a Heart Failure Program which provides care for outpatients by a multidisciplinary team of clinical experts.

The DeMatteis Center for Cardiac Research and Education, St. Francis Hospital's satellite campus, provides the services of a Lipid Center and Cardiac Fitness and Rehabilitation Program. Located in Old Brookville, the center is also the site of Long Island's first Ultrafast CT scanner, a simple and painless non-invasive method of detecting early coronary disease years before symptoms occur. This scanning device is offered in addition to the Cardiac Research Institute which studies new therapies and technology relating to the diagnosis, treatment, and prevention of heart disease.

CHS Ambulance Services

CHS Ambulance Services (CHSAS) was established in 1998 to assure high-quality, compassionate patient transportation services to residents of Long Island, Queens, and Brooklyn. Superior training and continuous quality improvement at CHSAS create the foundation for the best and most appropriate patient care. CHSAS offers services ranging from advanced high-risk critical care emergency transports, to non-emergency services, including prescheduled admissions and discharges, and transporation to and from visits to doctors and other treatment centers. CHSAS' ambulette division serves the needs of patients who require other than ambulance transport.

CHS Co-sponsored Organizations

Along with the Winthrop-South Nassau University Health System, CHS co-sponsors three other important healthcare resources on Long Island: New Island Hospital in Bethpage, South Oaks Hospital in Amityville, and Broadlawn Manor in Amityville.

New Island is a 223-bed acute care facility that provides high-quality inpatient, outpatient, and emergency services. South Oaks, with a proud history of almost 120 years, provides a comprehensive continuum of speciality mental health and substance abuse services to patients of all ages. On the same campus, Broadlawn Manor operates a full spectrum of rehabilitation and long-term care services for older adults. Care for Alzheimer's patients was pioneered by Broadlawn with its establishment in 1985 of Long Island's first such care unit. ∎

SIENA VILLAGE, PART OF THE CAMPUS AT ST. CATHERINE OF SIENA MEDICAL CENTER, OFFERS AN AFFORDABLE HOUSING OPTION FOR SENIORS.

PHOTO BY BRUCE BENNETT, BRUCE BENNETT STUDIOS.

VERIZON COMMUNICATIONS

Bell Atlantic and GTE have come together to form one of the world's premier communications companies—Verizon Communications. The new company is at the forefront of the communications and information industry with nearly 109 million access line equivalents and more than 27.5 million wireless customers. A Fortune 10 company, Verizon is among the ranks of America's top 10 employers, with approximately 260,000 employees and $63 billion in annual revenues. Verizon's global presence extends to 40 countries in the Americas, Europe, Asia, and the Pacific.

Verizon Wireless is the largest wireless communications provider in the U.S. with more than 27.5 million wireless voice and data customers and nearly 4 million paging customers. Its footprint covers over 90 percent of the U.S. population, 49 of the top 50, and 96 of the top 100 U.S. markets.

Verizon Information Services (VIS) is a world leading print and online directory publisher and a content provider for communications products and services. The largest directory publisher in the world, VIS has annual revenues of more than $4.1 billion and employs more than 11,000 people. The company provides sales, publishing and other related services for nearly 2,300 directory titles in 48 states, the District of Columbia and 17 countries outside the U.S. This includes more than 1,600 Verizon directory titles with a total circulation of approximately 110 million copies in the U.S. and 37 million copies internationally. Verizon Information Services also produces and markets SuperPages.com http://www.SuperPages.com, the Internet's preeminent online directory and shopping resource. SuperPages.com has received up to 4.2 million visits and 2.3 million unique visitors per month. BigYellow was the first Yellow Pages on the Internet.

ACROSS NASSAU AND SUFFOLK COUNTIES, DEDICATED VERIZON EMPLOYEES BUILD AND MAINTAIN THE VERIZON NETWORK TO PROVIDE OUTSTANDING CUSTOMER SERVICE EVERY HOUR, EVERY DAY.

Spurring Long Island's Economic Growth

While Verizon now has a presence around the globe and ranks among the country's largest corporations, it is still the same company that has for more than 100 years served Long Islanders from Cold Spring Harbor to Great South Bay, from Kings Point to the Montauk Lighthouse. Be it resorts or wineries, dotcoms or farms, high-tech firms or single-family homes, no communications company understands Long Island's needs like Verizon.

Verizon is still Long Island's local phone company but now also brings the benefits of the latest in telecommunications to everybody. More than 5,000 of the company's employees live and work in Nassau and Suffolk counties. They are active in the same community groups and are the friends and neighbors of the company's customers. The children of Verizon employees attend the same schools, play on the same sports teams, and share the same interests. So, like everyone on Long Island, Verizon's employees who live, work, and are involved in Long Island communities are committed to the long-term economic and social well-being of Nassau and Suffolk counties.

Verizon and its customers on Long Island have been partners in the transformation and growth of the new economy on Long Island—the "Silicon Island" miracle, if you will. Nassau and Suffolk counties have made what has sometimes been a bumpy transition from an economy based on the defense industry to today's booming economy based on high-tech industries.

In fact, Verizon likes to think of its communications network as the backbone of the Long Island economy. Today, everyone is talking about the vast potential of the "information superhighway," "high speed data services" and "interactive services." The Internet is having a profound effect on the way business is conducted. And Verizon is on the leading edge of this revolution—a revolution that is transforming not only its own telecommunications industry, but also the way that people communicate, work, play, and live their lives. The Verizon public switched network is ideally suited to transport business and residential customers to wherever the information superhighway takes them.

In today's new, wide open, and highly competitive and evolving marketplace, Verizon is committed to helping its customers—Long Island businesses—succeed by providing them with the advanced telecommunications tools that are important to every type of endeavor. Increasingly, that success will depend on local business' ability to deliver information faster and more effectively than their competitors. Verizon is working to make that happen as the company owns the most efficient network in the world and Verizon makes sure everyone on Long Island has access to it.

Verizon continues to invest aggressively in its facilities with $250 million invested annually on Long Island. The company has installed more than 150,000 miles of fiber optic lines on Long Island. In fact, Verizon was the first regional telephone company to deploy fiber optics all the way to its customers' doorsteps.

ON JUNE 30, 2000, BELL ATLANTIC AND GTE COMPLETED A MERGER AND BEGAN DOING BUSINESS AS VERIZON COMMUNICATIONS. CELEBRATIONS WERE HELD ACROSS THE COUNTRY AT VERIZON BUILDINGS LAUNCHING THIS NEW ERA IN TELECOMMUNICATIONS.

To help its customers achieve that success and to stay ahead of the curve, the company has expanded the scope of its business. Verizon can meet a large business' complex telecommunications requirements with super-fast data transmission products. Or the company also can provide DSL service to someone who works at home and simply needs a faster connection to the Internet.

Committed to the Communities It Serves

Even as Verizon redefines itself as a global communications player, the company's roots remain firmly planted in the diverse communities where it does business. Verizon's customers and the communities they live in have always been—and will remain—a top priority.

WHETHER AT HOME OR IN THE OFFICE, EDUCATION HAS TAKEN A MAJOR LEAP FORWARD. THANKS TO LIVE, TWO-WAY, INTERACTIVE VIDEOCONFERENCING AND ONLINE COURSES, PEOPLE CAN NOW PURSUE DEGREES WITHOUT ACTUALLY LEAVING THEIR HOMES OR DESKS.

The Verizon Foundation is the philanthropic arm of Verizon Communications. It was established to transform its nonprofit community partners with innovative e-solutions. Verizon Foundation is committed to "venture philanthropy"—investing in the development of capacity infrastructure to create new leadership models for our communities. It invests in over 12,000 nonprofit organizations a year based on strategic partnerships and innovative technology programs. Foundation partners include organizations that support literacy and education, health and human services, arts and humanities, community development, workforce development and the environment. Verizon employees will earn over $8 million dollars in grants for nonprofit organizations where they volunteer their time and financial resources. They will also clock over 10 million volunteer hours annually to various philanthropic organizations including mentoring programs like Aspira, Literacy Volunteers, Junior Achievement, and local programs in partnership with the United Way, the Long Island Blood Services and global concern programs including disaster relief efforts, and the fight against cancer and AIDS. With annual grants reaching about $70 million, the Verizon Foundation is among the nation's top 10 corporate foundations in monies distributed annually. Its overriding goal is to make information technology accessible to everyone, regardless of economics, demographics, or education.

The Foundation, while active across the country, supports a variety of projects on Long Island, with an emphasis on new technology applications in education, health and human services, the arts and humanities, and civic development.

Among the Long Island organizations that receive Foundation support are the Babylon Village Educational Foundation, the Chamber Players International, Friends Assisting Nassau Seniors, John T. Mather Memorial Hospital, L.I. First Robotics Competition, Long Island Association for AIDS Care Inc., Long Island Works Coalition, Minority Breast Health Partnership, National Center for Disability Services, St. Joseph's College, Suffolk County Organization for the Promotion of Education, Suffolk County Independent Living Organization, The Institute for Student Achievement, and the Ward Melville Heritage Organization.

Leading the Way in Telecommunication Education

One area of special emphasis on Long Island focuses on innovative ways to use the telecommunications network to aid in learning. Verizon was one of the founders and drivers of the formation of the Long Island Works Coalition. The Coalition is a partnership between the Long Island business community and the Long Island school districts that prepares students, grades K though 16, with the skills they will need to participate in the thriving Long Island economy. It utilizes an on-line internship clearinghouse to create work-based opportunities for students.

Verizon is also proud of is its partnership with the New York Institute of Technology (NYIT) and the development of the school's Verizon Technology Lab. The Central Islip-based college has done pioneering work in the distance learning field and Verizon has funded and been a major sponsor of NYIT's state-of-the-art Verizon Technology Lab.

Verizon and NYIT were among the creators of a consortium called the Educational Enterprise Zone. Members of this consortium create programming for K-12 classrooms to be delivered via videoconferencing. Research sites, hospitals, museums, cultural institutions, businesses, and government agencies will develop curricular programs with this consortium. The Educational Enterprise Zone puts in place the technology infrastructure and management structure that allows the students at their schools or from their homes to connect to resources worldwide.

While there is corporate support, individual Verizon employees can and do make a difference in their communities. Cissy Morturano, who works in the Patchogue central office, approached co-workers and asked them to participate in Suffolk County's "Adopt-a-Child" program. The Verizon's employees' efforts have snowballed from the first year where Verizon employees bought gifts for one family to the recent holiday season, where Verizon's Suffolk County employees supported 24 families with 80 children with gifts and fixings for holiday dinners. Tracy Riess, in the Garden City office, has organized three to four blood drives annually with the Long Island Blood Services and is the volunteer coordinator for Junior Achievement in Long Island classrooms.

Helping Long Islanders Communicate

Even though Verizon is now a global company, it is still Long Island's local service provider.

So whatever the information superhighway brings, Verizon is competitively positioned to provide Long Islanders with access to all its benefits. That means all Verizon customers—businesses, public service organizations and residential consumers. They will have access to advanced tools such as voice, video, and high-speed data services; wired and wireless communications; electronic and printed directory services; and access to information and entertainment.

Verizon will continue to enhance Long Island's public telecommunications network and create easier, more efficient ways for its customers to communicate. Through the efforts of the Verizon Foundation and the Verizon employees, the company will continue to give something back to the communities on Long Island.

Verizon looks forward to the future of Long Island, a future Verizon will no doubt help shape with its customers for the benefit of generations to come. ■

THE VERIZON PUBLIC SWITCHED NETWORK WITH ITS LATEST ENHANCEMENTS IS IDEALLY SUITED TO TRANSPORT VOICE AND DATA AT THE HIGHEST SPEEDS, WITH MAXIMUM SECURITY AND RELIABILITY FOR BOTH OUR RESIDENTIAL AND BUSINESS CUSTOMERS.

KeySpan Corporation

Based in Hicksville and Brooklyn, KeySpan is a geographically and functionally wide-ranging energy company with roots in the New York metropolitan area that reach back to the mid-19th century. Formed as the parent of the Brooklyn Union Gas Company in 1996, KeySpan merged with certain businesses of the Long Island Lighting Company on May 28, 1998, to create the foundation for the multi-faceted regional and national company that it is today.

FOR MORE THAN A CENTURY, KEYSPAN AND ITS PREDECESSORS HAVE PROVIDED GAS SERVICE TO THE NEW YORK METROPOLITAN REGION. WHETHER IN 19TH CENTURY HORSE-DRAWN WAGONS OR TODAY'S NATURAL GAS POWERED VANS, KEYSPAN'S MISSION IS UNPARALLELED CUSTOMER SERVICE.

The company delivers natural gas to, and generates electric power for, homes and businesses in New York City and Long Island. KeySpan Energy Delivery, known for more than a century as Brooklyn Union, is the fourth-largest natural gas utility in the country, with 1.6 million customers from Staten Island to Montauk. The recent acquisition of Eastern Enterprises raises that customer base to more than 2.4 million gas customers in New York, Massachusetts, and New Hampshire. KeySpan also owns and operates more than 6,000 MW of electric power generation on Long Island and in New York City, and manages the electric transmission and distribution system, as well as customer services, for the Long Island Power Authority's 1.1 million customers. "We decided to focus primarily on the Northeast region, and took the steps needed to fulfill our corporate vision to become a premier energy and services company," said Robert B. Catell, KeySpan's chairman and chief executive officer. "We created the first utility-initiated energy holding company in New York State. We diversified, with investments in gas-and-oil exploration and production, gas processing, pipelines, and storage, and made select international investments with local partners. We opened up our gas distribution system to

marketers, and launched our own unregulated energy commodity marketer. We created other unregulated businesses as appliance repair rolled out of the utility, and we increased our portfolio of energy-related services to better serve our customers' needs."

Opportunities in Deregulation

The recent and ongoing deregulation of the gas and electric industries has challenged KeySpan to be innovative and resourceful. It has become more agile, more competitive, and more responsive to customer needs. While some energy companies view deregulation negatively, KeySpan sees it as an opportunity to distinguish itself in the marketplace.

Deregulation of the gas industry began in the 1980s; electric deregulation began in the 1990s and continues today, as states consider legislation allowing new providers to enter the marketplace. New York has embraced deregulation, and consumers and businesses here can now choose their energy suppliers. As a result, a large number of buying pools have emerged to negotiate group rates, and several "dot-coms" have formed to help customers search for the best prices and service. In this environment, KeySpan not only must compete against providers of other kinds of fuel, but it also must battle for market share with new providers of gas and electricity. "Years ago, few of us knew what to expect. Some saw deregulation as a threat," said Catell. "Some, like KeySpan, saw it as a challenge. But whatever your view, it has caused a change to sweep through the energy industry, providing an opportunity for new players to meet the needs of the customer."

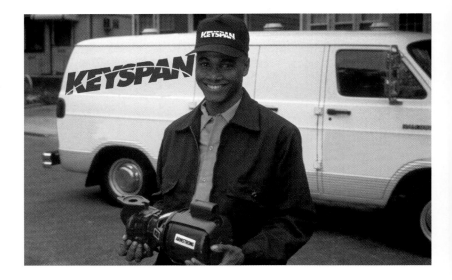

KEYSPAN HAS LONG BEEN COMMITTED TO PROVIDING THE HIGHEST QUALITY CUSTOMER SERVICE TO ITS 2.4 MILLION NATURAL GAS CUSTOMERS, AS WELL AS THE 1.1 MILLION ELECTRIC CUSTOMERS IT SERVES UNDER CONTRACT TO THE LONG ISLAND POWER AUTHORITY. MEETING CUSTOMER NEEDS IS THE NUMBER ONE PRIORITY OF THE COMPANY'S SKILLED, EXPERIENCED WORK FORCE.

THE ELECTRIC TRANSMISSION & DISTRIBUTION
SYSTEM MAINTAINED BY KEYSPAN HAS BEEN
RECOGNIZED AS THE MOST RELIABLE OVERHEAD
SYSTEM IN NEW YORK STATE. KEYSPAN IS A
RECIPIENT OF THE EDISON ELECTRIC INSTITUTE
EMERGENCY RESPONSE AWARD FOR ITS ACCOM-
PLISHMENTS IN EMERGENCY SYSTEM RESTORATION.

The company is positioning itself as a diverse, regional energy company that is able to deliver the products and services needed by different kinds of customers in many different locations. In the rapidly changing energy environment, it has steadily expanded its product and service offerings, many of which are provided by affiliated companies. KeySpan companies, for example, repair appliances, heating systems, and cooling systems for residential and commercial customers, as well as install, operate, and maintain turn-key energy systems, and provide fuel-management, energy-consulting, and project-financing services to high-volume energy customers. Other affiliates supply gas and electricity in six states, and provide natural gas and energy-supply-management services to industrial and commercial facilities in the Northeast.

Additional services include natural gas exploration, production, processing, transportation, and storage in the United States and around the world. The company has invested in a pipeline distribution system in Northern Ireland and owns a 64 percent interest in The Houston Exploration Company, which explores for and produces natural gas in the Southwestern United States.

Clean Energy

KeySpan and its predecessor companies have long been committed to protecting the natural environment. One of the company's basic principles is that stewardship of the environment and commitment to customers go hand-in-hand. It continuously strives to identify and develop new technologies that will help ensure the existence of clean energy—and a clean environment—for generations to come.

The foundation of the company's environmental advocacy is its long-standing promotion of natural gas as the country's cleanest, most efficient, and most abundant fossil fuel. A study released in 1999 found that, from 1990 to 1997, KeySpan helped reduce carbon dioxide emissions by nearly 850,000 tons through residential heating-system conversions. That figure is expected to increase by 180,000 tons when 1998 figures are tallied. KeySpan also has been a national leader in the natural gas vehicles market.

In March 2000, a subsidiary, KeySpan Technologies, Inc., began an aggressive testing program to perfect fuel-cell technology, a chemical process that produces electricity by converting the energy of hydrogen in natural gas directly into electricity. Properly applied, fuel cells would be a stable, clean, and efficient energy source, affordable and practical for residential and small-business customers. GE MicroGen, a subsidiary of GE Power Systems, and KeySpan Technologies have joined as partners to purchase and test 30 residential natural-gas-powered fuel cells, 29 of which will be placed on Long Island and in the New York metropolitan area. "With commercial availability anticipated by 2001, fuel cells will provide an outstanding opportunity to provide homeowners and small businesses with safe, efficient and cost-effective green power systems to meet their energy needs," pointed out Catell. "KeySpan will continue to research and develop other forms of distributed power, including micro-turbines and co-generation, to provide additional sources of clean, dependable power."

AS THE LARGEST INVESTOR-OWNED ELECTRIC
GENERATOR IN NEW YORK STATE, KEYSPAN IS
COMMITTED TO ENVIRONMENTAL STEWARDSHIP. THE
COMPANY'S SIX ELECTRIC GENERATING FACILITIES,
LIKE THE NORTHPORT POWER STATION SHOWN
HERE, ARE EQUIPPED TO BURN CLEAN, EFFICIENT
NATURAL GAS AND HAVE STATE-OF-THE-ART
ENVIRONMENTAL CONTROLS.

FOR MORE THAN THREE DECADES, KEYSPAN'S CINDERELLA PROGRAM HAS BEEN HELPING REHABILITATE BUILDINGS AND STOREFRONTS AND REVIVE DECLINING NEIGHBORHOODS. RECENTLY, A CINDERELLA GRANT FUNDED THE LIGHTING OF FREEPORT'S FAMED "NAUTICAL MILE."

The company is also a member of the Clean Energy Group, a coalition of electric producers that works with the U.S. Environmental Protection Agency and the Natural Resources Defense Council to decrease emissions throughout the industry. Internal recycling programs are in place at all KeySpan locations, and employees participate in a variety of community-based clean-up and environmental-preservation programs.

Community Commitment

The two energy companies that combined as KeySpan in 1998 both brought long traditions of promoting the well-being and quality of life of the communities they serve. In the new and farther-reaching company, this commitment has been extended and expanded. The company's corporate giving program supports more than 2,000 not-for-profit organizations.

Since 1998, a major new philanthropic program has been coordinated by the KeySpan Foundation, which administers grants in the areas of environmental preservation, community development, health and human services, education, and culture and the arts. Launched with an initial endowment of $20 million from KeySpan, most of the foundation's grants have been targeted to organizations in KeySpan's service territory. Among the organizations it has awarded funds to are Long Island Works Coalition, United Way of Long Island, United Way of New York City, Junior Achievement of Long Island, Museums at Stony Brook, and Maurer Foundation for Breast Health Education.

KeySpan Energy Delivery—the former Brooklyn Union—earned a national reputation for good corporate citizenship through its Cinderella program, which was started in 1966 to spur revitalization of Brooklyn's brownstone neighborhoods. Since then, the Cinderella program has contributed to the restoration of hundreds of buildings and storefronts throughout three boroughs of New York City, and lately on Long Island. In 1999, a $15,000 Cinderella grant helped fund the renovation of Northport Theater, a 1930s vaudeville playhouse— the first grant bestowed upon a Long Island community. The program has since participated in the restoration of downtown Glen Cove and in the lighting of Freeport's "Nautical Mile."

More than one-third of KeySpan employees are active in charitable organizations, including Long Island Blood Services drives, United Way's matching-gift program, the Row for a Cure for breast cancer, and The Points of Light Foundation. Through a company-sponsored Meals on Wheels program, employees give up their lunch-hours to deliver meals to the elderly and the infirm. In 2000, the Long Island Association awarded its Medal of Honor to KeySpan's employees for their commitment to the Long Island community. "We're privileged to have scores of KeySpan employees who generously give their personal time, their experience, their money, even their own blood, for the benefit of others," said Catell. "They demonstrate the kind of personal commitment that makes the greatest difference in the lives of so many people all throughout the Long Island and New York City region."

RICK SHALVOY'S ANNUAL "ROW FOR A CURE" AROUND LONG ISLAND IS AN EXAMPLE OF THE MANY FUND-RAISING EFFORTS THAT HIGHLIGHT KEYSPAN'S COMMITMENT TO COMMUNITY INVOLVEMENT. THE COMPANY CONTRIBUTED FINANCING AND EMPLOYEE SUPPORT TO THE ROW, WHICH HELPED RAISE MORE THAN $50,000 FOR BREAST CANCER RESEARCH.

Future Prospects

The energy industry has never been more uncertain, nor ever as exciting and promising. The future belongs to companies that plan wisely and adapt quickly, that are innovative and versatile in providing a wide range of products and services for a wide range of customers. That is the kind of company that KeySpan has become and will continue to be.

KeySpan's commitment to leveraging technology will enable it to serve customers more conveniently and resourcefully. The company has developed online service capabilities that allow customers to pay bills, input meter-readings, and activate or de-activate accounts from their desktops. It is now pursuing an equity interest in an Internet venture that would help it build an energy portal, which would give customers fast, 24-hour access to the company's energy products and home-management services. And, as a partner with e-business and community-services providers, KeySpan could offer a variety of additional products and services online. At the KeySpan energy portal, a customer could perform a range of tasks from changing environmental controls to ordering prescriptions.

KeySpan also owns a high-speed fiber-optic network that stretches 450 miles around Long Island and New York City. The company plans to use this network to provide its customers with communications products and services, and to become the "carrier's carrier" by selling network capacity and data transmission to other providers. Several key connections to trans-Atlantic cable systems give KeySpan improved access to customer homes and businesses, as well as links to Europe that may offer opportunities for overseas ventures.

"As deregulation continues I think that the Northeast is the most exciting place for an energy company to be doing business at this time," concludes Catell.

LONG ISLAND'S BOOMING ECONOMY MEANS INCREASED DEMAND FOR ENERGY. KEYSPAN IS HELPING TO MEET THAT DEMAND IN AN ENVIRONMENTALLY FRIENDLY WAY BY INSTALLING MORE THAN A MILLION FEET OF NEW NATURAL GAS PIPE PER YEAR.

"The Northeast region has about 43 percent of the country's population, 36 percent of the country's gas consumption, and 40 percent of the country's electricity consumption. I see that as 100 percent opportunity. In order to take advantage of that opportunity, the energy company of the future must utilize technology to focus on where the old economy and new economy converge, at the customer." ∎

ROBERT B. CATELL IS CHAIRMAN AND CHIEF EXECUTIVE OFFICER OF KEYSPAN, A MULTI-FACETED ENERGY SERVICES COMPANY SERVING MORE THAN 3 MILLION CUSTOMERS IN THE NORTHEAST REGION.

RUTTURA & SONS CONSTRUCTION CO., INC.

When you start out making sidewalks and curbs, there's nowhere else to go but up. And that's exactly where Ruttura & Sons Construction Co., Inc., has gone. The company that Dominick Ruttura founded in 1918 has long since moved on from the walkways of Freeport to major concrete and excavation projects across Long Island and the New York Metropolitan area.

Ruttura & Sons performs demolition, excavation, storm drainage, sanitary systems, water service work, as well as all phases of cast-in-place concrete. The Farmingdale company is well known in the construction industry and is often called upon by primary contractors to do the concrete and excavation work on new office, retail, educational, and industrial buildings.

"It's really amazing to me how the tiny business my grandfather started 83 years ago could become such an integral part of Long Island's growth," said Thomas Ruttura, president of the company. "We take great pride in our contributions to that growth."

Growing Long Island

Recent Ruttura & Sons projects include foundation excavation/backfilling, concrete work, foundations, slab on grade, and reinforcement for Korean Airlines at John F. Kennedy International Airport. Ruttura & Sons also did demolition work, as well as drainage, excavation, foundation, slab-on-grade, and other site concrete work on a new residence hall at Fordham University in the Bronx.

A new parking garage and day care center at Computer Associates in Islandia, N.Y., bears the Ruttura stamp, as does a tower addition to the software company's office complex. Stabile Hall at Brooklyn's Pratt Institute hired Ruttura & Sons to do site development, drainage, excavation, foundation and slab-on-grade work. The Asian Center at SUNY Stony Brook has a

BASEBALL COMES BACK TO BROOKLYN 2001.

foundation from Ruttura & Sons, as does the Cradle of Aviation Museum in Garden City, and the Kraft Center at Columbia University.

Ruttura & Sons has also played a major role in the expansion of the retail industry on Long Island. The company worked on the construction teams for the Target store in Bayshore, the Lord & Taylor shop in Bayshore, the Riverhead Center, Saks Fifth Avenue in Huntington, the Fortunoff Mall in Westbury, Office Depot in Syosset, and the Circuit City Service Center in Hicksville.

Weathering the Storms

Times have not always been good for the construction industry on Long Island. There was the Great Depression of the 1930s, the recession of the 1970s, and various periods of little, if any, economic expansion. When the economy suffers, companies don't build new buildings, and they don't upgrade old ones. So, construction and renovation companies are at the mercy of the ebb and flow of the general economy. Ruttura & Sons has weathered every storm.

CHARLES WANG ASIAN CENTER— STONY BROOK UNIVERSITY.

CARGO FACILITY JFK AIRPORT 2000.

"My grandfather had incredible vision," said Thomas Ruttura. "Despite the fact that Long Island was ripe for unbridled expansion back in the early 20th century, he knew that there would be bumps along the way. That's why he insisted the company change with the times. Every time new techniques and equipment came out, he was right there. We always had to have the latest toys."

Those "toys" are what enabled Ruttura & Sons to compete for the best jobs. With some of the best pieces of equipment in the industry, the company has been able to implement the most innovative techniques in concrete and excavation work.

What the company cannot do with equipment of its own, it does through partners. As recycling became an increasingly important part of the construction process in the 1990s, Ruttura & Sons began sending out old steel beams and other materials to be recycled at steel mills. When the company performed demolition work on the Centereach Mall, for example, it sent the old steel beams to be recycled by New Jersey Steel Corporation's mini mill in Sayreville, N.J. Much of the steel was returned to the job for reuse.

"We recognize the importance of recycling," said Thomas Ruttura, president of the company. "Everyone in the construction industry realized that in the 1980s when the landfills on Long Island began refusing heavy construction materials. With the high cost of transporting the materials to other landfills, we had no other choice but to recycle. But that option has worked out well for the industry and the Long Island environment."

Through diligence the company has earned a number of accolades. McGraw Hill Publications named Ruttura & Sons the number-one concrete and excavation company in New York and Long Island in 2000. The Engineering News Record named it number 356 out of 600 specialty contractors. In 1999, the same publication named Ruttura & Sons the 19th largest concrete company in the United States.

A Family Affair

Although Ruttura & Sons takes on projects in Queens, Brooklyn, the Bronx, Manhattan and New Jersey, the bulk of its work remains on Long Island. The company takes great pride in its workforce. Richard Pearsall, Ruttura & Sons' assistant vice president, has referred to its employees as "the greatest workforce in greater New York."

That is important to the Ruttura brothers, particularly because their company has always been a family owned business. That's why Ruttura & Sons provides its workers with an attractive benefits package and a flexible work environment. Every worker—even those without Ruttura for a last name—is treated like family.

"Our employees give us the best that they have each and every day," says Thomas Ruttura. "Most of them have been with us for years. At Ruttura & Sons, we take care of our own." ■

IMAX THEATER CRADLE OF AVIATION 1999.

E.W. HOWELL CO., INC.

If you measure a firm by the quality of its clients, E.W. Howell Co., Inc. is in good company. In the construction firm's early days, it built some of the largest and most prestigious mansions on Long Island.

The administration building at the C.W. Post Campus of Long Island University, once the home of Marjorie Merriweather Post of the Post cereal dynasty, is an E.W. Howell creation. The firm also built several homes for E.F. Hutton, one for Theodore Roosevelt, Jr., and one for Mrs. John D. Rockefeller in Tarrytown, N.Y. When Teddy Roosevelt's summer White House at Sagamore Hill was being prepared as a national shrine, E.W. Howell did the necessary renovations. And when the Guggenheim family wanted a home on Long Island, E.W. Howell created "Falaise," now a Nassau County Park in Sands Point. Other celebrated clients from those early days included Charles Lindbergh, Marshall Field, John T. Pratt, Jr., Robert Gardiner, Henry Luce, Harry Paine Whitney, Vincent Astor and Robert Moses.

"Our early work certainly helped to paint a colorful past," says Howard Rowland, the company's president and chief operating officer. Colorful, indeed. How many construction firms, which come and go about as quickly as the seasons, can claim such illustrious clientele? And how many can trace their origins back to 1891? E.W. Howell is certainly among the construction industry elite. But it didn't get there by dropping famous names.

E.F. HUTTON RESIDENCE, BUILT IN 1929.

From the Ground Up

Elmer Winfield Howell established E.W. Howell Co. on Long Island in 1891. From then until the 1920s, the company concentrated on building palatial homes on Long Island's famed Gold Coast. It gradually expanded into commercial construction, largely at the request of its residential customers, who had construction needs for their businesses. E.W. Howell eventually secured repeat business from such well-known companies as Saks Fifth Avenue, Target Stores, Sunrise Assisted Living, Hewlett Packard, Bank of Tokyo-Mitsubishi, Sanwa Bank, Columbia University, North Shore University Hospital, Estee Lauder, Underwriters Laboratories, Long Island University, and Northrop Grumman.

Now based in Woodbury, N.Y., the company concentrates on the construction and renovation of factories, power plants, retail malls and stores, hospitals, hotels, office buildings, laboratories, distribution facilities, nursing homes, university buildings, and schools. Recent projects include the Cradle of Aviation Museum at Mitchel Field, an athletic facility for Suffolk Community College's Brentwood Campus, six Target stores, three Kohl's stores, four Sunrise Assisted Living facilities, and the Saks Fifth Avenue store at the Walt Whitman Mall.

Every so often, E.W. Howell returns to its roots by building yet one more beautiful home. Several years ago, the company built a mansion in Pawling, N.Y., for the Ziff family of Ziff-Davis Publishing fame. And while the company performs most of its work in New York City and on Long Island, it also does work in the surrounding tri-state area. When Obayashi Corporation of Tokyo, Japan, purchased the company in 1989, E.W. Howell expanded into the Atlanta and Chicago areas, where it now has offices.

GOOD SAMARITAN HOSPITAL, 1982.

"Although we're owned by a Japanese firm, our focus remains in New York City and on Long Island," says Rowland. "We live and work in this community, and our reputation is second to none. So, there's an inherent commitment here that goes beyond ownership of the firm."

Sharing the Wealth

Throughout its long and storied history, E.W. Howell has weathered many an economic storm. The company's commitment to quality and customer service is the best explanation for that staying power. When Elmer Howell established the company 110 years ago, he insisted that quality be placed ahead of profit. That philosophy remains very much intact today.

"We place our reputation ahead of our bottom line, sometimes to our financial detriment," says Howard Rowland, president and chief operating officer. "But construction companies come and go; our long-term view of things has helped us to survive and thrive for more than 100 years."

E.W. Howell employs 100 full-time Long Islanders, in addition to another 100 or so tradesmen during the height of the construction season. In addition to employing the people of Long Island, the company supports a number of charitable organizations. It raises funds for Suffolk Community College and has teamed up with Target to build two homes for Habitat for Humanity.

KING OF PRUSSIA MALL, 1995.

"I think our biggest commitment to Long Island is evident in the number of local people we employ and the millions of dollars in salaries that go into this community," Rowland says. "That has the most lasting impact. Our philanthropic attempts are really minor in the long run, although they certainly galvanize our employees and bring attention to some of the causes that we think are important."

In addition, we continue to bring a quality alternative to the people of Long Island through our determined efforts in the public work arena, where quality is all too often sacrificed for a profit.

Building for the Future

You know what they say about things that aren't broken: Don't fix them. So, E.W. Howell has no intention of changing its approach to business. Rowland admits that the general reputation of building construction companies these days is not the best. E.W. Howell, on the other hand, enjoys an excellent reputation in the industry, and it plans to keep it that way.

"We've always maintained a philosophy of slow, controlled growth that provides opportunities for our employees," says Rowland. "We're not anxious to grow for the sake of growth. We're comfortable in the markets that we're in. We think we provide a competitive alternative to the private contracting community and a quality alternative to the public work arena." ∎

FRIENDS ACADEMY LIBRARY, 2000.

ST. JOSEPH'S COLLEGE

Named one of the 25 top liberal arts colleges in the North in a *U.S. News and World Report* survey, St. Joseph's College (SJC) is a private, independent institution which was chartered in 1916 as St. Joseph's College for Women. Founded in Brooklyn, the college has experienced unprecedented growth in the last two decades, and today is a coeducational, two-campus institution serving more than 4,200 students, nearly 3,000 of whom attend classes at the newer Patchogue campus. With personal growth a parallel goal to academic achievement, SJC stresses "Find Yourself Here" in defining itself to its present and future students.

The college motto, *Esse non videri*, "To be, not to seem," has been a guiding principle of SJC since its founding. As a result, an SJC education is designed with the understanding that students will assume responsibility for directing their own lives and contributing to local, national, and international communities. In this way the college aims to prepare each of its students for a life characterized by integrity, intellectual and spiritual values, social responsibility, and service.

SJC's annual Social Awareness series plays a critical role in guiding students toward meeting this commitment. Produced and sponsored by S.T.A.R.S. (Students Taking an Active Role in Society), the purpose of the series is to focus attention on cultural, ethnic, racial, and religious diversity, and also to sponsor events that assist less fortunate people in the community. Social Awareness

STUDENTS GATHER NEAR THE ENTRANCE TO O'CONNOR HALL, NAMED AFTER PRESIDENT EMERITA SISTER GEORGE AQUIN O'CONNOR, WHO GUIDED THE COLLEGE FOR 28 YEARS.

activities in recent years have included student participations in a Walk-a-Thon for cancer; National Make a Difference Day; Hunger Banquet; Living with AIDS; International Campaign for Tibet; *Kristallnacht* Remembrance; Nicaraguan Students Sharing their Culture; Women of the Calabash; Traditional Music from Africa, Latin America, the Caribbean, and Black America; Kwanzaa Celebration; and Women in Long Island History.

Burgeoning Curricular Choices

Reflecting the dramatic growth in academic offerings and enrollment, SJC renamed the Division of General Studies as the School of Adult and Professional Education in May 1999. Particularly responsive to the needs of career-oriented adults, this division offers a graduate program in management and undergraduate and certificate programs tailored to students who may already be working in their chosen fields.

Geared more to the traditional-aged student, the School of Arts and Sciences offers majors in a variety of areas: pre-professional, career-readiness, and certificate programs; and a master's in infant/toddler theraputic education.

Meeting Long Island's growing need for a highly skilled information technologies labor force, SJC now offers a combined bachelor's and master's program in collaboration with Polytechnic University. This unique collaboration allows students to earn an undergraduate degree from St. Joseph's and an M.S. in Computer Science from Polytechnic within a five year period .

SISTER SUZANNE FRANCK, ASSISTANT PROFESSOR OF RELIGIOUS STUDIES AND CAMPUS MINISTER, CHATS WITH STUDENTS. SISTER SUZANNE OVERSEES THE STUDENT ORGANIZATION, S.T.A.R.S. (STUDENTS TAKING AN ACTIVE ROLE IN SOCIETY), WHICH SPONSORS THE ANNUAL SOCIAL AWARENESS SERIES.

THE SIX-LANE, 25-YARD SWIMMING POOL, LOCATED
IN THE JOHN A. DANZI ATHLETIC CENTER, IS
HOME TO THE GOLDEN EAGLES SWIM TEAM AND IS
THE SITE OF SWIM MEETS, SWIMMING LESSONS FOR
CHILDREN AND ADULTS, LIFEGUARD TRAINING, AND
WATER AEROBICS CLASSES.

The Department of Business Administration and
Accounting features faculty members who each bring
to the classroom many years of experience in the field.
Four areas of concentration are offered: finance, marketing, international business, and information systems.
The curriculum for each is highlighted with internships
at prominent area businesses, among them Computer
Associates, Northrop Grumman, American Express,
Canon, USA, and Prudential Preferred Financial Services.
A measure of the department's success is that 100 percent of accounting graduates are employed in the field
and 96 percent of the business administration graduates
are employed in the field of their choice.

On the horizon for St. Joseph's College's Patchogue
campus is a new Business Information Technology Center.
Expected to open later this year, the $8-million, 33,380-
square-foot center will permit expanded computer-based
and computer-related learning with 13 new classrooms
(five computer labs), videoconferencing and seminar
facilities, and faculty offices. Here students will train for
careers in data processing, computer science, and information technology. The distance-learning facility will
accommodate expanding course offerings and enhance
SJC's move toward integrating computer science across
the academic curriculum.

SJC, which is noted for its strong teacher education
programs, is a mecca for those seeking teacher training.
Graduates of SJC's education program, which requires
at least 90 credits in the liberal arts and a senior thesis,
receive a bachelor in child study rather than in education. The unusual SJC program stresses child psychology
and development over teaching methodologies. Among
the newer SJC education degree offerings is a master of
arts in infant/toddler therapeutic education, a part-time
program which prepares teachers to work in home-
or center-based settings with infants and toddlers with
special needs.

Balancing Studies and Sports

While the emphasis at SJC is on training the "whole"
student within a social and environmental context, and on
providing training to meet the evolving needs of the local
business community, the school has also provided facilities to promote the scholar/athlete ideal. In 1997 it
unveiled the John A. Danzi Athletic Center, which has
since become a hub of campus and community activity. It
is comprised of a gymnasium, indoor track, six-lane pool,
fitness rooms, and facilities for SJC's 13 intercollegiate
teams. The Danzi Center was host for the 1999 Empire
State Games Women's Basketball competition, and regularly welcomes community groups for charity events and
fundraisers. It is also the site of SJC's winter graduation.

Ever-changing and always innovating, SJC's plans for
the immediate future call for addressing the long-term
needs of both the Brooklyn and Patchogue campuses,
including faculty development, scholarships, building
projects, and endowment expansion. ■

ASSISTANT PROFESSOR OF BUSINESS MARY
CHANCE IS ALSO DIRECTOR OF THE M.S. IN
MANAGEMENT PROGRAM, THE COLLEGE'S SECOND
GRADUATE OFFERING, WHICH DEBUTED IN THE FALL.

THE DEMATTEIS ORGANIZATIONS

Ranked among the top 25 real estate developers in the nation, The DeMatteis Organizations has one of the most familiar corporate logos on Long Island. They are builders of EAB Plaza, Nassau Coliseum, the Riverhead Court Complex, and a substantial portion of Long Island's school buildings. As integral as this company now in its third generation of family leadership is to the fabric of Long Island, its far-flung projects have also brought the DeMatteis name around the globe.

Family owned and operated since its inception in 1918, The DeMatteis Organizations has come to symbolize excellence in construction and development. It is hard to begin to picture the landscape of the New York metropolitan area without including a DeMatteis building. The firm also owns the RY Management Company, Inc., managing more than 15,000 residential apartments as well as the Morristown Municipal Airport in Morristown, New Jersey.

Best known as both a residential and commercial real estate developer, the diverse capabilities of The DeMatteis Organizations have involved the company in projects as designer, planner, developer, owner, and construction manager. Among the company's most notable projects are the 1.1 million-square-foot glass-enclosed twin towers of EAB Plaza in Uniondale and Museum Tower in New York City, a showcase 52-story residential project built over the Museum of Modern Art that represents the first time a building was constructed in the air right over a museum. Also of note are Rupert Yorkville Towers, a 1,852 residential unit urban renewal project in Manhattan's Yorkville neighborhood, formerly the Ruppert Brewery, and Confucius Plaza in Chinatown, a complex providing 800 apartments and office space over a public school serving 1,200 students. Current large-scale

MUSEUM TOWER—BUILT ABOVE THE MUSEUM OF MODERN ART, THIS 52-STORY LUXURY RESIDENTIAL BUILDING, REPRESENTED THE LARGEST "AIR RIGHTS" TRANSACTION IN NEW YORK CITY AT THAT TIME.

projects include the $300 million expansion of St. John's University, which will redefine the commuter university with its first student resident complex, and the development of South Cove Plaza at Battery Park City.

The DeMatteis Organizations have brought their design, construction, and development expertise to projects around the world. One of the most important is Nation Wealth Plaza in Beijing, China, a massive, 2.25 million-square-foot mixed-use commercial development with three office towers and one apartment tower atop a five-level podium of retail and entertainment space. DeMatteis was also selected as general contractor for the Saudi Arabian National Guard Headquarters Complex in Riyadh, a project equal in size to the Pentagon building and used as NATO headquarters during the Gulf War.

The roots of The DeMatteis Organizations lie in Brooklyn where Leon D. DeMatteis, who brought the traditions of old-world craftsmanship to his projects, founded the Leon D. DeMatteis Construction

THIS HIGH-QUALITY 1,852 UNIT RESIDENTIAL, BUILT ON A FORMER BREWERY SITE, REVITALIZED THE MANHATTAN'S UPPER EAST SIDE ABOVE 86TH STREET.

WITH OVER ONE MILLION SQUARE FEET OF OFFICE SPACE,
THE 15-LEVEL, TWIN TOWER IS THE LARGEST, TALLEST, AND
MOST SOPHISTICATED OFFICE BUILDING ON LONG ISLAND.

Corporation. His son Frederick joined the business in
1945 following his service in the Army Air Corp which
had garnered him a Presidential Citation and a Purple
Heart. Joining in the post-war shift to suburbia, in 1952
Fred DeMatteis moved the company's base of operations
to Elmont, Long Island.

Through the 1950s, the company built many of the
schools, college dormitories, hospitals, libraries, and
housing units needed to support Long Island's burgeoning suburban communities. During the '60s and '70s,
DeMatteis became involved in developing and building
large-scale middle-income and luxury housing as well
as major office complexes throughout the metropolitan
area. It was in the early 1970s that DeMatteis built Long
Island's landmark indoor sports arena, the Nassau
County Veterans Memorial Coliseum. By the 1980s and
into the 1990s, DeMatteis' focus widened to include
more nationwide and worldwide projects. During this
period, the company completed projects in New York
City such as the $22.5 million renovation and addition at
the Brooklyn Botanic Gardens, the extensive Oak Park
Townhouse complex in Douglaston, the dramatic 52-
story residential tower at 100 United Nations Plaza, the
492,000-square-foot JFK Airport Parking Garage, and the
renovation of the 70,000-square-foot central passenger
terminal at LaGuardia Airport. Closer to its home base,
DeMatteis constructed the Riverhead Criminal Courts
Building and the Nassau County Correctional Facility as
well as the $50 million, 400,000-square-foot renovation

of the Pilgrim Psychiatric Center in West
Brentwood, an assignment done for the New
York State Office of Mental Health.

In 1983 they constructed a Long Island
landmark, EAB Plaza, and moved the company
headquarters to this glamorous new facility.
While tenants appreciate the sophisticated
engineering and architectural features at EAB
Plaza, the Long Island public knows the complex best for its Christmas tree and skating
rink. Fred DeMatteis decided that Long Island
deserved the world's tallest Christmas tree and
so each year, the lighting of the towering tree,
taller than the one at Rockefeller Plaza, and
its accompanying community events have
become a beloved local tradition for thousands
of families. Other Long Islanders value the
DeMatteis family's commitments to the community when they use the facilities at The
DeMatteis Center in Old Brookville, the
region's only free-standing campus dedicated
to cardiac research and education.

Fred DeMatteis, still active in the company,
serves The DeMatteis Organizations as their
chairman. His sons, Richard and Scott, joined
the business during the 1970s and 1980s to
form the company's third generation of leadership.
Richard now serves as president and Scott as senior
vice president. Under their collective guidance, The
DeMatteis Organizations continues to be recognized as
one of the oldest family owned and operated construction companies in New York, and one of the largest
such firms in the country. ∎

LEFT TO RIGHT: RICHARD, FRED, AND SCOTT DEMATTEIS,
UNDER WHOSE COLLECTIVE GUIDANCE DEMATTEIS HAS
BECOME RECOGNIZED AS ONE OF THE LARGEST
BUILDER/DEVELOPER ORGANIZATIONS IN THE COUNTRY.

STATE UNIVERSITY OF NEW YORK AT FARMINGDALE

The history of the State University of New York at Farmingdale reads like the history of Long Island. As the region evolved from an agrarian society into a high-tech hub, so too did SUNY Farmingdale. Today, the college is one of the premier educational institutions—and the only public college—on Long Island dedicated to training the next generation of technologists.

"Our mission is to prepare students to solve real-life problems in traditional as well as emerging fields," said Michael J. Vinciguerra, Ph.D., acting president of the college. "We want them to be well-trained to contribute to the economic vitality of Long Island, our state, and our nation. Our original agrarian focus was no longer helping us meet that mission. Technology has."

BROAD HOLLOW BIOSCIENCE PARK AT SUNY FARMINGDALE. PHOTO BY K.S. COLEY.

Technology Transition

Established in 1912, SUNY Farmingdale was the first public college on Long Island. It was initially dedicated to serving the needs of the large farming community in the region, a mission it remained true to until the early 1970s, when shrinking farmland and a growing high-tech sector spurred college officials to develop a strong emphasis on the applied sciences and technology. Today, the college sits on 380 acres in suburban Farmingdale, on the border of Nassau and Suffolk Counties.

In 1993, SUNY Farmingdale became a four-year educational institution. Now, students can choose from more than 20 academic programs, including bachelor degrees in aeronautical science-professional pilot, aviation administration, automotive management technology, computer technology, construction management technology, electrical engineering technology, facility management technology, management of technology, manufacturing engineering technology, security systems, and visual communications. In early 2000, the B.S. in Technical Communications was offered for the first time.

Associate in Science Degrees are awarded in business administration, computer information systems, computer science, criminal justice, dental hygiene, food and nutrition, medical laboratory technology, and nursing. Associate in Arts degrees are available to graduates of the Liberal Arts and Sciences curriculum, and Associate in Applied Science degrees are available to graduates of degree-granting career programs.

The college has set ambitious goals for itself. It is committed to offering programs designed to prepare graduates to apply and integrate new knowledge in emerging fields. Across every discipline, a broad curriculum is designed to enhance students' appreciation of culture, ethics, aesthetics, and cultural diversity. The idea is to motivate students to participate in the community beyond the campus and to continue learning throughout their lives.

INSTITUTE FOR MANUFACTURING RESEARCH AT SUNY FARMINGDALE. PHOTO BY VICTOR PHOTOGRAPHERS.

A Relevant Education

SUNY Farmingdale has implemented its hands-on, real-life education through a variety of partnerships with private industry. The Broad Hollow Bioscience Park, a joint project between the college and Cold Spring Harbor Laboratory, opened in September 2000. The $22 million facility serves as a business incubator for biotechnology companies and provides focus for Long Island's biotechnology industry. SUNY Farmingdale officials anticipate that this project will help the college strengthen its biotechnology programs, as well as facilitate student internships and permanent placements with incubated companies.

The Institute for Manufacturing Research, located in the Technology Transfer and Utilization Center (TTUC), provides small- and medium-sized manufacturing companies with product development assistance. Since it opened in 1996, the center has worked with more than 50 such companies. In March 1999, the college signed an agreement to transfer management of industrial outreach for the IMR to the Long Island Forum for Technology (LIFT). Since that time, LIFT's assistance has translated into new products and lucrative contracts for numerous manufacturers.

The Long Island Manufacturing & Applied Engineering Incubator, managed on behalf of the college by LIFT, houses several start-up companies in Conklin Hall. With rent that is substantially below market rates, business assistance from college professors, and support from LIFT's administrative staff, these companies are able to fully develop—and begin implementing—their business plans before leaving the incubator.

The college's Small Business Development Center (SBDC) provides financial planning and business training to clients on campus and in its outreach office at the Hempstead Educational Center.

SOLAR ENERGY CENTER PANELS AT SUNY FARMINGDALE. PHOTO BY VICTOR PHOTOGRAPHERS.

At the Center for Rehabilitation Research and Technology, faculty and students designed a pediatric wheelchair for children ages six to 10. Visual communications students created child-friendly graphic designs for the chair, while students in the mechanical engineering technology program developed the structural design. The center is a consortium among Nassau University Medical Center, Touro College, the Long Island Forum for Technology, and SUNY Farmingdale. Other projects include the invention of pressure relief cushions for the wheelchair-bound elderly and disabled, and the development of a method of providing long distance medical diagnosis of skin ulcers for the homebound disabled and elderly.

In the summer of 2000, SUNY Farmingdale teamed up with Keyspan and the Long Island Power Authority to open the Solar Energy Center and launch the Long Island Solar Roofs Initiative (LISRI). Under the initiative, the faculty in the School of Engineering Technologies are conducting applied research in the field of solar energy as well as providing training to the community and the industry in the maintenance, installation, repair, and operation of photovoltaic units. The Solar Energy Center serves as a demonstration site for product testing by private companies. Students enrolled in electrical engineering, manufacturing engineering, and architectural engineering technology curricula will have opportunities to complete internships in this emerging industry.

"It is truly amazing to watch the interaction between our students and private industry leaders," said Vinciguerra. "When they team up to provide solutions to real-life problems, we know that we are preparing them well for the future." ■

SUNY FARMINGDALE AVIATION EDUCATION CENTER AT REPUBLIC AIRPORT. PHOTO BY VICTOR PHOTOGRAPHERS.

THE FALA DM GROUP

Not many organizations can claim eight-and-a-half decades of success. The Fala DM Group, a family of direct marketing and Internet marketing companies can. Still fewer are successful family businesses with three generations of leaders who have left—or are leaving—their own dynamic brand of innovation on an entire industry.

A Heritage Rich in Innovation

The Fala story began in 1916 when a 16-year old typist, Beatrice Goodman Robins, working in a struggling Manhattan stenographic company, suggested using a multigraph machine to produce personalized letters in large volumes. Her ingenuity was rewarded with a partnership in a newly formed lettershop business which she subsequently came to own. That company, Fifth Avenue Lettershop Associates, would be the forerunner of Fala Direct Marketing. Following years of steady growth, Fala's next major innovations would come under the leadership of Ms. Robins' son-in-law, Bob Jurick, Fala's current chairman, who joined the company in 1952.

After learning the business, Bob focused on its further expansion. In 1957, he spearheaded Fala's first print division. In 1960, he harnessed the power of emerging computer technology to create the industry's first computerized direct marketing mass mailing system for Business Week. He followed this innovation in 1972 with the industry's first check donation package for a presidential campaign.

FALA GRAPHICS IS A FULL-SERVICE COMMERCIAL PRINTER WITH STATE-OF-THE-ART SYSTEMS.

The legacy of Fala innovation advanced to the third generation in the presidency of Jeff Jurick, Bob and Fala treasurer Lyn Jurick's son. Jeff, who also serves as chief executive officer, has brought his own brand of entrepreneurism. Like his father, he too learned the business from the ground up. Buoyed by this knowledge and a family that encourages big, "out-of-the-box" thinking, Jeff led the organization through its longest leap from small family business to industry leader.

Heightened Focus, Broader Resources

Recognizing the market's demand for a more complete direct mail resource, Jeff began a corporate restructure in 1997. The end result would be today's Fala DM Group, consisting of: Fala DM, specializing in data processing, laser personalization, high-volume mail, lettershop, and fulfillment; Fala Graphics, commercial printing division; Fala Response Management, offering direct response, fulfillment, and customer relationship management; Fala Sorting Services, its mail commingling and presort service which includes Fala International Mailing Services; Fala Imagine That!, specializing in integrated strategic planning, creative services, database analytics, marketing, and e-business solutions; and Long Island Logistics, for streamline inbound and outbound freight transportation.

FALA SORTING SERVICES OFFERS HIGH QUALITY, COST-EFFECTIVE MAIL COMMINGLING AND PRESORT SERVICES.

FALA DM, THE ORGANIZATION'S FLAGSHIP COMPANY, USES HIGH PERFORMANCE LASER PRINTING TECHNOLOGY.

Facilities on the Leading Edge

Nineteen ninety-nine marked Fala's construction of new corporate headquarters. The facility, located at 40 Daniel Street in Farmingdale, NY, occupies 150,000 square feet and serves as Fala's primary production center. Housed there are Fala DM's volume mail, fulfillment, lettershop, production management, mail loading, warehousing, and finance operations. Additionally, Fala maintains a 78,000-square-foot building at 70 Marcus Drive in Melville, NY, for data processing, personalization, and bindery operations. Fala also has a 50,000-square-foot facility at 75 Marcus Drive housing Fala Graphics and other ancillary support buildings. In total, Fala's East Coast operations consist of over 300,000 square feet, staffed with over 700 employees, capable of handling over one billion direct mail pieces annually. All Fala facilities display the latest technologies. For example, Fala Graphics was among the first on the East Coast to obtain the Sanden Quantum-1500 ten-color press with operating speeds of up to 1,500 feet per minute. Fala Sorting Services' technology includes the Olympus remote video encoding system and Lockheed-Martin Tray Management System, moving 800,000 to 1.3 million mail pieces daily.

Recognized for its Leadership

Nationally recognized as one of the leaders in direct mail communications, Fala has received numerous awards. In 1997, Fala was named to Long Island's "Top 50 Companies" and "25 Fastest Growing Private Firms," and "Family Business of the Year." In 1998, Jeff and Bob Jurick were named "Entrepreneurs of the Year." In 1999, Fala was named "Direct Marketer of the Year" by Card Marketing and received the U.S. Postal Service's highest honor, the "Partnership for Progress Award." Year 2000 saw Bob Jurick, already the direct marketing industry's "Silver Apple" award winner, inducted into the Long Island Direct Marketing Association's "Hall of Fame."

Good People, Good Values

At Fala, a high value is placed on philanthropy. Jeff is a trustee for the North Shore-Long Island Jewish Health System and chairman of the Children's Medical Fund of New York, which honored him with its Bernard L. Martin Memorial Award for Humanitarianism. Bob serves on the Parker Jewish Geriatric Institute's Board, and is a commissioner of the Nassau County Bridge Authority. He and Lyn are ongoing supporters of The Ronald McDonald House of Long Island which was founded by Lyn, who is also a North Shore-Long Island Jewish Health System trustee, which honored her with its Distinguished Trustee Award and co-chair of its Long Island Cancer Campaign. Fala's corporate-wide initiatives include FalaCares, education and business partnerships, and sponsorship of the Beatrice and Samuel Robins Educational Scholarship Foundation. ∎

FALA DM'S LETTERSHOP IS HOUSED IN A MODERN, FULLY-EQUIPPED FACILITY.

ADELPHI UNIVERSITY

Now embarked on its third century, Adelphi University, the first liberal arts institution of higher education on Long Island, was chartered on June 24, 1896, by the New York State Board of Regents. The charter was one of the earliest granted to a coeducational college in New York State.

Over the course of the next century, Adelphi grew and changed significantly. For more than three decades, beginning in 1912, Adelphi served only women. But in 1946, as young men returned from World War II hungry to restart their lives, the university returned to its original model of coeducation. Initially located in Brooklyn, with an enrollment of 57 students taught by 16 faculty members, Adelphi moved in 1929 to its present location in Garden City. Today, on a much expanded campus, a full- and part-time faculty of more than 500 serves a student body of 6,300 undergraduate and graduate degree candidates.

On the undergraduate level, Adelphi is the most selective private institution of higher education on Long Island—about two-thirds of freshman applicants are awarded acceptance. Increases in enrollment and the number of applicants, as well as in their class standings and test scores, all signify a period of significant flourishing and growth at Adelphi.

DR. ROBERT ALLYN SCOTT, PRESIDENT OF ADELPHI UNIVERSITY.

The university is home to a broad diversity of programs, each of which originated in different times and contexts. The School of Nursing has its roots in 1943, when, as a part of the war effort, Eleanor Roosevelt inaugurated the first Cadet Nurse Corps School at Adelphi. After the war, the needs of returning servicemen and a rapidly expanding economy led to the establishment of other academic paths. The School of Social Work was founded in 1949; doctoral education began in 1950. The program in clinical psychology was formally organized in 1951. Known today as the Gordon F. Derner Institute of Advanced Psychological Studies, it has the distinction of being the first university-based graduate school in clinical psychotherapy. In addition to traditional disciplines of art, science, and the humanities, the College of Arts and Sciences houses University College, which offers two highly regarded programs: ABLE, Adelphi's undergraduate degree program for adults, and the General Studies program, which provides an opportunity for a small group of freshmen who have not met traditional qualifications for admission to Adelphi, but whom the university believes can succeed and therefore permits them to take an enhanced first-year curriculum and qualify after its successful completion.

In 1963, after another decade of expansion, Adelphi was granted University status by the New York State Board of Regents. By the 1970s, the original Garden City campus of three buildings had been extended to 21 buildings on 75 acres, including the Leon A. Swirbul Library, which currently holds a fully computerized collection of over 1.7 million volumes, microformat and audiovisual items, and electronic access to libraries worldwide.

Today, there are seven schools at Adelphi: the College of Arts and Sciences; the Honors College; the Schools of Business, Education, Nursing, and Social Work; and the Derner Institute of Advanced Psychological Studies. These schools' programs are shaped by the belief that professional and disciplinary study are best developed on a strong foundation in the liberal arts and sciences. Each school's faculty has been chosen to meet the twin standards of professional excellence and superb teaching. With a student/faculty ratio of 13 to 1, Adelphi students are educated by an outstanding faculty that includes many internationally renowned scholars, scientists, artists, and critics.

Uniting this panoply of liberal education and professional programs is a shared tradition of academic innovation and rigor and a common philosophy of education.

Dr. Robert A. Scott, president of Adelphi, has said that, "All of the particular activities that take place at Adelphi—in the classroom, in the laboratory, on the playing field, and in the residence hall—contribute to the education of the whole individual, whether a resident

ADELPHI'S BEAUTIFULLY LANDSCAPED CAMPUS DELIGHTS THE EYE AND PROVIDES A SENSE OF ORDERED SERENITY THAT COMPLIMENTS THE LIFE OF THE MIND.

or commuter. Preparation for a lifetime of learning is the hallmark of an Adelphi education—and our students find that principle embodied in their dedicated faculty, who work with students in small classes and one-on-one to help them achieve their best, in the classroom and out, in everything they do."

Students at Adelphi also find the principle of lifelong learning embodied in a far-reaching technology program that brings together teaching, research, learning in the classroom, curriculum and library resources onto a web-based educational platform. Adelphi commits millions of dollars annually to equipment, infrastructure and extensive training so that its students enter the workplace and the world not merely ready to handle the technological demands of the moment, but also ready to meet the rapid pace of technological change and the demands of learning posed by new technologies and other voices of learning in the years to come.

Students at Adelphi further their development in a wide array of extracurricular activities, including superb athletic programs that boast a long list of recent championships and titles, student newspapers and magazines, and clubs, societies, fraternities, and sororities. With an ethnically diverse student body recruited from most states and nearly 50 foreign nations, Adelphi provides a cosmopolitan atmosphere conducive to intellectual questioning, surprise, and growth.

Adelphi has been built on the fundamental principles of transmitting knowledge, transforming minds, and empowering students to thrive in their lives and professions. While focusing its rich resources on the needs of

ADELPHI MOVED TO ITS CURRENT SITE IN GARDEN CITY IN 1929. LEVERMORE HALL IS ONE OF THE THREE ORIGINAL BUILDINGS DESIGNED BY THE FAMOUS FIRM OF McKIM MEADE & WHITE.

students, Adelphi also seeks to serve schools, communities, and businesses throughout the locality, state, and nation. The university does so through the research and practice of its renowned faculty; the strengthening of ties between the professional schools and the community; the staging of distinguished cultural events and performances; and, most importantly, the education of a new generation of future leaders and informed citizens, professionals, and community leaders. ∎

PANTHER TEAMS COMPETE IN 16 SPORTS. THE MEN'S SOCCER, LACROSSE, BASEBALL, AND BASKETBALL TEAMS ARE NATIONALLY RANKED NCAA PROGRAMS WHOSE SUCCESSES INCLUDE RECENT NATIONAL CHAMPIONSHIPS AND A HOST OF TOURNAMENT BIDS. WOMEN'S SOFTBALL AND SOCCER ARE PERENNIAL TOURNAMENT TEAMS AS WELL.

COLD SPRING HARBOR LABORATORY

In cancer research, neurobiology, plant genetics, and bioinformatics, some of the world's most significant scientific discoveries have come from researchers working at Cold Spring Harbor Laboratory (CSHL), a research and teaching center of international importance.

JAMES D. WATSON, PRESIDENT, COLD SPRING HARBOR LABORATORY.

Nestled in a bucolic setting on one of Long Island's most beautiful North Shore areas, CSHL has been home base for many Nobel Prize winners, including Barbara McClintock, whose discovery of "jumping genes" in maize was awarded the 1983 Nobel Prize. Other Nobel laureates whose work was nurtured at CSHL were Alfred Day Hershey, Richard Roberts, Max Delbrück, Salvador Luria, and Phillip Sharp. James D. Watson, CSHL's director from 1968 to 1994 and its president since 1994, was awarded the 1962 Nobel Prize for his landmark research at Cambridge University with Francis H. C. Crick on the structure of DNA. In all, more than 80 Nobel laureates have been associated with CSHL.

The roots of CSHL lay in the founding in 1890 of the Biological Laboratory of the Brooklyn Institute of Arts and Sciences, a "summer camp" for biology teachers to study organisms found on the shores of Cold Spring Harbor. In 1905 the Carnegie Institute established the Station for Experimental Evolution, a year-round research institute at Cold Spring Harbor that shared land and buildings with the Biological Laboratory. By 1924, the BioLabs had attracted the support of scientists and wealthy Long Islanders who assumed the responsibility for the Lab's management. In 1962, the merging of the BioLab and Carnegie Institute's Genetics Research Unit created the Cold Spring Harbor Laboratory of Quantitative Biology. When James Watson became director in 1968, he initiated a major cancer research effort, recruited outstanding scientists from around the world, and dropped "of Quantitative Biology" from the Lab's name. In 1972, under Watson's leadership, CSHL received its first five-year Cancer Research Center grant from the National Cancer Institute; it has since continually maintained its status as a prestigious NCI Cancer Center.

Cancer research remains central to CSHL's mission and accounts for 67 percent of its funding. This research program focuses on genes and molecular components of cells in the campaign to better understand the processes that change normal cells to cancer cells. Former CSHL researcher Richard Roberts won a Nobel prize for his discovery of "split genes," and a CSHL team led by Michael Wigler was among the first to identify a human oncogene—a gene involved in the development of cancer.

CSHL neurobiologists are at the forefront of exploring the events that take place in the brain during learning and the formation of memory. The Lab's current neurobiology program was launched in 1990. In 1994, CSHL scientists Tim Tully and Jerry Yin identified a link between the CREB protein and the formation of long-term memory in fruit flies, as Alcino Silva discovered the same association in mice.

Many important advances in plant genetics have also taken place at CSHL. In 1905, CSHL researchers developed the first hybrid corn on fields adjacent to the building that now serves as the Lab's library. Barbara McClintock's research in the early 1950s in transposable elements ("jumping genes") led to her later Nobel Prize.

BRUCE W. STILLMAN, DIRECTOR, COLD SPRING HARBOR LABORATORY.

In the field of bioinformatics, CSHL scientists are now using and developing sophisticated computers and programs to organize, analyze, store, and communicate biological data.

Cold Spring Harbor Laboratory figures importantly in training tomorrow's top-flight scientists. In 1999, the Lab established its first degree-granting program—the Watson School of Biological Sciences—which will award Ph.D.s in the biological sciences. Its 25 post-doctoral courses offered each year are attended by an international audience of young scientists and established researchers. CSHL's undergraduate research program trains college students who live and work at the Lab. The CSHL DNA Learning Center, the world's first museum of molecular biology, conducts workshops in DNA science for high school and college science teachers and other special interest audiences. In collaboration with Long Island's school districts, the CSHL Partners for the Future program affords high school seniors the opportunity to work on original research projects at the Lab. And each summer, the Lab sponsors a summer camp with outdoor nature study courses for children.

The modern Grace Auditorium on the CSHL campus, with its dramatic lobby sculpture of Watson's double helix, is the site for 20 international scientific meetings each year in topics such as cell cycle, gene therapy, and dynamic organization of nuclear function. Grace Auditorium is also used for the benefit of the community as the site of various lectures, concerts and art exhibitions sponsored by the Lab.

CSHL Press publishes the scientific journals *Genes & Development*, *Learning and Memory*, and *Genome Research*, as well as laboratory manuals, science textbooks, and instructional videotapes for laboratory training.

Bruce Stillman, a member of the National Academy of Sciences and a Fellow of the Royal Society (London), was named Director of CSHL in 1994.

Cold Spring Harbor Laboratory is a multi-campus facility. In addition to its main campus—102 acres along Cold Spring Harbor's western shore—the Lab operates the DNA Learning Center and Uplands Farm in Cold Spring Harbor, the Banbury Conference Center and McClintock Meadows in Lloyd Harbor, and the Genome Research Center in Woodbury. The Lab's 700+ employees include a faculty of Ph.D.s and M.D.s, postdoctoral fellows, visiting scientists, and graduate students.

Together, Cold Spring Harbor Laboratory's faculty, students, and researchers are poised to discover the great—but as yet unanswered—questions of biological science. ■

LOOKING WEST AT THE SHORELINE OF THE COLD SPRING HARBOR LABORATORY GROUNDS.

P.C. RICHARD & SON

More than 91 years ago, in 1909, P.C. Richard & Son was established on the basic principles of customer service, Taking Care of the Customer Before, During, and After the Sale, with Honesty, Integrity, and Reliability. This commitment has allowed the company to flourish and grow on Long Island, the New York Metropolitan Area, and New Jersey, to become the dominant leader in retailing of appliances, electronics, and computers. President and CEO Gary Richard points out: "So many retailers in our industry have come and gone, but P.C. Richard & Son, with its philosophy of Honesty, Integrity, and Reliability, is unbeatable. We've put our value into living, working, and enjoying the Long Island communities we serve." As P.C. Richard & Son has expanded throughout the Metropolitan Area with 42 showrooms, Farmingdale, Long Island remains the heart of the organization. It is the center for all administrative functions, purchasing, warehousing, training, installations, advertising, and a state-of-the-art service center.

THE ORIGINAL P.C. RICHARD HARDWARE STORE—
BENSONHURST, BROOKLYN 1909.

The history of P.C. Richard & Son began in 1909 when Peter Christiaan ("P.C.") Richard opened a hardware store in Bensonhurst, Brooklyn. That same year, P.C.'s son, Alfred J. Richard (A.J.) was born. A.J. started his career in the business when he was still a youngster. To accommodate the company's growth during its first decade of business, P.C. Richard & Son started an eastward movement in 1919 with a new facility in Ozone Park, Queens. During the mid 1920s, A.J. added radios to the store's hardware inventory, the start of a tradition of product and service expansion which continues to the present day. A true entrepreneur, A.J. encouraged sales of electric irons by virtually inventing payment through installments.

Beyond the crucial decision to add the appliances, electric refrigerators...wringer washers and radios—and later, televisions—that were to become the company's future, in 1935 A.J. launched the very first non-manufacturers' service department offering manufacturers' authorized repair service, a move that was to forever set P.C. Richard & Son apart from its competitors. That service business has grown to become a very important component of P.C. Richard & Son as hundreds of electronics are repaired each day by the company's skilled, factory-trained technicians. The repair service business is central to the company's commitment "to make every customer happy. While you're standing in front of your product, we're standing behind it."

Beginning in the 1940s, A.J. led an expansion of company locations throughout Queens and Long Island. The interest in television during the '40s and '50s was a major spur for the company's growth. A.J. established a beachhead at the forefront of the trend, adding the stocking and repairing of television sets. He helped create consumer interest by putting a console TV set in showroom windows and then watching enthusiastic crowds gather to view this new electronic marvel.

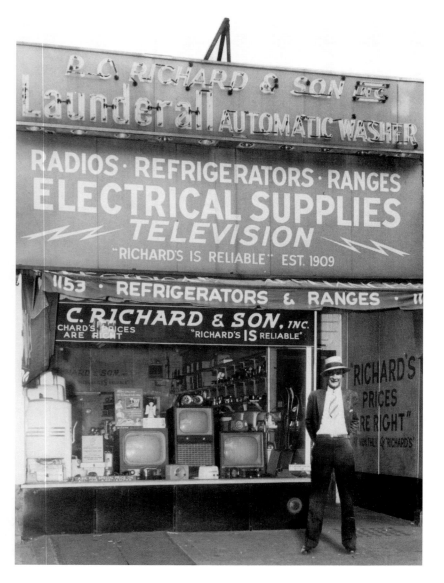

A.J. RICHARD CITY LINE, BROOKLYN 1948.

GRAND OPENING CO-OP CITY, BRONX, MAY 1999.

Coming into the business during the 1960s, the third generation of P.C. Richard & Son family leadership—A.J.'s sons Peter and Gary—pursued their vision of the future. Gary and Peter have presided over the company's extraordinary expansions in product lines and locations. In 1978, A.J. became Board Chairman, Gary was named President and CEO, and Peter became Executive Vice President. In 1980 there were ten P.C. Richard & Son showrooms. Today, as a result of an aggressive expansion campaign in Long Island, Manhattan, Queens, Brooklyn, Bronx, Westchester, and New Jersey, 42 P.C. Richard & Son locations dot the New York Metropolitan Area and New Jersey. During the 1970s, the third-generation of company leadership brought P.C. Richard & Son into the computer age. The result is that the company is managed with a state-of-the-art Management Information System that captures all customer and historical data originating from a point of sale system, tracks inventory, and automatically replenishes merchandise in the warehouse as well as at all 42 showroom locations.

Gary and Peter have also continued their father's tradition of making it economically feasible for customers to acquire appliances. In collaboration with Bank One, now G.E. Capital, a customized credit card program was created which offers customers extended payment terms...and special customer advantages.

The fourth generation has already begun to make an important impact on P.C. Richard & Son—Gary's son, Gregg, is credited with the company's entry into car-audio installation and 35-millimeter camera businesses.

When the day comes that Gregg and his cousin, Peter III, take over the leadership of P.C. Richard & Son, just as their fathers and grandfather before them, they will have been through each and every aspect and job description at P.C. Richard & Son. That's another company tradition that started with A.J. and continued with Gary and Peter II. Said Gary Richard: "That's how I learned the business...from the bottom up. You can't show or tell someone how to do the task if you can't do it yourself."

The fact that the company's leadership into the fourth generation has already been identified reveals yet another reason why P.C. Richard & Son has succeeded so stunningly as a friendly, family-owned and operated business. They know where they've been...where they are...and where they're going.

For 10 decades, members of the Richard family have watched the rise and fall of numerous competitors. Why has P.C. Richard & Son not only succeeded, but grown so dramatically, while these others have failed? Gary Richard said it's really pretty simple. He explained that the company's formula for success is its adherence to very strict standards of Taking Care of the Customer. Before, During, and After the Sale, consumers know they can trust P.C. Richard & Son and so they become and remain very loyal customers.

To Gary Richard and the members of his family, it's clear that what has assured the success of P.C. Richard & Son for more than 91 years is their strict dedication to satisfying customers: "We don't just make a sale, we make a customer." "Richard **IS** reliable."* ■

LEFT TO RIGHT: PETER RICHARD III,
PETER RICHARD II, A.J. RICHARD,
GARY RICHARD, AND GREGG RICHARD AT
CORPORATE OFFICES, JUNE 2000.

SOUTHSIDE HOSPITAL

A new Maternity Center, innovative therapeutic techniques, a full range of medical services, and a 90-year tradition of service ensures that Southside Hospital brings its community medicine as it should be—a patient-friendly blend of technology and personal touch.

The 439-bed hospital was founded in 1911 in Babylon and moved to Bay Shore two years later. Today, as part of the North Shore-Long Island Jewish Health System, Southside offers patients a solid network of healthcare that brings together medical specialties that, along with the physician specialists, ensure Southside's patients they have best care possible.

A new dedicated Maternity Center boasts its own parking lot, entrance, and elevator, with fast-track registration for women in labor. The seven Labor-Delivery-Recovery rooms in the center have all of the equipment needed for a normal birth. There are, of course, operating rooms nearby if necessary and three types of nurseries—one for well babies, one for special care, and one for neonatal intensive care.

Southside's Regional Center for Rehabilitation, with both in- and outpatient programs, fulfills a three-fold mission of comprehensive clinical care, education for medical specialists, and research, through four separate programs that are highly regarded in the medical community.

The In- and Outpatient Rehabilitation centers ensure continuity of care. The Regional Center for Adult Brain Injury Rehabilitation is the only state-designated hospital program on Long Island focusing on the adult population. The Southside Health Institute for Sports and Orthopedic Physical Therapy treats injured outpatients. Each program in the center is staffed with a team of physicians, nurses,

FOUNDED IN 1911, SOUTHSIDE HOSPITAL OFFERS A PATIENT-FRIENDLY BLEND OF TECHNOLOGY AND PERSONAL TOUCH.

therapists, and other specialists who work closely with patients on every facet of recovery.

Southside Hospital's Gulden Radiation Oncology Center—with an on-site linear accelerator—along with the Wound Healing and Vascular Institutes, mean that its patients do not have to travel to receive outstanding, top lever, care. The Family Practice Residency Program is the oldest on Long Island and, in conjunction with Long Island Jewish Medical Center, a residency in psychiatry is offered at the Regional Center for Rehabilitation.

Theodore A. Jospe, Southside Hospital's president and CEO says: "Our commitment to excellence has kept us in the lead with state-of-the-art technology and facilities that provide maximum comfort and benefit to our patients. We have opened a new maternity center with advanced labor and delivery suites, as well as new laboratories, a new radiology suite, and other new offices and treatment centers. We have provided expanded diagnostic services and hired more doctors,

A NEW MATERNITY CENTER AND LONG ISLAND'S ONLY STATE-DESIGNATED ADULT BRAIN INJURY REHABILITATION PROGRAM ARE AMONG THE MANY SPECIALIZED SERVICES AT BAY SHORE'S SOUTHSIDE HOSPITAL.

specialty nurses, and technicians of the highest caliber. It is a costly effort, but one worthy of the commitment made by many people dedicated to these goals. We know that Southside today offers the best care and will continue to do so in the future." ∎

PHOTO BY DEBORAH ROSS, BRUCE BENNETT STUDIOS.

CHAPTER FIVE

1918 TO 1945

There never was a time like it before and, probably, there never will be again. Despite passage of the federal income tax law in 1913 and the Volstead Act that ushered in fourteen years of prohibition, in the 1920s Long Island glittered—alive with celebrities, parties and, most important, a creative energy that would impact the entire world.

More people were moving to Nassau and Suffolk Counties. By 1920, there were 126,120 people in Nassau and 110,246 in Suffolk. Many breadwinners worked in New York City, turning the Island into a bedroom community. Farms were still plentiful and there were still fish to be caught in Long Island's waters. Shopping trips were still events, and people made annual or semi-annual excursions to towns like Patchogue, Huntington, and Jamaica to buy clothing and big-ticket items.

THE HAMPTONS ARE A SYMBOL OF THE GOOD LIFE, THE RESULT OF HUGE INCOMES AND INHERITED WEALTH, AND THE TYPE OF SOCIETY THAT PROVIDED INSPIRATION FOR F. SCOTT FITZGERALD'S *THE GREAT GATSBY*. PHOTO BY JOSEPH ROGATE, BRUCE BENNETT STUDIOS.

There remained small towns closer in spirit to the century just passed, but there were also people and places who took to the post-war years determined to prove the past was mere prologue.

Long Island was changing quickly. The waves of immigration that had risen in New York Harbor carried many newcomers east. As time went on there were settlements of immigrants from Germany, Ireland, Poland, Italy, Greece, Asia, and Eastern Europe across the Island. As the first of these immigrants found work and were able to begin building full lives, other countrymen followed. In Riverhead, Polish Town grew. Lindenhurst—originally called "Breslau"—and Yaphank had large German populations. These newcomers brought to the region a host of cultures, traditions, religions, and foods that endure today.

It was becoming more and more difficult to find a Long Islander descended from either an original settler or, in fact, of English background even similar to those settlers.

As in any other populous region, there was a broad range of wealth on Long Island. The great majority of people did not enjoy the benefits of inherited wealth or huge incomes. There were, however, some that did. And they used their money for maximum enjoyment.

As transportation improved, people with busy lives in Manhattan were able to enjoy the benefits of Long Island country life. George M. Cohan was referring to Great Neck when he wrote *45 Minutes From Broadway*. He was among the many prominent entertainers and writers who called the Gold Coast home.

In Great Neck, Cohan was joined by such contemporaries as the Marx Brothers, Paulette Goddard, Ed Wynn, Frederick March and Florence Eldridge, Norma Talmadge, Leslie Howard, Lillian Russell, and W.C. Fields.

F. Scott Fitzgerald is the most celebrated of the writers who lived in Great Neck. His book *The Great Gatsby* is believed by many to be a quintessentially American story. Fitzgerald wrote part it while he and his wife Zelda were renting a house at 6 Gateway Drive, Great Neck Estates.

In the book, narrator Nick Carraway lives in West Egg, which is, really, Great Neck. East Egg, home to Jay Gatsby, was in reality Sands Point. Carraway talks about West Egg:

"It was a matter of chance that I should have rented a house in one of the strangest communities in North America. It was on that slender riotous island which extends itself due east of New York—and where there are, among other natural curiosities, two unusual formations of land. Twenty miles from the city a pair of enormous eggs, identical in contour and separated only by a courtesy bay, jut out into the most domesticated body of salt water in the Western hemisphere, the great wet barnyard of Long Island Sound. They are not perfect ovals—like egg in the Columbus story, they are both crushed flat at the contact end—but their physical resemblance must be a source of perpetual wonder to the gulls that fly overhead. To the windless a more interesting phenomenon is their dissimilarity in every particular except shape and size."

AS TRANSPORTATION IMPROVED, PEOPLE WITH BUSY LIVES IN MANHATTAN WERE ABLE TO ENJOY THE
BENEFITS OF LONG ISLAND COUNTRY LIFE. GEORGE M. COHAN WAS REFERRING TO GREAT NECK WHEN HE
WROTE *45 MINUTES FROM BROADWAY*. TODAY, MANY PEOPLE STILL ENJOY THE AMENITIES OF FAMILY LIFE
ON LONG ISLAND WITHIN REACH OF NEW YORK CITY'S HUSTLE AND BUSTLE. PHOTO BY ROB AMATO,
BRUCE BENNETT STUDIOS.

In the 1920s, a host of entertainers and artists in all fields would call Great Neck home, much as today's famous gravitate to the East End.

Long Island's coastline was an invitation to rumrunners who used the sheltered coves along both shores, and on Shelter Island. Freeport boatyards built vessels for both the Coast Guard and the rumrunners, the latter capable of more speed. Freeport also was home to several after-hours speakeasies that catered to performers from Broadway whose workdays ended at 11 p.m.

The Prince of Wales was entertained in a suitably royal manner in the summer of 1924, when he traveled to Long Island for the International polo matches. He wrote upon his return, "the luxury I was accustomed to in Europe seemed almost primitive" when compared to the luxury he found in the United States. He was fol-lowed in 1927 by His Highness Sajjan Singh, Maharajah of Ratlam, whose retinue set up camp near the polo ponies at Mitchel Field.

While the grand party that was the Jazz Age was in progress on the Gold Coast, ugly forces were rising elsewhere on Long Island.

In 1923, more than twenty-five thousand people turned out in East Islip for a rally of the reborn Ku Klux Klan. Started by six veterans of the Confederate Army as a fraternal organization in Pulaski, Tennessee, in 1865, the KKK soon grew into a terrorist organization that,

by 1866, was indulging in "night rides" to harass local blacks. The organization became almost inactive but, in 1915, was revived, apparently propelled by the great tide of immigration.

On Long Island, Klansmen burned crosses and stood firm for morality and prohibition and against blacks, Jews, Catholics, and foreigners. Its membership included many leaders of Long Island. In fact, the Longwood School District's Charles E. Walters Elementary School is named for the wealthy local leader who donated the land on which the school was built. Mr. Walters was active in the Klan.

Within a few years the local Klan was riddled with internal strife and, by the mid-1920s, it was no longer a factor in local life.

Long Island's first public college, the New York State Institute of Applied Agriculture at Farmingdale, opened in 1912 as a two-year institution teaching horticulture and agriculture. Eventually, courses were added in aviation, business, construction, dental hygiene, and advertising art and design, among others.

Long Island's first 24-hour radio station, WGBB, began broadcasting in 1924. Adelphi University became the first private college on Long Island when its campus was moved from Brooklyn to Garden City in 1929. Six years later, it was joined by Hofstra. The first county police department, in Nassau, was formed in 1925.

IN F. SCOTT FITZGERALD'S GREAT STORY OF THE JAZZ AGE, *THE GREAT GATSBY*, NARRATOR NICK CARRAWAY LIVES IN WEST EGG, WHICH IS REALLY GREAT NECK. EAST EGG, HOME TO JAY GATSBY, WAS IN REALITY SANDS POINT. FITZGERALD WROTE PART OF THE BOOK WHILE HE AND HIS WIFE, ZELDA, WERE RENTING A HOUSE AT 6 GATEWAY DRIVE, GREAT NECK ESTATES. PHOTOS BY ROB AMATO (ABOVE) AND LISA MEYER (OPPOSITE PAGE), BRUCE BENNETT STUDIOS.

During the 1920s, Long Islanders were beginning to awaken to the realization that the region could serve as more than a bedroom for Manhattan; that it was itself a viable location in which to run a business.

Determined to attract businesses, the Long Island Chamber of Commerce was established in 1926, head-quartered at 20 West 34th Street in Manhattan. In 1930, the Chamber and the Long Island Rail Road recognized their mutual interests and teamed up to promote Long Island. The Chamber was given office space in Pennsylvania Station. Together, they focused on the cause of transportation to and from Long Island, lobbying for the completion of Jericho Turnpike, Sunrise Highway, Queens and Horace Harding Boulevards, the Midtown Tunnel, and the Triborough Bridge.

In 1936, the Chamber changed its name to the Long Island Association—the LIA—and, at the 1939 World's Fair in Flushing Meadow, welcomed four million visitors to its exhibit. The LIA moved to Garden City in 1940 and over the years made successive moves east until 1983, when it settled in Commack where it remains today.

If the "Roaring 20s" represented Long Island's adolescence, its adulthood began at the end of 1929.

On Thursday, October 24, the headline in *The New York Times* read, "PRICES OF STOCKS CRASH IN HEAVY LIQUIDATION, TOTAL DROP OF BILLIONS." A related story provided some hope: "SAYS STOCK SLUMP IS ONLY TEMPORARY: *Professor Fisher Tells Capital Bankers Market Rise Since War Has Been Justified.*"

The Friday, October 25, *Times* headline said, "WORST STOCK CRASH STEMMED BY BANKS; 12,894,650-SHARE DAY SWAMPS MARKET; LEADERS CONFER, FIND CONDITIONS SOUND."

Of course, there was no hope and conditions were not "sound." The Great Depression had arrived and with it came all of the misery that accompanies such a circumstance. There were hard times, but events were in play that made the lot of many Long Islanders easier than that of others in the United States.

Despite the efforts of the nascent LIA, the local economy was still to a great degree agrarian. Even though farms went a long way toward ensuring local residents had food, the times were not prosperous and were very difficult for most people.

Although private construction ceased almost entirely, the mid- and late-1920s saw the beginning of an unprecedented public works boom on Long Island and work on a variety of projects was available for local residents.

In June, 1929, Heckscher State Park opened; one month later, the Southern State Parkway. That August Jones Beach and the Wantagh Parkway were opened. Five years later, in 1934, Bethpage State Park and Bethpage State Parkway opened. The Meadowbrook Parkway followed the next year and Heckscher State Parkway one year after that.

Most of Long Island's banks were able to survive the 1933 Bank Holiday. They did so by working cooperatively to protect each other.

One notable casualty of the Depression was the dream of developer Carl Fisher to turn Montauk into a summer substitute for his successful development of the winter playgrounds of Miami Beach and Key West. He was also the builder of the Indianapolis Speedway.

Fisher saw grand things for the southern tip of eastern Long Island. He bought nine thousand acres of beach there and dredged Lake Montauk to create a deepwater harbor. He built the million-dollar Montauk Manor Hotel in 1926 and a seven-story office building for his "Miami of the North."

Unfortunately, Fisher's dream for Montauk crashed with the stock market. Today, all that remains are his hotel and office building, both looking somewhat odd sitting beachside.

As large as Fisher's failure at Montauk was, that's how great the success another Long Island businessman found in the Depression. He was Michael J. Cullen, who, in 1930, opened the first "super market," where all foodstuffs could be purchased in one place. The idea, as we know, took off and today King Kullen can lay rightful claim to the title, "America's First Supermarket."

Long Islanders wishing amusement in the Depression could visit the Frank Buck Zoo that opened in 1934 just off Sunrise Highway in Massapequa. The adventurer and big-game hunter whose exploits were detailed in several books and movies—most famously *Bring 'Em Back Alive*—kept a menagerie of exotic creatures collected from around the world.

Buck took his show to the 1939 World's Fair where advertisements for "Frank Buck's Jungleland" promised visitors an "educational, interesting, amusing" time as they learned "How Frank Buck Captures 'Em Alive." He promised "1,000 Indian Monkeys," "1,000 Exotic Birds," "mouse deer," a "whole troop of gibbons," "chimpanzees," "rare apes" and "orang-utans."

The chilling build-up in Europe leading to the cataclysm of World War II was felt on Long Island when the German American Bund opened Camp Siegfried in Yapbank, in 1936, calling it "Friends of New Germany Picnic Grounds."

It seemed at first as if the camp was as advertised, a place for youth to frolic and adults to socialize. But, by 1938, there were drills, German martial music, and speeches by Bund leader Fritz Kuhn, who spoke of the promise of an "Aryan paradise" on Long Island.

"German Gardens," a development adjoining Camp Siegfried, was laid out with streets named in honor of Nazi dignitaries. Although the development did not last and no streets in Yaphank bear these names, old maps still evidence the fervor that saw up to fifty thousand people coming to Yaphank on Sundays to watch the Nazis march.

Ultimately, Kuhn was arrested and discredited for a host of crimes and Camp Siegfried was shut down.

In a footnote to the recorded history of the Depression, photographer Walker Evans shot a portrait of writer James Agee, who collaborated with him on *Let Us Now Praise Famous Men*, when they visited Old Field Point. It is the most well-known picture of Agee.

If the Depression did not scar Long Island as it did other parts of the world, the hurricane of 1938 certainly did.

HORSE RACING RETURNED TO THE HEMPSTEAD PLAINS WHEN ROOSEVELT RACEWAY OPENED IN 1940 AND REMAINED THERE UNTIL 1988. THIS 25TH ANNIVERSARY PHOTO SHOWED THE ORIGINAL GRANDSTAND. PHOTO COURTESY OF THE NASSAU COUNTY DIVISION OF MUSEUM SERVICES/LONG ISLAND STUDIES INSTITUTE/HOFSTRA UNIVERSITY.

LONG ISLAND LEISURE, PART THREE

Roosevelt Raceway

With a 300-year-old heritage of horseracing, the Hempstead Plain should have been a natural spot for a track. But, Freeport attorney George Morton Levy and his consortium, the Old Country Racing Association, faced a host of obstacles when they wanted to open a track there.

Flat races, with the jockey sitting on the horse, were doing very well at Belmont Park. This new track would feature harness racing, or "trotters," in which horses are driven around the track by jockeys sitting in a small cart, a sulky. Physically, the Racing Association had most of what they needed. By using the former site of the Vanderbilt Cup auto races, they had a track and a grandstand. To popularize evening races, which had failed elsewhere, Levy rewrote the standard. Instead of successive elimination heats, there would be only one heat making up a race. In honor of its location, the track was called Roosevelt Raceway.

Opening night, September 2, 1940, brought out 4,584 fans who wagered a total of $4,734. But that was the best the track would do for years. It didn't make a profit at all for three years. World War II made it difficult to draw people with other concerns to the track and, when they did come, false starts and delays made it a long evening.

In 1946, Levy introduced the mobile starting gate that is still in use today, an innovation that improved fairness and raised the tempo of a full program of races.

That turned the tide. Roosevelt Raceway thrived and it grew. At its height the track drew an average daily gate of 20,000 and was home to the International Trot, the most prestigious harness race after the classic Hambletonian. The track was expanded to serve 60,000 people, and a high-end restaurant, the Cloud Casino, was opened. A new tote board developed by Levy showed both the odds and what each horse might pay to win.

Until children under age 18 were barred, racing was a family outing. Many children of the 1940s and 1950s can recall going to the track with their parents, learning how to read the racing form and how the system of odds worked.

Eventually, Long Islanders found other sports that engaged their interest more than racing. The advent of New York State's Off-Track Betting Corporation in 1971 was the onset of a lingering death for the track.

Roosevelt Raceway's final program was on July 15, 1988. Today, the site is a shopping center.

(CLOCKWISE FROM TOP LEFT) PHOTOS BY GARY FOX, ROB AMATO, LISA MEYER, AND ROB AMATO, BRUCE BENNETT STUDIOS.

Long Island's beachfront horizons, characterized by both rocky coves and sandy, shallow shoals, were often dotted with shipwrecks. The *Penobscot* went aground off Eaton's Neck in the early 1900s, as did a smaller vessel on the beach in Miller Place. Photos from the Fullerton Collection, courtesy of the Suffolk County Historical Society.

LONG ISLAND'S "GOLD COAST" INSPIRED THE PURSUIT OF PLEASURE THAT WAS CELEBRATED IN MUSIC, THEATER, ART, AND LITERATURE. IN THE 1920S, THE COASTLINE WAS AN INVITATION TO RUMRUNNERS WHO USED THE SHELTERED COVES ALONG BOTH SHORES AND ON SHELTER ISLAND. PHOTO BY GARY FOX, BRUCE BENNETT STUDIOS.

Hitting with almost no warning between four and five o'clock on the afternoon of September 21, the hurricane killed more than fifty people and destroyed millions and millions of dollars in property.

Hurricane winds thought to be traveling at 125 miles per hour caused floods that left much of eastern Long Island's south shore four feet deep in sand and water. Westhampton alone suffered the loss of thirty-two lives and more than 150 buildings. Hurricane damage stretched from Montauk to Babylon along the south shore, with damage estimated at six billion dollars in 1938 money.

During the 1930s, government on Long Island was changing. In 1936 a Nassau County Charter was adopted that centralized government under the leadership of a County Executive, with a Board of Supervisors representing the interests of the three towns and the cities of Glen Cove and Long Beach.

Long Island's status as the "Cradle of Aviation," dating back to the early 1900s, made it a natural home for a flourishing aircraft industry.

In 1929 two engineers who worked at Loening Aircraft declined to move with the company to Pennsylvania. Leroy Grumman and Jake Swirbul stayed on Long Island to start the Grumman Aircraft Engineering Company. Grumman opened on January 3, 1930, and swiftly secured a contract from the Navy for innovative floats with retractable landing gear. In 1931, the gear was used on Grumman's first airplane, the XFF-1. By 1939, Grumman employed seven hundred people at its Bethpage plant.

From the beginning, it was a very successful enterprise. During World War II, Grumman built 17,013 Navy planes, accounting for two-thirds of all enemy planes shot down by the Navy in the Pacific theatre. Grumman's three planes—the F4F Wildcat, the F6F Hellcat, and the TBF-1 Avenger—made aviation history. Some of the Hellcats were built of steel from the razed Second Avenue Elevated subway system.

After the war, Navy Secretary James Forrestal said, "Grumman saved Guadalcanal."

But Grumman was not the only aircraft manufacturer on Long Island. Its neighbor to the east, Republic Aircraft's P-47 Thunderbolt, fought the Luftwaffe in Europe. Sperry Gyroscope moved from Brooklyn to more spacious headquarters in Lake Success. There and in a Garden City plant, thirty-two thousand employees made instruments for flight.

Smaller companies, too, contributed to the war effort. Liberty Aircraft Products in Farmingdale made aircraft parts and Columbia Aviation in Valley Stream built an amphibian plane called the Duck. Airborne Instruments Laboratory, AIL, employed 350 people in a Mineola plant producing electronics.

At the height of the war, ninety thousand Long Islanders worked in aircraft plants, twenty-five thousand at Grumman; twenty-three thousand at Republic, the rest at smaller plants. The majority of the wartime workforce was women.

The Coast Artillery set up Camp Hero at Montauk Point and there was a Navy torpedo testing ground at Fort Pond Bay there. Carl Fisher's Montauk Manor provided housing for the servicemen stationed there. Camp Upton was reactivated.

Of course, Long Island's civilians did their part, too. There was rationing, practice air raids, Civil Defense and air raid wardens. There were blackouts and brownouts. People grew victory gardens and saved aluminum and bought war bonds. Aware that Long Island's location near Manhattan and extensive shoreline made enemy attack possible, residents learned to identify aircraft and patrol the beaches.

World War II and, specifically, the role Long Island and Long Islanders played, was chronicled daily by *Newsday*, the newspaper whose first edition came out on September 3, 1940. Published and edited by Alicia Patterson, the first press run of fifteen thousand was produced on a used press in a converted Hempstead garage. Harry F. Guggenheim, Ms. Patterson's husband, was president of the paper. *Newsday* was sold to the Times-Mirror Corporation in 1970, joining a roster of papers that included *The Washington Post* and *The Los Angeles Times*.

The first *Newsday* headline read, "U.S. GIVES BRITISH 50 WARSHIPS" and, anticipating the coming election, asked, "Will F.D.R. Gain or Lose in County?" In the years ahead, *Newsday* would grow with the Island and, even in the first few years, had a host of interesting stories to report. One of the more interesting stories was in the June 13, 1942, edition.

The day before, patrolling the beach at Amagansett, 21-year-old Coast Guard Seaman Second-Class John C. Cullen became the only person to directly confront the enemy on Long Island. On his regular three-mile shoreline patrol route, Cullen encountered three men. When challenged by the unarmed Cullen, they explained they had lost their fishing boat. Cullen asked the men to accompany him to the Coast Guard station to file a report. At that moment, a fourth man stepped out of the brush dragging a duffel bag.

Cullen tried to leave, but was detained by the men who, after conferring with each other in German, offered him a bribe to "forget" he ever saw them. He took the money, $260, and ran back to the station to report the incident.

Cullen and his fellow guardsmen returned to the beach but found no one and saw nothing suspicious. They did feel a vibration of the type that would be made by a diesel engine and thought they saw the outline of a u-boat, but they left the beach to return to search in daylight. At that time, Cullen found a pack of German cigarettes and the buried duffel bag filled with German uniforms and explosives.

The night before, when the four Nazis left the beach, they walked to the Amagansett train station and were soon safe in New York City hotels. It turned out they were part of an elaborate German plot, called "Operation Pastorius," after the first German immigrant in America, to destroy key American defenses. Four other German agents who were part of the same plot landed off Florida a few days later.

George Dasch, leader of the eight saboteurs, surrendered one week later and turned in his fellows. Six

were executed. Dasch and one other, who testified for the United States government, were jailed and later deported to Germany.

John Cullen was awarded the Legion of Merit and won a special citation from President Roosevelt.

French pilot and poet Antoine de Saint-Euxpèry settled briefly in Northport, having moved there from his native France during the Nazi occupation. His book *The Little Prince* was written while he lived on Long Island. In 1944, Saint-Euxpèry was shot down and died in battle over Africa.

World War II ended with joyous celebrations in 1945. The end of war, however, was just the beginning of deep changes, the first chapter in the story of the Long Island we know today. ■

LONGS ISLAND'S WEALTH WAS HERCULEAN ENOUGH TO IMPRESS VISITORS SUCH AS THE PRINCE OF WALES, WHO, AFTER HIS 1924 VISIT WROTE, "THE LUXURY I WAS ACCUSTOMED TO IN EUROPE SEEMED ALMOST PRIMITIVE" WHEN COMPARED TO THE LUXURY HE FOUND IN THE UNITED STATES. THE FIGUREHEAD OF HERCULES SAT IN A FIELD IN HAMPTON BAYS. TODAY, IT'S IN A PAVILION AT STONY BROOK HARBOR. PHOTO FROM THE FULLERTON COLLECTION, COURTESY OF THE SUFFOLK COUNTY HISTORICAL SOCIETY.

ARGUABLY THE GREATEST AMERICAN POLO PLAYER, THOMAS HITCHCOCK OF SANDS POINT IS SHOWN HERE
AT A MID-1920S MATCH AT THE MEADOWBROOK CLUB. PHOTOS COURTESY OF THE NASSAU COUNTY
DIVISION OF MUSEUM SERVICES/LONG ISLAND STUDIES INSTITUTE/HOFSTRA UNIVERSITY.

THE PRINCE OF WALES WAS ENTERTAINED IN A SUITABLY ROYAL MANNER IN THE SUMMER OF 1924, WHEN HE
TRAVELED TO LONG ISLAND FOR THE INTERNATIONAL POLO MATCHES. IN 1935, THE PRINCE OF WALES
(CENTER) GOLFED AT THE MEADOWBROOK CLUB, WHERE HE HAD, A DECADE EARLIER, BEEN A GUEST FOR
POLO. THE CLUB WAS DEMOLISHED TO MAKE WAY FOR THE MEADOWBROOK PARKWAY.

ROBERT MOSES STANDS IN FRONT OF THE UNISPHERE AT THE 1964 NEW YORK WORLD'S FAIR. HE WAS PRESIDENT OF THE WORLD'S FAIR CORPORATION. PHOTO COURTESY OF *NEWSDAY*.

ROBERT MOSES: HE BUILT IT AND THEY DID COME

Robert Moses was a phenomenon and, no matter which side people take in the debate over the worth of his legacy, there is no arguing that his impact on Long Island is unmatched and unlikely to be matched.

Born in New Haven on December 18, 1888, Moses was raised in Manhattan. A Phi Beta Kappa graduate of Yale, he attended Oxford and was the first American to head the famed debating society, the Oxford Union at that university. Moses received a Ph.D. from Columbia in 1914.

At Columbia Moses became interested in municipal administration, He worked for the mayor after he graduated and during World War I in the Emergency Fleet corporation. In 1918, Democrat Alfred E. Smith was elected governor of New York and he took Republican Robert Moses to Albany as chief-of-staff of a bipartisan Reconstruction Commission to study problems left by the war. In 1927, Smith appointed

Moses New York Secretary of State, a job he lost when Smith was succeeded as governor by Franklin Delano Roosevelt.

From the start, Moses was a towering, impressive man, standing more than six feet tall with a build that reflected his time on the swim teams at Yale and Oxford.

Moses' rise in government was rapid. In 1924 the State Park council was created and he was chair of that, as well as President of the Long Island State Park Commission.

In an admiring 1939 *Atlantic Monthly* "portrait" of Moses by Cleveland Rodgers, the author explains what happened next:

"When Moses became head of the Long Island State Park Commission the only state 'park' in the section was on Fire Island, a sand reef reached only by boat…Moses' first big undertaking…was the now famous Jones Beach. This stretch of

(continued)

clean, wide ocean beach, some thirty miles from the centre of the city, was almost inaccessible. Only a man of unusual vision would have selected the site as a likely seaside resort for a vast population. Engineers, architects, and experts thought he was dreaming, but he persuaded Al Smith to visit the beach and secured an initial appropriation for a bathhouse. There are now two miles of developed ocean beach, a mile-long stillwater swimming area in Zach's Bay, and a large salt-water enclosed pool for both swimming and wading....

"Architecturally the two immense bathhouses, with a picturesque water tower dominating the vast expanse of beach and water, are impressive and pleasing. Between four and five million people enjoy this park during the summer, yet there is no crowding. Sunday crowds run to 125,000. Concerts are given in the Music Shell on the Marine Boardwalk, and popular-priced operettas, operas, and concerts are staged over the water in Zach's Bay.

"Although a maximum of freedom is permitted, this is perhaps the cleanest and best regulated of public beaches. Robert Moses believes that giving the public the best arouses cooperation in maintaining high standards"

Following Jones Beach, Moses acquired and developed an astounding network of parks and beaches, along with the parkways, bridges and tunnels that carry people to those places. With federal programs put in place to fight the Depression, Moses was ready with plans that would put people back to work.

In all, *Newsday* enumerates fifty-two projects in the metropolitan area for which Moses was directly responsible, stretching from the Harlem River Drive and Henry Hudson Parkway to Montauk Point State Park. His highways bisect Long Island from the Northern State Parkway to the Southern State, with the Long Island Expressway in between.

Financier Otto Kahn objected to Moses' plans to have Northern State Parkway built in the middle of his Old Westbury golf club. Moses agreed to allow Kahn to foot the $10,000 bill for a new survey and neither that parkway, nor the later Long Island Expressway, touched Old Westbury.

With all of his will to benefit the public, the *Atlantic Monthly* piece noted, "It helps to an understanding of his activities to know that Moses himself drafted the laws creating every position he has held or now holds," [with the exception of Secretary of State for New York]. In 1933, New York Governor Herbert Lehman made Moses chairman of the Emergency Public Works Commission

and he took on expansion of the Saratoga Springs Spa, the Catskill Bridge Authority, the Thousand Islands Bridge Authority, the Triborough Bridge, the Jones Beach State Parkway, and the Bethpage State Park.

Moses worked closely with Mayor Fiorello LaGuardia, creating new projects that employed 75,000 people in 1,700 projects, including the 1939 World's Fair in Flushing Meadow and its sister event 25 years later in the same location.

The 1939 article includes this assessment of Moses: "His career, unique in so many ways, is our best example of what can be accomplished in the field of public service by one who decides early what he wants to do, thoroughly prepares himself for the task, and possesses the character, energy, and singleness of purpose to keep going."

He took little or no salary for his work, continuing to develop projects for Long Island and New York City, notably under Mayors LaGuardia and Paul O'Dwyer.

Railing against thoughtless suburban development in a 1950 *Atlantic Monthly* article, Moses wrote entitled, "Build and Be Damned," he concluded by saying, "A community must have leadership and conscience to resist the ruthless modern developer. These are commodities no outsider can supply. The most we as public officials can do is to hold the mirror up to nature, point the moral, and hope for the best."

Robert Moses was successful in carrying out his vision of a metropolitan area in which recreation was accessible through a network of roads. But, he apparently did not foresee the effect his roads would have in creating today's legendary traffic jams on a Long Island on which accessible mass transit was never built.

Moses rejected a proposal, for example, to put railroad tracks in the middle of the Expressway so that commuters could easily commute by rail, with homes within walking distance, that would use fewer automobiles.

Moses was defeated in his quest to build a cross-Sound bridge to Westchester from Oyster Bay and in his effort to put roads on Fire Island, on which, even today, automobiles are banned.

But the legacy of Robert Moses lives on Long Island and, in the summertime, when it shines especially bright in the parks and beaches that attract millions of visitors, it is fairly easy to forgive any planning trespasses he might have committed.

Robert Moses died in 1981 at age 92.

In all, *Newsday* enumerates fifty-two projects in the metropolitan area for which Moses was directly responsible, stretching from the Harlem River Drive and Henry Hudson Parkway to Montauk Point State Park. His highways bisect Long Island from the Northern State Parkway to the Southern State, with the Long Island Expressway in between. Photo by J. Giamundo, Bruce Bennett Studios.

Fire Island, Long Island's first state park, is still accessible only by boat, with no automobiles allowed on the island even to this day. Photo by Lisa Meyer, Bruce Bennett Studios.

THE LEGACY OF ROBERT MOSES LIVES ON LONG ISLAND, AND IN THE SUMMERTIME IT SHINES ESPECIALLY BRIGHT IN THE PARKS AND BEACHES THAT ATTRACT MILLIONS OF VISITORS. PHOTO BY LISA MEYER, BRUCE BENNETT STUDIOS.

(ABOVE) THE MONTAUK MANOR HOTEL, PICTURED IN THE MID-1940S, WAS BUILT IN 1926 BY ENTREPRENEUR CARL FISHER, WHO DREAMED OF RECREATING THE SUCCESS HE HAD FOUND IN MIAMI BEACH AND KEY WEST. PHOTO COURTESY OF THE NASSAU COUNTY DIVISION OF MUSEUM SERVICES/LONG ISLAND STUDIES INSTITUTE/HOFSTRA UNIVERSITY. (LEFT) FRANK BUCK'S ZOO OFF SUNRISE HIGHWAY IN MASSAPEQUA PROVIDED LOCAL ENTERTAINMENT FOR DEPRESSION-ERA LONG ISLANDERS. HERE, BUCK STANDS NEXT TO AN ELEPHANT IN FRONT OF "MONKEY MOUNTAIN" IN 1935. PHOTO COURTESY OF THE NASSAU COUNTY DIVISION OF MUSEUM SERVICES/LONG ISLAND STUDIES INSTITUTE/HOFSTRA UNIVERSITY.

SITUATED ON THE EASTERNMOST TIP OF LONG ISLAND, MONTAUK CONTINUES TO BE A DESTINATION FOR ESCAPE AND RELAXATION. PHOTO BY ROB AMATO, BRUCE BENNETT STUDIOS.

CHARLES LINDBERGH AND HUMORIST WILL ROGERS POSE IN A PHOTO REPRODUCED ON A 1930 POSTCARD. PHOTO COURTESY OF THE NASSAU COUNTY DIVISION OF MUSEUM SERVICES/LONG ISLAND STUDIES INSTITUTE/HOFSTRA UNIVERSITY.

FLYING INTO THE PAGES OF HISTORY

In 1904, aviator Glenn Curtiss was called "the fastest man on earth" when he was clocked at 136.6 mph. That feat was accomplished during a motorcycle race in Florida.

Like the Wright Brothers, Curtiss had started out manufacturing bicycles. But he switched to motorcycles and, like the Brothers who would become his lifelong rivals, he was interested in flight. He experimented with planes and, on July 17, 1909, won $10,000 from a magazine that had offered the prize to the first American who could fly 15.5 miles. Curtiss flew his plane, the June Bug, for 58 minutes between Westbury and Mineola.

In addition to winning a prize, he won Long Island the distinction of begin known forever as the "Cradle of Aviation." Curtiss moved his aircraft manufacturing operation to Curtiss Field in Mineola and Long Island's reputation as an aviation Mecca emerged.

The Hempstead Plains were as ideally suited for flight as they had been for pasturing animals and horseracing. Flat with little high-growth vegetation,

they offered the space and the clearance needed for airplane flight.

Curtiss' flight was the beginning of an industry whose development its early practitioners could likely never imagine.

A patchwork of airfields blanketed the Hempstead Plain. World War I brought the military in and technological developments brought in the aircraft factories that, later, would see their products travel to the moon with the Grumman Lunar Module.

At the beginning, though, the fliers were risk-takers and their planes were risky. The first monoplane was designed by Dr. Henry Walden, a dentist who in 1910 became the first person ever to fly a plane with only one set of wings.

Aviation was for years Long Island's most successful spectator sport. Crowds jammed the Hempstead Plain as new "firsts" happened and records were broken. Thus, on Long Island "those magnificent men in their flying machines" became the first to fly three passengers, to fly across the

(continued)

(LEFT) FREEPORT TEENAGER ELINOR SMITH SET AERONAUTICAL RECORDS. FREEPORT HISTORICAL SOCIETY PHOTO COURTESY *NEWSDAY*. (RIGHT) CHARLES LINDBERGH STANDS BY *THE SPIRIT OF ST. LOUIS* IMMEDIATELY BEFORE HIS TRANS-ATLANTIC FLIGHT MAY 20 AND 21, 1927. THE BAG AT HIS FEET CONTAINS HIS PERSONAL BELONGINGS FOR HIS STAY IN PARIS. PHOTO COURTESY OF THE NASSAU COUNTY DIVISION OF MUSEUM SERVICES/LONG ISLAND STUDIES INSTITUTE/HOFSTRA UNIVERSITY.

Long Island Sound, and the site of the first airmail delivery. A few years later, Long Island would lead the nation in aviation training for combat with Roosevelt Field and Mitchel Field providing pilots for the Navy and Army, respectively.

And, in 1927, Long Island's aviation reputation was cast in stone with another first. At 7:54 a.m. on May 20 of that year, Charles A. Lindbergh left Roosevelt Field in his plane *The Spirit of St. Louis* and, 33 hours, 29 minutes and 30 seconds later—at 10:22 p.m. Paris time—landed at Le Bourget Field outside Paris.

Lindbergh had done the unthinkable; the unimaginable. And, because he had done it with dignity and self-effacement, he immediately became the symbol of all that Americans believe is good in America. Despite his later political problems, Lindbergh is forever burnished in the nation's collective memory as the first and the best.

Of course, it wasn't only "magnificent men" who flew into aviation history on Long Island. Bessica Raiche, who flew out of the Hempstead

Plains, became known as the "First Woman Aviator of America" when she made a solo flight on September 26, 1910.

Purists, however, are always sure to note that, in fact, Raiche was the second to solo in America. For, just two weeks before Raiche's flight, another woman had flown alone, but she was lifted off the ground by wind while practicing her taxiing skills. Thus, Raiche got the first "official" credit.

On January 31, 1929, when Freeport teen Elinor Smith landed at Roosevelt Field after being aloft in her plane for 13 hours, 16 minutes and 45 seconds, she had set a world record. Smith followed Bessica Raiche of Mineola who, in 1910, became the first woman to pilot a plane solo.

Even the briefest recap of local aviation history would be incomplete without the tale of Douglas Corrigan, who attracted national attention by flying a plane non-stop from California to Roosevelt Field in 27 hours, 50 minutes, on July 10, 1938.

What makes Corrigan most memorable, however, is that his planned return flight to

(continued)

THE FIRST MEETING OF THE INTERNATIONAL WOMEN PILOTS ASSOCIATION WAS HELD AT CURTISS FIELD IN VALLEY STREAM IN 1929. AMONG THE MEMBERS OF THE ORGANIZATION, KNOWN AS THE "NINETY-NINES," WERE AMELIA EARHART (SHOWN THIRD FROM RIGHT) AND ELINOR SMITH (SECOND FROM RIGHT). PHOTO COURTESY OF THE NASSAU COUNTY DIVISION OF MUSEUM SERVICES/LONG ISLAND STUDIES INSTITUTE/HOFSTRA UNIVERSITY.

California went awry and, 28 hours after taking off from Roosevelt Field, ostensibly headed west, he landed in Dublin, Ireland. He claimed he had been lost and was known forever after as "Wrong Way" Corrigan.

The aviation tradition on Long Island continues today with six American astronauts—Mary Cleave, Robert Gibson, Kevin Kregel, Michael Massimino, William Shepherd, and James Weatherbee—all graduates of local high schools. Gibson also graduated from Suffolk Community College.

Today, Long Island is home to several small airfields and three large fields.

The Air National Guard station at Francis S. Gabreski Field in Westhampton Beach, named in honor of one of the two top aces in the World War II European theater, has been key to air missions in the region. Planes from Westhampton Beach took part in the search for survivors of Flight 800 in 1996 and were part of the rescue effort detailed in the book and film *The Perfect Storm*.

In addition, Long Island is also home to two large public airfields.

Republic Airport in Farmingdale has been in existence for more than seventy years, first as a test field for local airplane manufacture and now, owned by the NY State Department of Transportation. During the past thirty years Republic has served as home base for five hundred general aviation (non-commercial) aircraft.

The Town of Islip owns Long Island MacArthur Airport in Ronkonkoma. When it opened on Veterans Memorial Highway in 1942, there were 51,182 people in the Town of Islip and less than 200,000 in all of Suffolk County. It was a small airport in a small town and was used mostly for general aviation and business flights.

The rise in air traffic and the perception in the mind of travelers that Islip is a solid alternative to the larger airports in New York City has led to enormous growth. Islip is now home to ten commercial airlines and, in 1999, served 1.9 million passengers.

(LEFT) EARLY IN ITS LIFE, BELMONT PARK WAS USED AS THE SITE FOR AIR SHOWS. THIS IS THE COVER OF
THE 1910 INTERNATIONAL AVIATION TOURNAMENT. (RIGHT) THE *STARS AND STRIPES*, A FAIRCHILD
FC-2W2, BUILT AT FARMINGDALE IN 1928 FOR ADMIRAL RICHARD E. BYRD'S ANTARCTIC EXPEDITION.
PHOTOS COURTESY OF THE NASSAU COUNTY DIVISION OF MUSEUM SERVICES/LONG ISLAND STUDIES
INSTITUTE/HOFSTRA UNIVERSITY.

THE FF-1, THE FIRST GRUMMAN DESIGN USED BY THE UNITED STATES NAVY IN 1933.
PHOTO COURTESY OF THE NASSAU COUNTY DIVISION OF MUSEUM SERVICES/LONG ISLAND STUDIES
INSTITUTE/HOFSTRA UNIVERSITY.

LONG ISLAND UNIVERSITY

Within reach of the world's most exciting city, the campuses of Long Island University span Long Island, from the bustling streets of Brooklyn to a former Gold Coast estate to the beaches and woodlands of Suffolk County's East End. Each campus has its own character; students on all of them draw on the resources of what has become the nation's eighth-largest independent university.

This comprehensive doctoral institution, by far the largest on Long Island, reaches well beyond the island. Its Friends World Program has six overseas centers; instructional programs take place in Europe, aboard tall ships, on site at schools and some of the nation's largest corporations, and at the United States Military Academy at West Point.

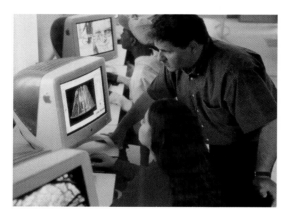

COMPUTER GRAPHICS LABORATORIES STIMULATE PRACTICAL CREATIVITY WITH UP-TO-DATE EQUIPMENT.

The university's distinctive place in higher education, said President David J. Steinberg, stems from its dual roles. It not only attracts "thousands of outstanding, nationally-competitive students who seek a nurturing learning environment," but also "is boldly determined to offer that same supportive environment to highly motivated students whose potential has yet to be realized." Many students represent the first generation of their families to attend college.

Long Island University provides access to the American dream, Steinberg said, by educating its 30,000 students "one at a time." Innovative, personalized activities include award-winning Honors Programs, where students take on academic challenges rivaling those at the nation's finest elite colleges, and the Higher Education Opportunity Program, which offers tutoring, counseling, and financial assistance to academically and economically disadvantaged students. The nearly 150,000 alumni often maintain lifelong links with the school and provide networking and mentoring for graduates.

Long Island University celebrates its 75th anniversary in 2001, having been chartered in downtown Brooklyn in 1926. (Its Arnold & Marie Schwartz College of Pharmacy and Health Sciences traces its roots to 1886.) In the years after World War II, the university followed the Island's population growth to the east, establishing the C.W. Post Campus in 1954 and Southampton College in 1963.

Regional and national leaders in government, banking, law, manufacturing, entertainment, broadcasting, scientific research and development, and civic affairs oversee the university as trustees, under the leadership of their chair, Roger Tilles, a director of the Tilles

THE UNIVERSITY'S C.W. POST CAMPUS NESTLES IN THE ROLLING HILLS OF THE ISLAND'S GOLD COAST ESTATE AREA BUT IS ONLY 20 MILES FROM NEW YORK CITY.

Investment Company. One trustee serves as Chancellor of each major unit: for the Brooklyn Campus, Edward Travaglianti, chairman and CEO of EAB and current chairman of the Long Island Association; for the C.W. Post Campus, Theresa Mall Mullarkey, the former president of Mall Associates; for Southampton College, Robert F.X. Sillerman, Chairman and CEO of The Sillerman Companies; for the regional campuses, Ronald J. Sylvestri, Vice President of Institutional Sales of Fleet Investment Group.

President Steinberg, a Harvard-educated historian, has directed the university since 1985. His initiatives have increased the university's academic quality and breadth by adding degree and certificate programs at all levels including doctoral programs, expanded internships and cooperative education placements, increased scholarships, and launched information technology projects. Centers of excellence now include nationally recognized programs in writing and in marine and environmental science at Southampton College, a theater program at C.W. Post that was selected to perform at the Kennedy Center; and natural science programs at the Brooklyn Campus that have won millions of dollars in grants from the National Science Foundation. During Steinberg's tenure the university has committed $175 million to construction projects.

THE STUDENT POPULATION OF THE BROOKLYN CAMPUS REFLECTS THE NEW YORK AREA'S RICH CULTURAL DIVERSITY.

Brooklyn Campus Educates a Dynamic Urban Population

Led by Provost Gale Stevens Haynes, an attorney and Long Island University graduate, Long Island University's Brooklyn Campus is a key part of downtown Brooklyn's recent renaissance. The six schools and colleges offer students degree programs up to doctoral education in clinical psychology, pharmaceutics, and pharmacy. A United Nations program holds graduate classes near UN headquarters; other programs draw talented students pursuing careers in the sciences, medicine, urban education, and business.

The oldest of the university's campuses, Brooklyn boasts some of its newest facilities, thanks to comprehensive recent renovations and building. The William Zeckendorf Health Sciences Center (1995) provides up to date facilities for the College of Pharmacy and Health Sciences, and classrooms and labs for programs in physical therapy, sports medicine, and nursing. The Jeanette and Edmund T. Pratt Jr. Center for Academic Studies (2000), funded with a gift from the former head of Pfizer Inc, conveniently centralizes student services and is the new home for the School of Education. The landmark Brooklyn Paramount Theater has been renovated as a dazzling student center, housing the home games of the Division I basketball Blackbirds and a dining commons named in honor of a former University board chairman and CEO of Brooklyn Union Gas, Eugene Luntey, and his wife.

SPORTS ARE HIGH ON THE AGENDA AT THE BROOKLYN CAMPUS, WHICH HAS DIVISION I TEAMS.

THE MARINE SCIENCES PROGRAM AT LONG ISLAND UNIVERSITY'S SOUTHAMPTON COLLEGE IS A LURE FOR STUDENTS FROM ALL OVER THE U.S.

Perhaps the most ethnically and racially balanced campus in the country, the Brooklyn Campus consciously draws insights and strength from its pluralism. It is, for example, the center for a rich variety of cultural offerings including literary readings, jazz, choral music, dance concerts, and exhibitions in its two galleries and landscaped plaza.

C.W. Post Campus Combines Liberal Arts and Practical Training on Gold Coast Estate

Only 20 miles from Manhattan, the C.W. Post Campus of Long Island University is distinguished by rolling green lawns, formal gardens—and involvement with its surrounding suburban community. Headed by Provost Joseph Shenker, C.W. Post melds strong liberal arts with degree and certificate programs in professional areas ranging from business, public administration, and the health professions to information studies and visual and performing arts.

C.W. Post's School of Education certifies a high proportion of New York State's teachers, administrators, and counselors; it recently attracted foundation grants to work with the Westbury public schools using the techniques of Yale reformer James Comer. The campus is the home of the Palmer School of Library and Information Science. Also unique to the Campus is the School of Professional Accountancy, with a highly regarded graduate tax program; the school is part of an up-and-coming College of Management. Programs offered by C.W. Post's School of Visual and Performing Arts include ceramics, fine arts, computer graphics, photography, music, public relations, theater, broadcasting, and journalism. Especially notable are the state-of-the-art computer facilities for graphic design and music, and a television studio that affords students the opportunity to master animation and television production.

Among recent campus developments, Billy Taylor, the legendary jazz pianist and educator, became the Rose Tilles University Professor in the Performing Arts and Distinguished Artist-in-Residence. (See page 380). A new recreation center is being named for the donors Edmund T. and Jeanette Pratt.

Founded in 1954, C.W. Post is built on former estates including that of Marjorie Merriweather Post, the cereal heiress. Her Tudor mansion, regarded as among the finest examples of Gold Coast architecture, continues to be a focal point, its Great Hall often serving as the setting for important campus and university events. This historic building is being renovated with a record grant to the campus from alumnus Gary Winnick, an investment banker and philanthropist, and his wife, Karen.

Small Southampton College Produces Top Scholars

Producing 35 Fulbright Scholars since 1975 would be a remarkable achievement for any institution of higher learning, but it is nothing less than extraordinary for a young college with an enrollment of 1,330 undergraduates. The college prides itself on "caring for students who will care for the world." Under the leadership of Provost Timothy H. Bishop, it draws on the environmental, artistic, and literary resources of the celebrated Hamptons and was the only campus highlighted by *The New York Times* in a special "Best of Long Island" issue.

The college is achieving a national reputation as a center for writers, thanks in part to the essayist Roger Rosenblatt, the Parsons Family Professor of English and Writing. Each spring, the East End literary season unofficially starts with an art gallery benefit for the college's writer's sanctuary, named for the author John Steinbeck. Peter Matthiessen and Dava Sobel are among the renowned East End writers who regularly teach in the college's M.F.A. program in English and Writing. In the visual arts, two galleries host exhibitions and lectures by prominent artists and photographers, and the artist and critic Brian O'Doherty (a.k.a. Patrick Ireland) is University Professor of Fine Arts and Media.

THE DISTINCTIVE TRADEMARK AT SOUTHAMPTON COLLEGE IS AN HISTORIC WINDMILL.

Yet for all its artistic and literary bent, Southampton College is equally well-known for nationally recognized programs in marine and environmental science. The ocean, bays, and salt marshes are nearby; students have access to a fleet of boats including a 44-foot ocean-going research vessel; the college is the North American affiliate of the Jacques Cousteau Society.

Environmental policy issues receive attention in courses under James Larocca, KeySpan University Professor of Public Policy, an environmentalist who has headed New York State's transportation and energy agencies as well as the Long Island Association. Students in the SEAmester program sail aboard tall ships for nine weeks, gaining first-hand experience in coastal ecology, marine history, and nautical adventure. Thanks to generous gifts from Chancellor Robert Sillerman and his wife, Laura Baudo Sillerman, a renovation and expansion of the library is underway and a new Chancellors Hall holds classrooms, science laboratories and the headquarters of the University's Public Radio Network. (See page 434).

Friends World Program Specializes in International Education for Social Change

International travel by Long Island University students is not confined to the marine programs. The Friends World Program, based at Southampton College, is a non-traditional institution in which faculty members guide students in devising their own plans of study.

STUDENTS ENROLLED IN LONG ISLAND UNIVERSITY'S COOPERATIVE EDUCATION PROGRAMS GAIN REAL WORLD EXPERIENCE BEFORE GRADUATION.

THE FRIENDS WORLD PROGRAM'S COURSE IN COMPARATIVE RELIGION AND CULTURE VISITS THE FAMED SIKH TEMPLE OF AMRITSAR, INDIA.

After a first year at the North American Center, students study in at least two of Friends World's six overseas centers, where the goals include total linguistic and cultural immersion. Friends World students are encouraged to take the world's most pressing problems as the focus of their curriculum. While other experimental programs have foundered, since 1992 the Friends World Program has experienced a significant enrollment surge.

Westchester, Rockland, and Brentwood Campuses Provide Fast Tracks for Adult Learners

The university welcomes adult students on all its campuses, but graduate and certificate courses are the specialty of three regional campuses—Brentwood, Long Island; the Westchester Graduate Campus in Purchase; and the Rockland Graduate Campus in Orangeburg. Graduate degree programs, some taking advantage of distance education, are offered in the arts and sciences, business administration, education, and the health professions. Brentwood additionally offers undergraduate programs.

Elsewhere, elementary and secondary teachers and employees of companies like Verizon, Symbol Technologies, and Northrop-Grumman pursue graduate degrees in university programs taught right in their places of business. The university's continuing education program, the largest on Long Island, offers courses ranging from current events to conflict resolution.

By serving diverse populations in personal ways and linking sophisticated training to humane, globally relevant education in the liberal arts and sciences, Long Island University today is enhancing its place in the vanguard of what higher education is becoming in the new century. ■

Also, see related sections on Long Island University Public Radio Network, page 434, and Tilles Center for the Performing Arts, page 380.

SOUTH NASSAU COMMUNITIES HOSPITAL

South Nassau Communities Hospital is responsive to the diverse and growing health care needs of the communities it serves. Focusing on innovative and compassionate service, this tradition of responsiveness ensures that the hospital will continue to fulfill its mission of providing efficient and effective health care for all.

Founded in 1928, South Nassau is one of the region's largest hospitals, with 429 beds, more than 820 physicians, and 1,900 employees. Located in Oceanside, the hospital is an acute care, not-for-profit, voluntary teaching hospital. It offers a comprehensive range of standard and specialized health care services, including ambulatory, home health, curative, restorative, preventive, and emergency medical care. It excels in cancer and cardiac care and offers comprehensive diagnostic treatment and behavioral health, rehabilitation, and support services.

Since its founding, South Nassau has continually responded to the need for more specialized health care. A state-of-the-art Outpatient Dialysis Center, a Physical Rehabilitation and Sports Medicine Center, a free-standing Family Medicine Center, and expanded Pediatric Unit are just some of the new and enhanced services recently introduced.

The new Women's Health Center and centers for Wound Care, Diabetes Education, Cardiac Rehabilitation, and Minimally Invasive Surgery are among the other specialized services offered by South Nassau. The

UNDER THE LEADERSHIP AND VISION OF JOSEPH A. QUAGLIATA, PRESIDENT AND CEO, SOUTH NASSAU FULFILLS ITS PROMISE OF "TOUCHING LIVES, ONE PATIENT AT A TIME."

Women's Health Center opened in March, 1999. Located in Bellmore, it is designed to meet women's health care needs, including physical, emotional, mental health, nutrition, and wellness. Its Day Spa, which opened in October, 1999, provides a complete range of beauty and wellness services, including facials, body treatments, cosmetics and skin health regimens. Featuring 18 spacious, individual, state-of-the-art dialysis stations, South Nassau's new Outpatient Dialysis Center, opened in May 2000, offers patients maximum privacy, comfort, and care. Each station features private telephone lines, satellite-linked television sets, high-speed Internet access, and individually-controlled heating and lighting systems. The completely refurbished Pediatric Unit offers children and their families the comforts, care, and security of home. Environmental enhancements include a softer, warmer decor, and increased parent/child playroom space. To facilitate physician accessibility and ensure constant coverage, physician offices are located on the unit. The unit also includes a Special Care area that features sophisticated monitoring systems and a 24-hour nursing staff. The comprehensive Physical Rehabilitation and Sports Medicine Center opened in the fall of 2000. Located in Oceanside, the center is founded on a team approach to delivering quality, individualized care. The center's specialists offer evaluations of pain emanating from injury, post surgery, fractured joints, arthritis, and subtissue muscle sprain; diagnose and prescribe treatment for neuromuscular conditions such as Parkinson's, muscular dystrophy and strokes; and conduct Electrodiagnostic testing and nerve conduction studies to help diagnose pinched nerves in the back or detect carpal tunnel syndrome.

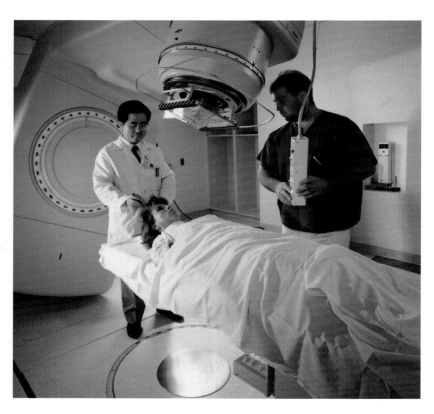

FOR ALMOST 75 YEARS, SOUTH NASSAU HAS BEEN TREATING PATIENTS WITH A POWERFUL COMBINATION OF ADVANCED MEDICAL TECHNOLOGY AND SKILLED, COMPASSIONATE CARE.

THE REGION'S NEED FOR CONVENIENTLY LOCATED, HIGH-QUALITY SPECIALIZED CARE IS THE BACKBONE OF SOUTH NASSAU'S INITIATIVE TO DEVELOP CENTERS OF SPECIALTY HEALTH CARE SUCH AS ITS OUTPATIENT DIALYSIS CENTER.

Recognizing current and future needs, long-range expansion plans are in progress for the Ambulatory Surgery Unit and Emergency Department. The Ambulatory Surgery Unit's four-phase expansion initiative will increase its space to 9,000 square feet and includes construction of private patient areas. To address the current and future projections for visits, the Emergency Department, which is one of the most utilized in the region, will increase in size to 18,000 square feet. When complete, the department will house a Chest Pain Center for cardiac patients, a spacious waiting room, and private, individual patient areas.

South Nassau employs the latest advancements in medical technology and skilled physicians. It was the first Long Island-based hospital to use 3-D imaging diagnostic technology that locates rapid heartbeats and is used to cure them with advanced therapies. Its Endoscopy Unit combines the expertise of specially trained physicians with the benefits and capabilities of advanced endoscopic technology. The delivery of high-tech, cutting-edge medicine is central to the mission of South Nassau Communities Hospital, but that tells only a part of the hospital's story. Joseph A. Quagliata, the president and CEO of South Nassau, stated: "The people who work here believe that we have only one reason to exist—to serve the people of the community." He explained that South Nassau's employees at every level are from the community and thus, "tend to view every patient as mother, father, sister, brother, or friend." "We share a sense," said Mr. Quagliata, "that we must treat each patient as someone who is important to us." While he and his staff are always striving to be even more responsive, feedback from patients and their families suggests to Mr. Quagliata that "we are successful in our quest to treat each patient as family."

South Nassau also operates a teaching program that is recognized for educating well-rounded medical professionals. The hospital is affiliated with more than 20 educational institutions, operates an accredited Family Practice Residency Program and a School of Radiology, and has residency program affiliations with major teaching institutions in surgery, obstetrics/gynecology, pathology, rehabilitative medicine, pediatrics, and nuclear medicine.

To support its many growth initiatives, South Nassau partnered with Winthrop-University Hospital in 1996 to form the Winthrop South Nassau University Health System, Inc. Through joint ventures and alliances with health care organizations such as Long Island Health Network, South Nassau continues to expand its continuum of care.

This tradition of delivering high-quality health care that is responsive to the needs of the communities it serves will continue at South Nassau. So will its mission of "attaining the highest quality of life for our patients and communities by providing personal, efficient, and effective health care without regard to race, creed, sex, age, national origin, or the ability to pay, in a professional, innovative, and learning environment." For more information, please visit www.southnassau.org or call 1-877-SOUTH NASSAU. ■

ENHANCING THE QUALITY OF LIFE OF THE PATIENTS AND COMMUNITIES IS ACHIEVED THROUGH SATELLITE SERVICES SUCH AS THE CENTER FOR CARDIAC REHABILITATION AND A COMPREHENSIVE COMMUNITY MEDICINE PROGRAM, WHICH OFFERS MORE THAN 20 SUPPORT GROUPS, FREE HEALTH SCREENINGS, AND MORE THAN 35 LECTURES AND SEMINARS ANNUALLY.

WIEDERSUM ASSOCIATES, P.C. ARCHITECTS

If you grew up on Long Island, chances are the schools you attended were designed by The Wiedersum Organization. The family owned and operated architectural design firm is best known for the more than 1,400 school buildings it has designed on Long Island and elsewhere in New York and New Jersey. But then there are also the hospitals, libraries,

CRADLE OF AVIATION MUSEUM AND THEATRE—
MITCHEL FIELD, UNIONDALE, NEW YORK.

churches, banks, community centers, and even the prisons that have been developed by the talented, creative Wiedersum team. Just as the Levitt organization introduced the homes that served to fuel Long Island's suburban boom, Wiedersum Associates' designs for the buildings that have served the Island's growing neighborhoods have contributed significantly to Nassau and Suffolk counties' present status as one of the nation's most thriving communities.

A Monument to Long Island's Prominence In Aviation

One of Wiedersum's highest-profile design projects to date is near the very site where Charles Lindbergh took off for his famed 1927 flight to Paris. The new Cradle of Aviation Museum at Mitchel Field, celebrating Long Island's importance in aviation history from the Lindbergh flight to the role played by Grumman and Long Island in the development of aerospace technology and the lunar module which first landed man to the moon, encompasses 85,000 square feet of new space and renovation of 50,000 square feet of existing hangar space. The award-winning Wiedersum design is described by President Richard C. Wiedersum as "a complete concrete circle which encompasses the theater and a glass-enclosed Visitors' Center, as well as the conversion of two hangars to house and exhibit the museum's collection of aircraft and aerospace vehicles." The theater is Long Island's only "Imax Dome" Theater, featuring a screen that soars several stories high in the shape of a dome.

Wiedersum is also responsible for the handsome new face presented by Good Samaritan Hospital Medical Center in West Islip. The Wiedersum team designed a 110,000-square-foot addition that creates an entirely new facade for the hospital. Within the addition are a new Women's Pavilion and expanded facilities for radiology and pediatrics. The lobby, reception area, and cafeteria have also been expanded. With the hospital's future needs in mind, the flexible Wiedersum design for the three-story addition allows for the construction of three additional stories atop the addition. Once completed, the Wiedersum design will feature a dramatic six-story glass-enclosed atrium for the pleasure of Good Sam's patients, visitors, and staff.

AUGUSTA HENES GULDEN EMERGENCY PAVILLION AT THE GOOD SAMARITAN HOSPITAL MEDICAL CENTER IN WEST ISLIP, NEW YORK.

NEW MIDDLE SCHOOL—WILLIAM FLOYD UNION
FREE SCHOOL DISTRICT.

Creating Educational Environments

Given its acknowledged expertise in designing buildings sensitive to the needs of students and educators,
Wiedersum was called upon by the William Floyd Union
Free School District to design its new 187,000-square-foot
middle school. Planned to house some 1,200 students,
this school will be Wiedersum's 1,415th school design in
the metropolitan area. It is slated to greet its first students
at the opening of the 2002 school year.

Other important Wiedersum designs for the educational community have been the Helen Keller Center for
the blind, deaf, and mute, a protype facility for future
locations nationwide, and new campuses for Suffolk,
Queensboro, Kingsboro, and Staten Island community
colleges. In a project which combined the company's
expertise in education and aviation, Wiedersum collaborated in the design of Dowling College's NAT Center, a
facility devoted to aviation and transportation education.

Wiedersum is responsible for the designs for Suffolk
County's prisons in Riverhead and Yaphank; the firm
also designed a minimum security prison for Nassau
County. The communities of Valley Stream, Smithtown,
Patchogue, and Rockville Centre are among those with
churches designed or restored by Wiedersum Associates.

A Family-Directed History

Wiedersum Associates was founded in Valley Stream
in 1926 by Frederic P. Wiedersum, the grandfather of the
company's current president. Wiedersum is now in its
fourth generation of family leadership with Richard
("Rick") Wiedersum, the great-grandson of the founder,
serving as vice president. Atypical for the architectural
profession, as compared to the construction and development industries, Wiedersum has maintained its privately
held, family run status throughout its history. Right from
its earliest years, Wiedersum became closely associated

with school design: among its first projects was Valley
Stream High School. Moving eastward along with the
development of Long Island, Wiedersum relocated to
Hauppauge in 1980 and remains in this important
business hub.

Wiedersum Associates built its reputation and continues to maintain it, by designing functional structures
for the community through its superior design abilities
and long-standing commitment to remain with its projects through to successful conclusion and beyond. As
Richard C. Wiedersum said: "We never leave the job."
He explained that once the construction process
begins "we're out on the project sites, administering
the development of the projects, sometimes acting as
the project's construction manager." ■

DOWLING COLLEGE'S NATIONAL AVIATION AND
TRANSPORTATION CENTER IS A 63,683-SQUARE-
FOOT UNIQUE EDUCATIONAL, TRAINING, AND
MAINTENANCE FACILITY.

BAE SYSTEMS

When a branch of the U.S. military needs to bolster its ranks through technology, BAE SYSTEMS often gets the call. The company was born in November 1999 out of the merger of British Aerospace and Marconi Electronic Systems, both with long histories and strong reputations in the defense industry. Several mergers and acquisitions prior and since have helped the company develop into a major force in the industry—and on Long Island.

ALTHOUGH THE **BAE SYSTEMS** ADVANCED SYSTEMS HEADQUARTERS HAVE BEEN LOCATED IN GREENLAWN, NEW YORK SINCE 1971, THE COMPANY FIRST MOVED TO LONG ISLAND IN 1930, WHEN IT MOVED ITS OFFICES TO BAYSIDE, QUEENS FROM MANHATTAN. PRIOR TO THAT, THE COMPANY HAD ORIGINATED IN HOBOKEN, NEW JERSEY. IT HAS SPENT THE MAJORITY OF ITS HISTORY SOMEWHERE ON LONG ISLAND.

With capabilities in naval platforms, military aircraft, electronics, and other technologies, BAE SYSTEMS offers an outstanding performance as a prime contractor in all of the main defense sectors and the civilian market. "We have built a strong business upon innovative solutions to the electronic challenges faced by the defense and civilian markets," said CEO John Weston. "Innovation is the key in this industry."

The Advanced Systems unit of BAE SYSTEMS bases its headquarters in Greenlawn, New York, with other facilities located in Mt. Vernon, New York, Braintree, Massachusetts; Lansdale, Pennsylvania; and Gaithersburg, Maryland. The 550 employees in Greenlawn help engineer and manufacture products that focus on communications, electronic identification, displays, and antenna design.

The Identification Friend or Foe (IFF) line, which helps military personnel determine the identity of outside forces, is under continuous improvement. The first airborne IFF interrogator antenna—the "invisible dipole," as it's called—was built in the early 1960s. More than 7,000 versions have since been sold.

In the 1990s, Advanced Systems in Greenlawn developed the Combined Interrogator/Transponder (CIT) for fighter aircraft. Various IFF products have since been developed for the F-16 Fighting Falcon and the F/A-18 Super Hornet. A Man-portable Digital Interrogator (MDI) is a compact, ground-to-air interrogator that is portable and can be mounted on air defense weapons. The Greenlawn facility has developed different antenna designs for different situations, as well as interfaces between the sensors and the communications systems of land-based, naval, and airborne vehicles.

Early Defenses

Advanced Systems can trace its Long Island roots to a company called Hazeltine. Alan Hazeltine, head of the Electrical Engineering Department at Stevens Institute of Technology in Hoboken, New Jersey, founded that company in 1924 to build a Neutrodyne receiver circuit. Because this new kind of circuit was more sensitive and easier to tune than other circuits at the time, it was widely used in radios, televisions, and medical and photographic equipment.

IN FEBRUARY 2001, THE ADVANCED SYSTEMS UNIT IN GREENLAWN, LONG ISLAND WON CONTRACTS VALUED AT MORE THAN $33 MILLION FOR CONTINUED PRODUCTION OF ADVANCED IDENTIFICATION FRIEND OR FOE (IFF) AVIONICS SYSTEMS FOR THE F-16 FIGHTING FALCON. DESIGNATED THE AN/APX-113, THE ADVANCED IFF SYSTEM IS A COMBINED INTERROGATOR TRANSPONDER CURRENTLY EMPLOYED ON FIGHTER AND SURVEILLANCE AIRCRAFT OF 12 NATIONS. THE AN/APX-113 HAS BEEN IN PRODUCTION SINCE 1992, WITH MORE THAN 800 ALREADY BUILT FOR DEFENSE USERS AROUND THE WORLD.

The company's first facility was in Hoboken, New Jersey, but by 1939 the company had a building in Little Neck, New York. During the 1940s, Hazeltine established itself as a major force in the defense industry by developing a variety of electronic defense systems and equipment, including mine detectors, direction finders, and multi-frequency radio tuners. Later projects included a Lifesaver Antenna, which was mounted on the surface of every Allied ship to guard against friendly fire. Hazeltine also provided the U.S. Navy with ground-based radar stations.

During the 1950s and 1960s, Hazeltine expanded its non-defense work. It developed, for example, the technology of precise color imaging and the Color Film Analyzer, which simulated the motion picture film development process for which it was awarded an Academy Award for Technical Innovation.

Both defense and commercial work also continued in full force throughout the 1970s and 1980s. But the end of the Cold War brought big changes, including several mergers and acquisitions. During that time, the company was called Emerson, ESCO, GEC-Marconi Hazeltine, Marconi Aerospace, and now BAE SYSTEMS Advanced Systems. Current products include IFF, airborne displays, stealth technology, visual guidance systems, and a tornado warning system.

Innovative Vision

Much of BAE SYSTEMS' success can be attributed to its vision and values. The company has one basic goal: to be the benchmark aerospace and defense systems company worldwide. It works toward this goal every day by maximizing the value of its existing business and capabilities, as well as by business growth and

DESPITE ITS SIMPLE APPEARANCE, THE NEUTRODYNE CIRCUIT RECEIVER, INVENTED BY PROFESSOR ALAN HAZELTINE IN 1923, REVOLUTIONIZED THE RADIO INDUSTRY AND WAS THE FOUNDATION FOR ONE OF LONG ISLAND'S MOST WELL-KNOWN AND SUCCESSFUL COMPANIES.

leading the global consolidation of the aerospace and defense systems industry.

In keeping with that mission, the company operates according to five guiding values:
- Customers are its top priority.
- People are the company's greatest strength.
- Performance is the key to winning.
- Partnering is the future.
- Innovation and technology help achieve a competitive edge.

It is this kind of vision that helped BAE SYSTEMS develop the BAE SYSTEMS Virtual University in 1998. By combining its expertise and technology, the company provides its employees with a continuous learning environment. The Virtual University is available to all BAE SYSTEMS employees worldwide. However, the Advanced Systems unit in Greenlawn also offers online training, as well as a year-round curriculum of on-site classes to maintain certification and keep its employees up to date on the latest technology. In March 2000, BAE SYSTEMS joined forces with Boeing, Lockheed Martin, and Raytheon to create Exostar SM, an online B2B exchange for the aerospace and defense industry.

"We are committed to pioneering the latest technologies, and the Web is no different," said Weston. "We're on the cutting edge at BAE SYSTEMS—and we plan to keep it that way by striving higher every day." The Advanced Systems facility in Greenlawn, New York, is proud to play an ever-growing role in reaching that goal, and knows that in the Long Island region, rich with high technology, it will continue the legacy begun by Alan Hazeltine well into the 21st century. ■

IN AN ONGOING EFFORT TO IMPROVE AND STREAM-LINE PRODUCTION, THE GREENLAWN FACILITY IMPLEMENTS LEAN MANUFACTURING TECHNIQUES. PICTURED, THE DIGITAL INTERROGATOR TOOLING SYSTEM IS DEDICATED TO THE VERTICAL MILLING CENTER, REDUCING ERRORS AND INCREASING PRODUCTIVITY.

LONG ISLAND ASSOCIATION

The Long Island Association (LIA) is the region's major vehicle for promoting business growth. One of the world's largest such enterprises, it currently represents more than 5,000 businesses, civic groups, labor unions, not-for-profit organizations, and educational and governmental institutions. But to liken the LIA to a business boosterism organization would be to greatly understate its powerful presence on Long Island.

LIA PRESIDENT MATTHEW T. CROSSON.

Founded in 1926, the LIA has evolved to become the leading voice of business and economic development. Further, the LIA initiates studies into Long Island's growth needs and then, in a collaborative and proactive manner, works to define the steps and solutions needed to meet those needs. An example of the LIA's commanding approach was the establishment of the Long Island Works Coalition in January 1999. Its multifaceted charge included the identification of critical skills needed by Long Island's employers, and the development of the resources which would assure that the region has a sufficiently large workforce in possession of these skills, particularly in the high-tech and other growth sectors. To ponder these issues, the Coalition brought together 100 of the region's top business CEOs along with their human resource officers, 100 school superintendents, and 100 school board presidents during the Island' first-ever Workforce Summit. The goal of putting this powerhouse group under one roof was to have participants examine workforce issues from all sides and from all points of view. Gary W. Wojtas, the LIA's director of communications, explained: "We're action oriented. This is not just to discuss future needs; it's to develop the ways in which we're going to meet those future needs." Noting Long Island's many very talented young people, Wojtas said: "We want them to stay, or if they've received their training elsewhere, to come back to Long Island, to fill job openings here."

Affordable Housing a Priority

But if that's to happen, said LIA President Matthew T. Crosson, there must also be an increase in the availability of affordable housing. So that too is an issue that the LIA has placed its formidable resources behind. According to Crosson "it is wholly unrealistic to believe that we can have an adequate, skilled workforce here unless we, as a community, provide our young people affordable and attractive places to live." To this end, the LIA is working with various levels of government to encourage the building of additional rental units. A particular target is the redevelopment of underutilized industrial and commercial property for housing purposes and the granting of government incentives to encourage builders to incorporate affordable housing into their developments. The push to expand Long Island's supply of low-cost housing options has long been an area of endeavor for the LIA. Indeed, this issue was among the major elements identified by the Long Island Action Plan, a comprehensive six-month initiative begun by the LIA in 1994 in which more than 1,000 of Long Island's most prominent leaders were called upon to reach consensus on a plan of action for Long Island's future economic health. Participants were asked to identify which industries held promise for future economic growth and how Long Island could establish these industries. Its findings became the basis for the Long Island Action Plan, implementation of which continues to the present day. According to Crosson, an encouraging measure of how far the community has come in recent years is that some 85 percent of the 250 items identified in the Long Island Action Plan have either been accomplished in their entirety or have been significantly advanced.

GENERAL COLIN L. POWELL SPEAKS DURING AN LIA ANNUAL MEETING AND LUNCHEON.

GENERAL H. NORMAN SCHWARZKOPF (U.S. ARMY, RETIRED) SPOKE TO MORE THAN 1,100 LIA MEMBERS AND GUESTS DURING A RECENT ANNUAL MEETING.

LIA NETWORKING EVENTS REGULARLY BRING MANY LONG ISLAND BUSINESS PEOPLE TOGETHER.

Beyond housing, some of the other items deliberated by creators of the Long Island Action Plan included boosting world trade, improving infrastructure and transportation, protecting the environment, enhancing tourism, and diversifying the economy into high-tech businesses.

Meeting Members' Needs

While the LIA speaks and acts for the business community as a whole, it also sponsors many programs designed to serve the individual needs of its member businesses. In addition to its many networking events, the organization is proud of bringing to Long Island business people the speakers they most want to hear. General Colin Powell kicked off the launching of the Long Island Works Coalition with a talk about business and education partnerships. During another meeting, LIA members heard General H. Norman Schwarzkopf discuss the nature of leadership. Former President George Bush, New York State Senator Charles Schumer, New York State Attorney General Eliot Spitzer, former First Lady Hillary Clinton, Bill Bradley, Bob and Elizabeth Dole, Tom Brokaw, New York State Governor George Pataki, U.S. Senator Daniel Patrick Moynihan, Tim Russert, and the chairman of NASDAQ, Frank Zarb, have been among the other preeminent speakers who have enlightened and intrigued LIA members.

The membership is also served by the LIA's comprehensive website which now offers virtual networking in which visitors may view and post business opportunities, an Island-wide community calendar of business, social and cultural events, and a daily Long Island stock ticker. Hoping that members will use this site as a portal to all of electronic Long Island, the site offers links to all news and business-related Long Island sites. In addition to this site, the LIA recently created TheSmallBusinessStore.com, designed to meet the many varied needs of small business owners. "The site offers a remarkable range of assistance—from business tools and advice, to savings on goods and services, to answers to questions small business owners might have. And, it is available 24/7/365," Crosson said. ∎

THE LIA ANNUAL GALA HONORS LONG ISLAND'S PHILANTHROPIC LEADERS.

NEWSDAY

*N*ewsday is Long Island's homegrown newspaper, its history intertwined with the growth of America's first suburb, linking the diverse communities from Long Island City in Queens to Nassau's Gold Coast to Montauk Point. At the same time, *Newsday* is consistently ranked as one of the nation's best newspapers and has earned 16 Pulitzer Prizes.

Sixty years after founder and publisher Alicia Patterson threw the printing press switch in Hempstead for *Newsday's* first edition, the paper has grown to become one of the nation's largest newspapers, ranked fifth among metropolitan dailies.

Newsday's reach spans the world with news bureaus in Beijing, Jerusalem, Moscow, Mexico City, and Johannesburg. Its writers have covered wars, genocide, disease, famine, and major political trends throughout the world. The stories have included Pulitzer Prize-winning coverage of ethnic cleansing in Bosnia, friendly fire casualties in the Gulf War, and Africa's Ebola virus outbreak.

Newsday was founded by Alicia Patterson in 1940, just prior to Long Island's extraordinary growth years of the post-World War II era. Riding the waves of the building and baby booms, the newspaper grew as Long Island matured into an independent economic and cultural market. Many *Newsday* articles and editorials defined and spurred that growth.

Guided by Patterson until her death in 1963, *Newsday* began in a former automobile showroom in Hempstead. In 1947, it moved to a plant in Garden City and, in 1979, to its present home in Melville. In 1970, Patterson's heirs sold *Newsday* to Times Mirror Company, owner of the *Los Angeles Times* and the *Baltimore Sun.* In June, 2000,

HOISTING *NEWSDAY*'S "LONG ISLAND: OUR FUTURE" FLAG MARKING THE PAPER'S YEARLONG LOOK AT THE FUTURE OF NASSAU AND SUFFOLK COUNTIES ARE (LEFT TO RIGHT) PUBLISHER RAYMOND A. JANSEN (LEFT) AND MANAGING EDITOR AND VP/CONTENT DEVELOPMENT HOWARD SCHNEIDER.

Times Mirror merged with Tribune Company, publishers of *The Chicago Tribune* and other newspapers, and owners of 22 TV stations and the Chicago Cubs. The combined company is now the nation's third largest newspaper company in terms of total circulation.

NEWSDAY'S EDITORIAL STAFF CELEBRATES NEWS OF THE PAPER'S 16TH PULITZER PRIZE—THIS ONE FOR COVERAGE OF THE CRASH OF TWA FLIGHT 800 OFF THE COAST OF LONG ISLAND.

EACH DAY, 600,000 COPIES OF *NEWSDAY* ARE
PRINTED IN THE STATE-OF-THE-ART PRESSROOM
IN MELVILLE.

The heart and soul of *Newsday*, the news operation,
under the direction of veteran reporter and editor
Anthony Marro, gives readers depth as well as the
broad scope of the news. Its unparalled coverage has
ranged from prize-winning international and national
stories, to top-flight sports stories and features, to local
stories on schools and government. In addition to 16
Pulitzers, *Newsday*'s coverage has earned countless
other prestigious local and national awards.

With these stories, *Newsday* creates an ongoing
dialogue of the critical issues affecting Long Island,
including inequitable property assessments, breast
cancer, and race relations. In-depth investigations have
examined abuses among cops on disability, the failure
of HMOs to notify customers of problem doctors, and
the lack of oversight of day care centers.

President, Publisher and Chief Executive Officer
Raymond A. Jansen works closely with Editorial Page
Editor James Klurfeld and the editorial board in *Newsday*'s
efforts to educate, lead, and stimulate decision makers
and voters. Through these in-depth editorials, *Newsday*
explores the significance of news issues and events to the
everyday lives of its readers, and also points to solutions.

Newsday readers can express their own views in
the paper's Viewpoints section or through letters to the
editor. Reader feedback is encouraged via letter, phone,
fax, e-mail, in person at one of the community forums,
at luncheons or breakfasts that bring readers together
with the paper's editorial and business staffs, or at
regularly sponsored focus groups.

Newsday's commitment to the community is exemplified by the highly interactive Student Briefing Page in
which Chip Tracer, *Newsday*'s comic book cyberjournalist/
superhero, engages young readers in dialogue while

teaching them about history and journalistic ethics.
Newsday also reaches thousands of students through its
Newsday in Education (NIE) program, which serves teachers and students with teacher training and educational
materials. During 1997, NIE was used by 97 percent of
Long Island's school districts. Additionally, students from
many of these districts visit *Newsday* for a first-hand
glimpse of how the paper is produced.

The paper's editorial content reflects the increasingly
diverse communities it covers, and is written and edited
by a staff composed of many ethnic and cultural backgrounds. In 1998, *Newsday* launched *Hoy*, a Spanish-
language newspaper designed to meet the needs of the
burgeoning Hispanic population in the metropolitan
area. *Hoy* and *La Vida Hoy*, its weekend arts and
entertainment edition, provide Hispanic readers not
only with local, state, national, and international news,
but also news from their native countries.

Newsday also reaches out to Long Island through its
Speakers Bureau, which provides non-profit organizations
with expert discussions on topics of interest to their
members. *Newsday* online—Newsday.com—is updated
throughout the day with breaking news, sports, and
features, and also has many interactive features, and
extensive archives from the "Long Island: Our Story",
and "Long Island and Queens: Our Future" series.

Through these and other activities, *Newsday* has
become an integral part of the Long Island community
and maintains its commitment to the improvement of
Long Island's economic and cultural quality of life.

Looking toward the future, *Newsday* continues to
build on its already strong commitment to the kind of
local, national, international, sports, and feature news
coverage that its readers have come to rely on over the
60 years since Alicia Patterson embarked on her remarkable enterprise. In the future, *Newsday* will continue to
be a newspaper that changes with the communities it
serves and provides the people in those communities
with information essential to their daily lives. ∎

MORNING NEWSPAPER DELIVERY BEGINS WITH
BUNDLING IN THE MAILROOM. THE PAPERS ARE
THEN STACKED ON PALLETS FOR LOADING ONTO
NEWSDAY'S DELIVERY TRUCKS.

NORTHROP GRUMMAN

There was a time when Northrop Grumman Corp. was one of the most powerful companies on Long Island. Today you could say it is one of the smartest. The defense contractor—the fourth largest in the country—has successfully reinvented itself in the post-Cold War era through innovative practices and by focusing on what it does best.

While cutbacks in defense spending led to the demise of many contractors, Northrop Grumman remains a major provider of world-class technologies and core competencies to military and commercial markets. The company has become a leader in defense electronics, systems integration, and information technology, with strengths in military aircraft systems and modifications and marine systems.

"There are people who would say that we have downsized. I would say we have rightsized," says Kent Kresa, chairman, president, and CEO of Northrop Grumman. "We tailored our organization to the amount of business available, and we developed our capabilities in new and emerging markets. That approach has helped us remain a major force in government and commercial sectors."

Glory Days

That approach is not surprising coming from the company that built the Apollo Lunar Module. Indeed, Northrop Grumman has a stellar history of leadership and innovation dating back to its first product—a float that enabled airplanes to land in the water. From there, the company built an airplane for the U.S. Navy and a reputation as one of the premier defense contractors in the nation.

The company grew from its humble beginnings in 1929 to the point where it employed 27,000 people on Long Island during the heyday of the Cold War. In fact, one out of every six Long Island families depended on

Northrop Grumman is investing more than $15 million to modernize and improve its facilities in Bethpage, which is the headquarters of the Integrated Systems Sector's Airborne Early Warning and Electronic Warfare Systems business area.

Bethpage-based Northrop Grumman for its income. People liked working for what was then known simply as Grumman. They had a sense of pride that extended beyond Long Island to the nations where Grumman planes were being used to fight for freedom.

When the Cold War ended in the early 1990s, the defense contractor saw programs canceled and was forced to scale back its organization and lay off thousands of workers. By working with the Suffolk County Department of Labor, Northrop Grumman established an extensive cooperative education program to retrain laid-off workers and to place them in new jobs. A booming economy also helped outgoing employees land on their feet. Today the company employs almost 2,000 people here on Long Island.

The dawn of peace proved to be a defining period in Northrop Grumman history. The Grumman Corporation became part of Los Angeles-based Northrop in 1994, forming a new company and expanding operations to Texas, California, and other parts of the country.

Ongoing Strengths

Today, Northrop Grumman comprises the Integrated Systems Sector (ISS), the Electronic Sensors and Systems Sector (ES3), and Logicon, Inc., a wholly-owned subsidiary. ES3, based in Baltimore, Maryland, has about 150 people working in its marine systems operation in Melville.

Herndon, Virginia-headquartered Logicon, a leader in advanced information technologies (IT) systems and services, has a Bohemia-based unit for the commercial IT market called Logicon Commercial Information Services. Logicon, with over 500 employees on Long Island, also provides an on-site IT and support and maintenance services to ISS on the Island.

Engineers in Bethpage are developing advanced systems such as information warfare, command and control, and others to meet the requirements of their U.S. and international customers.

TODAY, MILITARY SYSTEMS SUCH AS AIRBORNE EARLY WARNING OR ELECTRONIC WARFARE UTILIZE TECHNOLOGIES DEVELOPED BY THE COMMERCIAL ELECTRONICS INDUSTRY. NORTHROP GRUMMAN ENGINEERS ARE RENOWNED FOR THEIR ABILITY TO LEVERAGE NEW DEVELOPMENTS SUCH AS IN THE COMMAND AND CONTROL AREA OF THE E-2C HAWKEYE.

ISS, headquartered in Dallas, Texas, is a prime contractor for some key military programs, including the Joint Surveillance Target Attack Radar System and the B-2 Stealth bomber. It produces major portions of the F/A-18E/F strike fighter and is teamed with Lockheed Martin in the Joint Strike Fighter competition. Headquartered in Bethpage is its Airborne Early Warning and Electronic Warfare Systems business unit with about 1,300 employees. They work on two major programs. One is the E-2C Hawkeye airborne early warning and control aircraft. Though built in Florida, its designers and program managers live and work on Long Island.

A similar arrangement involves program management and engineering for the EA-6B Prowler electronic warfare aircraft, also based in Bethpage, and a new, advanced systems group. One of its projects is the Broad Area Maritime Surveillance System. This is a new concept offered by the Bethpage team to the U.S. Navy to lower the cost while improving the capability for this critical mission.

Corporate Values

Northrop Grumman has a commitment to quality, customer satisfaction, leadership, integrity, and its employees. Suppliers are essential members of the Northrop Grumman team. By putting those values into practice, the company has created long-term benefits for shareholders, customers, employees, and suppliers.

The company extends that commitment to quality into the communities in which it operates. Nationwide that translates into support for pre-college education, dropout prevention, child care, housing and the homeless, youth and family counseling, health services, the arts, job training/employment, and Welfare to Work. On Long Island, Northrop Grumman supports a diverse list of charitable, educational, cultural, and healthcare entities, including the Cradle of Aviation Museum, St. Joseph's College, Good Samaritan Hospital Medical Center, and the Boy Scouts.

A group of employees calls themselves the Care Cats, after the cat names given to most of Northrop Grumman's World War II, Korean, and Vietnam era aircraft. They volunteer in a variety of ways—cleaning the yards at non-profit organizations and tutoring high school students.

"Northrop Grumman is a long-time supporter of philanthropic activities in the local community," says Phil Teel, sector vice president for Airborne Early Warning and Electronic Warfare Systems. "Our presence has changed, but our commitment to the people of Long Island is stronger than ever." ∎

IT IS THE SYSTEMS INSIDE THE AIRCRAFT THAT KEEP OUR MILITARY AHEAD OF ANY THREAT. FOR EXAMPLE, THE E-2C HAWKEYE HAS GONE THROUGH FIVE GENERATIONS OF CHANGES, THE LATEST NOW IN TEST WITH THE NAVY. ALL SYSTEM ADVANCES WERE DESIGNED IN BETHPAGE.

TELEPHONICS CORPORATION

One of the world's foremost providers of communications and radar equipment, Farmingdale's Telephonics Corporation was founded in 1933 as a defense contractor that manufactured headsets for military aircraft. More than a decade ago, as the cold war thawed, Telephonics began a broad transition of its core technologies and products. Extensive technology conversion programs in parallel with continued investment in advanced technologies have enabled Telephonics to strategically expand into new markets. From its original defense industry focus, Telephonics has successfully widened its vision to embrace a much broader global, commercial business horizon.

Today, as a subsidiary of the Griffon Corporation (NYSE,GFF), Telephonics offers broad-based, high-tech engineering capabilities that provide integrated information and communications system solutions to both the military and commercial sectors, at home and abroad. The company serves a prestigious customer base that includes such internationally prominent customers as Sikorsky, Boeing, BAE SYSTEMS, Northrop Grumman, Lockheed Martin, Kawasaki, Bombardier, Siemens, TRW, and Eaton.

Telephonics is organized into four operating units: Communications Systems Division, specializing in aircraft intercommunications, mass transit communications, and wireless and audio products; Command Systems Division, specializing in electronic sensors, traffic management systems, maritime surveillance and weather radar, and aerospace electronics; TLSI, a subsidiary of Telephonics, specializing in application-specific integrated circuit products; and Telephonics Wireless, another wholly owned subsidiary, providing wireless infrastructure products for broadband, high-speed, data networks.

With more than 60 years of experience in the design, production, and integration of communications systems and components, Telephonics' Communications Systems Division is the leading supplier of commercial and military interior communication and audio distribution systems, wireless communication products, mass transit communications, passenger entertainment, integrated radio management systems, and audio products. Born out of Telephonics' intercommunication systems experience on USAir Force's C-17 transport aircraft as well as the NASA Space Shuttle and the Presidents airplane, Air Force One, the company has successfully ventured into the transit industry. Through global alliances with major rail car suppliers and transit authorities, Telephonics has worked to develop and integrate communication systems as well as central diagnostics systems, multiplexing, and network control systems for the transit industry.

Among its highly-diversified roster of customers served are NATO, the U.S. Air Force, the U.S. Navy, the

TELEPHONICS EMPLOYEES PARTICIPATING IN 2000 CHASE CORPORATE CHALLENGE.

TELEPHONICS CORPORATE HEADQUARTERS IN FARMINGDALE, NEW YORK.

UK's Navy and Air Force, the New York City Transit Authority, the Long Island Rail Road, Philadelphia's SEPTA, California's CALTRANS, Boston's MBTA, and New Jersey Transit's Hudson/Bergen Light Rail System.

The distinguished origins of Telephonics' Command Systems Division span back to the earliest days of radar, identification friend-or-foe (IFF), and air traffic control (ATC) technology. Long recognized for its high-tech applications in space and defense systems, Command Systems is gaining equal recognition domestically and internationally for a wide array of successful commercial applications. This division's products include maritime patrol, surveillance and weather radar systems including imaging capability; air traffic management systems, command and control systems, microwave landing systems, and related products. Global advances have come primarily through its ATC, IFF and maritime radar technologies. Having pioneered the use of multi-radar fusion processing over 20 years ago, Telephonics is now gaining market share in China and Korea, working with those two nations to develop their air transportation infrastructures. The company's tactical landing systems have been put into use by the air forces of Finland and Sweden, and Telephonics' multimode radar system has become vital to the navies of many countries around the world.

Telephonics' TLSI subsidiary, is a broad-based integrated circuit manufacturer that provides integrated circuit solutions for a wide range of applications. TLSI was established in 1977 to support the company's internal custom integrated circuit needs. In 1981, TLSI expanded to include external customers in industrial, consumer, commercial, and military markets. TLSI provides analog, digital, and mixed signal integrated circuits manufactured in various technologies including CMOS, Bipolar and BiCMOS. Supplying both custom and standard integrated circuits, TLSI has grown into a leading supplier of custom integrated circuits to the automotive, security and telecommunications equipment markets.

Telephonics' new Wireless subsidiary based in Melbourne, Florida is addressing the demand for wireless communication systems to seamlessly move large amounts of data further and faster. The goal of Telephonics Wireless is to provide wireless data infrastructure products that fundamentally increase the speed, capacity and performance of cellular communication networks.

Though its business is global, Telephonics maintains strong ties to Long Island, supporting many local charities. Telephonics' more than 1,000 employees are often found participating in activities that raise funds for community non-profit groups. Telephonics' associations with local colleges such as Dowling, SUNY-Stony Brook, SUNY-Old Westbury, New York Institute of Technology, and Polytechnic Institute of New York have helped students and faculty alike gain vital workplace experience and have also served to introduce Telephonics to some of the region's brightest young engineers.

With a solid business footing in traditional defense markets and an expanding presence in commercial and international markets, Telephonics is well positioned to provide advanced technology with a global reach. ■

TILLES COMPANIES

From the dawn of the space age to today's tech-oriented new economy, the Tilles Companies have been in the vanguard of developing and managing Long Island's finest office buildings—facilities which are designed to meet tenants' business, technological, and aesthetic needs. With more than 4 million square feet of office space in its portfolio, Tilles Companies is Long Island's own premier builder of office properties, and is a major force in the Island's business and commercial real estate sector. The Tilles brand on a building is widely respected as the mark of first class, technologically advanced office development which meets the complex needs of tenants while also honoring the company's commitment to the environment.

Reflective of Tilles Companies' past is the Tilles-built Grumman facility in Bethpage where the lunar module that brought Americans to the moon was developed. Demonstrating its ability to grow with the times, the company's newest project is the development of Expressway Corporate Plaza in Melville, a property popularly known as the Pumpkin Farm. The two-building, 690,000-square-foot complex includes a day care center, restaurant, a teleconferencing facility, a fitness center, and other tenant amenities all within the context of a state-of-the-art, fiber optic, high-speed connectivity corporate environment.

ROGER (LEFT) AND PETER (RIGHT) TILLES, THE THIRD GENERATION OF LEADERSHIP AT TILLES COMPANIES, RANK HIGH AMONG THE ISLAND'S POWER BROKERS IN THE COMMERCIAL REAL ESTATE AND PHILANTHROPIC COMMUNITIES.

Tilles Companies' recently completed Gateways 88 in Woodbury is Nassau County's first spec-built office building in 10 years. Addressing the technological needs of today's tenants, Gateways 88 boasts a back-up generator along with specialized heating, ventilation, and air conditioning systems customized for computer environments.

Gateways 88 adjoins Nassau Crossways International Plaza, creating a one-square mile corporate park immediately adjacent to major parkways. Although once strictly a research and development center, Crossways has evolved over the years to become a first-rate office park. Created almost 40 years ago by Gilbert Tilles, the second generation of his family in the commercial building business, this complex was revolutionary for its time. Where other builders of the era created industrial parks surrounded by a sea of asphalt, Tilles Companies created a planned complex which preserved open space and the natural environment of trees, shrubs, and grass. The buildings of Nassau Crossways International Plaza are surrounded with plantings, a pond, and a nesting ground for migratory birds. Tilles Companies' officials recognized that tenants would appreciate the calming effects of a naturalistic environment of a park-like setting. Honoring the recreational needs of its tenants and the surrounding community, the company also donated adjacent property to the Town of Oyster Bay for construction of a 40.5 acre park and recreational center.

AN AERIAL VIEW OF TILLES COMPANIES' NASSAU CROSSWAYS INTERNATIONAL PLAZA REVEALS ITS CONVENIENCE TO THE REGION'S MAJOR TRAFFIC ARTERIES. THE LONG ISLAND EXPRESSWAY AND JERICHO TURNPIKE AFFORD SWIFT EAST-WEST ACCESS, AND THE SEAFORD OYSTER BAY EXPRESSWAY, AT THE PROPERTY'S WESTERN EDGE, ALLOWS IMMEDIATE NORTH-SOUTH ACCESS.

THE NEWEST ENTRY IN TILLES COMPANIES' PORTFOLIO OF CLASS A PROPERTIES IS 88 FROEHLICH FARM BOULEVARD. BUILT ON SPEC, IT WAS FULLY OCCUPIED UPON ITS OPENING THIS YEAR.

Residents of the Woodbury community, in what was likely the first such outreach effort by a Long Island developer, actually had a voice in what this new corporate park would be. Judy Jacobs, then a civic activist and now the presiding officer of the Nassau County Legislature, recalled that she and her fellow activitists realized quickly that they were dealing with a very different kind of developer. She said that officials of Tilles Companies "really have the ability to make a community feel that they are part of a project; they welcome input and give residents the opportunity to have an impact on what affects them."

Future growth factored in

Nassau Crossways International Plaza was able to evolve through the past three decades because of its builder's foresight in providing for enough space, parking facilities, and set backs to allow the buildings to be retrofitted to serve succeeding generations of businesses. Proactive rather than reactive, the company's commitment to continually upgrading its properties has meant that even the oldest buildings in the Tilles portfolio offer tenants the technological advances and energy efficiency featured in its newer buildings.

Because of Tilles Companies' enormous portfolio of properties on Long Island, the company has the flexibility to meet tenants' changing space requirements within the Tilles family of office buildings.

Given Tilles Companies' record of building fine properties and then staying with their projects, many of the nation's most visible corporations have been long-term

Tilles tenants. This loyalty stems from the commitment that Tilles Companies has to building relationships. Intrinsic to the way the Tilles organization does business is that each tenant, no matter how large or small, is treated as though it is the sole tenant with every effort made to meet that business' needs and create a special relationship.

Now in its third generation of leadership, Tilles Companies is headed by brothers Peter and Roger Tilles. They have continued and advanced upon the company's traditional concern for the quality of its building projects—for corporate and industrial development which protects the environment, enhances the surroundings, and also serves to strengthen the regional economy.

That commitment to their tenants is extended to the Long Island community in which the Tilles family, their employees, and their tenants live. Individually, and through their business, the members of the Tilles family have been among Long Island's most prominent supporters and benefactors of the cultural, educational, environmental, healthcare, and religious communities.

Through the leading-edge buildings they offer to Long Island's businesses, through the respect for the environment which is central to each project, and through their numerous philanthropic initiatives, Tilles Companies and its principals have come to exemplify a corporate consciousness working at many levels to create and maintain Long Island's high quality of life. ■

ON THE DRAWING BOARDS AT TILLES COMPANIES IS EXPRESSWAY CORPORATE PLAZA. SLATED FOR OCCUPANCY DURING 2002, THIS JEWEL IN THE CROWN OF THE TILLES PORTFOLIO IS RISING ON THE FAMED "PUMPKIN FARM" PROPERTY IN MELVILLE.

AEROFLEX INCORPORATED

Just before Charles A. Lindberg flew the Spirit of St. Louis out of Mitchell Field on his famous nonstop, solo transatlantic flight in 1927, a man named George Margolin made sure that the engine was working properly. The Russian immigrant went on to launch Aeroflex Incorporated in 1937, a company that played a major role in the development of Long Island's technology industry.

THIN FILM ADVANCED INTERCONNECTS FOR
ELECTRO-PHOTONIC CIRCUITS.

"Margolin was a well-trained and gifted mechanic, who was known for his skill and his use of the latest techniques. That's why Mr. Lindberg chose him to give the Spirit of St. Louis a final check before takeoff," said Michael Gorin, Aeroflex' president and chief financial officer. "Today, we continue that tradition of leading-edge technology with our microelectronics, and test and measurement products."

From its worldwide headquarters in Plainview, Aeroflex oversees an international company that designs, develops, and produces state-of-the-art microelectronic module, integrated circuit, interconnect, and testing solutions used in broadband communication applications.

The Latest and Greatest

Aeroflex has a long tradition of leveraging the power of the latest technology. In the early 21st Century that happens to be broadband and wireless communications as exemplified by fiber optic networks and high speed testing of chips and devices for mobile systems, with data expected to exceed voice traffic early in the next decade. Companies like Aeroflex, whose mission is to develop and market products that support and enhance bandwidth, speed, and mobility for global communications systems, will drive this growth.

Through its various subsidiaries, Aeroflex produces two main types of products: microelectronics and test and measurement instruments and systems. While not the vocabulary of casual conversation, these terms are used to describe components found in everything from mobile phones to Internet-enabled computers.

Aeroflex microelectronics products include interconnect substrates, assemblies, and modules, for high bit-rate fiber optic networks as well as multi-chip modules for satellite communications, commercial avionics, and telecom markets. Some are used in modern wireless, communications satellite, video, and microwave systems, and some provide increased power handling, improved thermal management, and miniaturization of high frequency electronic and electro-optic devices. Aeroflex designs and manufactures its microelectronics products using the technological expertise of three subsidiaries: Aeroflex Circuit Technology in Plainview, N.Y.; Aeroflex MIC Technology Corp. in North Andover, Massachusetts, Pearl River, N.Y., and Richardson, Texas; and Aeroflex UTMC Microelectronic Systems in Colorado Springs, Colorado.

Test, measurement, and other electronics—including frequency synthesizers, electronic test systems, and specialized modules—are designed for fiber optic systems, high-speed automated testing of communications chips, satellite payload testing, and automated wireless component and system testing. Those products come out of Aeroflex Comstron in Plainview, N.Y., Aeroflex Motion Control Systems in Farmingdale, N.Y., Aeroflex Lintek Corp. in Powell, Ohio; and Europtest S.A. in Elancourt, France.

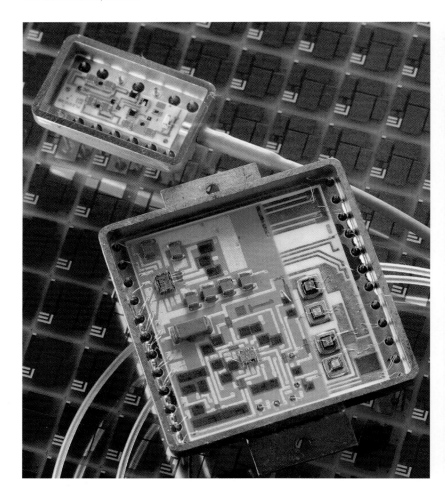

FIBER OPTIC COMPONENTS.

A Thriving Business

Aeroflex has its origins and business headquarters on Long Island, but the company is global in scope. That's why you'll find Aeroflex subsidiaries throughout the United States and in Elancourt, France. It is a company listed on the Nasdaq Stock Market under the symbol ARXX. The company's technological and geographic reach is substantial and it has been achieved through a combination of internal growth and strategic acquisitions.

"Acquisitions have been an important part of our growth strategy," said Gorin. "That approach has given us the ability to build a company that serves every aspect of broadband communications, from fiber optics to wireless and satellite cable TV. We've filled our gaps in technology through acquisitions. That's allowed us to grow much more quickly than we could have solely through in-house development."

That strategy has apparently paid off in more than technology development. In 2000, Aeroflex posted $186 million in sales, a 26 percent five year compounded growth rate. Microelectronics, the firm's top business, was responsible for $110.3 million of those sales, a 40 percent five year growth rate. Operating profits rose to $22.7 million, while net income hit $14.4 million.

Some of that growth can be attributed to the acquisition in 1999 of UTMC Microelectronic Systems. That

FIBER OPTIC COMPONENTS.

brought UTMC's fabless silicon semiconductor capabilities into the Aeroflex fold and also gave Aeroflex the ability to provide total solutions by adding its substrate and packaging technologies to UTMC's silicon chip capabilities.

This breadth of capabilities appeals to pretty big names in the global broadband communications market such as Lucent Technologies, Motorola, Nortel, JDS Uniphase, and Alcatel, as well as leaders in state-of-the-art automatic test equipment and manufacturers of advanced systems such as Hughes Space and Communications, Teradyne, and Lockheed Martin.

Riding the Wave

If the growth in the broadband market is any indication, the future is bright for Aeroflex. Gorin says the company plans to ride the broadband wave in whichever direction it goes. And in the process, it will contribute to the Long Island economy through the building of new facilities and the hiring of additional staff to help the company maintain its impressive level of growth.

"We've always been in the technology business, even before Long Island was a technology center," said Gorin. "Our history is in the defense market, but wherever the broadband market goes our technology will take us there." ■

FIBER OPTIC NETWORK CLOCK/DATA RECOVERY MODULE.

HOFSTRA UNIVERSITY

During its short 66-year history, Hofstra University has risen in the ranks from a primarily-commuter college to an international liberal arts university with seven schools of study, 32 accreditations, a student body of more than 13,000, and a resident population of more than 4,000. Hofstra is highly regarded as one of the busiest and most inventive, cultural and academic centers in New York. The university's current student/ faculty ratio of 13:1 offers students the opportunity to study in a small college environment. Yet, the campus boasts a level of resources equal to or greater than any large university might offer.

There are approximately 130 buildings located on Hofstra University's 240-acre campus, including classroom buildings, computer laboratories, residence halls, recreation facilities, an indoor olympic-size swimming pool, a 15,000-seat stadium, and a 5,000-seat indoor sports arena. The campus is 100 percent accessible to people with physical disabilities.

Half of Hofstra's 8,000 full-time undergraduates live on campus in an exciting variety of modern, comfortable, and secure residence facilities situated throughout the north campus. Both resident and commuter students have access to all the academic and recreation facilities that Hofstra offers. There is a tremendous sense of community on campus, due to a full schedule of weekday, weekend, and evening events.

The north campus features three sports complexes. The new Hofstra Arena is host to NCAA Division I men's and women's basketball, wrestling, and volleyball, as well as concerts, trade shows, and conventions. The Physical Fitness Center, adjacent to the arena, is home to many intramural sports and Hofstra's olympic-size swimming pool. Nearby, the Recreation Center, includes an indoor track, weight room, playing courts, and exercise rooms available seven days a week to all members of the University community.

HOFSTRA STUDENTS STUDY ELECTRONIC JOURNALISM AND BROADCASTING WITH STATE-OF-THE-ART EQUIPMENT AT GEORGE G. DEMPSTER HALL. PHOTO BY BRIAN BALLWEG.

Hofstra USA, the student night club, is host to capacity crowds who enjoy an extensive schedule of concerts, parties, and other student-oriented activities. An adjacent deli and dining area have made the Hofstra USA complex into a full-service dining and entertainment complex.

The Hofstra Student Center joins Hofstra's north and south campus. The Student Center includes the largest of Hofstra's 12 dining facilities. While in the Student Center, students can enjoy a full-course meal, hold student organization meetings, grab a slice of pizza, visit the multi-level Hofstra bookstore, or watch a first-run movie.

Walking through the Hofstra Unispan, an enclosed climate-controlled walkway crossing over Hempstead Turnpike, students prepare to enter the academic community of the university. The 1.6-million volume Joan and Donald E. Axinn Library, located at the south end of the Unispan, is one of the largest and most utilized libraries in the nation. The open stacks of the fully-automated Hofstra Library are supplemented by the latest in computer resources, allowing students full access to all of the library's volumes and services.

Academic highlights on the south campus include George G. Dempster Hall, home for Hofstra's School of Communication and the studios of the WRHU-FM radio station. Dempster Hall includes three well-equipped television studios, a computer laboratory, control rooms, editing suites, and other equipment that places this facility among the largest and most up-to-date of such facilities in the east.

THE 1.6 MILLION VOLUME JOAN AND DONALD E. AXINN LIBRARY AT HOFSTRA IS ONE OF THE MOST UTILIZED LIBRARIES IN THE NATION. PHOTO BY JOHN GIAMUNDO.

Hofstra's newest classroom buildings are the
Chemistry/Physics Building and C.V. Starr Hall. The
Chemistry/Physics Building boasts state-of-the-art laboratories and an observatory on the roof. C.V. Starr Hall
is a technology building that will primarily be used for
business classes. Every seat in every classroom in the
building will allow students to plug into the Hofstra
Network and the Internet.

Many across the nation who may not be familiar
with Hofstra's academic programs know about the university because of its Presidential Conference Series,
which began in 1982. The series, which has won international recognition, has featured scholarly seminars on
the administrations of most of the nation's presidents
since Franklin D. Roosevelt. The Hofstra Cultural Center
offers more than 500 lectures, conferences, plays, and
concerts every academic year.

Additionally, Hofstra's Department of Music and
Department of Drama and Dance offer a fantastic array
of concerts, plays, and musicals, including the annual
Shakespeare Festival. Performing Arts at Hofstra will get
a boost in the coming years when a new Performing
Arts Center opens. The new center will feature studios,
a theater, and art galleries.

Hofstra students enjoy the many benefits of small
classes (average 24 students to a class). Each professor
has an individual computer-equipped office, aiding his or
her ability to work with students. Many faculty members

are leaders in their fields who have authored books,
spearheaded innovative research, and/or served as
experts in the media.

An in-person visit is a must for those haven't yet met
the Hofstra of the new millennium. From the student ath-
lete competing in the newly-renovated Hofstra Arena, to
a Fine Arts class exploring the galleries of the nationally-
accredited Hofstra Museum, from the lectern of a Hofstra
professor inspiring her class, to an aspiring journalist
learning the basics of electronic journalism in Dempster
Hall—Hofstra University is an example of the best that
American higher education has to offer today. ∎

LONG ISLAND MacARTHUR AIRPORT

Long Island MacArthur Airport (LIMA) has evolved from a small, box-like terminal into a thriving, state-of-the-art, modern regional airport that serves more than 1 million passengers on an annual basis. However, LIMA didn't achieve its star status overnight, rather, it took careful planning and vision to create one of the most efficient regional airports in the country, used by both business and leisure passengers traveling to and from virtually every city in the United States.

The airport, which opened in 1942, is located in the hamlet of Ronkonkoma off Veteran's Memorial Highway, about 40 miles east of New York City. Situated on approximately 1,300 acres of land, LIMA is less than two miles away from the Long Island Rail Road Station (LIRR) in Ronkonkoma. It is centrally located between Sunrise Highway and the Long Island Expressway, and offers Long Island travelers a viable and convenient alternative to LaGuardia and JFK Airports. However, people have been known to come from as far away as Connecticut to take advantage of low fares and uncongested accessibility. MacArthur accommodates approximately 130 commercial flights a day on its four runways, two of which are lighted, and one of which is both lighted and equipped with an instrument landing system.

MacArthur's prime location along the Veteran's Memorial Highway industrial and business corridor has

MacArthur Airport, circa 1942. Known as the Islip Airport, it was developed by the Federal Civil Aeronautics Administration at the request of then-Supervisor Charles Duryea.

attracted several renowned companies to the area, including Nortel Networks, Symbol Technologies, Twin Labs, Atkins Nutritional, and Computer Associates World Headquarters. In fact, officials from Computer Associates have noted that the presence of the airport has been key in their ability to do business effectively and efficiently.

LONG ISLAND MacARTHUR AIRPORT AT PRESENT. PHOTO COMPLIMENTS OF EAGLE EYE AIR PHOTO.

THE BUSINESS AND INDUSTRIAL CORRIDOR AROUND
MACARTHUR AIRPORT IS ONE OF THE FASTEST
GROWING AREAS ON LONG ISLAND. MANY NATIONALLY
BASED CORPORATIONS, SUCH AS TELLABS, SHOWN
HERE IN THEIR NEW $60 MILLION FACILITY LOCATED
ADJACENT TO AIRPORT GROUNDS, HAVE CHOSEN TO
LOCATE THERE. PHOTO BY GREG HANCOCK.

Islip Town's Economic Development Director
William Mannix agreed, pointing out that he often cites
MacArthur's benefits when meeting with companies
intending to locate in the town. He notes that LIMA
has most certainly been a magnet for industrial and
economic growth. "In fact, several companies have
solidified their decision to locate or expand in Islip
because of the airport," said Mannix.

Another business advantage of MacArthur Airport is
the Foreign Trade Zone (FTZ), conveniently located just
next door. An FTZ is a site where foreign and domestic
merchandise is generally considered to be in international
commerce. Merchandise entering this enclave does not
need a formal U.S. Customs entry and isn't charged
Customs duties or government excise taxes until it leaves
an FTZ for sale in the domestic market. There are no
quota restrictions or limitations on goods housed in the
FTZ and the FTZ Authority is a tax-exempt body.

The FTZ adjacent to MacArthur Airport comprises
approximately 435,000 square feet of office, warehouse,
and industrial space on 52 acres of land. Here, merchandise may be stored, repaired, salvaged, manipulated,
mixed, assembled, repackaged, or destroyed, and no
duties are paid on goods that are re-exported directly
from the FTZ. Additionally, occupancy costs are included
in a single monthly rental fee, so businesses may
optimize their earnings.

While MacArthur Airport has historically been a
convenient option for travelers, September 1999 saw the
beginning of a new era, for it marked the grand opening
of an entirely renovated passenger terminal. The $13
million renovations included the addition of four baggage
carousels, new ticketing counters, the addition of 1400
parking spaces and brand-new bathroom facilities. All
of this was done on time and under budget, without
the use of town tax dollars.

Since the renovations, a number of air
carriers with service to virtually every city in
the United States have added their presence
to MacArthur, including Southwest Airlines,
the popular no-frills air carrier that offers
discount fares. Other airlines offer travel
options that include domestic flights, as
well as connections for international travel,
and MacArthur's popularity with both the
business and leisure traveler is reflected in
passenger numbers which have soared to
new heights. In 2000, the airport saw more
than two million passengers.

"Our goal was to create the most
efficient, modern regional airport that we
could without burdening the taxpayers," said Islip Town
Supervisor Pete McGowan. "Today, that goal is a reality,
and virtually every city in the country is served out of
MacArthur Airport."

When arriving at LIMA, passengers may park in the
hourly, daily, long-term, or economy lot, where a shuttle
bus awaits to take them to the main terminal. There is
also an exclusive parking lot where Islip Town residents
with a permit may park free of charge. For added convenience, a private jitney delivers travelers to and from
the LIRR station to the airport for a nominal charge.

Upon entering the terminal, travelers check in at the
expanded ticketing area and then have the opportunity
to visit the recently refurbished gift shop before going
to their gate. The airport also has a snack shop and
restaurant on premises.

However, as prosperous as MacArthur Airport may
become, Supervisor McGowan remains adamant in his
belief that, as a municipally owned and operated airport,
LIMA will retain its hometown flavor. ∎

WITH THE MODERNIZATION OF THE AIRPORT TERMI-
NAL AND THE ADDITION OF POPULAR NO-FRILLS AIR
CARRIER SOUTHWEST AIRLINES, ACTIVITY HAS
CLIMBED MORE THAN ONE MILLION PASSENGERS
ANNUALLY. PHOTO BY GREG HANCOCK.

LONG BEACH MEDICAL CENTER

From routine family health care, to emergency services and extensive rehabilitation facilities, to today's advanced medical procedures, Long Beach Medical Center (LBMC) has been a critical resource for the island communities of Long Beach, Lido Beach, Atlantic Beach, Island Park, and Point Lookout for almost eight decades.

The hospital's roots lay in the founding of a beachside emergency first aid station in 1922. Within five years, services had expanded and the hospital began operations at its present site. Today, LBMC is a 203-bed community hospital that is particularly noted for its extensive geriatric and rehabilitative services. Many of these services for older people are offered within the 200-bed Komanoff Center for Geriatric and Rehabilitative Medicine, a facility that in addition to subacute care and rehabilitation is a resource for chronic disease management and long-term skilled care.

While it fills the region's routine health care needs, LBMC is additionally a center for the most advanced medical procedures, assuring community residents that they will have access to the latest cutting edge treatment right at their hometown hospital. Through a collaborative venture with the Center for Molecular Medicine, LBMC now offers a revolutionary treatment for lethal brain tumors. The LBMC staff has also incorporated EECP, or enhanced external counterpulsation, an innovative technique that is being used to reduce or even eliminate the symptoms of angina without the pain or lengthy recovery of invasive surgical procedures.

LBMC's rehabilitation services include a 15-bed inpatient unit and outpatient therapy services. The LBMC Home Health Agency, established in 1982,

FOUNDED IN 1922 AS A BEACHSIDE FIRST AID STATION, TODAY'S MEDICAL CENTER INCLUDES A 203-BED COMMUNITY TEACHING HOSPITAL, A 200-BED SKILLED NURSING FACILITY, A HOME HEALTH AGENCY, AND NUMEROUS OUTPATIENT PROGRAMS.

works in concert with physicians to bring home-based nursing, rehabilitation, and other supportive services to community residents.

Primary and specialty medical care for people of limited financial resources is provided at LBMC's Family Care Center which is staffed by specialists in family practice, pediatrics, obstetrics, gynecology, cardiology, general surgery, and a full range of other medical specialties. LBMC's behavioral health services include a 25-bed inpatient psychiatric unit, inpatient medical detoxification, and outpatient services for the treatment of alcoholism, substance abuse, and mental health problems.

LBMC's commitment to community outreach is reflected in the hospital's numerous health screenings, support groups, and education programs which are offered throughout the year to educate the community about important health issues, and to provide screening for such conditions as alcoholism, diabetes, and depression. Smoking cessation and weight loss are among the programs included in LBMC's array of outreach activities.

From its humble beginnings, today's Long Beach Medical Center has evolved into a sophisticated community hospital with teaching affiliations with the New York College of Osteopathic Medicine and the New York College of Podiatric Medicine. Yet, it has never strayed from its mission of healing and its commitment to cater to the individual needs of its patients and its community. ■

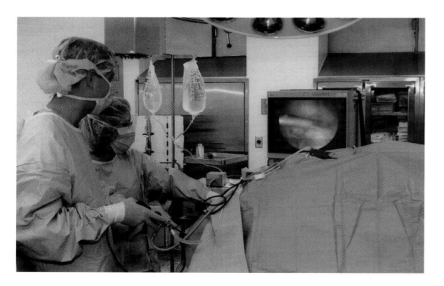

ORTHOPAEDIC SURGEON, ERIC FREEMAN, M.D., PERFORMS ARTHROSCOPIC SURGERY ON THE ANTERIOR CRUCIATE LIGAMENT OF THE KNEE. WITH FELLOWSHIP TRAINING IN ARTHROSCOPY, DR. FREEMAN IS ABLE TO PROVIDE STATE-OF-THE-ART CARE TO COMMUNITY RESIDENTS RIGHT IN THEIR HOMETOWN HOSPITAL.

SULZER METCO (US), INC.

Long before today's high-tech start-ups began setting up shop in garages across the United States, the predecessor of Westbury, N.Y.-based Sulzer Metco was operating out of a rented garage in Long Island City, N.Y. Though not as well known as Grumman, Hewlett-Packard, Apple Computer, and other celebrated garage alumni, Sulzer Metco is today a global leader in thermal spray coating services, materials, equipment, and automated coating systems.

Sulzer Metco offers coating solutions for thousands of different surfaces—from jet engines and ship hulls to bridges, gas turbines, automotive engine components, and playground equipment. The company makes its thermal spray coatings by heating powder or wire feedstock into a molten state. A stream of gas or compressed air propels that material onto a surface. The result is a metallic, ceramic, plastic, or combination surface that can be used to protect surfaces from wear and corrosion, restore dimensionality, maintain precise clearances, and modify thermal and electrical properties. Coatings can extend product life, increase performance, and reduce production and maintenance costs.

"Sulzer Metco has built a long history of providing our customers with unique solutions and high quality products," says Mario Kyd, CEO of Sulzer Metco. "We take that responsibility seriously. That's why we develop customized solutions and reinvest continuously in research and development."

SULZER METCO'S U.S. HEADQUARTERS ARE LOCATED IN A 160,000-SQUARE-FOOT FACILITY IN WESTBURY.

Innovative Beginnings

The Sulzer Metco tradition of excellence dates back to the company's earliest days. In 1933, Rea A. Axline founded Metallizing Engineering Corp. in a Jersey City, N.J., warehouse. In 1938, he and his five-man crew introduced their first wire spray gun and a selection of coating materials. By the 1960s, the company—now known simply as Metco—had developed such innovative thermal spray products as bonding wire, a powder spray gun, and one-step, self-bonding powders.

In 1971, Axline sold Metco to Perkin-Elmer for $65 million. In 1994, Metco was acquired by Sulzer Corp. The Swiss company promised to remain on Long Island, based on the skill of its workforce and its strategic location.

Coating the World

Today, Sulzer Metco, The Coatings Company, has a client list that includes General Electric, Boeing, Caterpillar, Fiat, Ford, Motorola, Rolls-Royce, Pratt & Whitney, and Westinghouse. Corporate headquarters are in Wohlen, Switzerland, with operations in Europe, Asia/Pacific, and the Americas. U.S. headquarters remain in Westbury, where approximately 250 employees work in the 160,000-square-foot production facility. Another 40 work in the company's 60,000-square-foot powder and wire manufacturing facility in Hicksville.

"People are our most important asset," says Jane Debbrecht, president of Sulzer Metco (US) Inc. "They are the ones who continuously research better ways to coat the surfaces of the 21st century. In the new millennium, we will continue to focus on providing our customers with innovative, value-added solutions." ∎

TO IMPROVE ABRASION RESISTANCE, TURBINE BLADES DESTINED FOR HYDRO-ELECTRIC POWER-GENERATING PLANTS ARE SPRAYED WITH A CARBIDE COATING APPLIED WITH SULZER METCO'S DIAMOND JET HIGH VELOCITY OXY-FUEL PROCESS.

ADP INVESTOR COMMUNICATION SERVICES

When most people think of ADP, their paycheck comes to mind. But Automatic Data Processing, Inc., provides far more than payroll services. The company's business includes brokerage services, dealer services, and insurance claims services.

ADP Investor Communication Services (ICS), part of the Brokerage Services division, is based in Edgewood. This division is one of the most profitable and fastest-growing members of the ADP family. It is the largest processor and provider of shareholder communication services, processing more than 700 million mailings, tabulating over 400 million shareholder ballots, and printing more than 700 million pages of statements, confirms, dividend checks and daily trade activity for 35 major brokerage firms in 2000 alone.

ICS also prints such shareholder communications as 10Ks, 10Qs, notice of proxy statements, prospectuses, and various marketing materials. A firm commitment to cutting-edge technology has enabled ICS to also provide Internet-based services, such as online proxy voting and the online delivery of investor communications materials.

"The Internet has enabled ICS to provide our customers with fast, streamlined, and cost-effective delivery of investor relations materials," said Richard J. Daly, president of ICS. "We combine those technical capabilities with outstanding customer service—a true value-add for the client."

ICS, which employs more than 2,000 people on Long Island during the industry's busy seasons, is one of ADP's most successful divisions. Clients include more than 800 brokerage firms and banks, over 450 mutual fund families, and more than 14,000 public corporations. The company attributes much of this success to its three-pronged approach to business. Start by producing the best products and services; then nurture and reward your associates. The two converge into a division that provides world-class service to clients and a strong revenue base for ADP.

ADP's COMMITMENT TO WORLD CLASS SERVICE FOCUSES ON ACHIEVING THE HIGHEST LEVELS OF ASSOCIATE AND CLIENT SATISFACTION.

Attracting, motivating, empowering, and retaining outstanding associates is paramount to ICS. That's why the company provides challenging opportunities, internal advancement based on merit, competitive compensation and benefits, and personal training and development. The atmosphere is fast-paced and demanding, yet flexible and family friendly.

"We know that our most important asset—and the one that touches our customers most closely—is our associates," said Daly. "That's why we provide them with one of the best places to work on Long Island. At the same time, we insist that they treat every client contact for what it is: an opportunity to present ICS in the best light possible."

ICS also serves the community through corporate sponsorship and employee involvement in local causes and events. Outreach activities include food drives, blood drives, the Walk to Cure Diabetes, the American Heart Walk, United Way, and Toys for Tots.

"Long Island has been good to ADP and ICS," Daly said. "We are only too happy to give something back." ∎

ADP INVESTOR COMMUNICATION SERVICES' FACILITY, LOCATED IN EDGEWOOD, LONG ISLAND, IS 430,000 SQUARE FEET.

PHOTO BY DEBORAH ROSS, BRUCE BENNETT STUDIOS.

CHAPTER SIX
1945 TO 1959

ROOSEVELT FIELD MALL WAS THE LARGEST MALL IN THE WORLD AT THE
TIME OF ITS CONSTRUCTION IN 1956, AND TODAY REMAINS A NATIONAL
LEADER. IT WAS DESIGNED BY FAMED ARCHITECT I.M. PEI.
PHOTO BY ROB AMATO, BRUCE BENNETT STUDIOS.

The national boom at end of World War II included Long Island. Soon, whatever was left of small family farms and of real, old-fashioned small-town life was to fade almost into oblivion. Over the next decades Long Island would become a stand-alone metropolis, stepping out of the shadow of New York City.

Former city-dwellers returned from service with a taste for a bit of space and a lawn. Many of them looked east to Long Island. The problem was, there wasn't enough housing to fill a post-war need fueled by housing and education programs put into place by a grateful federal government. But, enterprising Long Islanders rushed to meet those needs.

Fortune Magazine said in 1946, "This is a dream era, this is what everyone was waiting through the blackouts for. The Great American Boom is on."

Between 1940 and 1950, Nassau County's population grew by 266,017 people to 672,765. Suffolk grew by 78,774 people to 276,129 by 1950. In that same period, the value of the average home in Nassau County went from $5,807 to $12,914. Suffolk's average was less: $3,506 in 1940 and $9,228 in 1950. Most people owned their own homes. Nassau County renters in 1940 paid an average of $37.21 per month. In Suffolk, the average was $24.10 monthly. In 1950, rents rose to an average of $56.57 in Nassau; $42.61 in Suffolk.

STONY BROOK PHILANTHROPIST WARD MELVILLE HAD A LASTING IMPACT ON THE THREE VILLAGE AREA OF SUFFOLK COUNTY. LONG A SUMMER RESIDENT OF STONY BROOK, HE DECIDED TO CARVE OUT A NEW VILLAGE NEAR ITS HARBOR. AFTER CONSULTING WITH AN ARCHITECT AND DRAWING UP PLANS, HE UNVEILED HIS CONCEPT AT A MEETING OF BUSINESS OWNERS AND RESIDENTS AT THE THREE VILLAGE INN IN 1939. IN THOSE DAYS, HIS IDEA WAS REVOLUTIONARY—A PLANNED COMMUNITY WITH SEPARATE BUSINESS AND RESIDENTIAL AREAS. BUILDINGS WERE BOUGHT AND, SOMETIMES, RELOCATED TO CREATE THE TWO-ACRE GREEN OVERLOOKING THE HARBOR. THE PROJECT WAS COMPLETED IN 1941. LATER ON, MELVILLE CALLED IT "A LIVING WILLIAMSBURG," A COMMUNITY FEATURING MODERN STORES, A MUSEUM, HOMES, AND A COLLEGE. HE DONATED THE LAND FOR WHAT LATER BECAME THE STATE UNIVERSITY AT STONY BROOK, ENVISIONING A SMALL, LIBERAL ARTS INSTITUTION AKIN TO WILLIAMSBURG'S WILLIAM AND MARY COLLEGE. MELVILLE WAS DEEPLY INVOLVED IN THE DEVELOPMENT AND HISTORIC PRESERVATION OF THE ENTIRE AREA. FOR EXAMPLE, THE COMMUNITY'S PUBLIC SCHOOLS ARE ALL BUILT IN THE FEDERALIST STYLE HE ADOPTED FOR THE VILLAGE GREEN. THE STONY BROOK POST OFFICE FEATURES A CARVED WOODEN EAGLE ABOVE THE ENTRANCE. IT HAS A 20-FOOT WING SPAN, AND ON THE HOUR BETWEEN 8 A.M. AND 8 P.M. IT FLAPS ITS WINGS. IT WAS THE FOCAL POINT OF THE COMMUNITY WHEN MELVILLE'S PROJECT WAS COMPLETED. THE POST OFFICE IS THE BUILDING WITH COLUMNS AND A CUPOLA ON THE RIGHT. PICTURED AT TOP, PHILANTHROPIST WARD MELVILLE STANDS ON THE GREEN IN STONY BROOK VILLAGE CA. 1961. PHOTOS COURTESY WARD MELVILLE HERITAGE FUND.

THE QUIET HOMES AND OPEN SPACES IN AND AROUND STONY BROOK MAKE IT SOMEWHAT DIFFICULT TO
BELIEVE THAT THIS TOWN AND ITS UNIVERSITY ARE ON THE FOREFRONT OF RESEARCHING AND DEVELOPING
THE TECHNOLOGIES OF TOMORROW. PHOTO BY DEBBIE ROSS, BRUCE BENNETT STUDIOS.

In 1941, a brick veneer house on a 60-by-100-foot lot in Franklin Square sold for $3,900. By the end of the war, however, even those willing to pay more could not find housing. It just wasn't available.

To the rescue came Levitt & Sons, builders of single-family homes who a sold their first home for $14,200 in 1929 and sold two hundred more in their Strathmore development in Manhasset. The Levitts attracted upper middle-class families to enclaves on the north shore and in Westchester County.

Following the war, family patriarch Abraham, sons William J., the company's president, and Alfred, its architect, had a new idea. Their plan was to apply Henry Ford's assembly line principle of building cars to building homes. They bought twelve hundred acres on the Hempstead Plain in Island Trees, announced plans for two thousand houses, and approached the Hempstead Town Board.

To get the necessary permits to build what he planned, William J. Levitt had to convince the Hempstead Town Board to make a change in the building code, that at the time required each dwelling have a basement. Levitt's houses were on cement slabs.

The Levitt plan was not secret and opponents of the proposal didn't stand a chance. Before a single house was built, thousands of people had put down deposits. Each was given a letter asking for support in the fight against the Town Board. In addition, the local daily and weekly newspapers wrote strong pieces supporting Levitt. Lobbying on behalf of the plan was intense. At the meeting, eight hundred ex-servicemen turned out in support of the code change.

STONY BROOK VILLAGE TODAY REMAINS A VITAL
PART OF COMMUNITY LIFE, CA. 1960S, COURTESY
WARD MELVILLE HERITAGE FUND. PHOTO BY
DEBBIE ROSS, BRUCE BENNETT STUDIOS.

Levitt & Sons, along with their prospective tenants, carried the day. The requirement for a basement was dropped and building could proceed.

The first two hundred families moved in just four months later. At first, the homes could only be rented. Later on, the house could be bought for $6,990. A few months later, Levitt named his new community Levittown.

By the time he was finished building, William J. Levitt had employed fifteen thousand non-union laborers to build a total of 17,447 four-room Cape Cod homes complete with appliances and expandable attics. He planned for schools, shopping, parks, and houses of worship, and planted more than a half-million trees.

"POLLOCK WAS A GREAT PAINTER; AT LEAST HE PAINTED SOME GREAT PICTURES, WHICH CHANGED THE FACE OF AMERICAN ART, AND LOOK AS FRESH AND STRONG TODAY AS THEY MUST HAVE 50 YEARS AGO, WHEN THEY EMERGED FROM HIS SHACK OF A STUDIO ON NEW YORK'S LONG ISLAND."—ROBERT HUGHES. WILFRID ZOGBAUM PHOTO, ARCHIVES OF AMERICAN ART, COURTESY POLLOCK-KRASNER HOUSE AND STUDY CENTER.

LONG ISLAND ARTS AND LETTERS, PART THREE

Jackson Pollock

Almost a half-century after his death, Jackson Pollock remains the undisputed leader of the Abstract Expressionist movement in painting.

Born in Wyoming in 1912, Pollock studied at the Art Students League under Thomas Hart Benton and his early works reflect Benton's influence in their representations of American life. He was further influenced by Picasso, Miró, and Mexican muralist José Clemente Orozco.

With the advent of the Works Progress Administration (WPA), Pollock was able to continue working as an artist while expanding his own artistic horizons. Eventually, after participating in an exhibition of works by French and American artists, he caught the attention of Peggy Guggenheim, owner of the Art of This Century gallery, a showcase for American and European avant garde art. She became Pollock's dealer and patron, introducing his work to the audience that hungered for the latest in art.

Pollock married artist Lee Krasner in 1945 and they moved to the hamlet of The Springs near the Village of East Hampton. It was there that Pollock created the works that became his hallmark and earned him the nickname, "Jack the Dripper." Using liquid paint, he painted canvases thickly layered with webs of color and line that spread the artistic emphasis across the entire surface.

To say simply that Jackson Pollock's work was controversial is an understatement.

(continued)

(LEFT) JACKSON POLLOCK AND LEE KRASNER IN POLLOCK'S STUDIO IN 1949. SEVERAL OF HIS IMPORTANT PAINTINGS LEAN AGAINST THE WALL. ON THE LEFT IS THE 1944 WORK *GOTHIC*. THE 1946 PAINTING, *THE KEY* IS AT THE RIGHT. AN EXAMPLE OF POLLOCK'S CELEBRATED "POURED" WORK LEANS AGAINST THE BACK WALL. WILFRID ZOGBAUM PHOTO, ARCHIVES OF AMERICAN ART, COURTESY POLLOCK-KRASNER HOUSE AND STUDY CENTER.

(RIGHT) ARTHUR DOVE, WHO LIVED IN CENTERPORT WITH HIS ARTIST WIFE HELEN TORR, WAS CONSIDERED AN "ARTIST'S ARTIST," OFTEN MORE ADMIRED THAN HIS CONTEMPORARY, GEORGIA O'KEEFE. THIS IS *INDIAN SUMMER*, A 1941 OIL. PHOTO COURTESY HECKSCHER MUSEUM OF ART.

Art critic Clement Greenberg championed Pollock, saying he was "the most powerful painter in contemporary America and the only one who promises to be a major one."

Throughout his adult life, Pollock battled alcoholism and suffered from episodic depression. There is speculation that, in the early 1950s, these were the factors that led him to temporarily eliminate the vibrant colors from his work. In this period, he also produced a series of black paintings on plain canvas that contained clear representations of people and animals.

In the end, his demons won the battle and Pollock was unable to work for the last two years of his life, although his work was beginning to sell very well. He died in a 1956 car crash at the age of 44.

Reviewing a 1998 Pollock retrospective at the Museum of Modern Art, *Time* magazine's Robert Hughes compared him to "a meteor that plows into the earth and wreaks havoc on its climate, filling art's air with fallout."

Hughes went on to say: "Pollock became an exemplar of risk and openness. It wasn't just that, as de Kooning said, he 'broke the ice' and forced American art onto an international stage, where it had never had a place before. It was that the freedom implied in his work challenged and provoked other artists to claim an equal freedom in theirs—not only in painting but also in sculpture, performance art, dance, and music."

The home and studio in which Jackson Pollock and Lee Krasner lived and worked has been preserved as a National Historic Landmark and is a museum and study center sponsored by the University at Stony Brook. Students and interested members of the public are offered a full schedule of lectures and symposia dealing with various art-related topics.

The Pollock-Krasner House and Study Center is located at 830 Fireplace Road, East Hampton, NY 11937-1512. The phone number is (631)-324-4929.

FROM 1946 TO 1951, FLAGS OF THE MEMBER NATIONS FLEW OUTSIDE THE UNUSED SPERRY GYROSCOPE BUILDING IN LAKE SUCCESS IN WHICH THE UNITED NATIONS SECURITY COUNCIL AND SECRETARIAT WERE HOUSED. PHOTO COURTESY OF THE NASSAU COUNTY DIVISION OF MUSEUM SERVICES/LONG ISLAND STUDIES INSTITUTE/HOFSTRA UNIVERSITY.

Ultimately, the rentals were phased out, ranch homes were added, and the entire development featured only homes for sale that were ultimately priced at $7,990.

The headline in a 1949 advertisement for the houses said: *"This is Levittown! All yours for $58!"* adding, *"You're a lucky fellow, Mr. Veteran. Uncle Sam and the world's largest builders have made it possible for you to live in a charming house in a delightful community without paying for them with your eyeteeth."*

Levittown was wildly successful, the prototype for a new suburbia in which everyone could own a house and some land. Levitt & Sons went on to build in Pennsylvania, Florida, Maryland, and Europe.

However, barred by restrictive covenant from owning or living in a home in the original Levittown development—as they were from Levitt's earlier Strathmore developments—was anyone who was not Caucasian. The only exception would be employees of the homeowner.

STEPPING INTO THE WORLD'S SPOTLIGHT

The United Nations on Long Island

World War II taught Americans that, perhaps reluctantly, they were the major players in world politics and isolationism was not acceptable. The name "United Nations" was coined by President Franklin D. Roosevelt and was first used in the "Declaration by United Nations" on January 1, 1942, when representatives of twenty-six nations pledged that their governments would continue fighting together against the Axis powers.

Representatives of fifty countries at the United Nations Conference drew up the United Nations Charter on International Organization, in San Francisco from April to June, 1945.

Delegates at that meeting deliberated proposals worked out by the representatives of China, the Soviet Union, the United Kingdom and the United States at a Dumbarton Oaks meeting in 1944. The United Nations charter was signed on June 26, 1945 by the representatives of the original fifty

countries. Poland, which was not represented at the Conference, signed it later and became one of the original fifty-one member states.

The United Nations was officially born on October 24, 1945, after its charter had been ratified by China, France, the Soviet Union, the United Kingdom, the United States, and by a majority of other signatories.

Once formed, this new organization needed a home. An offer from New York City to be housed temporarily at the site of the 1939 World's Fair at Flushing Meadow was ultimately accepted. That site was not large enough to serve the needs of the entire organization. The suggestion was made to utilize empty space in the Sperry Gyroscope plant on Marcus Avenue in Lake Success. After a village vote, an invitation was extended and, from 1946 to 1951, with the Security Council and Secretariat in Lake Success, Long Island took its place on the world's stage.

Dr. Barbara M. Kelly, Director of Long Island Studies Institute at Hofstra University, has studied Levittown. She says restrictive covenants "go back to the Colonial period. They were part of the 1934 Housing Act that established the FHA because, as the insurer, the federal government wanted to make a sound investment and recoup its money.

"The thinking was," she continued, "without these rules to ensure harmonious communities, a development would fail and they wouldn't get their money back. It's important to remember that the FHA did insure minority developments."

After World War II, when for the first time in America people from every walk of life could afford to buy a home, the covenant against non-Caucasians became an issue and, in 1949, it was lifted.

Dependent on federal loans for the GIs who bought his houses, William J. Levitt played to the funding sources, the American Legion National Housing Committee, the Federal Housing Administration (FHA) and, at one point, Senator Joseph McCarthy toured Levittown.

When communism became an issue, William Levitt went on record. He said, "No man who owns his own house and lot can be a communist. He has too much to do."

Although Levitt & Sons did not restrict future developments, other post-war builders stepped in with housing open to all, notably in North Amityville, Wyandanch, and Gordon Heights.

Older, established communities saw a post-war resurgence in which new construction and resales of older houses swelled Long Island's population.

Along with all of the houses came the need for stores, schools, hospitals, police—all of the services required by twentieth-century life.

STEEPLECHASE RACING WAS STILL A POPULAR SPECTATOR SPORT AT BELMONT PARK IN 1950. PHOTO COURTESY OF THE NASSAU COUNTY DIVISION OF MUSEUM SERVICES/LONG ISLAND STUDIES INSTITUTE/HOFSTRA UNIVERSITY.

It was as if Long Island was exploding. Almost no institution that had been in place before the war was large enough to serve the post-war population. For example, the one-room schoolhouses that still dotted the landscape quickly disappeared, replaced by large centralized school districts serving thousands of students.

Today, there are fifty-eight school districts in Nassau County; seventy-one in Suffolk. As of 1999, there was a combined total of 443,318 students attending public school kindergarten through twelfth grade in the two counties.

In the mid-1950s, Harvard Professor James B. Conant named the Great Neck School District in Nassau the best in the United States.

To meet the higher education demands entailed in the GI bill, Long Island's educational community began to expand. Adelphi University started to admit men in 1946; and, in 1948, the New York State Institute of Applied Agriculture at Farmingdale joined the State University system. The 1950s brought a more higher education growth.

In 1954, Brooklyn's Long Island University added campuses on Long Island. C.W. Post was opened in Brookville at the former Marjorie Merriweather Post estate and the Southampton campus opened on the East End of the Island. New York Institute of Technology was chartered by the State of New York in 1955 and opened a campus on the C.V. Whitney estate in Old Westbury. Later, another campus was added in Central Islip.

The emphasis in Long Island colleges then tended to be on the liberal arts. To remedy this, in 1957 New York State opened a college for the preparation of secondary school teachers of mathematics and science in Oyster Bay. In 1962, the college was moved to a nine-building, 480-acre campus in Stony Brook donated by philanthropist Ward Melville. There were 175 faculty members teaching a thousand students.

RIDING TO HOUNDS—FOX HUNTING—WAS A POPULAR LONG ISLAND PASTIME WITH MEMBERS OF THE MEADOWBROOK CLUB IN THE 1940S. PHOTO COURTESY OF THE NASSAU COUNTY DIVISION OF MUSEUM SERVICES/LONG ISLAND STUDIES INSTITUTE/HOFSTRA UNIVERSITY.

AN AERIAL VIEW OF LEVITTOWN TAKEN IN 1947. PHOTO © 1947 *NEWSDAY*.

In 1958, when the only opportunity for students in Suffolk County to receive a private college education in Suffolk lay in an Adelphi University's county extension, a group of prominent businesspeople organized Dowling College. Dowling's classes were first offered in a school building in Sayville. Quickly outgrowing that space, Dowling relocated to Idle Hour, the William K. Vanderbilt estate in Oakdale.

At the end of the decade, both Nassau and Suffolk opened community colleges that awarded associate's degrees. Today Nassau and Suffolk are the two largest community colleges in the State University system.

Even after World War II, Long Island remained a good employer, with many of the wartime factories continuing to build airplanes and components, while engaging in research and development projects.

Expansion and prosperity were to change Long Island's landscape forever.

Retailers found Long Island attractive. Following the home building boom, there was an influx of suburban outposts of stores familiar to everyone from the five boroughs. Garden City, Hempstead, and Manhasset eventually became shopping centers. Stores like Best & Company, Lord & Taylor, Arnold Constable, Ohrbach's, Franklin Simon and B. Altman, Saks Fifth Avenue, Bloomingdale's—most of them gone today—served the shoppers who knew them elsewhere.

E.J. Korvette, one of the earliest and best-known discount stores, opened in 1950. It was an in-between store, better than the old five-and-dimes, but not offering "real" department store quality.

Then, of course, came the malls.

In *Fish-Shape Paumanok*, Robert Cushman Murphy tells of his friend:

"Edwin Way Teale, one of the gifted writers on natural history of our time, has told me of his last sighting on Long Island of the plains-inhabiting sandpiper known as the upland plover. The bird was perched atop a wooden sign, and when Teale came within range he read: 'A supermarket will be erected here.' Exit plover!"

Three major malls opened in just one year, 1956. Long Island shoppers could choose from Green Acres in Valley Stream, Mid-Island in Hicksville, and the largest of all, Roosevelt Field in Westbury.

The latter was, truly, to be more than a shopping center. It was the largest mall in the world at the time, built at a parkway interchange for maximum access. It was to feature restaurants, a theater, bowling alley, a hotel, and medical offices. World-renowned architect I.M. Pei designed the original space. While not all of the amenities remained in place at Roosevelt Field and, indeed, the management of the mall changed over the years, it has remained a national leader.

Along with the new landscape, a new day of shopping had arrived on Long Island, bringing the first generation of teenagers who treated the mall like a second home. Suburban teens, often too young to drive, and lacking both public transportation and places to congregate, found their way to the malls. There they could shop, have a snack, meet their friends. It was a defining image of suburbia.

Malls offered shoppers a complete world in one spot. At first, along with the anchoring department stores, there were independent small shops, chain stores and service

THE SAME AERIAL VIEW OF LEVITTOWN IN 1987, AS THE DEVELOPMENT CELEBRATED ITS 40TH ANNIVERSARY. PHOTO © 1987 *NEWSDAY*.

providers, like dentists and doctors. Within the next several years, other malls opened, including the Sunrise Mall in Massaspequa and Suffolk's first mall, Walt Whitman in Huntington, and Smith Haven in Lake Grove.

As Long Island grew, the people moving out from the boroughs were making sea changes in their lives. They were, most of them, owning homes for the first time. In fact, many of them were living in homes, rather than apartments, for the first time. Many bought their first cars and the wives who stayed at home in the daytime often learned to drive so they could join car pools for their children.

In addition, the new life in suburbia very frequently brought new politics.

Many new Long Islanders joined the Republican Party when they moved from the city. There has been debate about why this is so but in the end—like the "chicken and the egg" debate—it didn't matter. Huge enrollment enabled the Republican Parties in Nassau and Suffolk Counties to be among the strongest in the nation.

But, surprisingly, when Suffolk County residents cast their ballots for their first County Executive in 1959, they elected Port Jefferson Democrat H. Lee Dennison. He was joined two years later when Nassau County voters elected the first, and only, Democratic County Executive, Eugene Nickerson.

A tangible sign of growth was the 1957 formation of the Diocese of Rockville Centre, presided over by Bishop Walter Kellenberg. Formerly part of the Diocese of Brooklyn, the division of the Diocese brought Long Island into its own.

Post-war life on Long Island was pleasant and quiet, seldom interrupted by any untoward incidents. But, there were two of these that made headlines around the world.

In February 1950, a New York-bound Long Island Rail Road train crashed head-on into a train headed east toward Babylon. Thirty-two people were killed and scores were injured. Following official investigations of the crash, new procedures and equipment were put in place to improve safety. However they were not enough.

Just nine months later, on Thanksgiving Eve, 1950, the Long Island Rail Road suffered an even more devastating crash. The 6:09 train from Penn Station to Hempstead had stalled on the tracks at the Richmond Hill section of Queens when the operator was unable to deactivate the brakes he had used to slow to 15 miles per hour on a curve. The 6:09 was stuck on the tracks and crowded with people anxious get home to celebrate Thanksgiving.

As technology was then, there was likely no way to prevent the crash. The 6:32 train headed for Babylon came hurtling down the tracks and plowed into the stalled train. In a flash, seventy-nine people were killed. It was the second worst rail disaster in the history of the United States. In its aftermath, the Public Service Commission insisted on several procedural changes.

A happier ending closed the story of Benjamin Hooper, Jr., a 6-year-old who fell down a newly dug well on his family's Manorville property on May 16, 1957. All manner of press rushed to the site of the hole that was 18 feet deep, six inches wide, and Americans held their collective breath.

TODAY, LEVITTOWN IS STILL A POPULAR NEIGHBORHOOD ON LONG ISLAND. PHOTOS BY DEBORAH ROSS (ABOVE) AND ROB AMATO (BELOW), BRUCE BENNETT STUDIOS.

The plan to get the child out revolved around the excavation of a parallel shaft and the digging of a tunnel from the new shaft to the one that imprisoned Benny. Ultimately, when a power shovel caused sand to fall into the parallel shaft, the rescue had to be accomplished using volunteer teams who took turns digging by hand.

It seemed to take forever. The outcome was so in doubt that his priest gave Benny conditional last rites. After 24 hours, at 7:40 p.m. on May 17, Benny was rescued and the nation celebrated.

Long Island in the 1950s was seen almost everywhere as the prototype of suburbia. Planners and sociologists debated the development of Levittown and all that it meant for a modern society. A film made in the 1970s about the early days of rock 'n roll showcased a newsreel clip of the president of a Hicksville PTA as she expounded on proper dress for students and railed against the influence of this new music.

Long Island teenagers listened to AM radio from New York City. They heard Alan Freed and Murray the K on WINS; Peter Tripp on WMGM and, way down on the left of the dial, the WMCA "Good Guys."

Through all of growth that came in the fifteen years after the war, Long Island remained a relatively quiet place, a suburban ideal.

But, even the great post-war growth was about to be eclipsed by a phenomenal influx of people and businesses that began to turn Long Island into a place with its own identity separate from the city to the west. ■

GROWING FROM LEVITTOWN'S EXAMPLE, QUIET NEIGHBORHOODS WERE DEVELOPED ALL OVER THE ISLAND, PROVIDING A HAVEN FOR GROWING FAMILIES. PHOTOS BY BRUCE BENNETT (LEFT) AND ROB AMATO (RIGHT), BRUCE BENNETT STUDIOS.

HOW DID THIS COMMUNITY GET HERE?

The story of Levittown is well known. It is also obvious that some communities on Long Island, such as Oakdale, grew around the great estates much as English villages have done throughout history. Other communities have more unusual origins.

Garden City, for example, pre-dated Levittown as a planned community by decades. The Town of Hempstead would at times entertain prospective buyers of the seven thousand acres of the Hempstead Plains owned by the town. Finally, in 1869, New York City merchant Alexander T. Stewart won a vote that allowed him to buy the land for $55 an acre.

Together with architect John Kellum, Stewart planned to build an entire village in which employees of his New York City store could rent homes. The beauty of the plan was, to Stewart, that his employees would have fine homes and he would make back the money he paid them in their rent.

But the employees balked, preferring to own rather than rent. Stewart died in 1876 and Garden City appeared doomed. The project was rescued by a private investment company that completed the development of Garden City and allowed people to buy the homes there.

Alexander T. Stewart is remembered today by the avenue that bears his name and by the Cathedral of the Incarnation, a Gothic church with a 220-foot spire that serves as the seat of the Episcopal Diocese of Long Island. It was built in 1885 by Stewart's wife to honor his memory.

Suffolk's north shore villages of Sound Beach and Rocky Point had more humble beginnings. The *New York Daily Mirror* wanted to boost circulation in the environment of fierce competition of 1920s newspapering. Toward this end, they bought land in these two communities and offered subscribers the opportunity to buy lots for as little as $90. Thus, for very little money, a person could have a summer cottage—for that's what most of the original houses were—and get a daily newspaper.

A similar scheme was used in San Remo by the publisher of *Il Progresso*, an Italian-language newspaper and by others in Mastic Beach.

In 1927, on land between Coram and Middle Island in Suffolk County, there was only Gordon's Hotel, run by "Pop" Gordon. Entrepreneur Louis Fife, who was white, bought land there and re-sold it by going door-to-door in black communities in New York City. Fife sold the land as farmland; the kind of land the buyers were used to back home in the South or the Caribbean. He called the community Gordon Heights and did manage to sell the land.

Though it was sold, it was not immediately developed. Much of the land sat for years before the owners built homes. It wasn't until the 1940s that houses got electricity and running water.

The neighboring communities were not welcoming as any homeowner whose house caught fire quickly learned. Therefore, the people of Gordon Heights formed their own volunteer fire department in 1947 and, today, it remains Long Island's only all-black fire department.

PHOTOS BY ROB AMATO (THIS PAGE) AND JIM McISAAC (OPPOSITE PAGE, BELOW), BRUCE BENNETT STUDIOS.

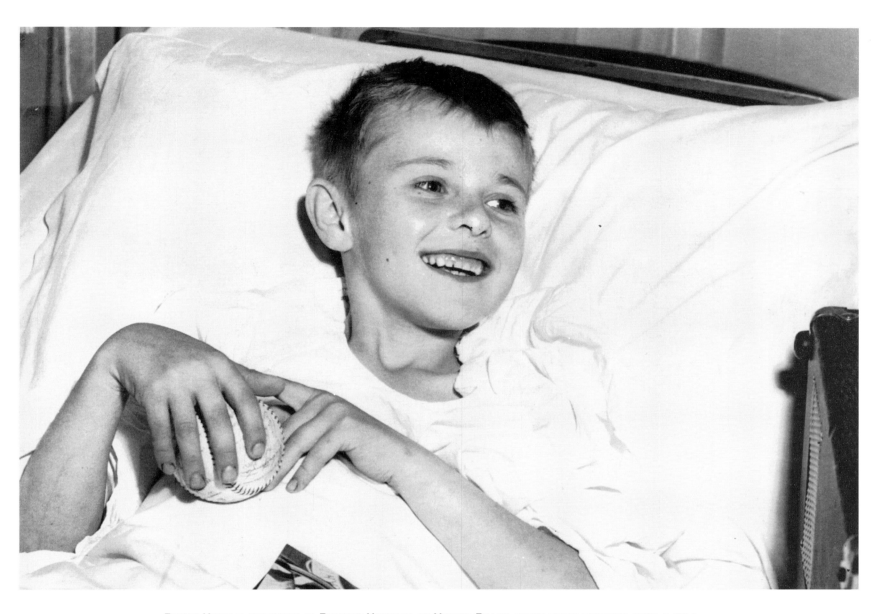

Benny Hooper recovers at Bayview Hospital in Mastic Beach after being rescued from a well.
Photo © 1957 *Newsday.*

AFTER WORLD WAR II, TO MEET THE HIGHER-EDUCATION DEMANDS ENTAILED IN THE GI BILL, LONG ISLAND'S EDUCATIONAL COMMUNITY BEGAN TO EXPAND. IN 1946, ADELPHI UNIVERSITY STARTED TO ADMIT MEN. PHOTO BY LISA MEYER, BRUCE BENNETT STUDIOS.

IN 1954, BROOKLYN'S LONG ISLAND UNIVERSITY ADDED CAMPUSES ON LONG ISLAND. C.W. POST WAS OPENED IN BROOKVILLE AT THE FORMER MARJORIE MERRIWEATHER POST ESTATE. THE SOUTHAMPTON CAMPUS OPENED ON THE EAST END OF THE ISLAND. PHOTO BY LISA MEYER, BRUCE BENNETT STUDIOS.

LOCATED 25 MILES EAST OF MANHATTAN IN HEMPSTEAD, HOFSTRA UNIVERSITY BECAME LONG ISLAND'S SECOND PRIVATE UNIVERSITY. ITS CURRENT STUDENT BODY APPROACHES 8,000. PHOTO BY LISA MEYER, BRUCE BENNETT STUDIOS.

BROOKHAVEN NATIONAL LABORATORY

Brookhaven National Laboratory covers only eight square miles, but its discoveries impact the entire world. The U.S. Department of Energy research facility, located in Upton, Long Island, is operated by Brookhaven Science Associates, LLC, a corporation founded by Stony Brook University and Battelle. The laboratory is home to about 3,000 scientists, engineers, and support staff, and each year approximately 4,000 visiting scientists come from around the world to conduct research there. Its world-class facilities include "big machines" for studies in physics, chemistry, biology, medicine, applied science, and advanced technology.

Sited at the former Camp Upton, which served as a training and induction camp for the U.S. Army during World Wars I and II, Brookhaven has evolved dramatically since it opened as a research facility in 1947. Today, approximately 360 facilities—including nearly a dozen particle accelerators, hundreds of research laboratories, a children's science museum, a research library, a post office, and a firehouse—support more than 600 cutting-edge research projects.

The laboratory's work has influenced the direction of science in many fields and has pointed the way toward technology of enormous practical benefit for society.

POSITRON EMISSION TOMOGRAPHY AT BROOKHAVEN PROVIDES A WINDOW INTO THE BRAIN FOR INVESTIGATING SUCH PROBLEMS AS COCAINE ADDICTION.

The Early Years

During World War II, major developments in nuclear physics and engineering created new opportunities for science, but most of the large-scale facilities needed for research were located far from the large community of scientists in the Northeast. After the war, a group of Columbia University scientists asked the federal government to construct advanced facilities close to the New York City region. Together, representatives from nine Northeastern universities—Columbia, Cornell, Harvard, Johns Hopkins, MIT, Princeton, Pennsylvania, Rochester, and Yale—formed Associated Universities, Inc., or AUI, to manage the new laboratory.

On January 13, 1947, the original staff moved to Brookhaven from Columbia, where they had spent the previous year preparing to launch the laboratory. By spring, Brookhaven Lab, with its 300 employees managed by AUI, was under the aegis of the newly created Atomic Energy Commission. Thirty years later, in 1977, Brookhaven was placed under the authority of the newly formed U.S. Department of Energy.

Big Machines

The new laboratory soon began construction for its first "big machine"—the Brookhaven Graphite Research Reactor (BGRR), which started operating in 1950. The world's first reactor built exclusively for scientific research into peacetime applications, the BGRR was important in the development of nuclear medicine. Three years later, the Cosmotron, the laboratory's first particle accelerator, was commissioned, becoming the world's highest energy proton accelerator of its day.

THIS 420-TON MAGNET AT BROOKHAVEN'S ALTERNATING GRADIENT SYNCHROTRON IS CRITICAL TO PHYSICISTS' ONGOING SEARCH FOR RARE DECAYS OF SHORT-LIVED SUBATOMIC PARTICLES CALLED KAONS—A SEARCH DESIGNED TO TEST A THEORY OF MATTER KNOWN AS THE STANDARD MODEL.

AERIAL VIEW OF BROOKHAVEN NATIONAL
LABORATORY. THE RELATIVISTIC HEAVY ION
COLLIDER (TOP, CENTER) IS 2.4 MILES IN
CIRCUMFERENCE AND DOMINATES BROOKHAVEN'S
5,300-ACRE CAMPUS.

Over the next half century, Brookhaven built
two more reactors and many more accelerators for
scientific research. The laboratory's big machines attract
scientists from around the world. In 1982, Brookhaven
commissioned the National Synchrotron Light Source
(NSLS), a scientific research facility used by over 2,400
researchers from 380 institutions annually—by far the
most used synchrotron in the U.S. With beams of
X-rays, infrared light and ultraviolet light at the NSLS,
researchers study materials as diverse as proteins and
moon rocks.

In 1999, Brookhaven began operating the Relativistic
Heavy Ion Collider (RHIC), the world's newest and
biggest accelerator for studies in nuclear physics. At RHIC,
physicists aim to recreate the conditions of the early
universe, just moments after the Big Bang. From their
pioneering experiments at this new collider, physicists
hope to gain insights into the fundamental nature
of matter—and extend the boundaries of scientific
understanding through the 21st century and beyond.

Physics Frontiers

Physics discoveries at Brookhaven have shaped
how scientists view the physical world today. In 1957,
scientists T.D. Lee and C.N. Yang won the Nobel Prize
in physics for their prediction at Brookhaven a year
earlier that "parity" would not be conserved in certain
nuclear interactions. In 1976, Samuel C.C. Ting shared
the Nobel Prize in physics for discovering the J/psi
particle at Brookhaven's Alternating Gradient Synchrotron
(AGS), the laboratory's premiere particle accelerator for
many years.

Two other discoveries at the AGS were recognized
with Nobel Prizes in the 1980s. The 1980 Nobel Prize
in physics went to James Cronin and Val Fitch for
their discovery of "CP" violation, which revealed a
"lopsidedness" among the particles and antiparticles in
the universe. In 1988, Leon Lederman, Melvin Schwartz,
and Jack Steinberger received a Nobel Prize in physics
for their discovery of an important elementary particle
known as the muon-neutrino.

Today, the AGS remains the brightest high-energy
proton source in the world, ideal for detecting extremely
rare phenomena involving elementary particles. For
example, a seven-institution collaboration recently found
evidence for a previously unobserved subatomic particle
known as an "exotic meson," and an international team
discovered the rarest decay ever observed of a short-lived
subatomic particle called a kaon. These results help to
fill out the theory of modern physics known as the
Standard Model.

As a new millennium began, Brookhaven launched its
largest and most powerful big machine: the Relativistic
Heavy Ion Collider, which is really two accelerators 2.4
miles around. Beginning a new era of research, collisions
of gold nuclei first occurred in RHIC in June 2000.

Nearly 1,000 scientists from around the world are
using RHIC's four state-of-the-art detectors to explore the
hottest, most dense matter ever created in a laboratory.
As the world's flagship facility for nuclear physics
research, RHIC promises to be the site of many new
discoveries in the new millennium.

A YOUNG VISITOR DURING ONE OF BROOKHAVEN'S
SUMMER SUNDAY TOURS HAS FUN LEARNING ABOUT
STATIC ELECTRICITY.

SCIENTISTS AT BROOKHAVEN'S NATIONAL
SYNCHROTRON LIGHT SOURCE BUILT THE
FIRST DETAILED ATOMIC MODEL OF AN IMPORTANT
LYME DISEASE BACTERIAL PROTEIN, INFORMATION
WHICH HELPED IN DEVELOPING A VACCINE FOR
THE DISEASE.

Medical and Biological Breakthroughs

Big machines can make big impacts in fields other
than physics. Over the years, Brookhaven has made
numerous important discoveries in the fields of biology
and medicine.

Nuclear medicine has been strong at the laboratory
since its earliest years. The Brookhaven-developed
radiotracer technetium-99m is used annually in 24
million nuclear medicine procedures performed
worldwide. Another important radiotracer is Brookhaven's
thallium-201, used in heart stress tests. In the early
years, Brookhaven scientists also conducted research
that led to the successful use of L-dopa to treat
Parkinson's disease.

In the 1960s, Brookhaven researchers developed a
novel detector for early brain-imaging studies that was a
precursor to today's position emission tomography (PET)
machines. Subsequently, Brookhaven researchers have
used PET to probe the brain chemistry of addiction,
mental illness, and aging, and have begun the work of
finding effective treatments. Recently, this work has
brought new insight into the chemical changes in the
brain induced by addiction, and the discovery that an
inexpensive epilepsy drug may prove to be an effective
treatment for addiction to cocaine, nicotine, and several
other substances.

In biological research, Brookhaven scientists were
the first to show DNA damage from ultraviolet light. In
the 1980s, Brookhaven biologists broke a genetic code
longer than 39,000 "letters" in a virus known as T7.
Today, the T7 process is a key to "expressing" large
quantities of proteins from their DNA blueprints, an
essential first step to determining a protein's structure.

Significant progress has been made in structural
biology studies at the NSLS, where researchers were the
first to view the process of AIDS infection on the atomic
scale. Using the NSLS, they created images that show the
AIDS virus as it makes contact with a human cell. Other
biological breakthroughs at the NSLS include building the
first detailed atomic model of an important Lyme disease
protein, a key step in the effort to develop a more
effective vaccine for the disease. Also, in what could be
the first step toward finding a cure for the common cold,
scientists discovered how one form of cold virus binds to
human cells.

Improving Everyday Life

Brookhaven capabilities have been harnessed using
U.S. Department of Energy funds to solve many practical
energy and environmental problems. In the environmental
area, Brookhaven scientists, working with W.R. Grace &
Co., developed an asbestos-digesting foam that renders
asbestos harmless, while retaining its functional properties.
Also, the discovery and development of bacteria that
consume oil, grease, and toxic waste have yielded
applications in purifying crude oil, recovering metals
from geothermal mining waste, and opening clogged
drains in homes and restaurants.

Laboratory researchers have teamed up with utility
companies to make a quieter, more environmentally
friendly alternative device to the jackhammer. In
another project with an industrial partner, Brookhaven
researchers developed materials with reduced toxicity for
light-weight, rechargeable lithium-ion batteries for use in
laptop computers, cellular phones, and, possibly, electric
cars. Brookhaven also anticipated a major industry when
one of its scientists created the world's first video game
to entertain visitors at a 1958 open house.

THE STAR DETECTOR AT BROOKHAVEN'S
RELATIVISTIC HEAVY ION COLLIDER, PART OF WHICH
IS SHOWN HERE UNDER CONSTRUCTION, TRACKS AND
ANALYZES THE THOUSANDS OF PARTICLES THAT ARE
PRODUCED BY EACH COLLISION OF GOLD IONS.

A Laboratory for the Millennium

In 1998, the U.S. Department of Energy named Brookhaven Science Associates to manage the laboratory in a new era in which excellence in science is matched by a new emphasis on environmental compliance and community involvement. The laboratory has reorganized itself and introduced new management systems to improve environment, health, and safety performance by minimizing waste and accelerating the cleanup of the soils and groundwater on the five percent of the site that is contaminated.

Brookhaven has also made significant strides in its outreach to the community. The laboratory established a Community Advisory Council that includes 30 representatives from the local community, including members from the Long Island Association, as well as various school districts, environmental groups, health-care organizations, and civic associations.

A Special Resource

While providing scientific leadership for the nation, Brookhaven strives to be a good neighbor to Long Islanders. Sunday tours for the general public during the summer months attract thousands of visitors, and a children's science museum welcomes 25,000 students per year. Brookhaven opens its facilities to students from kindergarten to the postgraduate level. Programs range from an annual elementary school science fair, which encourages budding scientists from Suffolk County, to summer research programs for high school and college students, and postdoctoral fellowships for students from universities around the world.

ENVIRONMENTALLY FRIENDLY BIOTECHNOLOGY HAS BEEN DEVELOPED AT BROOKHAVEN FOR ENERGY PRODUCTION. FOR EXAMPLE, MICROBES CAN ENHANCE OIL RECOVERY FROM WELLS OR CLEAN UP GEOTHERMAL BRINES.

Brookhaven also gives back economically to the local community. The laboratory is the fourth largest high-tech employer on Long Island, and it spends tens of millions of dollars per year on goods and services in the area. It also forms partnerships with industry, which take advantage of the large-scale facilities and expertise that the laboratory has available for research and development.

Already the world's premier center for nuclear physics, Brookhaven will focus future research on nanoscience, structural biology, high-energy physics, chemical and materials sciences, environmental science, and the production of new radioisotopes. With its top-notch staff and world-class facilities, Brookhaven is poised to remain on the forefront of scientific research well into the 21st century. ∎

A BROOKHAVEN SCIENTIST USES SPECIAL FISH TO STUDY THE LINK BETWEEN OZONE AND SKIN CANCER.

STONY BROOK UNIVERSITY

Nobel, Crafoord, and Pulitzer prizes; an Obie for playwriting; two Grammy nominations; Guggenheim, Sloan, Rockefeller Foundation, and MacArthur fellowships—all attest to the diversity, standards of excellence, and accomplishments of Stony Brook's faculty. The faculty has built a record of academic and scientific scholarship that is all the more extraordinary for an institution that is among the nation's youngest research universities. Stony Brook is a source of new ideas that fuel economic growth and business development, advance science and technology, improve health care, and strengthen government. The campus is part of a small national constellation of major institutions of higher learning known as research universities.

Stony Brook is the leading research university of the State University of New York. Among all public research universities, Stony Brook is second only to the University of California at Berkeley in terms of research generated per faculty member, according to a study published by Johns Hopkins University Press. The university generated more than $12 million in patent royalties licensed to industry, edging out Harvard for 12th among colleges and universities nationwide in 1998 and 1999. This represents 91 percent of all SUNY patent income for that year.

Groundbreaking research initiatives include the development of ReoPro®, used in cardiac angioplasties, the first drug from any SUNY campus cleared by the FDA for sale in the United States; the cause of and a new early-diagnostic test for Lyme disease; findings regarding elementary particles that *Science* magazine named as one of the top 10 discoveries of the year;

THE ANNUAL STUDENT/FACULTY CARDBOARD REGATTA IS A METAPHOR FOR HOW WE APPROACH EDUCATION—A COLLABORATIVE PROCESS BETWEEN LEARNING AND LIFE.

the first total synthesis of a virus outside a living cell; the identification of several new distant galaxies; establishment of the link between smoking and emphysema; development of 3-D computer visualization; and the discovery of the link between birds and dinosaurs.

Reinventing Undergraduate Education

Stony Brook President Shirley Strum Kenny is a dedicated national leader in the campaign to bring the resources of research universities into the lives and education of undergraduates. She emphasizes, "Our goal is to turn the prevailing undergraduate culture of receivers into a culture of inquirers—where faculty, graduate students, and undergraduates share an adventure of discovery that begins in the freshman year." To that end, President Kenny chaired the Boyer Commission, which made sweeping recommendations in the area of integrating research programs with the undergraduate curriculum. One outgrowth, The Reinvention Center at Stony Brook, is a national facility to promote new approaches to undergraduate education.

The Centers for Molecular Medicine and Biology Learning Laboratories are an example of the collaboration between education and research. The facility's interactive design fosters the rapid exchange of ideas between academic and clinical researchers and students from different disciplines. Stony Brook's Learning Communities—another innovative concept that is attracting national attention—are special programs for a select number of incoming students who register for a common group of courses, where material in one course relates to that in the others.

THE NEW FOUNTAIN, CENTERPIECE OF THE CAMPUS, IS AN OASIS OF TRANQUILITY ON THE BUSTLING STONY BROOK CAMPUS.

LONG ISLAND'S VARIED TOPOGRAPHY PROVIDES
AN IDEAL NATURAL LABORATORY FOR STONY
BROOK STUDENTS.

In recognition of its accomplishments in integrating education and research, Stony Brook was one of only 10 recipients nationwide of a National Science Foundation award. The university was also awarded the prestigious Theodore M. Hesburgh Certificate of Excellence, which recognizes outstanding efforts in undergraduate education. Stony Brook's groundbreaking Women in Science and Engineering (WISE) program for undergraduates—identified as a national model by the National Science Foundation—supports and mentors talented women in math and science.

In addition, the Graduate School was presented with the first-ever CGS/Petersen's Award for Innovation in Promoting an Inclusive Graduate Community, recognizing its commitment to promoting campus-wide diversity initiatives to advance a multicultural perspective among faculty, administrators, and students.

Degrees of Difference

Parallel to its sweeping success as a research institution, Stony Brook is committed to the education of its student body of more than 19,000—13,257 undergraduates and 6,574 at the graduate level. Enrollment figures are soaring, as are the qualifications of entering students: SAT scores of incoming freshmen have increased by 30 points over the past three years.

Students can choose from 85 undergraduate programs, 102 master's programs, 40 doctoral programs, and 32 graduate certificate programs. Among Stony Brook's doctoral programs are two that are ranked in the nation's top 10, four in the top 20, and 10 in the top 40. The primary care program at the University's School of Medicine is the number one ranked program in

New York State and the 18th nationwide. Undergraduates study in six schools: the College of Arts and Sciences with fields of study in physical and life sciences, mathematics, humanities and fine arts, and social and behavioral sciences; the College of Engineering and Applied Sciences with programs in engineering, computer science, applied mathematics and statistics, and business management; the Marine Sciences Research Center with fields of study in atmospheric and oceanic studies; the School of Health Technology and Management with upper-division programs in cytotechnology, occupational therapy, physical therapy, and physician assistant education, and four-year and upper-division programs in respiratory care and clinical laboratory sciences; the School of Nursing with upper-division programs in nursing; and the School of Social Welfare with an upper-division program in social work.

Long Island's Economic Engine

In President Kenny's words, one of Stony Brook's important missions is "creating, supporting, and staffing the Long Island industries of the future." In response to this mission, Stony Brook has appointed a vice president for economic development—the first position of its kind at a research university—who interacts with the business community to create new jobs, resources, and economic opportunities for the region. Based on a $120 million tax-levy appropriation, the university is estimated to have a regional economic impact of $2.5 billion, perhaps the highest return on any of New York State's investments. The school is the largest single-site employer on Long Island, with more than 12,000 full- or part-time employees.

UNDERGRADUATES WORK ON RESEARCH PROJECTS
WITH AWARD-WINNING FACULTY WHO RANK AMONG
THE BEST IN THE NATION.

THE ZEBRA PATH, DESIGNED BY KIM HARDIMAN, '82, LEADS TO THE STUDENT ACTIVITIES CENTER.

What sets Stony Brook apart from most other institutions of its kind is the university's commitment to support and partner with local businesses. President Kenny states, "to be a great national university, you must be a great local university." To that end, the university has developed several innovative economic development programs that provide vital assistance to Long Island's growing companies. Current programs have assisted 250 businesses, produced business volume of more than $180 million, and created or saved 3,200 jobs. The university also sponsors two Centers for Advanced Technology, which are designed to promote industry growth vital to the state's economic future. Also fueling new economic growth is the university's Long Island High Technology Incubator, where entrepreneurs occupy nearly 200,000 square feet of commercial space and have earned more than $100 million in gross revenues while employing 600 Long Islanders. A second incubator, founded in cooperation with Computer Associates International, Inc., is devoted to software development, making Stony Brook the only SUNY campus with two new business incubators. The Small Business Development Center at Stony Brook has assisted more than 4,000 clients in obtaining more than $50 million in business financing.

Through a recent $1 million planning grant from New York State, Stony Brook will play a role in a major initiative that may ultimately enable the region to rival Silicon Valley. Called the Millennium Technology Center, it will be a focal point for biotechnology and high-technology development throughout the state.

Selected to co-manage Brookhaven National Laboratory, Stony Brook joins an elite group of universities—including Cornell, Massachusetts Institute of Technology, and Princeton—that run federal laboratories. Brookhaven Lab supports 700 full-time scientists and hosts more than 4,000 visiting researchers a year.

President Kenny's vision for Stony Brook integrates the goals of education and enterprise. She states, "If New York State is to establish and maintain a leadership position in the high-tech global economy of the new millennium, it will need a highly educated workforce, cutting-edge technical expertise, and innovative thinking. Stony Brook has been providing—and will continue to provide—the intellectual fuel to power New York's economic engine."

Stony Brook's Thousand-Acre Universe

Located in mid-Suffolk County on Long Island's North Shore, the 1,100-acre campus is constantly growing to keep pace with its progress. Recently or nearly completed are the Charles B. Wang Asian-American Cultural Center, state-of-the-art child care facilities, an athletics stadium, a new undergraduate apartment complex, an ambulatory surgery center, and an $80 million renovation of all residence halls.

THERE ARE MORE THAN 100 ORGANIZATIONS ON CAMPUS: SORORITIES AND FRATERNITIES; SPORTS, RECREATIONAL, AND CULTURAL CLUBS; PLUS PRE-PROFESSIONAL AND EDUCATIONAL ASSOCIATIONS.

Stony Brook has become an invaluable leisure-time resource to residents of Long Island. The Staller Center for the Arts features productions by world-class artists in a Broadway-caliber theatre, a first-run cinema utilizing Suffolk County's largest screen, an art gallery that sponsors exhibitions by faculty and artists of the region, and its popular Summer Film Festival.

All 19 of Stony Brook's varsity teams compete in NCAA Division I athletics. Midnight Madness, signaling the start of basketball season, is a night of fun, games, and revelry. In the summer, the campus is home to two new camps for school-aged children: a day camp that provides athletics and recreation while stimulating the mind with science, technology, and computer programs, and a residential camp run in partnership with the New York City Board of Education that enhances literacy through hands-on learning and research.

Keeping Long Island Healthy

The University Hospital and Medical Center is Long Island's number one health care organization, providing primary medical services to more than half a million patients. It houses a 504-bed hospital, 350-bed nursing home, and dental care center.

The Medical Center has Suffolk County's only Level I Trauma Unit, AIDS Center, Burn Center, Skin Bank, Child Abuse Clinic, Lyme Disease Center, Autism Center, Neonatal Intensive Care Unit, and Transplant Center. The hospital has been ranked as one of the 100 best hospitals and one of the 15 best major teaching hospitals in the United States. The Heart Hospital is ranked first on Long Island in angioplasty/cardiac catheterization by the New York State Department of Health and is among the top heart centers statewide in open-heart surgery. The School

THE ACADEMIC MALL CREATES A STRONG SENSE OF PLACE FOR THE UNIVERSITY COMMUNITY.

of Medicine, ranked in the top 20 percent in the nation in terms of grant funding per faculty member, was recognized by *U.S. News & World Report* as having the best primary care program in New York State and as one of the top 20 nationwide.

Soaring to its Place Among the Stars

"Stony Brook Soars," according to the title of a *New York Times* article on the study, "The Rise of American Research Universities," that ranks Stony Brook as the third-best public research university in the nation by combining the top science, social science, and arts and humanities programs. President Kenny reinforces Stony Brook's stellar qualities, "Every day the university is making new discoveries and setting the standard for other institutions. Stony Brook is proud of its academic, medical, research, and economic accomplishments, and looks forward to meeting exciting challenges. That excitement is fueling a dynamic at Stony Brook, giving off an energy that is so unique and compelling that it touches every one of our more than 19,000 students." ■

Also, see related section on the University Hospital and Medical Center at Stony Brook, page 366-369.

ALL 19 STONY BROOK VARSITY TEAMS COMPETE IN NCAA DIVISION I ATHLETICS.

NEW YORK INSTITUTE OF TECHNOLOGY

How much do we know today? What will we know in the years to come? Some information theorists believe that 97 percent of what we will know in 50 years is still unknown today. With that in mind, a college education will be, perhaps more than ever before, the foundation for professional and personal success. New York Institute of Technology offers dynamic, career-focused educational programs that lead its graduates to the forefront of future advancements and information.

NYIT was founded in 1955 with a mission that was and remains unique among institutions of higher learning:
• to provide a career-oriented, technology-based education that gives students the means to excel in their chosen fields;
• to offer access to opportunity through moderate tuition, generous scholarships, hands-on technological facilities, and flexible learning options;

STUDENTS AT NYIT LEARN BY DOING, IN CAREER-FOCUSED HANDS-ON PROGRAMS OF STUDY THAT BRING REAL-WORLD SUBJECTS INTO THE CLASSROOM.

• to support applications-oriented research that enhances the quality of life in nearby communities and in the larger world.

This mission continues to drive every aspect of NYIT's educational strategy and serves as a strong foundation for the college's academic programs, development goals, and community relations efforts.

Career-Focused Education

NYIT offers more than 100 undergraduate and graduate programs of study on its campuses in Old Westbury and Central Islip on Long Island, at Columbus Circle in Manhattan, and online via the Internet. These programs lead to careers in a wide variety of fields, many of them the fastest growing and in-demand in the world. From telecommunications technology and management to physical therapy, from computer graphics to career and technology education, from interior design to international business—there's something for every interest in NYIT's eight schools:
• Allied Health and Life Sciences
• Architecture and Design
• Arts, Sciences, and Communication
• Education and Professional Services
• Extended Education
• Management
• New York College of Osteopathic Medicine.

Each school's technology-infused curriculum incorporates the vital elements that give every student a competitive edge in the 21st century business world: familiarity with and understanding of computers and their applications; oral and written communication skills; the ability to identify problems and devise solutions; and a cooperative, team-oriented work ethic. These elements combine with a solid core foundation in liberal arts and sciences—including history, literature, math, and physical, natural, and social sciences—and choice of comprehensive preprofessional courses within each academic program to prepare students for all of the rewards and challenges of a successful career.

NYIT'S MANHATTAN CAMPUS IS LOCATED IN THE HEART OF NEW YORK CITY, JUST STEPS AWAY FROM LINCOLN CENTER AND CENTRAL PARK AND A QUICK SUBWAY RIDE FROM WALL STREET AND THE WORLD FINANCIAL CENTER.

NYIT STUDENTS WORK WITH STATE-OF-THE-ART TECHNOLOGIES THAT MIRROR THOSE USED IN THE PROFESSIONAL WORLD, GIVING THEM A DISTINCT ADVANTAGE IN A COMPETITIVE JOB MARKET.

This complete approach to higher education is made possible by NYIT's faculty members, who hold advanced degrees and have years of quality professional experience in their fields. Their dual expertise gives students exceptional opportunities to learn from professors who understand both the theoretical and practical aspects of their work. NYIT faculty members serve as academic and professional mentors to their students, often maintaining these relationships long after the students have graduated. In turn, many NYIT alumni reciprocate by providing opportunities for student internships and returning to their mentors' classes as guest speakers.

The "real world" connection is at the heart of NYIT's career-oriented educational mission. NYIT students in different programs of study design community housing, produce the nightly news show *L.I. News Tonight*, help monitor water pollution, create public relations and advertising campaigns for non-profit organizations, build vehicles powered by alternate fuel sources, and so much more. Students in every degree program have the chance to participate in professional caliber projects and research, and to put their knowledge to work in internships and paid positions that often lead to permanent, career-track positions after graduation. In fact, more than 75 percent of NYIT students have job offers in hand at the time they graduate.

Access to Opportunity

Everyone at NYIT believes that a high-quality education should be available to every qualified student, regardless of financial status. As college costs around the nation continue to rise, NYIT's tuition remains moderate, among the lowest of private, senior-level institutions in the New York metropolitan area. Generous scholarships—both need-based and achievement-based—are available to nearly every student, along with work-study jobs and low-interest loans.

Understanding that many students have work, family, and other personal obligations in addition to their education, NYIT offers flexible schedules that allow students to incorporate classes into their busy lives. Courses are available mornings, afternoons, and evenings, on weekdays and weekends, on the three New York area campuses, on the Internet, and at a site in Fort Lauderdale, Florida. Most programs allow students to combine all of these options in designing their schedules, creating opportunities for students who otherwise would not be able to attend college or complete degrees.

AT NYIT, CLASSES ARE SMALL AND STUDENTS RECEIVE PERSONAL ATTENTION FROM PROFESSORS, SO NO STUDENT IS "JUST A NUMBER."

THERE ARE FIVE LIBRARIES AT **NYIT**, PROVIDING
STUDENTS WITH ACCESS TO EXCLUSIVE EDUCATIONAL
AND RESEARCH DATABASES, JOURNALS, PERIODICALS,
BOOKS AND OTHER RESOURCES, AS WELL AS
INSTRUCTIONAL FACILITIES.

NYIT also offers residential facilities on two of
its three New York campuses. Students who wish to
experience an on-site campus experience may opt for the
NYIT residence halls located on the Central Islip campus.
These dormitory- and apartment-style units are located in
the heart of the campus and offer opportunities for students to utilize the many on-campus amenities, including
a bowling alley, an indoor swimming pool, a 400-seat
auditorium, and student dining facilities. Shuttle bus
service is provided to the Old Westbury campus. Students
interested in an urban environment may opt to live in
the St. George Residence, located in Brooklyn Heights,
one of New York City's most dynamic and popular
neighborhoods. The residence is a short subway ride
from NYIT's Manhattan campus and offers opportunities
for students to directly experience all that New York City
has to offer.

NYIT's classes, even introductory courses, are small—
most with fewer than 30 students—and taught within a
supportive environment, where faculty members get to
know their students, and take personal interest in the
growth and development of each individual. At NYIT,
nobody is "just a number." Students receive hands-on
instruction using equipment and facilities that mirror
those used in the professional world. Each graduate
enters the workforce with a solid educational foundation
in his or her field and the self-assurance to be a decision-
maker with other professionals.

STUDENTS COME TO **NYIT** FROM AROUND THE CORNER AND AROUND THE WORLD, CREATING A DIVERSE
STUDENT POPULATION WHOSE VARIED EXPERIENCES ENHANCE THE EDUCATIONAL ATMOSPHERE.

Applications-Oriented Research

NYIT encourages its faculty to engage in research endeavors that benefit the communities the college serves and the larger world. Together with the faculty of NYCOM, NYIT professors work toward finding solutions to some of the world's most significant problems, including disease prevention and treatment, alternative energy resources, environmental conservation, improvement of public education, and bridging the "digital divide" between socioeconomic and geographic populations. These dedicated educators design their research not only to gather and publish information, but also to directly apply their findings in existing situations where the people affected can receive maximum benefits.

NYIT's CENTRAL ISLIP CAMPUS, LOCATED HALFWAY BETWEEN NEW YORK CITY AND THE HAMPTONS, OFFERS STUDENTS ALL THE BENEFITS OF ON-CAMPUS RESIDENTIAL LIFE, INCLUDING WORLD-CLASS ATHLETIC AND SOCIAL FACILITIES.

Some of the projects in which NYIT and NYCOM faculty are actively engaged include:
• studying osteopathic manipulation therapy in Parkinson's disease treatment;
• offering computer training to teachers in at-risk public schools to improve student test scores;
• analyzing the use of photovoltaic panels as an alternate source of energy in both residential and commercial buildings;
• developing a neural interface between a prosthetic limb and an amputee's nervous system;
• assessing the health risks and environmental impact of sanitary sewage overflows.

While conducting this research, NYIT professors maintain a strong classroom presence, continuing to teach and interact with students. Their dedication to both teaching and research allows them to share their expertise in a uniquely comprehensive manner that provides their students with unparalleled learning benefits.

Everyone at New York Institute of Technology is greeting the new millennium with excitement and enthusiasm, eager to explore the many challenges that the future will bring. NYIT's ongoing mission to provide career-focused, technology-infused education, access to an opportunity and applications-oriented research will continue to position the college as a leader in higher education, preparing students for the limitless possibilities of the 21st century in an environment that fosters knowledge, personal growth, and success. ■

NYIT's EXQUISITE OLD WESTBURY CAMPUS, NESTLED IN THE RURAL BEAUTY OF NASSAU COUNTY'S NORTH SHORE, IS HOUSED ON A FORMER GOLD COAST ESTATE AND USES MANY OF THE ORIGINAL ESTATE BUILDINGS AS CLASSROOMS AND OFFICES.

SBARRO, INC.

Right now, in hundreds of restaurants around the world, Sbarro is hard at work. Whether it's serving pizza and pastas in more that 900 worldwide quick-service restaurants or serving steaks and Italian cuisine in 28 mid-scale and fine-dining restaurants, the one thing you can count on is this—freshly prepared food and superior service that will more than surpass diners' expectations. For over 40 years of operating restaurants and meeting consumers' needs, this recipe has been the secret to Sbarro's success.

Financial results may tell the story for some companies, but at Sbarro they are only the consequence of an ongoing commitment to quality and service that has spanned three generations of the Sbarro family. "Sbarro is more than a business to us," says Mario Sbarro, chairman, president and chief executive officer. "It is our heritage and the life that my parents, Gennaro and Carmela, built over 40 years ago." It is one of the enduring qualities that make Sbarro's a unique company in the restaurant industry.

JOSEPH, MARIO, AND ANTHONY SBARRO OUTSIDE
SBARRO SALUMERIA IN BROOKLYN, NEW YORK.

A History of Excellence

Sbarro has its roots in Naples, Italy. In 1956, Gennaro and Carmela Sbarro left Naples and immigrated to the United States. They soon opened a Salumeria, or Italian grocery store, in Brooklyn, N.Y. "As young children, my two brothers, Joseph and Anthony, and I worked in the business along with our parents," says Mario Sbarro. "Starting an Italian Salumeria in a new country was hard work for my parents," says Mario Sbarro. "But because the quality of the food and service was exceptional, the Salumeria quickly became a neighborhood favorite." The Sbarro's offered freshly made mozzarella, imported cheeses, homemade sausages, salamis and many traditional Italian delicacies and desserts that were all based on family recipes. They also offered something else that was in rare supply—a passion for food quality and customer service that was unmatched.

After a short time, the Salumeria became a huge success. Because of the popularity of the original Salumeria and the demand for Sbarro food, the Sbarros opened two additional stores—one in Brooklyn and one in Manhattan. Each of the stores was managed by one of the three brothers under the direction of their father. While sales in the three stores continued to be good, Carmela (Mama) Sbarro developed a new aspect of the business—catering for birthdays, graduations, showers, and other family events. The catering business soon grew and became an integral part of the Sbarro business.

The Sbarro family prepared Italian dishes and recipes for the three stores fresh each day in a central kitchen. In 1971, the family introduced a self-service style restaurant on Lexington Avenue and 57th street. The restaurant was supplied daily by the central kitchen. Elaborate food displays with a wide range of choices, along with the traditional family quality made this location an instant success. Several additional self-service-style units were opened in Manhattan.

Soon the central kitchen reached its capacity and the family was faced with deciding whether to build a larger central kitchen or limit growth. Recognizing the potential for growth outside New York City and insisting on freshly prepared foods, the family reinvented their business so that all cooking could be done on premises. Open-display kitchens with attractively presented food selections in a fast-moving, self-service style became the Sbarro hallmark that is still used today.

The family quickly identified shopping malls as a possible expansion vehicle. Malls had many of the characteristics of a city street location, with their weekend, weekday, lunch and dinner traffic patterns. When the first mall opened in Brooklyn, Sbarro was one of its anchor quick-service restaurants. As the business continued to expand and the three Sbarro sons—Mario, Joseph, and Anthony—moved east, Sbarro developed a presence in all the major malls on Long Island.

CARMELA "MAMA" SBARRO.

By 1985, Sbarro had become so successful that it went public with 60 units and $30 million of revenue. After a secondary offering a year later, the company was able to internally fund a rapid national expansion. During that time, Sbarro was repeatedly named as one of Forbes magazine's "Best 200 Small Companies" and was listed on the New York Stock Exchange in 1994. By 1999, Sbarro had grown to more than 900 restaurants with more than $500 million in system wide sales when circumstances permitted the Sbarro family to take the company private. Going private has allowed the company to operate the way it always has: as a family business that is rooted in three generations of outstanding quality and commitment to excellence.

Sbarro Today

Today, Sbarro is the largest shopping mall-based, cafeteria-style restaurant in the world. Sbarro's system-wide sales are more than $575 million. The Company operates 960 restaurants in 48 states and 28 countries, including the United Kingdom, Puerto Rico, Canada, Russia, and Israel. Approximately 300 restaurants are franchised.

Over the past several years, Sbarro has expanded into various casual dining concepts. In partnership with other successful restauranteurs, Sbarro operates a number of other concepts, including steak houses, pizzerias, full-menu restaurants, and high-end, full-service Italian/Mediterranean restaurants located on Long Island and in New York City. These restaurants have been highly successful and represent a significant growth vehicle for Sbarro.

Sbarro's corporate headquarters is in Melville, N.Y. It has an operations center in Commack, N.Y., which provides administrative services to all Sbarro restaurants worldwide. The company employs more than 7,500 employees. Sbarro is one of Long Island's largest employers.

"My brothers and I are proud to have expanded this company from a single Italian store in Brooklyn to a global company with almost 1,000 restaurants in 28 countries," says Mario Sbarro. "But the most rewarding aspect of our success is that we are continuing the dream of our parents and maintaining the family passion for excellence and commitment to fresh and high quality food." It is interesting to note that over the next few months, Sbarro's international expansion will bring the family back to Italy—where the newest Sbarro restaurant will open shortly. Mario, Joseph, and Anthony Sbarro look at each other and smile at this newest restaurant. It's the birthplace of their father and mother, the place where the family recipes were first introduced, the place where the Sbarro story originally began.

Dynamic Leadership

Today, the company is headed by Mario Sbarro and his two brothers, Joseph and Anthony. Joseph is senior executive vice president and Anthony is vice chairman of the board and treasurer. Even Carmela (Mama) Sbarro, the family matriarch, retains an active role in the company. In addition to serving as director emeritus and vice president, Mama Sbarro continues to run the daily operations at Sbarro's Salumeria in Brooklyn, N.Y., the family's original Italian deli.

GENNARO SBARRO, FOUNDER.

SBARRO UNITS FEATURE DISPLAY KITCHENS,

unique advantages that differentiate Sbarro from many of its competitors. Says Mario Sbarro, "we are fortunate to be able to blend the traditions of the family with executives who bring their expertise and combine it with our core traditions and values."

Operational Excellence

Despite the global scope of the Sbarro business, each restaurant—whether franchised or company owned—maintains the family commitment to quality and service.

All food at all Sbarro restaurants is prepared daily and made from the best ingredients. Even the sauce and pizza dough is made fresh in each restaurant from long-standing family recipes. Many consumers are initially attracted to Sbarro by watching the pizza makers spin pizza dough behind the counter. However, once the guests become better acquainted with Sbarro, they find that the menu is quite extensive and varied. In addition to traditional Italian specialties, the menu features fresh salads, grilled chicken, steamed vegetable dishes, and delicious desserts.

Family and family traditions are important to the Sbarro's. While the company is a global organization with sales of more than $575 million, the company's unique success is due not only to the quality of its food, but also to the continuing influence of the Sbarro family. Today more than 20 third-generation family members have joined the business. They continue to operate the business today, utilizing the long-cherished traditions of quality and excellence started more than 40 years ago by their grandparents.

Today, the Sbarro family works side-by-side with a non-family management team who is among the best in the restaurant industry. The unique combination of family and non-family management is one of the

Long Term Vendor Relationships

In its early development, specialty Italian products and high-quality ingredients used in the family recipes were difficult to obtain outside the New York metropolitan area. Sbarro's local distributor, Lisanti Foods, recognized the potential growth opportunity and was willing to deliver these products throughout the country at the same price as if delivered locally. "This was a critical success factor in Sbarro's rapid development into a national restaurant chain," said Joseph Sbarro. Today Lisanti Foods and its president, Joseph Lisanti, is a national distributor servicing Sbarro and many other successful restaurant chains. The Lisanti and Sbarro families maintain a close and long-lasting relationship.

SBARRO: DELICIOUS ITALIAN FOOD FOR PEOPLE ON THE MOVE.

Franchising

About 300 of Sbarro's restaurants are franchised. Sbarro believes that its established brand name, standardized operating systems, support services, and superior economic model provide tremendous value for its franchisees.

The company only considers experienced food-service operators as potential franchisees. Franchisees must demonstrate a proven track record in the food service industry and at least five years of restaurant ownership or operations experience. They must also have experience in commercial leasing or real estate development, and an interest in developing multiple locations. Most importantly, franchisees must continue the Sbarro family traditions of quality and excellence in food, customer service and facilities.

"Our franchisees are our ambassadors," says Anthony Sbarro. "They must understand the Sbarro family approach. If a franchisee doesn't understand that, our customers won't have an authentic dining experience." The franchising of Sbarro restaurants worldwide is a key element of Sbarro's future growth strategy.

Sbarro's Future

"Sbarro's future is bright," says Mario Sbarro. "We have a long and proud history, and a future that is filled with challenges and extraordinary opportunities."

"Our company has extraordinary fundamentals." "We have a product that is unmatched in quality and excellence, a capable management team, several successful concepts, a worldwide presence, a proven business model, and three generations of commitment to family traditions, recipes, and values."

FRESHLY PREPARED FOODS OFFER GUESTS A MEMORABLE DINNING EXPERIENCE.

"We are making substantial investments in our future from our operating systems to our recipes to our restaurant designs and future expansion plans. We are committed to being the best. It's that simple. All of our 7,500 Sbarro employees in 28 countries around the world are clearly committed to one thing. The one thing that has been the foundation of Sbarro's enduring success—a passion for excellence, quality, and outstanding customer value." ■

SBARRO'S MELVILLE LONG ISLAND HEADQUARTERS.

CANON U.S.A., INC.

If a picture is worth a thousand words, as the old saying goes, then a snapshot of Canon U.S.A., Inc. speaks volumes. Known for imaging excellence in its cameras and business machines, the company also has demonstrated in many ways its outstanding support of the Long Island community—with employees cleaning up area parks and nature preserves, walking to raise money for breast cancer research, and biking across Long Island to help disabled children.

At the heart of all Canon activities is a corporate philosophy known as "kyosei," which is best described as "living and working together for the common good."

"We strive to live by this philosophy in all aspects of our business—from the research and development, manufacturing and shipping of our professional and consumer imaging solutions, down to and including our community involvement," said Kinya Uchida, president & CEO of Canon U.S.A., Inc. "That is the surest path to success."

The Business

Canon has operated in the United States since 1955, with the opening of its first branch office on Fifth Avenue in New York City. By 1966, Canon expanded its operations, and the New York office was officially incorporated under the name of Canon U.S.A., Inc., a division of Canon, Inc., based in Japan. The U.S. Corporate headquarters has been based in Lake Success, Long Island, New York, since 1971 and employs 800 people. The parent company has come a long way from its founding in 1937 as a camera manufacturer. It now has more than 40 divisions worldwide, with 10 locations in North America,

KINYA UCHIDA, PRESIDENT & CEO—
CANON U.S.A., INC.

and offices in South America, Europe, the Middle East, Africa, Asia, Australia, and New Zealand.

Canon technology is based on a concept the company calls "Canon KNOW HOW." The concept is meant to empower both the consumer and the professional who use Canon products to achieve optimum results with technology that is approachable, intuitive, and fun to use.

With the PowerShot S20, the world's smallest 3.3 megapixel digital camera, consumers get a high-quality image by simply pointing and clicking. The ELPH Series cameras, designed for use in a variety of environments, are simple and fun to use. Other Canon products, from the imageRUNNER™ digital imaging system to the Elura digital video camcorder and the DR-5080C Color Scanner, have won awards for their usability and ingenuity.

Canon business machines account for about 80 percent of the company's sales, followed by photographic products at 10 percent, and optical and other products. These products include full-color and black-and-white copiers; printers; micrographics and image-filing systems; facsimile machines; calculators; cameras and lenses; camcorders; and seimconductor, broadcast, and optical equipment.

Beyond the office and consumer markets, Canon's deep commitment to research and development has helped the company develop medical imaging technology and software for advanced semiconductor equipment.

Canon's sensor technology helped it develop the new Digital Radiography System, which produces high-resolution images that can be viewed in seconds

CANON U.S.A., INC. CORPORATE
HEADQUARTERS—LAKE SUCCESS, NEW YORK.

CANON EMPLOYEES VOLUNTEER THEIR TIME IN A VARIETY OF WAYS. LEFT: MEMBERS OF TEAM CANON STROLL ALONG THE BOARDWALK AT JONES BEACH STATE PARK FOR THE ANNUAL MAKING STRIDES AGAINST BREAST CANCER WALK. RIGHT: THE CANON CLEAN EARTH CREW DIGS ANOTHER CLEAN-UP PROJECT.

by radiologists and clinicians. The system's large sensor plate enables both quick and highly accurate diagnoses.

"At Canon, we strive to provide real solutions for everyday life," said Uchida. "Our advances in medical imaging technology are an example of this."

The Community

Canon U.S.A. has established a true home on Long Island. The role the company plays in the Long Island community extends beyond the people it employs and the products and services it provides.

Canon employees participate locally and nationally in a variety of charitable events, including the March of Dimes' WalkAmerica, a national fundraiser dedicated to fighting birth defects in babies; The LensCrafters Foundation's Give the Gift of Sight program, which delivers free eye exams and glasses to children on Long Island and around the world; and the annual Making Strides Against Breast Cancer Walk raising funds for the Long Island Chapter of the American Cancer Society.

The Canon Discover Long Island Bike Tour is an annual family bike ride through Long Island's south shore, and The Canon Long Island marathon offers runners of all ages the chance to compete right in their own backyard.

In keeping with the philosophy of "kyosei," Canon is committed to a healthy environment. Canon funds conservation research through the Canon National Parks Science Scholars program, which provides the nation's largest environment-related scholarships to Ph.D. candidates for research in U.S. National Parks. Canon also makes possible The Nature Conservancy's Wings of the Americas program, which protects birds and their habitats throughout the Americas. In fact, Canon's support helps The Nature Conservancy of Long Island preserve nesting areas for piping plovers and osprey.

The Canon Envirothon is North America's largest environmental science competition for high school students, while Canon's Clean Earth Crew, staffed by employee volunteers, conducts beach clean-ups and other activities in local parks and wildlife preserves. Canon also underwrites the Emmy award winning PBS television series NATURE.

Additionally, Canon is leading the charge to make its manufacturing and workplace processes "green" by operating the world's largest toner cartridge return program, designing energy efficient office equipment manufactured for end-of-life recovery, removing 100 percent of the lead from photographic lenses, and encouraging employees to practice workplace conservation.

"At the heart of Canon's commitment to the environment is the belief that we are building a better world for all generations to follow," said Uchida. "To succeed, we must take responsibility for preserving the ecology of our planet today." ∎

CANON DIGITAL VIDEO CAMCORDER.

SLANT/FIN CORP.

Slant/Fin is as predominant in baseboard heating equipment as Campbell's is in soup and Intel is in computer components. It is a favorite of professional heating contractors, fuel oil dealers, specifying engineers, homebuilders and homeowners. Slant/Fin Corp. is not only the nation's number one manufacturer of hot water baseboard heating systems, Slant/Fin is a leading producer of high-efficiency gas and oil-fired boilers.

THE CONSTRUCTION FEATURES THAT MAKE SLANT/FIN BASEBOARD SO DURABLE, ALSO MAKE IT FASTER AND EASIER TO INSTALL. SLANT/FIN BASEBOARD IS RECOGNIZED BY PROFESSIONAL HEATING CONTRACTORS AS AMERICA'S LEADING BRAND.

In addition, the Slant/Fin consumer division produces a variety of portable, electric home comfort products including heaters, air purifiers, personal coolers and germ-free humidifiers. Slant/Fin products are in millions of homes and buildings throughout the U.S., Canada, and 25 countries around the world.

The company's general office and main factory are on an 11-acre campus in Greenvale. Other manufacturing and administrative facilities are in Glen Cove, Ontario, Canada and Eastern Europe. Slant/Fin has maintained its commitment to manufacturing on Long Island since the company moved here from Queens in 1966. As a result, Slant/Fin has the distinction of being Long Island's largest outbound tonnage shipper. The company has also remained loyal to its long-time Canadian customers and employees. The Ontario plant continues to operate full-scale even though tariff changes have prompted many U.S. companies to close their Canadian factories.

The company has grown steadily from its founding in 1949 by Mel Dubin, an electrical engineer and inventor. What he started as a two-person operation in Brooklyn in an 800-square-foot converted bakery now employs over 400 people in multiple buildings encompassing 375,000 square feet. The focus for more than 50 years has been to produce energy-efficient, environmentally friendly products. The hallmarks of Slant/Fin operations are quality design, quality manufacturing, dependability, and service. Computer-assisted design and engineering combined with advanced metalworking technology are central to the company's superior capabilities in producing baseboard radiation, boilers, and other products.

President Donald Brown points out that in a highly competitive industry, Slant/Fin maintains its edge through superior research, development, and engineering: "Our company invests significant resources each year to keep us ahead of the field." According to Brown, many current Slant/Fin boiler models didn't even exist five years ago. He cited among recent product introductions, Concept 21, the industry's safest, most advanced computer-controlled boiler for commercial and residential applications.

Brown explains that Slant/Fin boilers and baseboard products are sold exclusively to plumbing and heating wholesalers. The wholesalers resell them to trade and commercial customers. However, the Slant/Fin consumer products division markets its products directly to retailers. While other manufacturers often produce consumer products under various private brands or store labels,

SLANT/FIN'S 11-ACRE CORPORATE HEADQUARTERS AND PRIMARY MANUFACTURING PLANT IS LOCATED IN GREENVALE. ADDITIONAL FACILITIES ARE MAINTAINED IN GLEN COVE, CANADA AND EASTERN EUROPE.

SLANT/FIN RESIDENTIAL AND COMMERCIAL HEATING PRODUCTS ARE INSTALLED IN MILLIONS OF HOMES AND BUILDINGS. THE COMPANY'S RANGE OF EQUIPMENT FEATURES AMERICA'S MOST POPULAR BASEBOARD HEATING AND INCLUDES BOILERS THAT LEAD THE INDUSTRY IN SAFETY AND ECONOMY.

all Slant/Fin consumer products are branded with the Slant/Fin name. They are available through home centers, hardware chains, department stores, catalogs, and other retail outlets. Slant/Fin produces hundreds of different products under strict quality assurance programs. More than 100 sales representatives sell these products to thousands of resellers.

Dick Thompson, vice president, sales, notes that many Slant/Fin employees have been with the company for 20, 30, and even over 40 years. "Since Slant/Fin is a 12-month-a-year manufacturing operation, we're able to offer our manufacturing personnel, steady, year-round employment," says Thompson.

Slant/Fin is also a good corporate citizen of Long Island. According to Brown, the company places its charitable support behind a number of regional organizations including North Shore-LIJ Health System, Tilles Center for the Performing Arts, and Long Island University.

Specifiers and buyers can review technical details of Slant/Fin products on a convenient CD-ROM. Company and product information can be accessed through the company's web site: www.slantfin.com.

Mel Dubin, who founded Slant/Fin, continues to play a key role as chairman of the privately held company. His son, Adam Dubin, executive vice president, says the company's mission remains what it has been for decades: "to be a dependable source for an expanding array of superior products and to provide the highest level of customer service to resellers, specifiers, installers, and end-users." ■

DOWLING COLLEGE

For students who seek a unique learning environment rich in history and replete with personal opportunity, Dowling College is an excellent choice. Situated on the picturesque banks of the Connetquot River in Oakdale, Dowling's main campus, now celebrating its 100th year, was once home to members of the William K. Vanderbilt family. The college mansion and many of its remaining artifacts are reminiscent of the Gilded Age, and serve as the perfect historical compliment to the College's state-of-the-art resources and curriculum offered at its Oakdale and Brookhaven campuses. Today, through its Schools of Arts and Sciences, Aviation and Transportation, Business, and Education, the College offers a wide range of Bachelor's and Master's degree programs, professional diplomas, and post-graduate certificate programs, as well as an Ed.D in Educational Administration. However, despite its expanded university-style curriculum, Dowling remains The Personal College.

A Foundation for Personal Growth

With its ideal student-to-teacher ratios, Dowling's dedicated and highly credentialed faculty strives to bring out the best in each student. "Smart" classrooms are designed and equipped with the latest technologies to facilitate student-teacher communications and the learning experience. Students are encouraged to participate in a wide range of personal growth venues including high-level academic, athletic and cultural programs. Whether a science student participating in a groundbreaking research study subsequently published in prestigious scientific journals; or a student pilot flying to the aviation industry's "Top Gun" status; Dowling students are taking advantage of every opportunity to grow.

TEACHER-STUDENT INTERACTION IS THE TRADE-MARK OF DOWLING, "THE PERSONAL COLLEGE."

Students whose personal goals reflect changing social and economic directives will find Dowling's programs a perfect fit to their educational requirements. As the world began a new millennium, the College launched several new academic programs that serve these evolving demands. Among them are the MBA in Intermodal Transportation, MBA in Information Systems Management, BS in Sports Management, BA in Visual Communications and MS in Integrated Mathematics and Science—the first of its kind on Long Island. Because fulfilling each student's educational goals is Dowling's top priority, the College treats each student as a member of its extended family. The new Student Services Center, staffed by caring and knowledgeable advisors, assist each student with matters ranging from course selections and financial aid, to academic support, counseling, internships, career planning and job placements.

An Educational Mission That Knows No Boundaries

The College's educational mission is not confined to its campuses. Dowling takes a leadership role on a local, national and global level through its various outreach initiatives. Locally, businesses depend on Dowling to help prepare their employees to meet changing industry requirement and future challenges. Many Long Island managers have successfully completed Dowling's Accelerated MBA programs. Other businesses take advantage of Dowling's corporate partnerships—facilitated through the Dowling Institute—which offer on-site informational and training programs. Another example of Dowling's commitment is the School of Education's service to local districts through its "Superintendents Roundtable."

DOWLING'S AWARD-WINNING CREW TEAM ON THE CONNETQUOT RIVER.

THE NEWLY RESTORED CENTRAL COURTYARD.

On a global scale, Dowling—through its internationally recognized faculty—has sponsored Mediterranean Conferences. These multi-discipline conferences are attended by representatives from colleges, universities, museums, governments and other institutions worldwide. Dowling's leadership in this prominent academic forum has gained the College international recognition. Further evidence of Dowling's position as a global ambassador is its recent appointment of a member of the Italian Ministry of External Affairs as its Chair of Italian culture. In addition, the College, through the Dowling Institute, has been offering English and technology courses to students of the People's Republic of China. The College extends its MBA offerings to Russia as well.

Award-Winning Athletics

Dowling's achievements are not confined to the world of academia. Its athletic teams have made news and garnered awards across several sports. For example, the College won the coveted Commissioner's Cup as the best overall program in the New York Collegiate Athletic Conference for two of the past three years. Dowling's widely acclaimed Crew Team gained the title of 1998 National champions and its Men's Soccer was a Top Ten Division II contender. On a more a personal level, Dowling produced the National Intercollegiate Flying Association's Top Pilot of the Northeast Region for four consecutive years, and the First Distinguished Scholar Award recipient named by The Wings Club, a prestigious group of top airline and aviation executives. The College also saw one of its rowing athletes represent his native country at the 2000 Olympics.

The Lion's Pride

Dowling students, faculty and administrators are not the only ones with great pride in the College's advancement over the past five decades. The College has a strong and active Board whose members represent diverse organizations from major manufacturers, real estate and high tech firms to leading financial institutions and other academic institutions. Dowling's alumni also have a strong allegiance to the college which, while changed over the years, has been steadfast in its mission to bring out the best in each student. Some of its alumni now serve on the College's Board, as members of its faculty or staff, or in other professional capacities. For all of these individuals and the existing student body, their pride in Dowling College; its historical roots and "Personal College" legacy, is ferocious. ■

DOWLING STUDENTS ENJOY THE BEAUTIFUL OAKDALE RUDOLPH CAMPUS.

AUSTIN TRAVEL

Austin Travel, Long Island's largest corporate Travel Management Company, has established itself as the region's most globally connected travel service while retaining its perspective as a family operated business with strong ties to the local business community, one which routinely turns up on Hofstra/KPMG's roster of 50 Top Businesses and 25 Fastest Growing Businesses.

As a member of First Travel Management, Austin Travel adds international clout to the company's famed level of local, personalized service. The company's prestigious corporate client list of companies such as Symbol Technologies, KeySpan Energy, Luxottica, Audiovox, the Jets and Islanders teams, Sbarro and others, benefit from travel services with an international reach from a company boasting 50 locations throughout the country and a strong Web presence.

Austin Travel was founded in 1955 by Larry Austin who now holds the posts of Chairman and CEO. His sons have brought the company into its second generation of leadership with Jeffrey as President and COO, Jamie as Senior Vice President of Sales and Account Management, and Stewart as Senior Vice President of Information Technology.

Although Austin Travel is perhaps best known for its corporate services, leisure travel accounts for a $35 million segment of the company's business.

OFFICIALS AT AUSTIN TRAVEL STRATEGIZE A COMPREHENSIVE TRAVEL SCHEDULE FOR ONE OF THE MANY CORPORATIONS SERVED BY THE COMPANY.

Of increasing importance to Austin Travel is its web-based business. Offering both corporate and leisure travel services, the Austin sites are upgraded constantly. Said Jamie Austin: "We see dramatic growth in future years. We're preparing for that growth all the time by continually updating our leisure and corporate websites." Their remarkable achievement in wedding their "brick and click" businesses hasn't gone unnoticed— Jamie finds that he's often sought after as a speaker by other Long Island companies hoping to replicate the Austin Web success story.

Austin also reaches out to the travel community with a relatively new division, Austin Associates, which affords smaller, independently-run travel agencies access to the national and international clout of Austin Travel. Combining the sales of associate members, Austin Travel is projecting over $800 million in sales for 2001.

Many Long Islanders are familiar with the company through its involvement in Long Island charitable and philanthropic endeavors. The pattern was set by Larry Austin whose many associations include being President of the Long Island Philharmonic, the Long Island Association (where he is Chairman of Transportation), and the Cinema Arts Centre, to cite just a few. Among the organizations which have garnered his sons' attention are the Arthritis Foundation, the Heart Council of Long Island, the Long Island Community Chest, and the Long Island Coalition for Fair Broadcasting.

While achieving an enviable level of sophistication and growth, the heart of Austin Travel remains its status as a family owned and operated business. ■

PROVIDING THE SECOND GENERATION OF LEADERSHIP AT AUSTIN TRAVEL ARE (LEFT TO RIGHT) JAMIE, STEWART, AND JEFF AUSTIN. THEY ARE SHOWN WITH COMPANY FOUNDER LARRY AUSTIN (FAR RIGHT).

AVIS GROUP HOLDINGS CO.

Mediocrity has no place in today's competitive business environment. That is why Avis Group Holdings Co. transformed itself from Avis Rent A Car, Inc., into a global, business-to-business vehicle management and information solutions company. Avis is now focused on providing a full array of automotive, transportation, and vehicle management solutions—all under the banner of personalized service that meets clients' needs.

"Providing an outstanding product or service is the first step toward excellence, but it is certainly not the last," said A. Barry Rand, chairman of the board and chief executive officer of Avis Group. "Everyone at Avis shares our commitment to providing outstanding, personalized service to every Avis customer. And by expanding our focus, we are able to offer our customers comprehensive information to manage their resources more efficiently."

The evolution of Avis gained momentum in May 1999, when the company acquired PHH and Wright Express. That transformed Avis from not only the world's second-largest, general-use car rental business into the world's leading provider of fleet cars and value-added fleet management services, and the second-largest provider of vehicle leasing services.

Hunt Valley, Maryland-based PHH manages the vehicles of more than 22,000 companies, including one-third of Fortune 500 companies and half of the FTSE 100. The acquisition brought to the Avis family PHH's fee-based fuel and credit card businesses, as well as award-winning data warehouse technology and a secure extranet site. PHH InterActiveTM enables PHH's customers to obtain real-time information about repair

transactions, maintenance schedules, employee driving activities, and the like.

This technology was key to the development of Avis InterActive, the first Internet-based information system in the rent-a-car industry. This sophisticated Internet-based application and data warehouse allows the company's corporate customers to access online aggregated

AVIS RENT A CAR FACILITY AT LONG ISLAND'S MACARTHUR AIRPORT.

information on car rental expenses and usage, as well as renter preferences. Wright Express provides information management, payment processing, and financial services to car, van, and truck fleets. It also owns the nation's most widely accepted electronic universal fleet card for controlling expenses and monitoring employee travel.

These new initiatives help support the Avis commitment to providing outstanding customer service and value, the foundation upon which the company was founded. The Avis Experience, which defines the quality service that the company provides to each and every car rental customer, is a total service ethic that encompasses employee training, customer choice, database tools, and front-line customer service.

"This is truly an amazing time for Avis," said Mr. Rand. "By leveraging our company's financial strength, award-winning technology, and strong customer service base, we are well on our way to becoming the business-to-business vehicle management and information solutions company of the 21st Century." ■

AVIS GROUP EMPLOYEES CELEBRATING EMPLOYEE APPRECIATION DAY AT EISENHOWSER PARK.

MOLLOY COLLEGE

Rooted in the Catholic and Dominican traditions, Molloy College promotes the ideal of truth by providing a value-centered education experience which seeks to enhance the intellectual, ethical, spiritual, and social development of its students.

Since its founding in 1955 by the Sisters of St. Dominic, Molloy has worked to do more than help its students get a solid education and a great job. The faculty and staff at Molloy are committed to helping young men and women achieve their full potential as productive, civic minded, complete persons who can truly make a difference in the world of today and tomorrow. Molloy graduates make significant contributions every day in business, education, nursing, criminal justice, and many other diverse fields. They don't just attain financial success, they apply the values that were nurtured at Molloy College to raise the level of their professions. They are leaders who make the people around them better, and reach out beyond their job descriptions to raise the quality of life for everyone.

Molloy College offers more than 30 graduate and undergraduate majors including Nursing, Education, Social Work, Business, Environmental Studies, Criminal Justice, Music Therapy, Speech Pathology, Computer Information Systems, and various Allied Health professions.

MOLLOY COLLEGE PROMOTES THE IDEAL OF TRUTH BY PROVIDING A VALUE-CENTERED EDUCATION EXPERIENCE WHICH SEEKS TO ENHANCE THE INTELLECTUAL, ETHICAL, SPIRITUAL, AND SOCIAL DEVELOPMENT OF ITS STUDENTS.

Facilities on the picturesque campus include a modern International Business Lab, Academic Computer Lab, Library, Media Center, TV Studio, and Professional Theater. Molloy College offers students the opportunity to expand their personal development by encouraging participation in any or all of the more than 35 clubs and honor societies, as well as a host of community service projects.

Intercollegiate athletics at Molloy is flourishing. Men and women compete in NCAA Division II sports that include basketball, baseball, softball, tennis, volleyball, soccer, lacrosse, and equestrian events. Recently, the men's basketball team advanced to the NYCAC championship game, and the men's lacrosse team was ranked sixth in the nation in Division II.

Community groups also make use of the campus. In addition to many community events, there are several meeting facilities and fine catering options available to accommodate just about any event. Molloy College plays a visible and active role in the business and civic community, and Long Island's business and civic leaders have traditionally shown strong support for Molloy and its students. The school's development office actively welcomes participation from the local business community.

For more information on how to become involved with programs at Molloy visit the college's website www.molloy.edu. ■

FACILITIES ON THE PICTURESQUE CAMPUS INCLUDE A MODERN INTERNATIONAL BUSINESS LAB, ACADEMIC COMPUTER LAB, LIBRARY, MEDIA CENTER, TV STUDIO, AND PROFESSIONAL THEATER.

ADECCO

Recruiting qualified workers has always been mission critical for most U.S. companies. With unemployment at historic lows, the issue is even more urgent. At the same time, job seekers want to explore career options, receive skills training, and pursue lifestyle choices. These trends present additional challenges to employers.

That's where Adecco enters the picture. The largest employment services company in the world, Adecco offers a comprehensive range of flexible staffing and career resources to corporate clients and qualified temporary associates. From local businesses to multinationals, Adecco has the talent and technology to meet clients' changing human resources needs. The company forms strategic partnerships with clients to address temporary and permanent staffing requirements, from clerical and light industrial to computer programming and software design.

ADECCO'S NORTH AMERICAN HEADQUARTERS IN MELVILLE, NEW YORK.

Adecco's North American network of 2,000 points of sales and service employs more than 800,000 temporary employees who provide a flexible workforce for 50,000 companies each year. Adecco provides innovative staffing solutions, from recruitment, screening, and evaluation to staffing and management. Adecco helps clients use its flexible staffing solutions as a key organizational tool, rather than simply as a temporary solution.

Technological innovation lies at the heart of Adecco's strategy. In addition to Adecco's website, which is effective in recruiting temporary and full-time candidates, Adecco offers three key technologies to its customers:

• *Job Shop*—Essentially ATMs for jobs, these interactive kiosks allow job seekers to apply for Adecco's temporary, contract, and temp-to-hire jobs. Adecco's Job Shops are located in high-traffic locations such as shopping malls, transit stations, universities, and civic centers.

• *Xpert*—Adecco's unique, proprietary candidate-matching and branch-automation system is networked throughout all Adecco offices. This evaluation methodology ensures that temporary associates are ideally matched to clients' specific staffing needs.

• *Connect*—This system provides customers with immediate PC access to staffing statistics and analysis—making the flow of information, resources, and people seamless and reliable, thus improving response time and increasing the quality of its service.

Despite Adecco's global reach and Swiss heritage, the company has strong roots on Long Island. When the company merged with Olsten Corporation in March 2000, it moved its North American headquarters from Redwood City, California, to Olsten's building in Melville. The move took advantage of the region's rich employer and employee base, as well as its proximity to New York City. From nearly a dozen other locations on the island, including Garden City, Hauppauge, Islandia, and Ronkonkoma, Adecco places more than 2,000 temporary associates at 500 client locations every week.

Adecco's reach extends beyond putting people to work. The company gives its temporary associates the means to discover and develop their interests, skills, and careers. It also helps to create a viable workforce that contributes meaningfully to the community and the next generation. ∎

MARCH 15, 2000: ADECCO LISTS ON THE NEW YORK STOCK EXCHANGE UNDER TICKER SYMBOL ADO. EXECUTIVES FROM LEFT TO RIGHT: STUART OLSTEN, FELIX WEBER, STEVE HARRISON, KLAUS JACOBS, DEBBIE POND-HEIDE, JOHN BOWMER, PHILIPPE FORIEL-DESTEZET.

The promise of a bright future pervaded the air as 1960 began. The United States was prospering. More people were able to attend college and buy homes than ever before in history. In 1960 John F. Kennedy, the youngest president since Theodore Roosevelt, was elected. Of special interest to Long Islanders was the fact that new First Lady Jacqueline Kennedy had deep family roots in East Hampton.

In most ways, Long Island was a microcosm of the rest of the nation, although no region was growing as quickly.

In the decade since the 1950 census, Long Island's population had more than doubled, to 1,300,171 in Nassau; 666,784 in Suffolk. Forty percent of the population was aged 19 or under. The median value of a home in Nassau was $18,500. In Suffolk it was four thousand dollars less. Rent in Nassau averaged $95 a month and $77 a month in Suffolk.

In 1940, there were approximately 80,000 children in Nassau County's public schools and 29,175 in Suffolk's, as well as 15,000 enrolled in Long Island's Catholic schools. By 1965, these numbers had grown to 331,872 students in Nassau, 221,303 in Suffolk, and 88,755 in the parochial schools.

As the decade began, there were 900 United States military advisors in South Vietnam. An early call to be wary of what was to come was sounded by Bob Dylan, in 1962, when he wrote that the times were *"Like the stillness in the wind 'Fore the hurricane begins."*

One storm brewing ever more strongly on Long Island was the battle over civil rights. When Martin Luther King led the marches in the South, Long Islanders were there with him. In 1964, Long Islander Michael Schwerner—along with Andrew Goodman and James Chaney—was one of three civil rights workers murdered in Mississippi in an incident that drew international attention.

At home, however, there was a great deal to be done. Communities and, therefore, their school districts, were essentially segregated. Even those communities in which integration was the planned ideal were not really integrated.

WITH A GROWING NUMBER OF MINORITIES, PARTICULARLY AFRICAN AMERICANS, MOVING OUT FROM NEW YORK CITY, PEOPLE WERE WORKING HARD TO SOLVE THE PROBLEMS OF SEGREGATION AND DISCRIMINATION THAT STILL COULD BE COMMON IN THE EARLY 1960S. PHOTO BY ROB AMATO, BRUCE BENNETT STUDIOS.

With a growing number of minorities, particularly African Americans, moving out from New York City, people were making attempts to solve the problem. Activist groups were formed. Long Island had branches of the Congress of Racial Equality (CORE) and the National Association for the Advancement of Colored People (NAACP). There were cross-burnings in Amityville, a refusal to comply with court-ordered integration in Malverne, and a proposal to bus minority city children to schools in Great Neck.

In a decade-long lesson, Long Islanders found out that the problems they generally believed to exist only in the South existed in their hometowns.

At the beginning of the '60s, the majority of people who lived on Long Island commuted to work in New York City. The aircraft industry that had brought the region wartime prosperity was foundering in peacetime.

Republic Aviation's Navy contract to build the F-105 Thunderchief was cancelled as the result of safety concerns. In 1965, Republic was taken over by the Fairchild Hiller Corporation.

Grumman Aerospace Corporation in Bethpage was also hit hard by the peacetime economy. Grumman, however, hit the jackpot on May 25, 1961, when President Kennedy told Congress: "I believe that this nation should commit itself to achieving the goal, before this decade is out, of landing a man on the Moon and returning him safely to the Earth."

Grumman won the contract to build a Lunar Excursion Module, a LEM, that would transport America's Apollo astronauts from their spaceship to the surface of the moon six times between the first landing on July 20, 1969, and the last three years later.

In a local footnote, twenty years after he was the first man to walk on the moon, Neil Armstrong was named Chairman of AIL, the Long Island company owned by Eaton Corporation. Both Eaton and Armstrong were based in Ohio.

LONG ISLAND ESTABLISHED BRANCHES OF THE CONGRESS OF RACIAL EQUALITY (CORE) AND THE NATIONAL ASSOCIATION FOR THE ADVANCEMENT OF COLORED PEOPLE (NAACP). PHOTOS BY DEBORAH ROSS, BRUCE BENNETT STUDIOS.

As the decade went on, the leadership of Long Island realized that the regional economy could not depend so heavily on the defense industry. Thus, an aggressive program of building office space and recruiting corporations began.

The business corridor along Route 110 in Melville began to grow, drawing nationally prominent businesses like Underwriters Laboratories, Inc. which, since its founding in Chicago in 1894, maintained its position as the leader in product safety testing.

Garden City, too, was growing as a business hub, with Avis establishing its world headquarters there in 1962 and the relocation of Dale Carnegie & Associates' international headquarters there in 1964.

The boom on Long Island gave rise to civic organizations that favored planned growth and environmental groups that worried about land use as it impacted natural resources.

Rachel Carson's 1962 book *The Silent Spring* laid out the dangers of commonly used pesticides like DDT, a long-lasting substance that impacts every link in the food chain, from single-cell plankton to fish to birds.

Carson's warning was heard by a group of citizens in Suffolk County who had been noticing that fish in Yaphank were dying in their lakes and ponds. Dr. Charles E. Wurster, a marine biologist at Stony Brook; Bellport High School teacher Arthur Cooley, who also chaired the Brookhaven Town Natural Resources Committee; and Brookhaven National Laboratory naturalist Dennis Puleston began speaking out about the problem.

Joined by Patchogue attorney Victor Yannacone, they sued to stop the Suffolk County Mosquito Control Commission from spraying DDT in Long Island's marshes. The plaintiffs brought scientific data to court to prove that DDT was causing the eggshells of ospreys and other birds break so that fewer offspring were hatched.

The judge in the case had to look in the dictionary for a definition of the word "ecology," but he decided in the end to ban the spraying of DDT.

Buoyed by that success, those involved in the suit incorporated as the Environmental Defense Fund on October 6, 1967. They began a series of legal actions across the country that led to a permanent, nationwide ban on DDT in 1972.

Today, with headquarters in Washington, DC, the organization has a membership of 300,000, a 1999 operating budget of $31.4 million, and is working around the world. In 2000, the group changed its name to "Environmental Defense."

The Suffolk County Legislature took the clean water campaign one step further in 1971, when they banned the sale of any laundry detergent that was not biodegradable. Residents who found the soap substitutes inadequate for getting their clothing as clean as they would like brought detergent in from Nassau and New York City. The ban was repealed after 10 years.

The 1969 opening of Smith Haven Mall in Lake Grove signaled for many Suffolk County's coming of age. For the first time, people in mid- and western Suffolk would not have to travel great distances to reach the closest mall.

PHOTOS BY SCOTT LEVY (ABOVE) AND LISA MEYER (BELOW), BRUCE BENNETT STUDIOS.

IN 1971, THE SUFFOLK COUNTY LEGISLATURE TOOK A CLEAN WATER CAMPAIGN A STEP FURTHER WHEN THEY BANNED THE SALE OF ANY LAUNDRY DETERGENT THAT WAS NOT BIODEGRADABLE. THE BAN WAS REPEALED AFTER TEN YEARS, BUT LONG ISLAND RESIDENTS STILL DEMONSTRATE CONCERN FOR THE WATERS THAT ARE SUCH AN INTEGRAL PART OF DAILY LIFE. PHOTOS BY DEBORAH ROSS, BRUCE BENNETT STUDIOS.

Louis Simpson, a Pulitzer Prize winning poet who taught at Stony Brook and lived near the mall, took a snapshot of Suffolk County suburbia in his poem, "The Beaded Pear:"

"Dad in Bermuda shorts, Mom her hair in curlers,
Jimmy 16, and Darlene who is twelve,
are walking through the Smith Haven Mall.

Jimmy needs a new pair of shoes.
In the Mall by actual count
there are twenty-two stores selling shoes:
Wise Shoes, Regal Shoes,
National Shoes, Naturalizer Shoes,
Stride Rite, Selby, Hanover...

...The Mall is laid out like a cathedral
with two arcades that cross -
Macy's at one end of the main arcade,
Abraham and Straus at the other..."

The national schism that was the Vietnam War divided Long Island, too. By the time the war ended in 1974, 574 Long Islanders had been killed in the service of their country.

As was true elsewhere, universities were often the centers in which the discontent with the war was expressed. Long Island's first anti-war teach-in was at Adelphi University in 1965.

In 1970, almost exactly five years to day of the teach-in, Long Islander Jeffrey Miller was one of four

GRUMMAN AEROSPACE CORPORATION IN BETHPAGE WON THE CONTRACT TO BUILD A LUNAR EXCURSION MODULE (LEM) THAT WOULD TRANSPORT AMERICA'S APOLLO ASTRONAUTS FROM THEIR SPACESHIP TO THE SURFACE OF THE MOON SIX TIMES BETWEEN THE FIRST LANDING ON JULY 20, 1969, AND THE LAST THREE YEARS LATER. PHOTO © *NEWSDAY*.

IN 1974, DR. JEROME SWARTZ CO-FOUNDED SYMBOL TECHNOLOGIES, WHICH TODAY IS HEADQUARTERED IN HOLTSVILLE. SWARTZ IS CREDITED WITH 125 PATENTS, INCLUDING THE REVOLUTIONARY BAR CODE TECHNOLOGY USED ON JUST ABOUT EVERY PRODUCT SOLD TODAY. PHOTO BY BRUCE BENNETT, BRUCE BENNETT STUDIOS.

students killed by the National Guard in the Kent State anti-Vietnam demonstration. John Filo, a photographer with the local *Valley News*, shot the definitive photo at Kent State. It was a picture of a teenage girl crying in anguish as she knelt over the body of Jeffrey Miller.

Two central figures in the Vietnam War protest movement were Long Islanders: one "Born On the Fourth of July," the other an adopted Long Islander.

The latter was Allard K. Lowenstein. Born in 1929, the New Jersey native entered the national spotlight as the force behind the "Dump Johnson" movement. The movement was key in forcing President Lyndon B. Johnson to withdraw from the 1968 presidential race. Lowenstein convinced Senator Eugene McCarthy to run in the 1968 Democratic presidential primaries. In that race, voters were encouraged to "Get Clean For Gene."

In 1968, he moved to New York's Fifth Congressional District in Long Beach and won a seat in the House of Representatives. He served one term.

Throughout his life, Lowenstein was politically active and outspoken, teaching law and political science at several universities. A former co-worker in Manhattan assassinated Lowenstein in 1980.

At a memorial marking the twentieth anniversary of his death, former Representative Patricia Schroeder said Lowenstein "had a knack for focusing in on issues that no one else was paying attention to and getting people to understand that these were vital struggles, That just shows you the energy and the passion of the man."

Ron Kovic, born in Massapequa in 1946, shared that anti-war passion but, unlike Lowenstein and others who did not directly experience war, Kovic came to his conviction after serving in Vietnam.

There were many people who believed in the axiom "my country, right or wrong." They were often the young men who enlisted in the service believing that it was an act of the type of selfless, responsible patriotism portrayed by John Wayne in the movies.

Ron Kovic was such a young man. He enlisted at age 18 and was sent to Vietnam. He returned home at age 21 in a wheelchair, paralyzed from the chest down.

In the late '60s, revealing a new view of what it was to be a patriot, Kovic began to speak out against the horror and futility of the war. He went to the 1972 GOP national convention, where he joined other protesters calling for President Richard Nixon to end the war. In 1976 he published his memoir, *Born On the Fourth of July.* That year, he spoke at the Democratic National convention in Madison Square Garden, reading a poem he had written:

> *"I am the living death*
> *the Memorial Day on wheels*
> *I am your Yankee Doodle Dandy*
> *your John Wayne come home*
> *your Fourth of July firecracker*
> *exploding in the grave."*

Kovic continued to work in the cause of peace both in the United States and abroad.

(ABOVE) RON KOVIC, BORN IN MASSAPEQUA IN 1946, BECAME AN IMPASSIONED ANTI-WAR PROTESTER AFTER VOLUNTARILY ENLISTING IN THE ARMY AND GOING TO WAR IN VIETNAM AT AGE 18, AND RETURNING HOME PARALYZED AT AGE 21. HIS EXPERIENCE WAS THE SUBJECT OF HIS BOOK, *BORN ON THE FOURTH OF JULY*, WHICH LATER WAS MADE INTO A FILM STARRING TOM CRUISE AS KOVIC. PHOTO © *NEWSDAY*. (BELOW) ON VETERAN'S DAY, NOVEMBER 11, 1991, A VIETNAM MEMORIAL WAS DEDICATED AT BALD HILL IN FARMINGVILLE, ONE OF THE HIGHEST POINTS ON LONG ISLAND. PHOTO BY J. MCISAAC, BRUCE BENNETT STUDIOS.

VETERAN'S DAY PARADE, BALDWIN. PHOTO BY DEBORAH ROSS, BRUCE BENNETT STUDIOS.

The Vietnam War remained on the minds of Long Islanders. On Veteran's Day, November 11, 1991, a Vietnam Memorial was dedicated at Bald Hill in Farmingville, one of the highest points on Long Island. It is in the form of an obelisk with a flag draped over the top.

With the national unrest over Vietnam continuing, the '60s also saw the rise of the feminist movement and the arrival of the Beatles, whose first concert in the United States was at Flushing's Shea Stadium.

Naturally, Long Island wasn't immune to new trends in the national culture. One of these was recreational drug use. On January 17, 1968 the Suffolk County police raided the campus, arresting a score of people on drug charges. The incident—the first time police in the United States raided a college campus looking for drugs—made national headlines and earned Stony Brook a reputation as a "drug school."

As it turned out, the majority of those people arrested spent no time in jail. It was an instance when facts were not allowed to interfere with a good story, and it took a long time for the university to live down the incident.

With all of the earth-changing events in the rest of the world, Long Island did continue to conduct business as usual. For example, in 1960, the business of Suffolk County government broadened to include a new county police department formed out of the individual departments of the five western towns. The five eastern towns still have individual departments.

Part of that business was building the public infrastructure to support growth. One of the largest projects begun in the 1960s was the Southwest Sewer District in West Babylon.

With drinking water—all of their water—supplied by the sole source aquifer underground, Long Islanders have had what outsiders might think is an inordinate

MANORHAVEN WATERWAY/MARSH. PHOTO BY
LISA MEYER, BRUCE BENNETT STUDIOS.

interest in sewage. Yet, because it all goes back to the water supply, this interest makes sense.

Thus, in 1967, when the residents of western Suffolk passed a referendum in favor of the project, expectations were high. The outcome, however, was dismal. Mired in a decade of scandal, the Southwest Sewer District took on legendary status as a political scandal. In the end, the sewage treatment plant cost tens of millions of dollars, some politicians their careers, and a host of funding problems over the years. Today, however, the plant is efficient and the scandal is a thing of the past.

One footnote to the scandal was pointed out in a recent *Newsday* story: "There is no bronze plaque on the treatment plant listing the officials responsible for the facility because no one wanted his name used."

Local sports fans had to travel west to watch major league sports, although there was one team on Long Island beginning in 1959. They were the original Long Island Ducks, a minor league hockey team that played in the Commack Arena until 1973.

Long Island entered big-time sports in the 1968-69 season when the New York Nets of the American Basketball Association (ABA) began playing in the Commack Arena, where they were less popular than the Ducks. The next season they moved to the Island Garden and, finally, in 1971, to the Nassau Coliseum, where they played until they left Long Island after the 1975-76 season.

In 1973, hometown hero Julius Erving of Roosevelt joined the Nets and brought nationwide attention to team, while also giving credibility to the ABA. In the next three years, Erving won the league's MVP Award three times. The Nets won the ABA title two out of those three years.

In 1972 the trip to the East End of Long Island became easier as the last stretch of the Long Island Expressway opened all the way out to Riverhead. The LIE had been built to serve the growing needs of a large population. It was one of the last growth spurts the Island was to experience for several years.

Unbridled growth began to exert pressure on the Island's resources to make more out of less. In particular, the state system of funding education through property taxes became onerous during a national recession. Thus, Levittown again made headlines.

It was the Levittown School District that led the way in 1974, filing suit against the State of New York seeking more equitable funding for the schools. Districts like Levittown—largely residential with little or no industry to pick up some of the tax burden—were finding they were unable to fund a host of programs, even those mandated by state and federal law.

Levittown was joined in the suit by twelve other districts on Long Island and by cities from New York to Buffalo. After an eight-month trial, in 1978, the districts won. That decision was reversed four years later by the Court of Appeals.

By 1970, the Nassau County population swelled to 1,428,838 people living in 410,379 houses. Suffolk's growth almost doubled to 1,127,030 residents living in 335,041 houses. The average monthly rent had gone up between 50 and 100 percent in just ten years. It was then that planners began to realize that natural resources on Long Island were limited and it would be in the best interest of all residents if growth were sensible.

Gone, therefore, was the willingness to build homes everywhere. Active civic associations made their feelings known at planning board meetings in towns across the two counties and land preservation moved to the top of civic agendas. Looking at Nassau's comparative dearth of open space following the almost untamed growth in the twenty-five years after World War II, people in Suffolk actively moved to preserve open space, especially in the Pine Barrens.

For the first time in its history, Nassau County would see a decline in its population in the 1970s. The post-War boom ended in the 1970s. Young people began to find living on Long Island prohibitively expensive. Schools would begin to see a decline in enrollment.

A GROUP OF SUFFOLK COUNTY CITIZENS, CONCERNED ABOUT THE ENVIRONMENT AFTER NOTICING THE DEATH OF FISH IN YAPHANK, JOINED TO STOP THE SPRAYING OF DDT IN LONG ISLAND'S MARSHES. THEY WENT ON TO CREATE THE ENVIRONMENTAL DEFENSE FUND IN 1967. TODAY, THE ORGANIZATION HAS A MEMBERSHIP OF 300,000 AND IS KNOWN SIMPLY AS ENVIRONMENTAL DEFENSE. PHOTO BY DEBORAH ROSS, BRUCE BENNETT STUDIOS.

The lush, resource-rich Long Island that had supported its residents for three hundred years or more was facing an era of change. As America celebrated its bicentennial, there was a vastly different mood in the nation when compared to the mood at the centennial. Gone was the national optimism. In the last fifteen years, the United States had lost one president to assassination, another to resignation, and a third gave in to public pressure and chose not to run for reelection. Watergate taught us cynicism. It was an unprecedented time.

The old Long Island was changing. In 1973, Stanford White's Garden City Hotel was razed to make way for a more modern structure. Long Island's venerable Franklin National Bank became the largest bank failure in United States history.

But, at the same time, hints of a better future for Long Island could be found. In 1970, Dr. Raymond Damadian first developed the technology that would lead to the Magnetic Resonance Imaging (MRI) scanner. The first MRI was done in 1977. Today, Damadian is President of Fonar Corporation in Melville, a manufacturer of MRI machines.

In 1974, Dr. Jerome Swartz co-founded Symbol Technologies, which is today headquartered in Holtsville. Swartz is credited with 125 patents, including the revolutionary bar code technology used just about on every product sold today.

It would, however, be a while before the technology developed by Damadian and Swartz would be commonplace and would help Long Island build a solid base in the late-century global market.

The nation and Long Island learned that life isn't always easy; that there might be difficult times ahead. And, as Long Islanders had shared in the easygoing good times, they would not be immune from the tough ones. ■

THE BUILDING AND POPULATION BOOMS ON LONG ISLAND GAVE RISE TO CIVIC ORGANIZATIONS THAT FAVORED PLANNED GROWTH AND ENVIRONMENTAL GROUPS THAT WORRIED ABOUT LAND USE AS IT IMPACTED NATURAL RESOURCES. PHOTOS BY BRUCE BENNETT, BRUCE BENNETT STUDIOS.

HARRY CHAPIN ENTERTAINS AT A BARBECUE HE HOSTED AT HIS HUNTINGTON BAY HOME IN 1975 TO BENEFIT HIS PERFORMING ARTS FOUNDATION. PHOTO © 1975 *NEWSDAY*.

THE LONG ISLAND FAMOUS

Harry Chapin:
The First Modern Performer Activist

Harry Chapin is remembered for his story songs—*Cat's In the Cradle* most of all—and for his involvement in the task of bettering the human condition.

Born in New York City in 1942, Chapin didn't become involved with Long Island until he was an adult. When he married Sandy Gaston they researched a host of locations and, finally, settled on Long Island. He had worked as a musician and

filmmaker but, as he wrote in an autobiographical program note around 1980: *"The end of 70 arrives, there are no film jobs and the movie industry is an economic disaster area. My daughter Jennie is 6 months on the way to being born and I panic. I set into New York City to sign up for a hack license. On the way I meet an old girlfriend who has married money instead of becoming an actress, and I contemplate the irony of 'flying in my taxi.' But the day I'm supposed to start driving fate again intervenes and I'm offered three film jobs. Relieved,*

(continued)

I plunge back into work, but find that the songs are still coming."

It took a year or so more but, eventually, he signed a recording contract and, in December 1974, *Cat's In the Cradle*, written by Sandy Chapin, became the number-one song in the nation. Harry Chapin was a success and he wrote: *"All my brave words of the '60s about the social responsibility of successful people became bluffs to be called. I believe that success brings responsibility. It also does not bring immunity to the consequences of our quickening march toward oblivion. The bottom line is that all of us should be involved in our futures to create a world that our children will want to live in."*

With others, Harry Chapin created World Hunger Year and a Washington, D.C., lobbying organization, the Food Policy Center. This led to the creation of a Commission on World Hunger by President Jimmy Carter. Chapin was a member.

Chapin concluded his autobiographical note: *"This commitment to end world hunger, and my music and story songs, are ways of dealing with the world as I see it. I'm playing 200 concerts per year—half of them benefits—all of them attempts at getting across the footlights to people I would enjoy spending time with in non-concert situations. And over the past 4 years of musical fun, millions of dollars have been raised for things I believe in. Telling stories of our time, building a lasting body of work, new songs, new records, new audiences, new challenges, and still that painfully exciting process of growth that can make one's life into a richly woven tapestry."*

Chapin served on the boards of the Performing Arts Foundation, the Eglevsky Ballet, the Long Island Philharmonic, the Action Committee of Long Island, and Hofstra University.

On July 16, 1981, at age 38, Harry Chapin was killed in a crash on the Long Island Expressway. In the years during which he had made Long Island his home, Chapin had become symbolic of a Long Island that was compassionate, caring, and committed to making the world a better place.

In its editorial about Chapin, *Newsday* wrote, *"'The key to my life,' he once said, 'is that I am willing to make an ass of myself.' Behind the self-deprecation of that remark was a perceptive description of another of his gifts: He could express compassion with directness and simplicity that others might scorn as unsophisticated."*

Chapin was eulogized in Congress by members of all political persuasions, in the press, and by fans waiting in East Meadow's Eisenhower Park that July

16 for Chapin's scheduled free concert ("bring a donation of food"). His work is carried on by the World Hunger Year organization that each year presents a Chapin Award for activism and by a foundation that bears his name and continues his work.

Shortly after his death, Chapin was eulogized in *Rolling Stone*: *"Harry Chapin often described himself as a 'third-rate folk singer,' and judging from most of the reviews he received in these pages and elsewhere, he wasn't kidding. Yet Harry Chapin was something more than that. For many who knew him, he was a legitimate hero, not so much for his music as for his consistent and conscientious willingness to fight the right battles, to stand up for a just cause, no matter how hopeless."*

A Star-Studded Firmament

Harry Chapin was not the first Long Islander to become famous and he wasn't the most famous. He was one of the most unique, blazing a trail that many other artists have followed.

There are in fact hundreds of people born, or who settled, on Long Island, became famous in a variety of arts:

They include: Jerry Seinfeld; Billy Joel; Ben (Cohen) and Jerry (Greenfield), the famed ice-cream makers; Billy Crystal; Pat Benetar; Bud Abbott; Mariah Carey; Eddie Money; Telly Savalas; Edward Burns; Chuck D; Francis Ford Coppola; *Silence of the Lambs* director Jonathan Demme was born on Long Island, and the book's author, Thomas Harris, summers in Sag Harbor; *The Secret Garden* author Frances Hodgsen Burnett; actor George Segal; Eddie Murphy; Howard Stern; John Tesh; Paul Simon; authors Thomas Pynchon; Peter Mathiessen; Nelson DeMille, Nelson Algren; Truman Capote; Kurt Vonnegut; Michael Crichton; Susan Isaacs; WFAN's "Mike and the Mad Dog"; opera singer Richard Tucker; James Brady; Alan Alda; Patti Lupone; Kevin James; Lisa Gay Hamilton; Robert Keeshan, who was Captain Kangaroo; Susan Lucci; Rosie O'Donnell; all four Baldwin Brothers; cartoonist Charles Addams; Ed Wynn; Jim Brown; Lenny Bruce; Deborah Gibson; painters Willem deKooning and Larry Rivers; radio's Tex McCrary and Jinx Falkenberg; Rodney Dangerfield; Sid Caesar; Martha Stewart; Alan King; Guy Lombardo; Andy Kaufman; Betty Friedan; Al Oerter; Carl Yastrzemski; and Neal Marlens. When Marlens created television's *The Wonder Years*, the family home bore the address "516," then the area code for all of Long Island...and the list goes on.

THERE WAS A MAJOR LEAGUE SPORTS TEAM ON LONG ISLAND BEGINNING IN 1959—THE ORIGINAL LONG
ISLAND DUCKS, A MINOR LEAGUE HOCKEY TEAM THAT PLAYED IN THE COMMACK ARENA UNTIL 1973.
PICTURED IS ALL-STAR MOE BUNTOLI. PHOTO © BRUCE BENNETT STUDIOS.

TODAY, LONG ISLANDERS CHEER ON THE NEW YORK ISLANDERS. PICTURED IS DEFENSEMAN ROMAN HAMRLIK. PHOTO BY LISA MEYER, BRUCE BENNETT STUDIOS.

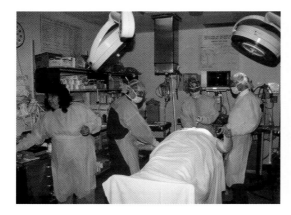 

MEADOWBROOK, THE FIRST PUBLIC HOSPITAL IN NASSAU COUNTY, OPENED IN 1935. IT BECAME NASSAU COUNTY MEDICAL CENTER AND, IN SEPTEMBER 1999, THE NASSAU COUNTY HEALTH DEPARTMENT RELINQUISHED CONTROL OF THE HOSPITAL AND THE CLINICS, AND THE FACILITY WAS RECOGNIZED AS A PUBLIC BENEFIT CORPORATION. IN 2000, THE HOSPITAL'S NAME WAS CHANGED TO NASSAU COUNTY UNIVERSITY HOSPITAL. PHOTOS BY J. LEARY, BRUCE BENNETT STUDIOS.

TO OUR GOOD HEALTH

Today in Nassau and Suffolk Counties there are a total of twenty-three not-for-profit hospitals, one private hospital and sixteen public health clinics, some with satellite services. But, before these systems, or managed care or mergers, local healthcare was largely dependent upon where on Long Island an individual lived.

Nassau Hospital—today's Winthrop University Hospital—opened in 1896 in Mineola, the first hospital in the county. Suffolk's first hospital, Eastern Long Island in Greenport, opened in 1905. From that time until the 1960s a network of hospitals opened across the region, assuring hospital care for those in need across the Island.

Some hospitals were built as hospitals and grew along with their communities. Others began life as something other than a hospital.

For example, Long Beach Memorial Hospital was born as a lifesaving station. The most unusual genesis of a hospital is that of St. Francis, today a dedicated cardiac treatment center with an international reputation. It opened in 1922 as a summer camp for children run by Sisters of the Franciscan Missionaries of Mary, on the Munson estate in Manhasset.

By 1936, it had become a country sanitarium for children with rheumatic fever. In 1954, it opened its doors to adults as St. Francis Hospital and Sanitarium. By the 1960s, the hospital began to evolve into the specialized heart center it is today.

Similarly, St. Charles Hospital in Port Jefferson was founded as the Brooklyn Home for Blind and Crippled Children in 1907. It changed its name to St. Charles Hospital in 1911, but today still offers

the rehabilitation services that are a natural outgrowth of its original mission.

The public health system, however, took longer to put into place.

Meadowbrook was the first public hospital in Nassau. It opened in 1935 in East Meadow. Three years later, the Nassau County Department of Health was organized out of several smaller agencies and eventually operated a clinic system that provided primary care at sites in Hempstead, Elmont, Freeport-Roosevelt, Inwood-Lawrence, Long Beach, and New Cassel-Westbury, and a school-based program in Roosevelt.

Meadowbrook became Nassau County Medical Center and, in September 1999, the Nassau County Health Department relinquished control of the hospital and the clinics. It was then that Nassau County Medical Center was reorganized as a public benefit corporation. The county no longer had any administrative responsibility for clinical care. In December 2000, the change was completed as the hospital's name became Nassau County University Hospital.

Today, the Nassau County Health Department focuses on protecting public health and wellness.

In Suffolk County, there were several community hospitals—in Greenport, Riverhead, Southampton, Patchogue, Bay Shore, West Islip, Smithtown, and two in Port Jefferson. Residents who were uninsured, or who could not afford a private physician, depended on the emergency department in the hospital closest to where they lived.

But access to healthcare in Suffolk's underserved communities remained an issue that was brought

(continued)

ST. FRANCIS HOSPITAL, TODAY A DEDICATED CARDIAC TREATMENT CENTER WITH AN INTERNATIONAL REPUTA-
TION, HAD ITS BEGINNINGS AS A SUMMER CAMP FOR CHILDREN AND, LATER, A COUNTY SANITARIUM FOR
CHILDREN WITH RHEUMATIC FEVER. PHOTO BY LISA MEYER, BRUCE BENNETT STUDIOS.

to a head in the mid-'60s, in the aftermath of vehement protests in Wyandanch.

Suffolk County Executive H. Lee Dennison began the process of change by working with community activists who wanted programs for prenatal and primary care. Over the next few years, Blue Ribbon Panels and various commissions were formed by the county to examine all facets of public health.

The Task Force on Community Healthcare advocated for placing clinics in all areas of the county. The first experimental clinic was opened in an abandoned grocery store in Wyandanch. It was to be staffed by volunteer physicians. That plan, however, was not a reliable method of providing care, so the county stepped in. The Suffolk County Department of Health Services eventually opened health centers in Coram, Patchogue, Bay Shore, Shirley, Amityville, Brentwood, Wyandanch, Riverhead, with smaller satellites in Central Islip, Southampton, Amagansett, and Greenport, and at the county-funded Dolan Health Center in Huntington Station.

Another Suffolk commission examined the question of a county hospital. They ultimately decided it would be impractical to do so for three reasons. First, in a county of 1,000 square miles, a central, easily accessible location was problematic.

Second, if the community hospitals were seeing to the needs of the underserved population through their emergency departments, was another hospital emergency department necessary if it would duplicate existing services?

Finally, they decided it was more important to establish a primary care network in which

people could be treated before hospital services became necessary.

Thus, the network of county clinics was structured over a period of several years. To help the local hospitals, the county did form a "Health Facilities Commission," empowered to guarantee bonds used to upgrade and expand emergency rooms in community hospitals to better serve the public.

Suffolk County finally got a public hospital in 1980, when University Hospital at Stony Brook opened in central Suffolk as part of the state university system.

In 1998, University Hospital recognized the work of nine citizen-activists they called "Women Pioneers in Suffolk County Healthcare." The nine came from all walks of life, represented a mix of races and religions, and collectively were credited with guiding the advocacy that resulted in the public health network in the county.

Today, the healthcare landscape on Long Island features three networks: Catholic Health Services, the Long Island Health Network, and, the largest in New York, the North Shore-Long Island Jewish Health System.

There remain concerns about access to health care, but the overall health picture has greatly improved over the last forty years. The infant mortality rate is much lower, prenatal care is more widely available, and free screenings for such illnesses as breast cancer and prostate cancer are available. The ability of underserved populations to access health care remains an issue, but it is being studied and taken seriously from one end of Long Island to the other.

CREATIVE BATH PRODUCTS, INC.

Common wisdom has it that Long Island's heyday as a manufacturing center is a thing of the past. Its expensive, educated labor force along with the generally high cost of doing business on Long Island have caused much of its one-time manufacturing base to flee to lower-cost southern states or even to abandon the country entirely in favor of manufacturing off-shore, in Asia.

Fortunately, nobody shared this "common wisdom" with Mathias Meinzinger, a Long Islander who's often been called the "king of the bath products industry." As a result of his not accepting that Long Island is an unpromising locale for a manufacturing company, his business, Creative Bath Products Inc., is a flourishing, ever-expanding manufacturing enterprise occupying a half-million square feet of space on a 32-acre campus in Central Islip and supplying its products to retail establishments worldwide. In recognition of his leadership of this remarkable company, Meinzinger, an immigrant to these shores as are many of Long Island's most prominent business leaders, was named Ernst & Young's 1997 Long Island Entrepreneur of the Year.

From its Long Island facility in two handsome glass-encased atrium buildings, Creative Bath Products designs and produces more than 4,000 different bath and houseware accessory items which are supplied to retailers all across the nation and to 50 foreign countries. Items manufactured by Creative Bath are found at a vast spectrum of retailers—from Fortunoff to Wal-Mart, with Bloomingdale's; Bed, Bath and Beyond; Sears; Linens N' Things; and JC Penney included among its valued customer base of department stores, linen specialty shops, national chains, and mass merchants.

CREATIVE BATH PRODUCT'S EXPANDED 10,000 SQUARE FOOT SHOWROOM ON MANHATTAN'S FIFTH AVENUE LURES RETAILERS FROM AROUND THE WORLD TO INDUSTRY MARKET WEEKS EACH APRIL AND OCTOBER.

Meinzinger, widely known as Mat, founded the privately-held company in 1973 with partner Guenther Bartsch, now vice president of Creative Bath. It was started with two employees and $10,000 in seed money. Today, the company employs 700 people. Product development and a full 80 percent of its manufacturing are fulfilled here on Long Island. Additionally, the company owns a 50 percent interest in a Toronto distributorship which brings items manufactured by Creative Bath Products to retail outlets throughout Canada.

The company's CFO, Ron Secker, credits Creative Bath's astounding record of manufacturing growth on Long Island in part to various governmental initiatives. According to Secker, it was New York State's designation of Central Islip's Empire Zone which afforded the company access to the real estate tax abatements and reduced electric costs which permitted cost-effective operation. Said Secker, "Because of our location in New York, and our industry sector, we've been eligible for such incentives." He explained that reduced electric costs were particularly central to the company's ability to do business on Long Island because "electricity is of major importance in manufacturing; we consume enormous amounts of electricity." Explained Secker: "The state's Empire Zone program has been paramount in allowing us to remain and grow on Long Island." Other programs which spurred growth for Creative Bath Products came from New York State's Urban Development Corporation and its subsidiary, the Empire State Development Corporation. Secker stated that these state government agencies "have assisted and

CREATIVE BATH PRODUCTS, A LEADER IN PRODUCT DESIGN, WAS THE FIRST IN THE INDUSTRY TO EMBELLISH PLASTIC BATH ACCESSORIES WITH LUXURIOUS 24 KARAT GOLD TRIM. SHOWN ARE SOPHISTICATED BLACK AND GOLD SELECTIONS FROM THE CHATEAU COLLECTION.

ONE OF THE TWO FACILITIES HOUSING CREATIVE
BATH PRODUCTS' RESEARCH AND DEVELOPMENT
AND DESIGN OFFICES, AS WELL AS MANUFACTURING
AND WAREHOUSING SPACE. PART OF ITS OWN
HALF-MILLION SQUARE FOOT, 32-ACRE CAMPUS IN
CENTRAL ISLIP.

encouraged our growth on Long Island with financial
assistance in the form of grants and low-interest rate
loans." He also cited encouragement and assistance
from the Town of Islip, including its Industrial
Development Agency.

Creativity at the Heart of Growth

Governmental incentive programs are clearly crucial
to the continued ability of Creative Bath Products to
do business on Long Island. But just as essential to its
success, and especially to its enviable reputation in the
bath accessories industry, are its creative functions.
President and CEO Meinzinger stressed: "Creativity is
the lifeblood of our company. This is the single most
important factor—our ability to design new, innovative,
and decorative merchandise for the bath."

These beautifully—designed collections of coordinated
shower curtains, jacquard embellished towels, bath mats,
lotion pumps, soaps, and other accessory items are the
stars at Creative Bath Products' newly-expanded 10,000-
square-foot New York City showroom, located on Fifth
Avenue near the Empire State Building. Representatives
of national and international retailers flock to the
sensational showroom for twice-a-year April and
October Market Weeks.

Where once the company was sharply focused on
decorative products for the bath, in recent years it has
diversified into housewares. While the company's bath
and houseware products are readily identified by those
in the business and are to be found just about anywhere buyers are likely to do their home shopping,
consumers typically have no idea that they're buying
a product produced by Meinzinger's Long Island-based
company. That's because, in another move which flies

in the face of current economic and marketing wisdom,
Creative Bath Products has never chosen to "brand" its
products. Said Meinzinger: "This is really not something
we've done a lot of." Instead, he said, the company
often manufactures its products through licensing or
under private store labels.

New Business Initiatives

This disinterest in branding may soon go by the
wayside with the company's entry into a whole new
business. Though the core business of Creative Bath
Products remains accessories for the bathroom, a recent
acquisition will result in expansion of Creative Bath's
product line into a wholly new area of household items,
including decorative pillows and bedding. Meinzinger
calls the product expansion "a logical, natural growth
direction for this company." He predicted that this "shift
of focus" is likely to result in greater branding efforts
on the part of his company—for the new CreativeWare
houseware product lines and the pillow lines distributed
by Creative Home Furnishings, Inc., an affiliate of
Creative Bath Products, Inc.

From his vantage point as CEO of a large successful
company, one which has already put into place the
moves to assure even greater growth in the future,
Meinzinger, who came to this country from Hungary by
way of Germany in 1956 without being able to speak a
word of English, surveys the background which took
him into the bath products industry, from assembly line
worker to company president. He used his years on the
line to learn and improve his English and to build the
savings which would eventually enable him to open his
own business. In 1973, Meinzinger formed Creative Bath
Products with an initial investment of $10,000. At the
outset, Meinzinger used his extensive knowledge of
tooling to design molds for coordinating plastic bath
products; eventually the products were wielded together
into coordinated design collections.

THE ENTRYWAY TO THE CORPORATE HEADQUARTERS
OF CREATIVE BATH PRODUCTS IS ENHANCED WITH
A GLASS CEILING WHICH POURS LIGHT INTO THE
GUEST RECEPTION AREA.

THE "KING OF THE BATH PRODUCTS INDUSTRY," MATHIAS MEINZINGER WAS NAMED 1997 LONG ISLAND ENTREPRENEUR OF THE YEAR.

Looking back on the beginnings of Creative Bath Products, especially its first three years when he didn't take a salary, Meinzinger recalls that in 1973, the company's first year, "sales were only $40,000 and I wondered if I would survive."

But within 10 years, Meinzinger's annual sales topped the $10-million mark. With that success under his belt, the bath products chief was emboldened to take the next step. In 1993, with an investment of $11 million, Creative Bath Products built a new 200,000-square-feet state-of-the-art facility. Since 1993, the company has expanded its facility to 500,000 square feet. Its local presence—versus foreign manufacturing sites for many of its competitors—has had a major impact in the company's responsiveness to the marketplace. While other suppliers are waiting on shipments from overseas, Creative Bath Products has already got its products on retail shelves. This flexibility is also seen in the company's ability to customize its products for major retailers who are offered "something different from the retailer next door, and at sharp price points." Key to its customized design ability is Creative Bath Product's in-house design team. But with an eye toward the future, Meinzinger said "we also look for innovation from outside of our industry, drawing in young people through our new internship program."

THIS STRIKING BATHROOM IS COMPLETELY OUTFITTED WITH COORDINATED ACCESSORIES FROM CREATIVE BATH PRODUCT'S SHADOWPLAY COLLECTION.

With people always the most precious resource of this or any other company, Creative Bath Products and its President sustain a profound commitment to its employees. That commitment is part of the reason the company has never seriously considered shifting its manufacturing functions from Long Island. Establishing and maintaining a collegial environment within the company, Meinzinger, a familiar presence at the company cafeteria, often becomes involved in the lives of his employees and has assisted at least 50 Creative Bath Products workers through the process of achieving U.S. citizenship. His loyalty is returned by his employees, many of whom have been with the company for many years.

Creative Bath Products is also supportive of the Long Island community. Meinzinger said "we contribute to many civic and charitable organizations, especially those serving the Central Islip area." The Congress of Racial Equality and the Long Island Head Injury Association are particular beneficiaries of the company's charitable giving. In addition, students of the Central Islip school district and the Central Islip campus of New York Institute of Technology are encouraged to join the Creative Bath Products' part-time workforce.

Recipe for Success

Several principles have guided the growth of Creative Bath Products from the day of its opening more than a quarter-century ago. According to Mat Meinzinger, he has grown his business by: staying close to the company's customers; establishing an aggressive approach in the marketplace; maintaining a continuous commitment to new product development; remaining flexible enough to produce custom products and programs for retailers; meeting specific customer requirements in terms of labeling, packaging and service; maintaining his commitment

THE SCROLLED BORDER OF CREATIVE BATH PRODUCTS' VERONA SHOWER CURTAIN IS INSPIRED BY ELEGANT ITALIAN DESIGN.

to global expansion; acquiring synergetic companies; staying focused on the core business; and maintaining a showroom presence in the heart of the bath design world at the New York Textile Building. ■

HOUSEWARES ARE AMONG THE NEW PRODUCT LINES AT CREATIVE BATH PRODUCTS. SHOWN ARE SEVERAL PLATES AND BOWLS FROM THE WINGS COLLECTION WHICH MAY BE USED INDOOR OR OUT.

SUTTON & EDWARDS INC.

The name Sutton & Edwards Inc. is synonymous in the Long Island real estate industry with quality, excellence, service, and value. It has fashioned its position as a service-oriented commercial real estate provider through innovative solutions, attention to detail, and a commitment to technology to create and enhance value for its clients. The result is a complete range of real estate services that rivals that of other real estate firms.

GATEWAY AT LAKE SUCCESS, 1981 AND 1993 MARCUS AVENUE, LAKE SUCCESS.

"Our firm successfully differentiates itself in the marketplace by providing customized service to a broad range of companies with diverse needs and objectives," "That approach has proved to be key in establishing ourselves as a competitive force in the Long Island commercial real estate market," said Chief Executive Officer, Herbert S. Agin.

The firm's mission is to provide comprehensive real estate solutions to its clients. It accomplishes this goal by applying solid real estate principles and creative problem-solving techniques that help customers develop and execute real estate plans that meet their ever-changing business objectives. As the needs of local businesses changed during the last 40 years, with Long Island evolving from a bedroom community into a thriving commercial marketplace in its own right, Sutton & Edwards adapted its capabilities and operations accordingly.

Solid Beginnings

Sutton & Edwards roots go back to 1962, when The Sutton Organization and Towne Affiliates merged to form Sutton & Towne. After successfully establishing a strong position in the Manhattan marketplace, the firm launched a planned expansion in 1969 opening a Long Island office, followed by Westchester (1970), Connecticut (1971), and New Jersey (1972).

In 1979, as part of a corporate plan to expand the scope of real estate services throughout the United States, Coldwell Banker negotiated the acquisition of Sutton & Towne, a tactical move that assisted the West Coast real estate organization in establishing a commercial presence in the New York Metropolitan area.

For the next three years the firm worked under the auspices of a corporate infrastructure, and reemerged in 1982 under new leadership as Sutton & Edwards Inc. to pursue the entrepreneurial approach that defined its previous successes.

Sutton & Edwards prospered during the mid- to late-1980s, maintaining multiple offices throughout the region. Then in the early 1990s a major downturn hit the market. The underpinnings of the real estate industry were being attacked, calling into question the solvency of the real estate business. Sutton & Edwards recognized this business cycle as an opportunity to reevaluate its corporate plan and implement a strategy that would consolidate operations in its most successful office, based in Lake Success, Long Island. An integral part of the strategy was to affiliate with TCN Worldwide, to service the local and global expansion needs of its clients.

"The Long Island office was our flagship," said President Alan H. Rosenberg. "So our decision to retain it was the natural choice. Concentrating on a single office enabled us to attract, train, and position our sales associates as highly skilled and competitive 'players' in the market."

With a solid staff in place, Sutton & Edwards was able to design a service plan that encompassed the diverse needs of its client/customer base, including comprehensive and flexible delivery programs that facilitated both local and global companies.

FRANKLIN AVENUE PLAZA, 1205, 1305, 1225, 1325 FRANKLIN AVENUE, GARDEN CITY.

PARKWAY PLAZA, 1400 OLD COUNTRY ROAD, WESTBURY.

Innovative Service

Sutton & Edwards continues to apply an entrepreneurial approach to the development and implementation of customized real estate plans. Its diverse group of professionals leverage innovative service applications and progressive technology to provide unique, proactive solutions to real estate challenges. The overriding principles guiding those solutions are service and value.

Sutton & Edwards offers a complete range of real estate services and acts as a catalyst to the internal collaboration necessary when developing and executing a real estate plan. As tenant representatives, the associates of the firm evaluate corporate business plans and present real estate alternatives to the best economic and functional advantage of the company. In a landlord representative capacity, the agents implement strategies to achieve maximum economic realization in line with market conditions. Understanding the relationship between landlord and tenant gives a unique perspective to Sutton & Edwards and far from presenting a conflict of interest, this dual client base gives Sutton & Edwards the insight necessary to serve both parties more efficiently

Institutions and entrepreneurs leveraging the real estate investment market have long relied on the investment specialists of Sutton & Edwards to initiate real estate acquisition/disposition decisions consistent with their objectives. Sutton & Edwards combines more than 40 years of experience in banking, investment, and finance, and provides extensive market knowledge and credibility to facilitate the sale or purchase of income-producing property. The risks and returns inherent in a real estate opportunity are evaluated utilizing advanced analytical software that assists the firm's analysts in the review and projection of cash flows and values necessary to define appropriate deal structures.

Sutton & Edwards rounds out its full-service approach as the exclusive Long Island affiliate of TCN Worldwide, a global consortium of independent real estate firms of more than 2,000 member-associates in 100 offices throughout the world. The entrepreneurial approach and streamlined corporate structure supported by the organization enable its members to serve their clients with more agility and personalized service than highly structured, multi-layered national and international real estate firms.

40 HARBOR PARK DRIVE, PORT WASHINGTON.

200 WIRELESS BOULEVARD, HAUPPAUGE.

Solid Relationships

Sutton & Edwards serves as a partner—an advocate, if you will—to its clients. The working relationships that the firm fosters, enables it to serve as an integral role in real estate planning and a facilitator during the implementation process.

"Providing traditional real estate services is only part of the equation," said Agin "If you want to differentiate yourself in this market, you need to do more. In our case, doing more involves strategic planning, process management, and coordinated service delivery—all with a global reach."

Sutton & Edwards helps its clients define their needs, objectives, and expectations. The firm initiates the evaluation of every level of their clients' organization to develop targeted real estate programs that coincide with corporate business plans. Not only does this assist Sutton & Edwards in becoming versed in the daily operations of its clients' businesses, but it enables the firm to establish real estate goals for its clients that account for anticipated growth.

Once goals have been set, Sutton & Edwards helps facilitate the execution of the client's real estate plan by keeping a central communication structure and overseeing accountability and quality control. At the same time, the firm looks for new ways to help its clients achieve their intended goals. Finally, Sutton & Edwards delivers on its promises by leveraging its extensive knowledge and experience base, as well as its global network and strategic alliances, to provide real-world real estate solutions.

The Team

The executives of Sutton & Edwards know that the success of the firm is a direct result of the diligent efforts of its sales and support staff. With a background in real estate training, Agin spearheads the new associate training program, adapted from training seminars he conducted in Washington, D.C., while serving as resident manager for Coldwell Banker's Long Island office.

Sutton & Edwards has developed a mentoring program where new associates pair with experienced agents who actively involve them in every aspect of the real estate process, from sales calls, lease analysis, and strategic planning workshops to negotiation roundtables. By "shadowing" their mentors, new agents get an inside view of how things really work in the real estate industry.

When pairing seasoned agents with recruits, the firm takes into account personalities, work styles and experience levels to develop the best potential partners while also encouraging new associates to study the approach of several agents giving them a comprehensive picture of the real estate process and the ability to develop their own work style.

EQUIPARK, 2905 VETERAN'S MEMORIAL HIGHWAY, RONKONKOMA.

The Community Beyond

The personnel of Sutton & Edwards understand that good corporate citizenship requires more than productivity. It calls for giving something back to the community. And that is exactly what Sutton & Edwards does—in both a formal and informal way. By creating relationships with a multitude of charities, the firm contributes funds and manpower to the Interfaith Nutrition Network, Parker Geriatric Associates Board of Trustees, March of Dimes, American Heart Association, and the Epilepsy Foundation, among others.

"We were fortunate to find a true home on Long Island," says Rosenberg. "Not only have we achieved commercial success, but we have been privileged to share the rewards of that success with so many deserving organizations in the area. Long Island has been good to us; it's only right that we should give something back."

As an active participant in the Long Island real estate community, the firm was a founder of the Commercial Industrial Brokers Society (CIBS). Sutton & Edwards works in conjunction with the membership to maintain a local voice in legislation regarding issues affecting the commercial real estate industry and a high standard of professionalism.

"Our main purpose is to elevate the professionalism of the brokerage community," said Agin. "The best way to do that is through the development of standards, seminars, and various other educational activities. We want the entire industry on Long Island to raise the bar. That makes us all better."

The Future

Sutton & Edwards has played a major role in the commercial development of Long Island during the past

RETAIL STRIP CENTER.

40 years. To maintain its leadership position the company plans several initiatives. First, it will continue to integrate technology into its operations enabling its workforce to be more productive and serve clients more efficiently.

Continued geographic expansion throughout Long Island and into Queens and Brooklyn will occur largely through the recruitment of new sales associates. Sutton & Edwards is committed to extending unique opportunities to the region's young professionals. This strategy will help the firm maintain a healthy cross section of talent and ensure its continued growth.

"Long Island has afforded us unique growth opportunities as a real estate firm," said Rosenberg "We are convinced that our future is here, and we are committed to pursuing it—for our continued success and the long-term prosperity of Long Island." ■

MULTI-FAMILY APARTMENT COMPLEX.

COMPUTER ASSOCIATES (CA)

The statistics of Computer Associates' growth on Long Island stagger the imagination. Founded 25 years ago with one product, the company now holds an undisputed global position as the world's leading provider of eBusiness management solutions. CA offers organizations the solutions to meet the challenges presented by the next generation of eBusiness and fully embrace the opportunities that lie ahead.

CA has strategically focused its innovative software solutions into three strategic categories: eBusiness Process Management to seamlessly manage business *processes* within and across the extended enterprise, eBusiness Information Management to cohesively manage vital business *information* and leverage it for new opportunities, and eBusiness Infrastructure Management to powerfully manage the core *infrastructure*, keeping the eBusiness up, running, and secure while connecting customers, suppliers, partners, and employees.

The company also launched a new corporate branding identity to reflect CA's renewed focus on customers, shareholders, employees and partners. A new CA logo represents the company's increased focus on eBusiness to accelerate growth, provide greater market visibility, and reinforce the company's position as an innovative and trusted global leader.

To ensure that its products reflect the most advanced technology, CA recognizes that no one vendor can do it alone, so CA leverages the strength and expertise of strategic partnerships with key industry giants including: Microsoft, Intel, Sun, EMC, Oracle, Cisco, Hewlett-Packard, Compaq, and Dell to offer unique eBusiness solutions that meet specific needs.

To support the growing Hosted Service Provider imarketplace, CA recently formed iCan-SP, Inc., a subsidiary that provides business and operations support software for the xSP (Service Provider). iCan provides customized service level management, application provisioning, billing, metering, and operations management solutions that enable xSPs to deliver quality, and highly reliable services. CA also launched interBiz, a division that helps financial, banking, and supply chain clients to capitalize on eBusiness opportunities through Web-enabled integrated and extended applications.

Pretty impressive for a company that started out in 1976 with four employees and one product! The driving forces behind CA's dynamic record of growth and innovation are CA Chairman Charles B. Wang and President and CEO Sanjay Kumar. Wang founded the company with Russell M. Artzt on the seemingly simple premise that in an industry driven largely by technology, there was great opportunity for people who actually asked clients about their needs and problems.

Wang and Kumar oversee a company that is remarkable both for its growth record and, for its dedication to a highly nurturing, model workplace environment.

CA CHAIRMAN (LEFT) CHARLES B. WANG AND CEO AND PRESIDENT SANJAY KUMAR.

CA WORLD HEADQUARTERS IN ISLANDIA, NEW YORK.

Recognized as a world leader in innovative management strategies, CA has been named one of *IndustryWeek*'s 100 Best-Managed Companies for three consecutive years. *Fortune* magazine also named CA one of America's "most admired companies." CA was the second highest ranked software company and was rated number one in social responsibility.

CA received the 2000 Dale Carnegie Training Leadership Award for its continuous demonstration of superior leadership in human resources development, in alignment with its dedication to promoting people-friendly, family friendly, and environmentally friendly corporate policies.

Worldwide network based in Islandia, New York

CA software is licensed and supported in more than 100 countries. Managing all CA computer environments is the state-of-the-art Global Command Center (GCC) at corporate headquarters in Islandia, which monitors the pulse of hundreds of Websites, business processes, and eBusiness applications. The GCC serves CA in several important ways. First, it centralizes and automates the management of a global network, allowing the company to be proactive in the management of its resources. Second, by deploying the same tools it offers its clients, CA is more effective in enhancing the tools and transferring knowledge on their use to clients.

Long Island Talents—Key to CA Growth

The worldwide company, with the original staff of four, all still with CA, is now joined by more than 18,000 dedicated and talented employees, in 100 countries—focused on making a difference for its customers. At CA's state-of-the-art headquarters in Islandia, New York

CA CEO AND PRESIDENT SANJAY KUMAR (LEFT) ACCEPTING ISO 9002 CERTIFICATION FROM KEITH KETHEESWARAN, MANAGING DIRECTOR FOR QUALITY ASSURANCE SERVICES (QAS). CA IS THE FIRST AND ONLY ENTERPRISE SOFTWARE COMPANY TO MEET THE EXACTING STANDARDS OF ISO CERTIFICATION.

CA CHAIRMAN CHARLES B. WANG AND CEO AND PRESIDENT, SANJAY KUMAR AT THE SMILE TRAIN BOOTH AT CA WORLD 2000. THE SMILE TRAIN IS A NON-PROFIT ORGANIZATION, SUPPORTED BY CA, WHICH IS COMMITTED TO ERADICATING THE PROBLEM OF CLEFT LIPS AND PALATES BY EMPOWERING LOCAL SURGEONS AND MEDICAL PROFESSIONALS IN DEVELOPING COUNTRIES TO PERFORM THE SURGERY THEMSELVES.

3,000 employees are located. With CA's standing as a major multi-national corporation that could base its headquarters anywhere in the world, the question is frequently raised—Why Long Island? The answer lies both in the attractiveness of Long Island's highly educated high-tech work-force, and in the commitment of CA's leaders to the Long Island community.

Attracting and retaining talent is a CA priority, one that is reflected throughout the company headquarters and in the company guiding philosophy that "If you want to attract the best people on the globe, you have to have the facilities for them." CA provides an award-winning, extremely progressive work environment that helps achieve balance between their personal and professional lives.

The company offers many opportunities for ongoing career development by offering interesting and challenging work on groundbreaking technology. CA also provides a healthy and supportive culture, with a host of progressive policies and benefits to help employees succeed and grow.

CA continues to win industry-wide acclaim for a progressive work environment that encourages teamwork while recognizing individual contributions. In its annual survey of leading information technology companies, *ComputerWorld* magazine recently cited CA as one of the "100 Best Places to Work in IT" for the sixth consecutive year.

CA OFFERS EMPLOYEES STATE-OF-THE-ART HEALTH AND FITNESS CENTERS EQUIPPED WITH EXERCISE AND WEIGHT ROOMS AND RECREATIONAL FACILITIES SUCH AS TENNIS AND BASKETBALL COURTS.

On-site Fitness Facilities

Worldwide, CA employees have breakfast on the company. Many arrive early, not only for breakfast, but for morning workouts at the company's extensive fitness center which is available to employees each day from 6:30 A.M. to 9:30 P.M. Throughout the world, CA offices with 100 or more employees each have these state-of-the-art health and fitness centers.

The Islandia fitness complex, with men's and women's locker rooms, features an aerobics room expansive enough to rival major dance studio facilities. The aerobics room is where classes are offered in such arts as yoga or jujitsu. Adjacent is a weight training room, outfitted with free weights and Cybex equipment as well as a panoply of exercise machines including treadmills, cycles, skiers, and Nordic tracks. Squash and racquetball courts are available, as is a full basketball court.

Outdoors, the CA Islandia property is dotted with yet other fitness facilities; tennis and basketball courts, soccer and football fields, and a running track integrated into the landscaping.

Crib to Child Development Center

Potential CA employees are often drawn to the company because of its remarkable, company-subsidized Child Development Center. The center is available to children of employees and is charged for on a sliding scale of modest fees. The award-winning, fully-licensed center, designed along Montessori educational philosophy lines, has been cited by *Parents* Magazine as among the top five such facilities in the nation.

As their parents work upstairs, children aged five years or younger spend their days in attractively decorated classrooms and play areas. Tight security is maintained,

but parents frequently visit with their children during the workday, particularly joining in on outdoor field days, and family celebrations of the many events of the company's international holiday calendar.

Designed to serve as far more than a baby-watching service, the CA Child Development Center offers extensive educational, cultural, and recreational activities including music, ballet, karate, tee ball, and soccer. Through Association Montessori Internationale, the center also offers teacher certification. Classes are held for parents so that they are able to follow through at home the practices applied in the classroom. Other family friendly CA offerings include company subsidized summer camp and holiday care programs.

Professional Growth Encouraged

But as much as elaborate fitness and top quality child development act as magnets for employees, what likely fuels the company's continuing ability to retain and attract employees is CA's free-wheeling entrepreneurial flavor, which emphasizes professional growth.

From the outset, CA was organized with no strict hierarchical lines. Eschewing cumbersome bureaucracy, the company designed a corporate system that encourages an entrepreneurial spirit and empowers employees to reach their potential through individual contributions and collective efforts as part of a team.

Employee growth at CA is bolstered through distance learning programs, special training events, on-site courses, and a twice-a-year Boot Camp for newly hired computer science graduates from around the world. Once assigned a particular job, the company encourages employees to try many different positions. These job shifts often serve to bring fresh outlooks to each CA department and provide excellent opportunities for individual career growth and advancement.

CA'S ON-SITE, MONTESSORI-BASED CHILD DEVELOPMENT CENTERS BOAST SPACIOUS, COLORFUL CLASSROOMS AND LARGE OUTDOOR AND INDOOR PLAYGROUNDS FOR CHILDREN AGES SIX WEEKS TO SIX YEARS.

The hard work and dedication of CA's valuable employees enabled the company to reach a historic milestone. CA was officially recognized as the first enterprise software company to globally achieve ISO 9002 quality certification, a accomplishment that simply would not have been possible if not for the collective efforts of a proud workforce. ISO represents an international consensus on good management practices, ensuring organizations consistently deliver products and services that meet their customers' quality requirements. This global certification demonstrates CA's overall commitment to quality.

Philanthropy and Community Involvement

CA and its employees are involved in a variety of charitable programs and philanthropic activities. The company's ongoing humanitarian efforts are far reaching—from a generous company-sponsored Matching Charitable Gifts program and private contributions from CA officers and employees, to millions of dollars in corporate donations. The company designed and is hosting Web sites for Missing and Exploited Children in the United States, Europe, and Asia, and also actively supports The Smile Train to provide surgery for children with cleft lips and palates, and the Make-A-Wish Foundation to grant wishes to terminally ill children.

Closer to home, CA support extends to the Nassau County Sports Commission, a non-profit organization that promotes and enhances the quality of life for area residents while improving the economy of the region through sports. The commission's "Let's Do It!" initiative, made possible through the efforts of the Sanjay Kumar Foundation and CA, exposes children of all backgrounds to various non-traditional sports.

COMPUTER ASSOCIATES KINDERGARTEN GRADUATION CEREMONY WHERE CA CHAIRMAN, CHARLES B. WANG CONGRATULATES THOMAS DONOHUE. OTHER GRADUATES IN BACKGROUND INCLUDE WILLIAM BENNETT AND STEPHEN CARR (LEFT TO RIGHT).

CA AND ITS EMPLOYEES CONTINUE THEIR COMMITMENT TO THEIR COMMUNITY IN WHICH THEY LIVE AND WORK THROUGH VOLUNTEER EFFORTS. CA HOSTED A CHARITY DAY WHERE OVER 30 LONG ISLAND CHARITIES WERE REPRESENTED.

CA also supports local and national chapters of Habitat for Humanity, which seeks to eliminate homelessness from the world, KaBOOM!, which builds safe playgrounds in local neighborhoods across the country, and CA's Charity Day, where representatives from over 30 Long Island non-profit organizations came to CA to discuss services they provide and ways in which CA employees can volunteer.

The underpinnings of CA's unique workplace environment and corporate culture can be traced to the leadership of Charles Wang, who founded CA and oversaw its growth into a multinational $6-billion software leader, and to Sanjay Kumar, who continues to increase the flexibility and efficiency of CA's business units to ensure that the company remains responsive to changing client requirements.

Today, CA's renewed focus is on the software that manages eBusiness and underscores our commitment to providing value through trusted, innovative business solutions, services, and support. The company's underlining strength has always been the ability to quickly adapt to tomorrow's changing landscape. CA has the experience and breadth of product and services to provide solutions enabling eBusiness to succeed and thrive in this new environment. ∎

BRIARCLIFFE COLLEGE

From the beginning, Briarcliffe's keen sensitivity to the needs of Long Island's business community helped shape its future. Its philosophy of providing higher education and career training to spur the region's economic growth has been the hallmark for its success.

BRIARCLIFFE COLLEGE, LONG ISLAND'S PREMIER PRIVATE COLLEGE SPECIALIZING IN BUSINESS, COMPUTER TECHNOLOGY, AND GRAPHIC DESIGN, HOUSES ITS MAIN CAMPUS IN THE SPACIOUS FORMER GRUMMAN CORPORATION BUILDING IN BETHPAGE WHERE THE LUNAR MODELE WAS ENGINEERED IN THE LATE 1960S. A LARGE BRANCH CAMPUS IS LOCATED IN SUFFOLK COUNTY.

Since Briarcliffe College was founded in 1966, it has been committed to producing graduates with marketable professional skills. Since then, thousands have graduated from a variety of programs of study well-prepared to meet the demands of the current business environment. Today, the college has a reputation for skillfully integrating the demands of the market's high-tech business environment into all its programs. Briarcliffe is regarded as a well-rounded educational institution, grounded in career training. Committed to the pursuit of personal and professional growth, the college offers relevant programs aimed at enriching the intellectual, cultural, ethical, and social development of its students. The college's motto is *Potentiam Ampliare Humanum*—"maximizing human potential."

Briarcliffe's main campus is in Bethpage, on the former Grumman Aerospace property. Past and present meet at Briarcliffe, where 2,000-plus students are learning to develop tomorrow's high technology in the same building where the historic Lunar Excursion Module (L.E.M.) was engineered. The college maintains a branch campus in Patchogue.

"With a focus on professional preparation, students' educational goals at Briarcliffe are primarily career entry, career advancement, and career change," stated Briarcliffe President C. Ronald Kimberling, Ph.D. "This is consistent with our mission statement of providing specialized academic programs that integrate theory and practice, utilize advanced technologies, and incorporate liberal arts course offerings."

Two- and four-year degrees at Briarcliffe range from Associate in Applied Science to Associate in Occupational Studies, Bachelor of Business Administration, and Bachelor of Fine Arts in Graphic Design. Programs focus on computer technology, graphic design, and business. Areas of study include accounting, business administration, computer information systems, graphic design (print, Web, and animation), networking and computer technology, computer application systems, and telecommunications. Briarcliffe also offers one-year diploma programs in a variety of disciplines including accounting, computer service technology, and computer programming.

From its inception, Briarcliffe has remained on the cutting-edge of the technological revolution. During the 1970s, Briarcliffe pioneered the use of computers in the classroom. In response to the growing technological needs of the business community during the 1990s, Briarcliffe added high-technology associate degree programs in information technology and design.

Drawing on its strengths in business and technology, Briarcliffe created its first bachelor's degree programs in 1998. The Bachelor of Business Administration in Information Technology degree reflects the dominant position technology has assumed in the local economy. In 1999, Briarcliffe added bachelor's degree programs in marketing and management. In 2000 a Bachelor of Fine Arts in Graphic Design was also added to the curriculum.

BRIARCLIFFE COLLEGE PRESIDENT, DR. C. RONALD KIMBERLING AND NEW YORK GOVERNOR, GEORGE PATAKI, CUT THE RIBBON FOR THE OPENING OF THE LISTNET HIGH-TECH INCUBATOR AT BRIARCLIFFE COLLEGE. THE INCUBATOR HOUSES 16 HIGH-TECH STARTUP COMPANIES AND PROVIDES AN ARRAY OF SERVICES AND PROGRAMS DESIGNED TO CONTRIBUTE TO BUSINESS DEVELOPMENT ON LONG ISLAND. BRIARCLIFFE IS PROUD OF ITS INVOLVEMENT WITH LISTNET (LONG ISLAND SOFTWARE AND TECHNOLOGY NETWORK), THE PREMIER HIGH TECH BUSINESS ASSOCIATION ON LONG ISLAND.

Briarcliffe's strong ties to the business community are best exemplified by the college's establishment of an on-site incubator in 1999. This high-tech incubator provides affordable rental prices to 15 start-up technology-based companies on Briarcliffe's main campus. To help tenants develop into successful business ventures, the college partners with the Long Island Software and Technology Network (LISTnet) to provide weekly business consultations, special-interest speakers and roundtable discussions, an on-premises manager, high-speed Internet connectivity, a professional library, and assistance from student interns. "The program is a win-win for all involved," Kimberling explained. "Start-up companies are given technical and professional assistance, allowing them to grow and prosper at a comfortable pace, while Briarcliffe students and graduates are provided jobs and hands-on experience. And, the businesses that are successful provide a tremendous boost to Long Island's economy," he added.

Members of the Briarcliffe faculty typically have had real-world career success in the fields they teach. Instructors often bring their experiences in the exciting world of business and cutting-edge technology into the classroom, providing an added dimension to the curriculum. Briarcliffe's business administration faculty, for example, includes experts in accounting, marketing, and management. The graphic design program is taught primarily by practicing artists. Experienced engineers and computer professionals use their real-world experience when teaching technology-based courses.

Briarcliffe College's School of Continuing Education and Professional Development is highly regarded by high-tech corporations for its accelerated technology training

BRIARCLIFFE COLLEGE'S MISSION IS TO EDUCATE AND PREPARE A DIVERSE STUDENT POPULATION FOR PROFESSIONAL CAREERS IN BUSINESS, COMPUTER TECHNOLOGY, AND GRAPHIC DESIGN. BRIARCLIFFE EMPHASIZES STRONG TIES TO THE BUSINESS AND TECHNOLOGY COMMUNITIES IN ORDER TO DESIGN AND OFFER CUTTING EDGE COURSEWORK USING INDUSTRY STANDARD HARDWARE AND SOFTWARE.

courses. In fact, the college has attained the credentials of Microsoft Certified Technical Educational Center, Microsoft Train the Trainer provider, a Cisco Regional Networking Academy, A+ certified computer repair program, and a Novell Education Academic Partner.

Briarcliffe College's continuing education programs combine instructor-led classes with e-learning and 24-hour, 7-day-a-week, real-time mentoring to create effective personalized learning paths. Course offerings range from one-day application classes to six-month comprehensive certification programs. Briarcliffe's corporate training programs offer customized training courses at workplace sites throughout Long Island.

Students also benefit from a full range of counseling and support services under the direction of a staff of professionals in various fields. Academic counseling, job placement assistance, educational testing and placement, extracurricular activities, and tutoring are all available.

As a member of the National Junior College Athletic Association, Briarcliffe College offers Division I intercollegiate baseball, softball, soccer, and bowling. In a very short period of time, Briarcliffe's teams have achieved national prominence, with men's baseball and women's softball going to the College World Series and its bowling team producing the women's all-around national champion two consecutive years. Additional sports opportunities include intramural activities in tennis, volleyball, and basketball.

On the leading edge of technology education, Briarcliffe College is prepared to maintain its commitment to academic excellence, while offering a wide range of programs and degree levels to its growing student body, well into the future. ∎

BRIARCLIFFE COLLEGE'S STUDENT-ATHLETES COMPETE IN THE NJCAA DIVISION I IN FIVE SPORTS: WOMEN'S SOCCER (FEATURED ABOVE), MEN'S BASEBALL, WOMEN'S FASTPITCH SOFTBALL, AND MEN'S AND WOMEN'S BOWLING. IN 1999 AND 2000, BOTH THE BASEBALL AND SOFTBALL TEAMS MADE BACK-TO-BACK VISITS TO THE COLLEGE WORLD SERIES.

EAB

❧

As a measure of just how dynamic a role EAB plays in the Long Island economy, a recent bank survey reveals that in Nassau County one in five households transacts business with EAB while in Suffolk County it is one in six households. At its 100 branches and several financial centers, EAB's hallmark is seamless service delivered by branch personnel, business advisors, insurance agents, and equity loan, mortgage, and financial consultants.

EAB's success in branch banking is matched by the bank's success in its other core businesses: Corporate Banking, Leasing, and Retail Credit. All have experienced remarkable double-digit growth in the last few years. EAB's Chairman and Chief Executive Officer, Edward Travaglianti, explains the company's winning strategy: "To keep ourselves current in a fast-paced and increasingly competitive marketplace, each year we at EAB develop business and community strategies that address our organization's fundamental mission: meeting our customers' financial needs. We believe that we are differentiated in the marketplace by our people and our personal service."

EAB invests in technology to provide value to its customers, with the goal of providing customer-driven choices with a personal touch. Along with innovative delivery options, the bank offers to its customers expansion of traditional branches in both familiar and new markets. And, with an eye toward increased customer convenience, EAB continues to add to the number of its in-store branches in supermarkets and other retail outlets.

Consistent with its commitment to maximizing customer convenience, EAB continues to implement new banking options and capabilities through its Call Center.

The bank also offers SpeedTr@de℠, its on-line investment and stock-trading capability available through its investment arm, EAB Financial Strategies. Transactions at www.eab.com include on-line account opening, bill paying, and transactional reporting services. EAB's cutting-edge aggregation platform, MySites℠, provides users with secure, convenient access to to all of their accounts from finances to frequent flyer miles—with a single click, a single ID, and a single password. While EAB believes that the Internet is a potent delivery tool, the bank offers its customers an array of service channels from which to choose.

EAB's Corporate and Retail Credit customers, like its Branch Banking customers, value the bank's level of service. EAB's highly trained personnel deliver products and services right across a client's organization, providing business and personal banking services that range from corporate cash management and insurance to mortgages and personal insurance for employees. Through its parent bank, ABN AMRO Bank N.V., EAB has a global reach that greatly enhances convenience for its corporate customers. The strength of EAB's leasing equipment business, one of the 20 largest in North America, exceeded U. S. borders when EAB undertook management of ABM AMRO Canada's leasing activities. EAB's own three leasing companies—WASCO Funding Corp., American Equipment Leasing, and Bankers Leasing Association—focus on small and niche leasing activities nationwide. Last summer, EAB added a fourth leasing company, Fidelity Leasing, Inc.

EAB leads the field in meeting the needs of small businesses. The custom-tailored services it offers to the

(LEFT) EDWARD TRAVAGLIANTI, EAB CHAIRMAN AND CEO. (RIGHT) BRENDAN J. DUGAN, EAB PRESIDENT AND COO.

EAB SUSTAINS A COMMITMENT TO UNDERWRITING LOCAL SCHOOL PROGRAMMING, BOTH FOR CLASSROOM AND AFTERSCHOOL ACTIVITIES.

small business community include fast-track loan approval, a special Call Center Small Business Line, multilingual small business brochures, the availability of Small Business Advisors, EAB Business FaxLink, and outreach that affords small business entrepreneurs access to networking and informational opportunities. EAB's achievements in serving small business were recognized when the U. S. Small Business Administration designated the bank a Small Business Preferred Lender.

Connected to the Community

EAB's commitment to the communities it serves is as notable as its commitments to its retail and business customers. Brendan J. Dugan, EAB's president and chief operating officer, has said: "At EAB, corporate and personal involvement in community activities is not optional. It is essential to the achievement of our mission." Corporate support from EAB thus means far more than funding for a much-needed community project—it frequently means the personal involvement of EAB employees, from an executive vice president who personally led a Long Island blood drive, to the EAB Employee Mentoring Program in the Uniondale public schools that is now in its eighth year.

EAB's Community Development Corporation (CDC) leads in supporting the revitalization of low- and moderate-income neighborhoods. Working in partnership with community-based organizations, real estate developers, government agencies, and other financial institutions, EAB's CDC has been instrumental in transforming neighborhoods with diverse redevelopment projects.

The cornerstone of EAB's community outreach efforts is advocacy for organizations and institutions whose goal is education and the general well-being of communities. An example is the bank's participation in the Long Island

Works Coalition. The bank is particularly supportive of literacy and health initiatives that prepare and encourage children to strive for scholastic achievement. Among the bank's well-known educational initiatives are its long-time sponsorship of the EAB/News 12 Scholar-Athlete Award, its partnership in the Newspaper in Education Program through which *Newsday* and *The New York Times* are made available in classrooms across the metropolitan area, and its support of various programs at Long Island museums that promote literacy in the visual arts. Additionally, many Long Island children have their first experience with live orchestral music through the Long Island Philharmonic's EAB Family Concert Series. In its recent sponsorship of EAB Park in Central Islip, EAB merged two of the focuses of its corporate outreach— families and community revitalization. ■

EAB PARK, CENTRAL ISLIP.

MSC INDUSTRIAL DIRECT

Walk into the customer support center of MSC Industrial Direct Co., Inc., in Melville, New York and you'll see some interesting things—like the sign that says, "Smile, it's the boss calling."

No, President and CEO Mitchell Jacobson isn't always on the line. The industrial and MRO supply company doesn't actually consider Mitchell Jacobson to be "the boss." That designation belongs solely to the company's customers. And it has plenty of those, thanks to a business mission that is built upon customer satisfaction.

MSC BIG BOOK & CD-ROM.

In addition to the small catalogues it publishes throughout the year, every August MSC puts out a 4,000-page catalogue—the "Big Book"—with more than 450,000 items. Customers can even get the book on CD-Rom. And last year, MSC developed MSCdirect.com, an impressive e-commerce Web site featuring a real-time database of all 450,000 items in the Big Book, easy search capabilities and customer-specific pricing. Customers can get everything from cordless drill kits and sanders to utility pumps and manifolds. And they can get most of them the next day, thanks to MSC's extensive network of distribution centers.

"Because we don't manufacture anything, our entire focus is on servicing and delighting our customers by providing real value to them. Our ultimate goal is to help our customers by addressing their specific needs while driving cost out of their overall procurement process," says Mitchell Jacobson. "That approach has been working for more than 60 years. We expect that it will work for another 60."

A Lucky Start

Sid Jacobson started MSC Industrial Direct in 1941 as Sid Tool Company, a general line mill supply house. When he was drafted into the Army later that year, his mother and sister supported him by minding the store while he was away. He returned in 1944 to find that they had kept the business in the black and maintained a strong following.

"Failure wasn't an option for me," said Sid, who worked at a supply house for seven years before venturing out on his own. "I just knew this business could be successful because of my earlier experience. All I had to do was work hard and treat my customers, my people, and suppliers with respect and consideration."

Throughout the years, Sid Tool Co. grew through internal growth and numerous acquisitions. In 1966, the company moved from Manhattan to Plainview five years after purchasing Manhattan Supply Company. Subsequent acquisitions gave Sid Tool Co. access to new products and new customers. By 1993, Sid Tool Co. had $142 million in sales, 20 branches, and 80 outside sales representatives. The company had opened its first major distribution center in Atlanta, Georgia in 1989, followed by one in Elkhart, Indiana in 1995, Jonestown, Pennsylvania in 1996, and Fernley, NEV. in 1999.

Since 1982, Mitchell Jacobson has served as president. He helped grow the company from $7 million in regional revenues to $793 million in revenues nationwide at the end of fiscal year 2000. In 1995, the company became MSC Industrial Direct, a publicly traded company on the New York Stock Exchange under the symbol MSM. Customers range from small tool shops to KeySpan, Ford Motor Co. and Pall Corporation. This year, *Newsday* named MSC number 15 out of the 100 top companies on Long Island.

MSC DISTRIBUTION CENTER IN HARRISBURG, PENNSYLVANIA.

A Unique Culture

MSC defines its success through a company culture that revolves around four key groups of people: Associates, customers, owners, and suppliers. That culture is what determines every aspect of the company, from the way people behave and how decisions are made, to the way in which information is shared, conflict resolved, and staff motivated.

MSC has no employees. (They call that the "e-word.") Instead, it has Associates. That's because the term "employee" conjures up images of someone who works for someone else, with little concern for the company's ultimate success. An Associate, on the other hand, is more like a partner or colleague. An Associate commits to the company's success. That's why you'll find a full house at MSC's Voice of the Customer meetings every other Friday morning. It doesn't matter that these meetings start at 6:30 a.m. or that they're voluntary. MSC Associates care about what's going on in the company, including who's being honored for a job well done and how they can better serve customers.

They also turn out in droves for the Big Book Rollout every August. That's when MSC releases the new Big Book and celebrates the achievements of the past year. And they do it in grand MSC style. Associates write jingles and perform skits, including a recent hit entitled, True Blue MSC. They admit to some very silly behavior, but it's all in good fun—and part of the enthusiasm they have for the company.

MSC WEB SITE.

There are no bosses at MSC—save the customer, of course. Instead, every Associate works together to ensure a total quality experience for every customer. Communication is encouraged, the environment is challenging, the quality is high, and the integrity is strong. Associates are expected to respect each other and to deliver on their promises.

"We set high standards, but our associates know what is expected of them," says Mitchell. "They know that by adhering to the MSC principles they will benefit from the ultimate success of the company." ■

MSC LONG ISLAND ASSOCIATES.

PALANKER CHEVROLET

It wasn't mere good fortune that Palanker Chevrolet of West Babylon, the tri-state area's largest Corvette retailer, and one of the region's top 100 businesses in retail sales, has been ranked number two in customer satisfaction within its class and region. Palanker's owner, Bill Adkins, has made happy customers the central focus in how his business is run. Reaching that coveted second ranking resulted from systems and priorities firmly set in place by Adkins.

REACHING OUT TO SUPPORT LONG ISLAND'S CULTURAL COMMUNITY, PALANKER CHEVROLET WAS THE SPONSOR OF A RECENT EXHIBITION AT THE HECKSCHER MUSEUM OF ART IN HUNTINGTON. SHOWN (LEFT TO RIGHT) ARE THE HECKSCHER'S BOARD CHAIRMAN, CATHERINE A. JANSEN; PAULINE ADKINS; AND BILL ADKINS.

For instance, Palanker's managers know that their bonuses, and indeed, their jobs, are tied into attaining higher levels of customer satisfaction. Every vehicle purchase and repair is followed up immediately by telephone and mail so that any problems can be addressed swiftly. New car purchasers even receive a gift box of cookies thanking them for their business.

Speaking of his unique brand of customer service, Adkins offered as an example a recent instance in which the keys of a car in for repair were misplaced, inconveniencing the customer when he arrived to pick up his vehicle. Though new keys were quickly cut to speed the driver on his way, both Adkins and his service manager called the customer to apologize and, as a courtesy, the customer was also offered a free detailing of his car during his next visit. But Adkins went even further. To assure that this type of mishap wouldn't recur and inconvenience yet another customer, he put into place new systems which track keys from the time a car is dropped off until those keys are placed back in the customer's hands. With service of this caliber, it's likely that the number one spot for customer satisfaction will soon belong to Adkins' Palanker Chevrolet.

In recognition of this extraordinary commitment to service, Adkins received a rank of distinction-the Time Magazine Quality Dealer Award (TMQDA). Each year, at the National Automobile Dealer Association Convention, out of some 23,000 new car dealers nationwide, a mere 63 receive this prestigious designation. The TMQDA, which was created by the national association to create a positive public relations forum for all new car dealers, looks at dealerships throughout the country and presents the award to those few who have demonstrated truly exceptional performance as well as distinguished community service.

Using Technology to Serve Customers in New Ways

The technological revolution has presented Adkins and his staff with new and swifter ways to communicate with and serve their customers. Speaking of e-mailed inquiries, for instance, Adkins noted: "Technological advances have changed what is considered an appropriate response time. Our customers now expect to hear from us almost immediately and we do respond that way."

The Internet is another area presenting communication and customer service initiatives for Palanker. Adkins and his wife and partner, Pauline, are actively planning for the electronic future of their business, a time when they anticipate that people will be able to complete the entire car buying process on the web—from investigating different models through three-dimensional images, right through to arranging favorable financing. Pauline Adkins predicted that one day "we'll be delivering cars to the front door of a customer who may never have stepped

A PROUD BILL ADKINS IS SHOWN SPORTING HIS BRAND NEW ELLIS ISLAND MEDAL OF HONOR. WITH BILL IS HIS WIFE, PAULINE.

into our dealership." For the nearer future, she is exploring the sales opportunities available through other web sites and utilizing the interactive Palanker web site to announce sales on routine maintenance procedures and special prices on various car models.

The Palanker web site is of particular value to Corvette enthusiasts all over the world. The dealership has long enjoyed a niche market as a specialist in Corvettes, the only world-class, luxury sports car manufactured in America. At any given time, at least 100 of these high-performance automotive machines are in stock at Palanker. So, in contrast to its customers for other Chevrolet models who tend to be from the surrounding community, Palanker's reputation among Corvette owners is nationwide, even international. On occasion, calls have come into the West Babylon dealership from Europe, inquiring about the availability of specific Corvettes.

Twice a year, thousands of Corvette owners from throughout the tri-state area converge upon Palanker for a showcase of their collections of vintage and current models. The attendees look around, shop the market, compare their own prized auto with others, enter their beloved Corvettes in various competitions, and also raise money for charity. The events are sponsored by the Long Island Corvette Owners Association and, through registration fees, funds are raised for the Marty Lyons Make A Wish Foundation, which grants wishes to critically or terminally ill children.

EACH HOLIDAY SEASON, PALANKER CHEVROLET GATHERS MOUNDS OF GIFTS FOR THE ANNUAL TOYS FOR TOTS CAMPAIGN.

Leasing Cars—A Growth Area

Another specialty area for Palanker Chevrolet is their expertise in luxury vans. Customers may purchase or lease these and other models as new vehicles or through the company's pre-owned vehicle division. As with other dealerships, leasing has become an increasingly important segment of Palanker's business. Adkins estimates that leasing at various times accounts for 40-60 percent of new car purchases, particularly when it comes to the higher priced models. With so many cars acquired on lease these days and still having high value when they come off lease, Adkins said, "We're leasing pre-owned and pre-leased vehicles, and that's become an important new business sector for us." If the vehicle had originally been leased from and serviced by Palanker, an additional advantage for his customers is that the vehicle's maintenance records are available. Adkins also noted that extended service contracts are available for these previously owned vehicles, just as they are for new vehicles.

For those who choose to buy rather than lease, Palanker sales personnel administer promotional incentive programs offered by General Motors and also seek out the most favorable sources of financing. The best financing may be found within a General Motors Acceptance Corporation (GMAC) program, or it may be at a local bank with which Palanker Chevrolet has built a relationship over the years.

BILL AND PAULINE ADKINS (SECOND AND THIRD FROM LEFT) ARE SHOWN WITH OFFICIALS OF OUR LADY OF CONSOLATION WHEN BILL WAS HONORED BY THAT ORGANIZATION AS ITS 7TH ANNUAL CELEBRATION OF LIFE.

Adkins regards his pre-owned vehicle division as "an important service to our customers." Most used vehicles come to the dealership through trade-ins, and others are privately purchased. By maintaining a used vehicle division, Adkins said, "We enable buyers to use their trade-ins as equity in gaining a new one." The new vehicle thus gained by the buyer may be the latest year's model fresh off the showroom floor, or it may be a recent model just acquired by the dealership through another trade-in or through the end of a lease.

At Palanker Chevrolet's service department, Adkins said, "We try to understand our customers' needs and are here to satisfy them." Because of this service-oriented philosophy, Palanker often finds itself taking care of repair items at no cost to the customer, repairs that typically would be charged for at other dealerships. For instance, under Palanker's Service Plus policy certain parts bought and installed by the dealership's service department are guaranteed for as long as the client owns

BILL ADKINS, A CORVETTE DRIVER HIMSELF, IS SHOWN WITH ONE OF THE DEALERSHIP'S SHINY SPORTS CAR DRIVING MACHINES.

ADVISING THE NEXT GENERATION OF BUSINESSPEO-PLE IS IMPORTANT TO BILL ADKINS. HE IS SHOWN WITH STUDENTS OF THE HALF HOLLOW HILLS SCHOOL DISTRICT AT A CAREER PLANNING FORUM.

the vehicle. According to Adkins, his service department goes the distance because "we want our customers for life, and we'll do what it takes to retain them." Further explaining his liberal service guidelines, Adkins noted, "If we're there for them, they'll come back and recommend family and friends to us."

Leading the Way in Community Service

Palanker Chevrolet and its president are not only there for their customers, they are also there for the community at large. Bill Adkins' numerous contributions to the community his company serves were recognized when he was honored last year by Our Lady of Consolation, a long and short term nursing and rehabilitative care facility in nearby West Islip. Adkins is a board member of Catholic Health Services, a far flung network of Long Island healthcare providers, of which Our Lady of Consolation is a part. He also serves on the board of directors of the Suffolk County Community College Foundation, the Harbor Country Day School, Long Island United Way, the Institute for Student Achievement and is an honorary trustee for the Long Island Aquarium. Last year, Adkins added Tilles Center for the Performing Arts, the region's leading art presenter, to the lengthy list of boards on which he sits. As a prominent African American businessman, Adkins also devotes much of his time and resources to the NAACP, the Urban League and the United Negro College Fund. Palanker was the corporate sponsor of a landmark exhibition of works by African American artists. The Heckscher Museum of Art exhibition, which showcased works from the holdings of collector Walter O. Evans, portrayed the diversity and vibrancy of artistic endeavors by African American artists over a 150-year period.

CHARITY GOLF TOURNAMENTS ARE ALL IN A DAY'S WORK—AND FUN—FOR PALANKER CHEVROLET'S PRESIDENT BILL ADKINS. HERE HE IS SHOWN (RIGHT) WITH FELLOW DUFFERS AT THE SUFFOLK COMMUNITY COLLEGE FOUNDATION TOURNAMENT.

Palanker's-and Adkins'-charitable commitments in the community are no less diverse. According to Adkins, "Youth and seniors are my particular commitments, especially the disadvantaged." Therefore, his dealership also supports local school and youth programs and works with the Town of Babylon providing contributions and services for programs geared to meet the needs of senior citizens. Area soup kitchens and Toys for Tots programs enjoy Palanker support as do the West Babylon Fire Department and the school district's PTA. When local youngsters compete in the Special Olympics, it's quite likely that their participation was made possible through support from Palanker Chevrolet.

Additionally, Adkins has become an important player in organizations which serve his professional field. He is on the board of directors of the General Motors Minority Dealers Association (GMMDA), National Association of Minority Automobile Dealers (NAMAD), and the Greater New York Dealers Association. Among the many honors that have been accorded Adkins' accomplishments are the Suffolk County Martin Luther King, Jr. Award, the Commission Public Service Award, the Ellis Island Medal of Honor Award, the Small Business Advocate Minority Award, and the Time Magazine Quality Dealer Award.

Planning for Future Growth

On the horizon for Palanker Chevrolet, said its president, will be acquiring more franchise opportunities in the automotive field and providing others with the opportunities for ownership. He and Pauline, the company's "futurist" who particularly dedicates her time to Palanker's long-range planning, are actively refocusing and recommitting their organization. Toward that end, they've already brought in "more experienced

people as key personnel-people who will help us get to that next step of success."

Casting his thoughts toward the future of his company, Adkins predicted that Palanker will grow through expansion and acquisition. Further explaining the commitment, which will spur this growth, Adkins stated: "I look toward our business expanding as long as we continue to exceed our customers' expectations. We want to keep creating win-win situations for our customers, our team members, and our community." ∎

SUFFOLK COUNTY EXECUTIVE ROBERT GAFFNEY IS SHOWN PRESENTING BILL ADKINS WITH THE COUNTY'S MARTIN LUTHER KING, JR. PUBLIC SERVICE AWARD.

SYMBOL TECHNOLOGIES, INC.

Symbol Technologies, Inc. is the global leader in mobile data transaction systems that improve productivity and competitiveness across industries by increasing speed and accuracy, lowering costs, and enhancing customer service. The company's technology solutions integrate portable bar code laser scanners and application-specific mobile computing systems, communicating over wireless local area networks (LANs). These innovations are driven by Symbol's advances in miniaturization, ergonomic design, and power management.

Symbol's strength in changing the paradigms of capturing and communicating data has fueled its impressive growth from a startup in the mid-1970s to an industry leader today, with revenue at $1.45 billion in 2000, nearly half of which is derived from export, and some 4,500 associates worldwide.

Today, more than 10 million Symbol bar code scanners, mobile computers, and wireless LANs are in use worldwide in markets ranging from retailing to transportation and distribution logistics, manufacturing, parcel and postal delivery, government, healthcare, and education. Symbol's wireless information appliances—intuitive, convenient, and easy-to-use "tools"—help connect the physical world of people "on the move," packages, paper and shipping pallets to information systems and the Internet, a linkage that's increasingly critical to unlocking the true potential of e-commerce.

THE EXECUTIVE MANAGEMENT TEAM: JERRY SWARTZ (LEFT) IS CHAIRMAN AND CO-FOUNDER; TOMO RAZMILOVIC (RIGHT) IS PRESIDENT AND CEO.

Symbol's record of technology achievement was recognized by winning the 1999 National Medal of Technology, the nation's highest honor for technology innovation. Symbol is only the 11th corporate recipient in the 20-year history of the award. President Clinton presented the award to Symbol at a ceremony at the White House on March 14, 2000.

Revolutionizing hand-held scanning

In the early 1980s, the company introduced the world's first Hand-Held Laser Scanner (HHLS), which revolutionized bar code scanning applications and proliferated the use of bar codes. Whereas scanning was previously limited to bulky fixed-station laser scanners used primarily at retail checkout, the HHLS is a mobile device that operates in tough retail environments from point-of-sale to the warehouse and enables supply chain logistics from the factory to the home. The HHLS comprises a laser diode optoelectronic system and decode software to translate the bar code pattern into data.

Since 1980, the company has driven the miniaturization of the bar code scan engine by a factor of several thousand, shrinking it from the size of a supermarket slot scanner to today's high-performance Symbol scan engine at 1/5 of a cubic inch and a fraction of an ounce—embedded in a wide range of OEM devices such as hand-held computers and palmtop PDAs, health monitoring, and photoprocessing equipment. This drive toward miniaturization has facilitated pervasive use of bar code-based mobile data capture in broad and diverse applications.

THE U.S. DEPARTMENT OF DEFENSE AWARDED SYMBOL A $248 MILLION CONTRACT—LARGEST IN COMPANY HISTORY—TO SUPPLY WIRELESS MOBILE COMPUTING AND SCANNING SYSTEMS FOR DEMANDING LOGISTICS APPLICATIONS.

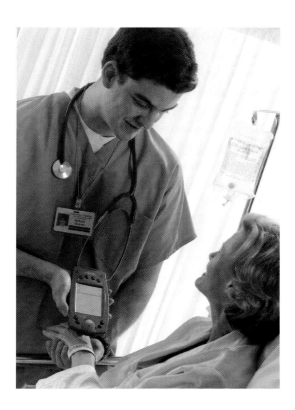

Advances in Hand-held Computing

In 1990, the Company introduced the first packet-switched, commercial spread spectrum wireless LAN for data communications. This mission-critical, real-time technology led to Symbol's LRT (Laser Radio Terminal)-the first hand-held computer system with an integrated bar code laser scanner and a digital radio. The LRT significantly increased the productivity and efficiency of retail store personnel, warehouse and factory workers, and parcel delivery drivers by allowing them to scan and wirelessly communicate in real-time to a host terminal.

Pioneered and led by Symbol, wireless LAN technology has standardized around the internationally accepted IEEE 802.11 specification, opening the market for more cost-effective, flexible system implementation and paving the way for the proliferation of wireless LANs worldwide, ultimately providing anywhere/anytime Internet connectivity. Symbol's open-architecture wireless LAN solutions support data, voice-over-IP, and multimedia applications at up to 11 Mbps with robust interference immunity. In 1998, Symbol introduced the first-ever voice-over-IP wireless LAN-based phone system, able to carry toll-free calls over an existing data network.

In the early '90s, Symbol also introduced the first wearable ring scanner and wrist computer, which provides major productivity advantage by leaving both hands free to perform handling-intensive tasks like sorting parcels and moving packages. The wearable and wireless scanning system is a technological breakthrough in ergonomics and miniaturization. It consists of two

lightweight components: a radio-integrated wrist computer for wireless data (and voice) communications, and a laser scanner-on-a-ring for aim-and-shoot bar code reading.

Continued Innovations in Bar Code Technology

Symbol has moved bar codes to the next generation when it unveiled today's world-standard two-dimensional portable data file symbology (PDF417). The information stored in a portable data file (PDF) can contain more than a kilobyte of machine-readable spatial data in a square inch or two at a fraction of a penny in cost, increasing the capacity of laser-readable bar codes by over 100 times. PDF acts as a bridge to EDI (electronic data interchange) by serving as a paper-based data communication protocol, versus linear bar codes that rely on data stored in a computer file.

As companies dramatically expand their use of technology to meet the demands of e-commerce—bar code data capture, mobile computing, and wireless LAN systems are clear solutions. In fact, Symbol has been producing e-commerce "tools" for nearly 20 years and continues to provide innovative productivity solutions for today's (and tomorrow's) data-intensive, Internet-driven world. ∎

CENTRAL SEMICONDUCTOR CORP.

In the ever-changing electronics industry, Central Semiconductor Corp. of Hauppauge, has continually answered the industry's demand for smaller, lighter, and more energy efficient discrete semiconductors. With consistent growth throughout its 25-year history, Central has maintained its headquarters here on Long Island and considers Long Island a valuable resource of talented individuals. Central is truly a Long Island company.

CENTRAL SEMICONDUCTOR'S CORPORATE HEADQUARTERS IN HAUPPAUGE.

1970s

Central Semiconductor Corp. was founded in 1974 by Jack Radgowski and his late wife Dorothy with the primary focus of manufacturing germanium and silicon discrete semiconductors. In the mid-1970s, discrete semiconductor manufacturers such as Motorola and Texas Instrument, began discontinuing germanium semiconductors in favor of silicon devices, leaving many electronics manufacturers in a quandary. Recognizing there was still a demand for devices of this technology, the company continued to manufacture them, providing an alternative to costly redesigns faced by many electronics manufacturers. Although customer demand for germanium ceased in the late 1980s, Central is still dedicated to the manufacture of other trailing edge devices, presently accounting for close to 25 percent of sales. At this same time the company began the manufacture of standard commodity products, which are used in most electronic circuits today. The latter products have the greatest sales volume.

1980s

Central's growth was maintained throughout the 1980s by focusing on quality and customer satisfaction. Keeping with the latest advances in the discrete semiconductor industry, the company developed its first Surface Mount Devices (SMD) in 1987. These devices were required for the newer portable electronic products. In addition, many manufacturers were requesting special, custom, or selected variations on the standard devices. With a strong engineering design team, Central found solutions for many unique problems. This was yet another niche the company would identify. Special, custom, or selected products would eventually account for 15 percent of sales.

1990s

In 1994, with an ever-increasing customer base, Central expanded to its present 30,000-square-foot manufacturing facility to meet its growing demand. With almost 100 employees dedicated to Total Customer Satisfaction, Central Semiconductor is proud to be an ISO9001 company and truly believes quality is built into a product. The company's extensive manufacturing facility boasts a Class 1000 Clean-room, high-speed automated wafer probing, in-process production test and quality control, marking, taping and reeling, and a Nicolet Real Time X-ray and JEOL scanning electron microscope.

Central has developed a long list of customers including many of today's leading companies. Among its more than 1500 clients are 3 Com, CISCO Systems, Eaton Corp., HP/Agilent, IBM, Lucent, Nortel Networks, Sony, TDK and Symbol Technologies. Almost two-thirds of its sales are in North America with significant business in the Far East and Europe. Central is privately held, with 1999 sales of $25 million and a projection for 2001 of $40 million. Over 200 million devices were shipped in 1999 alone.

PROCESSING OF SEMICONDUCTOR WAFERS IN CLASS 1000 CLEAN-ROOM.

Into the Millennium

Today, the company is still dedicated to supporting trailing edge devices with its EOL-Life Support program which includes over 700 devices discontinued by other manufacturers but still manufactured by Central. While maintaining the trailing edge niche it forged in the 1970s, Central has also continued developing its leading edge products, which account for 45 percent of sales, with the newest family of devices called Ultramini. This product family lives up to the company's commitment for smaller, lighter, and more efficient devices by being approximately 65 percent smaller, 60 percent lighter, and using 45 percent less energy, than the standard mini devices.

Central Semiconductor's dramatic growth within the last year included the promotion of long time staff member Susan Ryan to the post of President. In this capacity, Ryan oversees a company which has established an impressively inclusive corporate environment, one in which each employee is regarded as an essential team member. Recognizing these individuals as its most valuable resource, company officials have invested significantly in staff training and development, as well as having allocated funds toward social activities that have served to strengthen the bond within the Central Semiconductor family.

Senior Human Resources Representative Deborah A. Lange describes Central Semiconductor as providing "company programs designed to create a dynamic

CULTURE DEVELOPMENT THROUGH CONTINUOUS TRAINING.

environment for all members, to nurture their career development and enrich their education." She adds, "these programs have resulted in a high overall job satisfaction for our members."

What the Central team strives for is outlined in the company's statement of its four priorities: perfect quality, perfect service, perfect delivery, and a reasonable price. To further these goals, the company participates in many trade organizations, including the American Electronics Association, the Electrostatic Discharge Society, the National Electronic Distribution Association, and the Surface Mount Technology Association. As a good corporate neighbor, Central Semiconductor is also a member of the Long Island Association, the Long Island Forum for Technology, and the Hauppauge Industrial Association. Jack Radgowski, CEO, serves on the board of the Visiting Nurse Service of Suffolk County and is also involved with Mather Memorial Hospital in Port Jefferson, Family Service League of Huntington, and United Cerebral Palsy of Greater Suffolk.

Looking toward the future of the company he founded in 1974, one which has greatly evolved over the years, Radgowski foresees building on the company's strengths and flexibilities as it continues its pattern of solid growth. He concludes "we'll adapt our product lines to meet the ever-changing needs of our customer base in an industry where change is a constant." ∎

DEVICE ANALYSIS UTILIZING SCANNING ELECTRON MICROSCOPE.

FOREST LABORATORIES, INC.

Forest Laboratories, Inc., with its Long Island base in Commack, is an international developer, marketer, and manufacturer of branded, generic, and non-prescription pharmaceutical preparations used to treat a wide range of illnesses. Headquartered in New York City it sells its goods in the United States and Europe and is rapidly expanding. A public corporation with annual sales of over $1 billion, it trades on the New York Stock Exchange under the symbol "frx."

Founded in 1954 as a Delaware Corporation, Forest sold to a niche market in patented time release technology using its Synchron oral carrier base. The business grew internationally with the acquisition of a number of smaller pharmaceutical firms in the U.S., Puerto Rico, and England. Most notable of these early additions was the marriage of Forest with Barrow's Pharmaceutical of Inwood, Long Island, creating Inwood Laboratories, Forest's generic subsidiary. It was there that the company chose to move their main research and manufacturing operations from Elizabeth, New Jersey in the mid-1970s.

During the 1980s Forest continued to add new subsidiaries. The two main additions were O'Neill, Jones, and Feldman of St. Louis, Missouri and UAD Laboratories of Jackson, Mississippi, both of which possessed substantial salesforces. Forest's European presence was, at the same time, enhanced through the purchase of an Irish company, Tosara Products, makers of Sudocrem, the leading diaper rash ointment in the British Isles.

LONG ISLAND IS HOME TO SEVERAL KEY AREAS OF FOREST'S PHARMACEUTICAL BUSINESS, INCLUDING R&D, MANUFACTURING, PACKAGING, SALES TRAINING, ETC. FACILITIES ARE LOCATED IN COMMACK (PICTURED), INWOOD, FARMINGDALE AND HAUPPAUGE.

The 1990s saw substantial growth of Forest's marketing and manufacturing, mainly through the licensing and development of many novel new drugs. Naturally, with this increase in business came more personnel, equipment, and facilities. The research, sales, and manufacturing divisions all moved to expanded, new, or refurbished production buildings. Today, Forest employs more than 2,500 people worldwide and occupies more than 1.3 million square feet of floor space in over 20 buildings.

Forest's sales divisions—Forest Pharmaceuticals, Forest Therapeutics, Forest Specialty Sales, Inwood Sales, and Pharmax Ltd.—promote a wide range of drugs, from analgesics, to cardiovascular and pulmonary, to central nervous system specialities. Many of these products were developed and are produced at Long Island facilities. The most notable of these is the Celexa brand of Citalopram HBR tablets, a selective seratonin reuptake inhibitor (SSRI) used primarily in the treatment of clinical depression.

Celexa, already ranks as the company's largest product. Within one year of its introduction, prescriptions for Celexa had been written by more than 100,000 physicians. Against well-known giants, Celexa quickly captured 11 percent of new prescriptions in the $6.3 billion U.S. market for its class of antidepressants. Its market share continues to grow. The rapid success of the drug has been attributed to its minimal side effects, infrequent interactions with other drugs, and swift onset of action. Success is also due to the enhancement of the company's

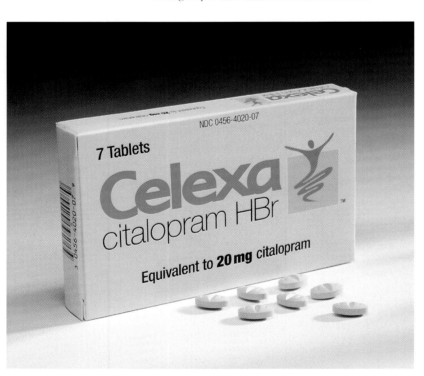

FOLLOWING ITS INTRODUCTION IN 1998, CELEXA, AN ANTIDEPRESSANT, ACHIEVED THE SIXTH BEST PHARMACEUTICAL LAUNCH IN HISTORY AND QUICKLY BECAME FOREST'S BIGGEST PRODUCT. TODAY IT REMAINS THE FASTEST GROWING PRODUCT IN ITS CATEGORY.

FOREST LICENSES PROMISING NEW COMPOUNDS—
AS EARLY AS THE CHARACTERIZATION OF NEW
MOLECULES TO PRODUCTS WITH FULL CLINICAL
DOSSIERS—AND DEVELOPS THEM IN TO PRODUCTS
THAT TREAT A WIDE RANGE OF ILLNESSES.

salesforce that grew from 650 to 850 representatives at
the launch and now totals in excess of 1,500. These
aggressive, representatives call upon primary care physicians, psychiatrists, and hospital personnel throughout the
country to introduce them to this new antidepressant and
to provide critical education as to its uses and benefits.
Their state of the art training program is developed and
administered at Forest's Commack Sales Training Center
with the assistance of the staff and services of many fine
area hotels and caterers.

The wide acceptance of Celexa and its anticipated
annual upward sales spiral have placed heavy demands
on Forest's manufacturing facilities, several of which are
undergoing expansion. This has also resulted in the
construction of a new distribution warehouse in St.
Louis, added space in Ireland, and three new facilities
in the Hauppauge/Commack area.

In the face of the company's dynamic growth following the introduction of Celexa, Forest Laboratories chairman and chief executive officer, Howard Solomon, has
recognized that the company will require products to
augment and succeed Celexa in several years when its
rapid sales curve is likely to moderate. Solomon plans
to continue to depend on licensing products which
have been initially discovered by other companies and
acquiring rights to these products at various stages in
their development, from as early as the identification of
a new molecule to as late as after FDA approval of the
new drug.

Recently introduced products, developed through
the efforts of these employees include Monurol, a single
dose urinary tract infection antibiotic; Infasurf, a lung sur-
factant, used for treating respiratory distress in premature
infants; Aerobid, an inhaled corticosteroid for asthma
and Tiazac, used for treating hypertension. Products in
development include the promising drugs Escitalopram
(next generation of Celexa), ML3000 (Arthritis),Memantine
(Neuropathic pain and Alzheimer's), Lercanidipine
(Cardioascular), Dexloxiglumide (Irritable Bowel
Syndrome), and many more that Forest intends to
formulate into new dosage forms for FDA approval at
its new Pharmaceutical Development Center now being
constructed at Commack. The facility brings together,
under one roof, the functions of Forest's Research and
Development Department's Administration, Formulation,
Methods Development, Technical Transfer, Clinical
Packaging, and Analytical Support.

Forest long ago recognized that its strength lies in
its personnel, their skills, and performance. Toward that
end, many forward thinking benefit programs have
been established to attract the finest available talent to
Forest's Long Island operations. These include medical,
dental, and life insurance, savings and profit sharing
plan (with company match), annual bonuses and salary
increases, summer hours, and flex time. ■

FOREST MEETS THE DEMANDS OF ITS GROWING
PRODUCT PORTFOLIO AND DYNAMIC NEW DRUG
DEVELOPMENT PIPELINE BY MAINTAINING STATE-OF-
THE-ART TECHNOLOGY THROUGHOUT ITS FACILITIES.

GODSELL CONSTRUCTION CORP.

When Arthur J. Godsell thinks back to the launch of his construction business in 1968, one feeling remains fresh in his mind—fear. He remembers vividly the night he and his wife, Gloria, sat down at their kitchen table in Hauppauge, New York, to decide whether or not to proceed with the venture.

"It was a little frightening for both of us," admits Art Godsell, who had been working as a salesman for a construction company. "Most people thought I was crazy. They said I wasn't big enough; I didn't have enough money. You had to be a giant to start a business like that. So, I was frightened."

TWO GENERATIONS OF PARTNERS; ARTHUR J., ARTHUR E., AND JOHN GODSELL.

The prospect of starting a business was so ominous, in fact, that when the company he was working for shut down, Art Godsell planned to take a job with a previous employer. Several of his current employers' clients, however, had other ideas. They suggested that Art Godsell start his own business—and promised to be his first clients. He was just 33 years old at the time.

Godsell Today

It turns out that their confidence was well-founded. Today, Godsell Construction Corporation boasts such well-known clients as Cushman & Wakefield, Helmsley Spear, North Shore—Long Island Jewish Health System, Winthrop Hospital, Rockefeller Center, and Andersen Consulting. The Hicksville-based company employs approximately 75 people, depending on its workload. Business spans Long Island and Manhattan, with rare jobs in New Jersey and Westchester.

The company is a union carpentry contractor. As such, it handles virtually all construction and renovation work,

from drywall and acoustics to carpentry and cabinet work. Electrical and plumbing jobs are about the only work Godsell Construction doesn't handle. Its projects include office space, showrooms, hospitals, nursing homes, and retail complexes. The recent renovation of North Shore University Hospital at Plainview, for example, is a project in which Godsell Construction was involved.

The Early Days

The company started out as Interboro Acoustics Inc., a lathing and ceiling specialist. Back in the late 1960s, plaster was a popular building material for walls. A lathing base was applied to the walls in order to enable it to accept the plaster. It was a good business to be in back then. But when drywall became popular, Art Godsell knew it was time to change. He started Interboro Contracting Company to take advantage of the trend. He partnered briefly with two men who ran a general contracting business. The arrangement was less than ideal. So, when the two men retired, Art Godsell vowed to never to go outside the family again.

In 1977, he and Gloria decided to "make bookkeeping easier" by incorporating their two businesses under the family name. Sons Arthur E. and John had worked in the business part-time during high school. Arthur E. joined the business in the mid 1970s. He began his career as a carpenter while studying architecture and business in the evenings at SUNY Farmingdale. Arthur E. progressed to foreman, then moved into the office as a salesman and field supervisor. He now serves as president. John joined the business in the late 1980s, after finishing his studies at SUNY Farmingdale receiving a degree in business administration. Starting in estimating and field supervisor he moved on to sales and also serves as vice president of the company. Art Sr., Gloria, Arthur E., and John each own a 25 percent share in the company. A third son, James, works as a jobsite general foreman.

The company was based in Manhattan for much of its history. The location was a natural choice, considering that Arthur, Sr., had worked there with his last employer, and nearly all of Godsell Construction's work was there. "My wife, who serves as our bookkeeper, would never go to Manhattan," says Godsell. "She kept an office in the house, and Arthur, John, and I would go into Manhattan each day. But we all lived on Long Island and often worked late into the evenings. In 1993, as the company expanded and business diversified into Long Island and the boroughs, we decided to move the main offices to Hicksville because of its central location and excellent commute to the city."

A sales office and warehouse remained in Manhattan until 1999. At that time, the company consolidated its offices and warehouse in one new location. Today, Godsell Construction Corporation operates from its own quarters on Duffy Avenue in Hicksville. A full-service building is jointly owned by Arthur E. and John.

Community Commitment

Godsell is committed to strengthening the construction business, particularly on Long Island. The company is a member of the New York chapter of the International Wall and Ceiling Association. Arthur E. serves as vice president of the board of directors, as well as a management trustee of pensions and welfare funds for the Suburban District Council of Carpenters.

Godsell's commitment to Long Island extends far beyond its business involvement. For years, Godsell has sponsored local baseball, softball, and soccer teams. The company also repairs sports fields and gives financial support to the local Police Athletic League, the fire departments, and other organizations and activities. While his four sons and two daughters were growing up, Arthur, Sr., managed many of their sports teams. Today, his sons carry on that tradition by coaching Godsell Construction-sponsored teams.

GODSELL CONSTRUCTION'S HEADQUARTERS AT 351 DUFFY AVENUE, HICKSVILLE, NEW YORK.

"Long Island has been good to us, both personally and professionally," says Arthur, Sr. "Our commitment to quality and personal service has not gone unnoticed by the business community here. We are grateful for the work we have secured here and for the home we have made here." ■

FATHER AND SONS PICTURED AT THE WALL & CEILING ASSOCIATION DINNER, MARCH 2000, HONORING ARTHUR J. AS CONTRACTOR OF THE YEAR.

LLOYD STAFFING

As the largest privately held staffing company on Long Island, Lloyd Staffing has dedicated the past 30 years to successfully answering the employment needs of the regional workforce.

Lloyd Staffing responds to direct hire and temporary career openings by providing people skilled in the demands of the current marketplace. The company, which is headquartered in Melville, also maintains Long Island offices in Holbrook and Great Neck, and has company-owned and franchised locations in New York City, Westchester, Connecticut, New Jersey, Pennsylvania, Florida, Maryland, and North Carolina.

Two generations of Lloyd leadership. Keith Banks, CTS, Executive Vice President (left), Jason Banks, CPC, Director, Spider Staffing (center), Merrill Banks, CPC, President/CEO and founder of Lloyd Staffing.

Specialized Knowledge of Every Market Sector

Hiring professionals have come to value Lloyd Staffing's expertise in Direct Hire placement using either contingency or retained search methods, particularly within niche market specializations. Client companies work with a Lloyd Staffing team who are specialists within a given marketplace. The placement staff of these divisions, such as Accounting and Finance, Biotechnology, Graphic Arts, Healthcare, Information Technology, Sales, Human Resources, Pharmaceuticals, Multilingual, Call Center/ Customer Service, Office Administration, Supply Chain Management, and eMedia are experienced in their respective industries and are thoroughly familiar with field terminology, salary levels, current job-related technologies, and the specific skill demands of the discipline. Two divisions, Lloyd Information Technology and Spider Staffing cater exclusively to the high-tech and eMedia needs of the millennium workforce, focusing on candidates and consultants whose skills and job descriptions must keep pace with technological innovations and practices.

As a result of its extensive executive search efforts, *Newsday* ranked Lloyd Staffing number one in the Long Island region based on the volume of its placements made annually by its Direct Hire placement professionals.

Lloyd's own internal workforce are certified professionals themselves. More than 80 percent of the placement staff and corporate management hold the designation of CPC (certified personnel consultant) or CTS (certified temporary staffing specialist). These prestigious rankings are awarded by the National Association of Personnel Services and are recognized in the staffing industry as a benchmark of excellence. The association has consistently granted Lloyd Staffing first place honors when it comes to commitment to employees, commitment to clients, and commitment to the industry.

As a full service, multifaceted staffing company, Lloyd also assists its client companies with a broad range of hiring and training services such as temporary and consultant staffing in the area of Office Support services, as well as many specialized niches of staffing, such as Healthcare and eMedia. Lloyd has also established a reputation for its abilities to recruit and supply employees for large scale staffing assignments requiring hundreds of workers—assignments which are typically beyond the capacity of a given company to staff on its own.

Employees granted benefits and training

The company was one of the first in its industry to provide benefits such as medical, dental, and a 401k plan to its temporary staffing associates. This benefits program builds employee loyalty and retention so that Lloyd can offer their client companies a high level of continuity and minimal turnover for temporary personnel out on assignment.

Lloyd Staffing corporate headquarters at 445 Broadhollow Road, Melville. Additional Long Island locations are in Holbrook and Great Neck.

Lloyd currently has more than 10,000 employees throughout its eight-state network, and thousands more in its database of prospective job candidates. What this means to employers is that Lloyd Staffing has the ability to swiftly reach out to recruit or identify an ideally skilled candidate for virtually any career opening or market sector. Within Lloyd Healthcare Staffing, for instance, hospital relief staffing is provided 24 hours a day, 7 days a week. Clinical and non-clinical personnel, people experienced in any and all nursing specialties, and others in allied health professions are provided around the clock to hospitals, clinics, and other medical related organizations.

Many of Lloyd's temporary staffing associates have opted for temporary careers on a full-time basis. They can choose to work a 40-hour week, or just one or two days a week depending on lifestyle need. This area of employment has become a recognized career alternative for people who value freedom and flexibility while earning good hourly pay. They also have the opportunity to build their computer savvy through a unique skills upgrading program. As they work, they earn credits toward classes in word processing, spreadsheets, presentation graphics, databases, and e-mail.

These educational services are offered by Lloyd's training affiliate, PC&Mac Central, which provides instruction in dual platforms (Windows and Macintosh) focusing on the areas of office productivity, graphic design, and the Internet. With course offerings mirroring today's most commonly used business applications, PC&Mac Central offers hands-on training at state-of-the-art workstations. Given its close ties to the corporations it serves in a wide

LOBBY OF LLOYD'S CORPORATE HEADQUARTERS IN MELVILLE.

variety of disciplines and niche markets, Lloyd is able to quickly react to changes in the workplace and provide the training needed to meet the evolving needs of the current workforce.

Founded in 1971 by Merrill Banks, CPC, who continues as Lloyd's president and CEO, the company is firmly entrenched in the Long Island business landscape. A second generation of family leadership has now come aboard and looks forward to equal success for Lloyd's next 30 years of service to the Long Island community. ■

CLASSROOM OF PC&MAC CENTRAL, LLOYD'S TRAINING AFFILIATE WHERE WORKFORCE TRAINING IS PROVIDED TO A CORPORATE AUDIENCE.

LACKMANN CULINARY SERVICES

Lackmann Culinary Services feeds Long Islanders at work or at play—from casual pizza services at offices and colleges to haute cuisine at the Island's poshest black tie galas.

Founded in 1968, Lackmann has grown to become the region's leader in the contract food management industry. It currently occupies a pinnacle as the largest privately—held food service in the New York/New Jersey, and Florida regions. Winner of the industry's prestigious Silver Plate Award, Lackmann's recipe for success is to go above and beyond the norm, providing its clients with innovative, creative solutions to their food service needs.

Tom Lackmann, the company's founder, chairman, and CEO, explained the philosophy that has guided the company to its present prominence: "Our vision is to remain an independent, strong organization, one that focuses on providing our clients and guests with a level of service our larger competitors can't even come close to." In practice, this means that Lackmann commits to being a strong business partner to its clients, responding immediately to needs, becoming personally involved at its most senior levels, developing quality customized solutions tailored to the customer's needs, and delivering appetizing menus within the client's budgetary restraints.

Lackmann and his management team have established a company with an ingrained culture of hospitality. From the chairman on down to unit managers—the people who are based at client sites—all share an intensive common denominator. Hospitality is the core value of the company, one that has been integral to the company's growth and guiding philosophies.

LACKMANN CULINARY SERVICES FOUNDER, CHAIRMAN, AND CHIEF EXECUTIVE OFFICER, THOMAS F. LACKMANN.

Lackmann's president, Peter Alessio, said that the company is also stressing "value-added services for our client community." Among these services are the addition of an on-staff certified dietitian, a renewed emphasis on training for field managers as well as the actual servers at client locations, and the development of what Alessio described as "faultless HACCP (hazard analysis critical control point)—a safe food handling procedure that is recognized by the industry and the federal government as a gold standard, one that is critical for today and for the future."

Prestigious Client Roster for Lackmann

Lackmann clients include leading corporations, investment banking companies, educational institutions, and private clubs. In New York City, Prudential Securities, Morgan Stanley Dean Witter, Rockefeller Foundation, New York Stock Exchange, and Tiffany & Co. are just a few of Lackmann's blue chip clients. Similarly, on Long Island, Lackmann services many of the region's most well-known corporations and educational institutions, among them JP Morgan, Chase Treasury Services, Astoria Federal Savings Bank, Geico Insurance, Olympus America, Reuters Information Technology, KeySpan, Friends Academy, and Hofstra and Adelphi Universities.

With headquarters in Woodbury, Lackmann is most active in its Long Island hometown and contributes in many ways to the continued health and prosperity of Long Island. Peter Alessio said that many of the Island's significant fundraisers and dinners are catered by Lackmann. Beyond sharing its hospitality expertise, Lackmann supports the local philanthropic community in other ways. Tom Lackmann served on the board of

ONE OF LACKMANN CULINARY SERVICES' FRESH TOSSED SALAD STATIONS WHERE GUESTS CAN SELECT FROM A WIDE VARIETY OF INGREDIENTS TO CREATE A DISH MADE JUST FOR THEM.

Long Island Cares, the regional food bank, for many years. Looking toward the future of the industry, Lackmann Culinary Services contributes significantly to the Culinary Institute of America (CIA) in Hyde Park, New York, one of the world's most prestigious professional culinary schools. Lackmann is also represented on CIA's corporate board and on the long-range planning committee.

Beyond its prominence in New York, Lackmann services organizations as far flung as the Kennedy Space Center in Florida, a contract that Lackmann was awarded by NASA following a feverish four-month bidding process. The agreement, with renewal options running into 2010, has the Lackmann team in orbit over this exciting new partnership. NASA is far from Lackmann's sole Florida client. In fact, business in Florida has been expanding by a rapid 30 percent with no sign of abating. Some of Lackmann's newest Southeast region clients include Ceridian Benefits Services, Rockwell Collins, BAE SYSTEMS, and GE Harris Railways. The company's growth in the Southeast has been fueled by its long association with the aerospace giant, Northrup Grumman. Said Peter Alessio, "our past association with Grumman on Long Island has resulted in an enhancement of the relationship at other Northrup Grumman sites in Florida." Alessio explained that this is one demonstration of how Lackmann is growing with its client base: "As our clients grow and expand, we move with them into new geographic areas. That's become our future growth strategy—providing the highest levels of client service and continuing client relationships."

What's clear is that this strategy is resulting in significant growth. With Lackmann poised to hit a $100 million sales goal by the end of next year, its president said: "The foundation and support for this growth is in place." ∎

A LACKMANN CULINARY SERVICES CHEF SERVES UP A SPECIAL PASTA DISH FOR A STUDENT AT CAFE BISTRO AT HOFSTRA UNIVERSITY.

CONTINUING THEIR EXCEPTIONAL SERVICE STRATEGY, LACKMANN CULINARY SERVICES' ATTENTION TO DETAIL AND PRESENTATION CARRIES OVER, EVEN INTO THEIR SELF-SERVE STATIONS.

STANDARD MICROSYSTEMS CORPORATION

S tandard Microsystems Corporation (SMSC) is a worldwide supplier of leading edge integrated circuit components. In recent years, the company has revamped its guiding business model and has completely reorganized. It is now sharply focused on two separate product families: Personal Computer Products and Embedded Products. According to Steven J. Bilodeau, the chairman, president, and CEO of SMSC, "The purpose of this change was to better realize the growth opportunities in each business by independently optimizing business strategies, tactics, and practices for these two very different businesses."

Having forged relationships with virtually every major personal computer manufacturer in the world, SMSC has enjoyed a long and successful history as the leading producer of PC input/output (I/O) chips. These devices have historically controlled communications between personal computers and peripherals such as keyboards, printers, and disk drives of all types. These products are continually evolving to serve the communication needs of the most advanced PC architectures for Commercial, Consumer, Desktop, and Notebook PCs, as well as Internet connectivity platforms.

To meet the needs of the legacy-free PC era, SMSC has strategically refocused its I/O product line to replace the resident legacy content with new features that will continue to flourish in future PC architectures. Further, a recent alliance with Intel Corporation, the market leader in PC chipsets, greatly strengthens SMSC's position and poises the company for significant market expansion. Under this agreement, Intel is providing its leading edge Memory Controller Hubs to SMSC. SMSC then combines the Intel product with its own I/O Controller Hubs to

SMSC'S VICTORYBX-66 CHIPSET.

create complete chipsets. Since the PC chipset market is 10 times larger than the PC I/O market, this Intel alliance has created explosive growth opportunities for SMSC's Personal Computer Products.

SMSC's Embedded Products focus on providing chips to be used in a vast array of industrial applications such as elevators, robotic devices, factory automation, transportation systems, "smart" buildings, and remote and wireless communication of all types. Given the ongoing intensive growth in computing and communications, SMSC anticipates that its Embedded Products will account for fully a quarter of its revenue in the year ending February 28, 2001, and that it will become even more significant to the total business of the company beyond that date. Further, the new emphasis on Embedded Products brings a greater measure of diversity to SMSC's business as these products are characterized by longer design cycles, higher margins, and longer product life cycles and are sold to a wider customer base than SMSC's PC Products.

SMSC CORPORATE OFFICES.

Andrew M. Caggia, SMSC's senior vice president and CFO, explained, "Our expertise and unique niche market leadership position in embedded systems will enable us to successfully participate in this high growth marketplace. Applications for our products in factory control systems, printers, scanners, mass storage units, digital cameras, and automotive networking are steadily increasing. Set top or cable/satellite boxes, which are transforming household TV sets into Internet appliances, represent another large potential market for our products."

SMSC was founded in 1971, at the very dawn of the semiconductor era. Early in its history, SMSC's development of COPLAMOS®, a patented semiconductor manufacturing technology which provided a better way to isolate active devices on silicon, signaled that it was to be a vital contributor to the industry. COPLAMOS became essential to the development of advanced metal oxide silicon (MOS) which drove the growth of the semiconductor industry. Noted Chairman Bilodeau, "We were there, right at the development of this technology revolution. The need that so many companies had for our technology granted us access to the intellectual

INTERNET APPLIANCES ARE AMONG THE MANY EMBEDDED APPLICATIONS FOR **SMSC** INTEGRATED CIRCUITS.

SMSC PRODUCTION TEST FACILITY.

property developed by other companies, creating a leading position that has been ongoing as the company has revamped itself to serve newer, expanding markets."

A public company trading on NASDAQ, SMSC was founded in Hauppauge and, though it has a growing worldwide presence, it continues to maintain its state-of-the-art semiconductor test facility in Hauppauge. This facility, even in the face of high, competitive labor rates on Long Island, is one that is run at world-class cost and efficiency levels consistently higher than those achieved in many low-labor-cost markets. In addition to its important Long Island operations and headquarters, SMSC maintains a significant presence in most of the world's major high-tech centers, including San Jose (CA), Austin (TX), Westborough (MA), Munich, Taipei, and Tokyo.

SMSC has a proud history of product innovation and technology leadership. The company has excelled in assessing market trends and responding to customers' needs with leading-edge silicon solutions. SMSC has consistently been recognized for its commitment to providing the highest quality products, supported by outstanding service. Changing and continually reinventing itself to serve new technologies, the company's newest strategies relate to advances in wireless communication and other significant outgrowths of the personal computer and Internet industries. Throughout this process, SMSC has remained true to its semiconductor roots and has retained its ascendancy in that market.

"Having emerged," as Bilodeau explained, "as a reinvigorated, focused semiconductor solution provider, SMSC has made significant strides in its goal to serve the ever-developing demands of the semiconductor market. By upgrading its engineering development tools, expanding its multiple design centers, constructing state-of-the-art validation and compatibility labs, and most importantly attracting world class industry talent to lead its product development programs, SMSC is poised to offer products which will meet the challenges of computing and communications in the 21st century." ■

DiCarlo Distributors, Inc.

If you're eating it, chances are Holtsville's DiCarlo Distributors, Inc. has played a role in getting it to you. This privately-held, family owned and operated company in Holtsville is a broadline food distribution service company, which sells meats, dairy, fish, produce, and groceries. The business distributes these food products, as well as many food-related tabletop items and cleaning supplies, to supermarkets, restaurants, company cafeterias, restaurant facilities, school cafeterias, grocery stores, and just about anywhere food is sold or served.

The company was founded in 1963. One of the founders, Vincent DiCarlo, Sr., is currently president and CEO. With his brothers, John and Michael, he has steered DiCarlo into its second generation of leadership with their children holding important executive posts. Along with leadership from outside of the family, they head up a company of 240 employees.

DiCarlo is Long Island's largest food service distributor and is one of the largest independently owned such businesses in the entire tri-state metropolitan area. Swimming against the tide of the mega-conglomerates, which dominate this industry, DiCarlo has grown and prospered as it follows its own strong, independent family style. Annual sales reached the landmark $100-million mark last year with substantial increases projected for this year. DiCarlo has exercised market clout beyond its Long Island base through participation in two trade associations: Unipro, a $23-billion multinational cooperative, and The Multi Unit Group, which enables the company to supply national food chains.

At its founding, DiCarlo was exclusively a distributor to supermarkets and dealt with only one company— Polly-O Dairy Products. But by the mid-60s, the DiCarlo's began to expand their horizons, adding to the product line, and also adding distribution services to schools and restaurants. That product line expansion has continued throughout the company's history. Today, the company distributes more than 9,000 items. It continues to be the

AERIAL PHOTO OF THE DICARLO FACILITY, HOLTSVILLE, NEW YORK.

exclusive distributor on Long Island for Polly-O Dairy Products and also for Constantia Food Products from Italy, and for Arneo brand food products from many parts of the world.

Supermarkets, once DiCarlo's exclusive distribution outlet, now account for only six percent of the company's sales. The great majority of DiCarlo's clients are now restaurants and institutions throughout the tri-state area.

On the horizon for DiCarlo Distributors, Inc. is expansion of the company's Internet-based services. While the company presently has a website, Vincent DiCarlo, Sr. said that the site's enhancements this year will result in interactivity that allows customers to accomplish their business with the company electronically. ∎

LEFT TO RIGHT: JOHN DICARLO SR., VINCENT DICARLO SR., AND MICHAEL DICARLO.

CONTEMPORARY COMPUTER SERVICES, INC.

Contemporary Computer Services, Inc., or as it is familiarly known, CCSI, is a broad-based technology services company which counts major corporations as well as private retail customers among its client roster.

Founded by the father of the current president and CEO, John R. Riconda, CCSI is a privately held company that has traveled a long road since its beginnings in 1974. According to Riconda, the technological marketplace a quarter of a century ago, before the age of PCs, was pretty much limited to IBM mainframe business and so that was the new company's focus and expertise.

Today, CCSI has evolved with the changed high-tech environment and now offers a wide range of technology solutions for medium and large business. They design, install, and maintain computers systems, as well as voice, video, and data networks. Riconda points to system maintenance—"really being there for the customer following installation"—as perhaps the most critical service his company offers, certainly the aspect of his business which sets him apart from others in the field.

From its Bohemia headquarters and from auxiliary offices in Pennsylvania and New Jersey, CCSI services customers throughout most of the Northeast, primarily

CCSI CORPORATE SOLUTION CENTER.

from Connecticut through to Delaware. The company has some 200 employees, about 140 of whom are here on Long Island. They are skilled high-tech professionals, trained and qualified by the leading edge companies whose products they install and service. Most of the nation's top tech hardware and software companies are CCSI partners, chief among them CISCO Systems, Microsoft, IBM, and Compaq.

As the company has evolved and broadened its range of services, it has garnered an ever more prestigious client roster. Among the Long Island businesses and municipalities utilizing CCSI installed and maintained systems are Nassau County, Reuters, LIPA, Nassau Community College, and a host of public school districts.

CCSI is a participant in the Long Island Software and Technology Network (LISTnet), an incubator for high-tech start-up companies which provides entrepreneurs with support, consultation, and resources that work to develop and grow their new companies. As these fledgling businesses prosper, they serve to grow Long Island's economy. Vitally concerned with the health of the region's business community, CCSI is also an active member of the Long Island Association.

But Riconda, the company's president and CEO, doesn't limit his community involvement to business-related organizations. He also works to improve Long Island's quality of life by serving as a board member of Huntington Hospital and as an active supporter of the Make-A-Wish Foundation. ■

JOHN RICONDA, PRESIDENT AND CEO.

DuPont Pharmaceuticals Company

DuPont Pharmaceuticals Company, a wholly-owned subsidiary of the DuPont Company, headquartered in Wilmington, DE, is a worldwide business focused on research, development, and delivery of pharmaceuticals and imaging products to treat unmet medical needs in the fight against HIV, Cardiovascular Disease, Central Nervous System Disorders, and Inflammatory Disease.

THE DUPONT GARDEN CITY SITE'S STATE-OF-THE-ART PACKAGING LINE WAS RECOGNIZED IN THE PACKAGING DIGEST SEPTEMBER 2000 ISSUE.

The company's fortress-like building on Stewart Avenue, Garden City, is a well-known landmark in Nassau County. When the building was being constructed, it was so unusual that Robert Moses, developer of the Long Island Parkway System and Jones Beach State Park, had fast growing poplar trees planted along the Meadowbrook Parkway to shield the construction from the view of motorists. Later, the building was praised by the New York Times as the "Concrete Building of the Year."

Many outstanding pharmaceutical compounds have been developed by DuPont. One of the oldest and most popular is Coumadin® For more than 40 years, this leading anticoagulant has been used for the prevention of pulmonary embolism and some forms of stroke. DuPont also markets Cardiolite®, the leading cardiac stress imaging agent in the U. S. DuPont recently launched Innohep®, a low-molecular weight heparin used to treat acute symptomatic deep vein thrombosis, with or without pulmonary embolism, when used with Coumadin®.

In September 1998, DuPont introduced its first therapy in the fight against HIV and AIDS. Sustiva™ is the first once-daily treatment approved in the U.S., Canada, and Europe for use in combination therapy for people living with HIV and AIDS. Sustiva™ is the first non-nucleoside reverse transcriptase inhibitor (NNRTI) to be recognized by the U.S. Department of Health and Social Services as a preferred first-line treatment option in combination with other drugs.

The Garden City site has been instrumental in the development and production of Sustiva™ and many other pharmaceutical products. Sustiva™ is the cornerstone on which the company will build a broad base of products to combat HIV/AIDS.

DuPont conducts business based on a culture of Shared Values.

Performance—No Excuses: Employees are action-oriented, innovative, and produce quality work, while maintaining the highest standards of safety.

Everyone Receives Special Treatment: Fair, honest, and respectful treatment from everyone is expected. As colleagues, relationships are built on a foundation of trust, mutual support, teamwork, and recognition.

Business is a Social Institution: By developing and respecting the rich talents of a diverse workforce, DuPont measures itself by its ability to serve society and improve the quality of life—through products, financial and personal commitment to our communities, and by maintaining rigorous ethical standards.

DuPont Pharmaceuticals' Garden City organization prides itself in its ability to support research and development while producing high quality pharmaceuticals. DuPont employees are highly valued for their outstanding contributions to the business and community. ∎

THE COMPANY'S FORTRESS-LIKE BUILDING ON STEWART AVENUE, GARDEN CITY, IS A WELL-KNOWN LANDMARK IN NASSAU COUNTY.

CABLEVISION SYSTEMS CORPORATION

Based on Long Island, Cablevision Systems Corporation is one of the nation's leading media, entertainment, and telecommunications companies. Its portfolio of operations ranges from high-speed Internet access and robust cable television offerings to championship professional sports teams and national television program networks. Central to Cablevision's mission is a commitment to enrich customers' lives by providing the greatest possible choice of entertainment, sports, information, and telecommunications services utilizing state-of-the-art technology.

Compelling content has always been the cornerstone of Cablevision's cable television offerings. Through Rainbow Media, Cablevision offers an unparalleled suite of local and regional programming, including its targeted New York line-up—the MetroChannels, News 12 Networks, MSG Network, and FOX Sports Net New York. Complementing these local and regional services are Rainbow's strong national networks: American Movie Classics, Bravo, The Independent Film Channel, WE: Women's Entertainment, and FOX Sports Net.

In addition to delivering quality programming, Cablevision provides exciting live sports, exhibitions, and other entertainment offerings through Madison Square Garden and its teams, the Knicks, Rangers, and WNBA Liberty; The Theater at Madison Square Garden; Radio City Music Hall and its world-famous Rockettes; and Clearview Cinemas.

Founded in 1973 as a cable television operator with 1,500 Long Island customers, Cablevision now serves about 3 million households in the New York metropolitan area. Expanding beyond traditional video services, the company's broadband network also connects

HAVE YOU BEEN OPTIMIZED?

customers to advanced, customized communications products, including Cablevision's residential Optimum Telephone service, its Optimum-branded high-speed Internet access, and its Lightpath integrated business communications services.

Cablevision's commitment to education is boundless. The Power To Learn is an educational initiative designed to enable teachers, students, and parents to leverage the power of the Internet in a commercial-free environment. As part of the initiative, Cablevision offers high-speed Internet access to schools and libraries, provides an online learning community, www.powertolearn.com, and trains teachers to integrate the Internet into their classrooms.

Today the company continues to strengthen its position as a leading broadband communications, sports, and entertainment provider in the New York market. To this end, Cablevision last year announced a landmark agreement with Sony to develop and deploy digital set-top boxes—the next-generation technology that will deliver advanced digital services, including expanded channel capacity, increased pay-per-view options, and a broad range of interactive television applications.

Completing the customer experience, THE WIZ, owned by Cablevision, provides customers with a valuable connection between the in-store purchase of equipment and the home use of Cablevision's telecommunications services.

Cablevision is utilizing its unique resources—its broadband telecommunications network, its live and televised entertainment properties, and its retail presence—to offer customers superior choice and unparalleled value in entertainment and communications. ■

CABLEVISION PROVIDES SCHOOLS WITH THE POWER TO LEARN.

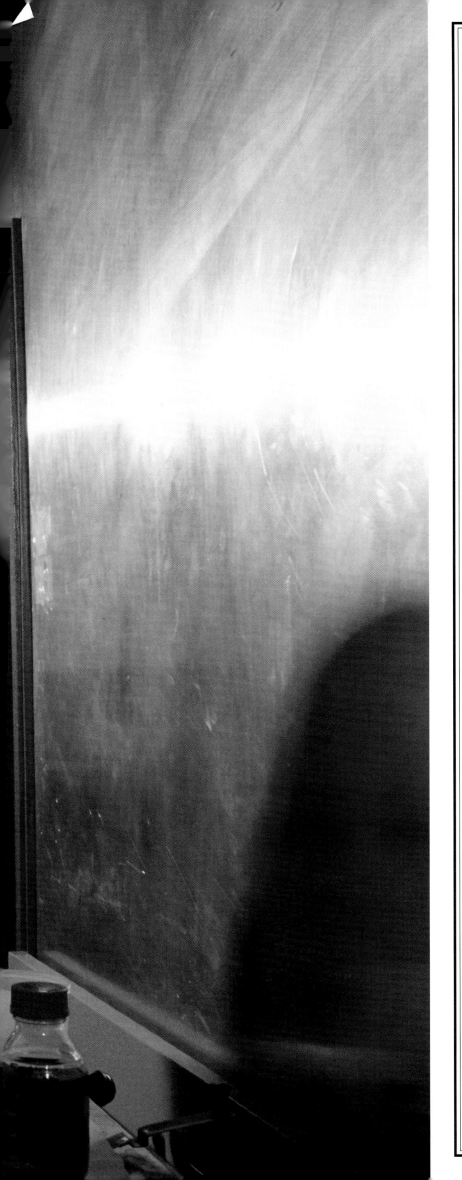

HISTORICAL COLD SPRING HARBOR'S CLOSE ALLIANCES WITH
STONY BROOK UNIVERSITY AND BROOKHAVEN NATIONAL LABORATORY
HAVE REDEFINED RESEARCH AND LEARNING BY ENCOURAGING STUDENTS
AND MENTORS TO DISCOVER NEW TECHNOLOGIES TOGETHER. HERE, A LAB
TECHNICIAN CONDUCTS AN EXPERIMENT AT COLD SPRING HARBOR
LABORATORY. PHOTO BY SCOTT LEVY, BRUCE BENNETT STUDIOS.

The generation that had fought World War II was aging and their children—the first modern suburban generation—were walking into a brand new world. These kids had learned the power of the individual. They learned about glass ceilings and childcare and feminism. They learned that there is no blueprint to follow through life; that an individual could set his or her own course in a new world.

Their parents were moving off Long Island, most of them headed south to Florida. In the last few years, the world had gotten a lot smaller, and parents who had worked so hard to build up Nassau and Suffolk weren't staying. Less expensive air travel and a national highway system made it easier to visit relatives who lived far away, and there were no snowstorms in Florida.

This pattern of older people moving off Long Island was so well established that when a talk show host asked Jerry Seinfeld if his parents still lived on Long Island, he said, "Yes, but they're moving to Florida. They don't want to, but they're 50, and on Long Island that's the law."

Although the population of Suffolk County grew between 1970 and 1980 by 157,001 people to a total of 1,284,231, the Nassau population declined in those years by 107,257 to 1,321,582.

America was not the same prosperous nation it had been in the 1950s and 60s. Gasoline shortages had made us conscious of the need to conserve our natural resources. It was getting more expensive to stay on Long Island and it seemed as if "open space" would become an alien concept to the children of the Baby Boomers.

The social unrest that touched the rest of the nation was felt on Long Island as people there began to grapple, for example, with the issue of choice. The region's national profile was raised—for better or worse—in 1977 with the publication of *The Amityville Horror*.

Over mounting protests and questions, LILCO continued its plan to open a nuclear power plant in Shoreham. Spiraling costs, passed onto ratepayers, totaled in the billions. Taxes levied on the plant by the local township and school district added to the ratepayers' burden. A whistleblower who spoke about poor management and low productivity at the plant lost his job, creating a public furor.

In 1978, there was a coolant leak at the Three Mile Island nuclear power plant near Harrisburg, Pennsylvania and the potential for a nuclear power plant disaster took center stage on Long Island. Adding to the fire of anti-nuclear sentiment was the 1979 movie *The China Syndrome*.

PUBLIC ACTIVISM AGAINST THE OPENING OF A NUCLEAR POWER PLANT IN SHOREHAM ULTIMATELY LED TO THE PLANT'S CLOSING AND THE DOWNFALL OF LILCO. HERE, IN FEBRUARY 1986, "MR. AND MRS. GRIM REAPER" ASK PEOPLE TO CONSIDER WHETHER THEIR FAMILIES COULD SAFELY EVACUATE LONG ISLAND IN THE EVENT OF A NUCLEAR PLANT ACCIDENT. PHOTO ©1986 *NEWSDAY*.

EAB PLAZA, TWO 15-STORY TOWERS CONTAINING 1.1 MILLION SQUARE FEET OF OFFICE SPACE, OPENED
IN UNIONDALE IN 1983. TODAY, THE SUCCESSFUL ENTERPRISE FEATURES AN ANNUAL CHRISTMAS TREE
LIGHTING CEREMONY, A SHOPPING MALL, AND AN ICE SKATING RINK. PHOTO BY DEBBIE ROSS,
BRUCE BENNETT STUDIOS.

The Federal government and LILCO were insistent
that Long Island could be evacuated in the event of an
accident at Shoreham. However, protesters pointed out
that local Routes 25 and 25A, the roads heading west
nearest to Shoreham, and the Long Island Expressway
eight miles away couldn't carry a half-million people
away from disaster quickly enough. Not enough people
had access to boats or planes to do the job, either.

The Shoreham Opponents Coalition, led by future
County Legislator Nora Bredes, grew stronger, regularly
demonstrating at the plant and at public meetings when
the topic was discussed. In 1983, new Governor Mario
Cuomo pulled state support from any evacuation plan
and, that same day, the Suffolk County Legislature, with
only a single "no" vote, decreed that no safe evacuation
plan could be put into effect. The dissenting legislator—
Amityville's Lou Howard—was defeated the next time
he ran for office. Huntington resident Frank Petrone,
the Regional Director of the Federal Emergency
Management Agency (FEMA) resigned in protest over
the federal government's insistence that FEMA coordi-
nate emergency evacuation drills on Long Island.

Ignoring the storm, LILCO completed the plant in
1984 and began to perform low-power tests. But the
utility could not adequately answer the questions about
safe evacuation and, in 1989, the plant was shut down.

FOUNDED IN 1979, COMPUTER ASSOCIATES
INTERNATIONAL, INC. REPRESENTED, LIKE
MANY OTHER EMERGING COMPANIES AND THE
ENTREPRENEURS BEHIND THEM, LONG ISLAND'S
NEW ECONOMY. COMPUTER AND OTHER HIGH-TECH
COMPANIES WOULD BLOSSOM IN THE '90S AND
SHAPE THE REGION'S FUTURE. PHOTO BY JIM
MCISAAC, BRUCE BENNETT STUDIOS.

SCORES OF LOCAL AND WORLDWIDE FANS ALIKE FOLLOW THE NEW YORK ISLANDERS, WHO HAVE BEEN A
LONG ISLAND HOCKEY TRADITION FOR DECADES. TOP PHOTO BY JIM MCISAAC, BRUCE BENNETT STUDIOS,
1996. BOTTOM PHOTO BY NORMAN Y. LONO, BRUCE BENNETT STUDIOS, 2000.

NEW YORK ISLANDERS

With the Nets off playing in New Jersey, local sports fans had the New York Islanders to cheer on.

The team finished their first season in 1972-73 in last place. By 1975, the Isles had made it to the playoffs, defeated the archrival New York Rangers, but had not won the Stanley Cup. They, and their fans, were hungry. The 1979-80 season looked promising, but the early season was beset with problems. By February, 1980, reports had coach Al Arbour and the players losing confidence. General Manager Bill Torrey made a deadline trade and found the magic formula. They finished the season second in their Patrick Division, fifth overall, with an 8-0-4 record. They made it through the playoffs beating the LA Kings, the Boston Bruins, and the Buffalo Sabres. They ultimately beat the Philadelphia Flyers in overtime in game six.

That was the birth of a hockey dynasty—four Stanley Cups in four years.

THE POPULARITY OF LACROSSE GAINED MOMENTUM ON LONG ISLAND DURING THE '80S AND CONTINUES
STRONGLY TO THIS DAY. PHOTO BY BRUCE BENNETT, BRUCE BENNETT STUDIOS.

IN 1890, A CLASS OF HIGH SCHOOL BIOLOGY TEACHERS STUDIED MARINE BIOLOGY IN COLD SPRING HARBOR. THE CLASS WAS HELD AT THE BROOKLYN INSTITUTE OF ARTS & SCIENCES' BIOLOGICAL LABORATORY, WHICH IS NOW COLD SPRING HARBOR LABORATORY. COURTESY OF COLD SPRING HARBOR LABORATORY.

SCIENCE ON LONG ISLAND

A Tradition of Investigation & Discovery

As the 20th century drew to a close, Long Island had won a firm place in the history of science.

The Island's scientific legacy has roots more than 100 years old. From the era of the eighteenth century experiments performed by Ezra L'Hommedieu to find the best fertilizer for his crops, Long Island has provided a hospitable environment for scientists.

In 1882, a fish hatchery was established in an abandoned mill in Cold Spring Harbor. There the culture of salt and fresh water fish was studied—and is still studied today. The hatchery benefactors were the Jones Family, members of a wealthy local business dynasty that had found success in a number of commercial ventures, from whaling to woolen goods. They agreed to donate the land for the laboratory and, at first, the site served as a "summer camp for scientists" who came to Long Island to study biology. From one summer course taught in 1890, the curriculum grew to year-round study and research covering all areas of biology, zoology, genetics, bacteriology, botany, and anatomy.

Cold Spring Harbor

The region's permanent place in the geography of scientific investigation exists in part because—if nothing else ever happened in the area—in 1890 Cold Spring Harbor Laboratory was born as the Biological Laboratory of the Brooklyn Institute of Arts and Sciences.

Cold Spring Harbor grew, housing three separate institutions, the original Biological Laboratory, the Carnegie Department of Experimental Evolution (established 1904), and the Eugenics Record Office

(1910). The latter, while contributing to the understanding of the genetics of several diseases, ultimately suffered from the very negative association fascists brought to theories of eugenics. That office was closed in 1940. In 1924, the Long Island Biological Association (LIBA) was formed to take over administration and funding of the Biological Laboratory. LIBA attracted philanthropic patrons and was successful in its mission.

The era of World War II brought more government oversight and funding of research. The study of molecular biology, viruses, genetics, and cancer have through the years made Cold Spring Harbor Laboratory one of the world's leading research institutions.

No less than fourteen Nobel Prize winners have been associated with Cold Spring Harbor. In fact, James D. Watson, who is now President of Cold Spring Harbor, shared the 1962 Nobel Prize for his work with Francis H.C. Crick on the structure of DNA.

Though today we are sophisticated about the possibilities of science and invention—and have real expectations of what science can bring to us—at the end of the nineteenth century there was a real sense of awe about the wonders waiting to be discovered. One of the most awe-inspiring discoveries of the day was the transmission of radio waves through the air as wireless communication.

For a half-century, Italian immigrant Guglielmo Marconi (1874-1937) was acknowledged as the inventor of wireless and, in fact, he was the first on record to transmit a code the great distance between England and Newfoundland in 1901. This communication so excited contemporary

(continued)

THE STUDY OF MOLECULAR BIOLOGY, VIRUSES, GENETICS, AND CANCER HAVE MADE COLD SPRING HARBOR LABORATORY ONE OF THE WORLD'S LEADING RESEARCH INSTITUTIONS. THE LEGACY THAT BEGAN IN 1890 CONTINUES TO THIS DAY. AS OF 2001, NO LESS THAN 14 NOBEL PRIZE WINNERS HAVE BEEN ASSOCIATED WITH COLD SPRING HARBOR. PHOTO BY MARGOT BENNETT, COLD SPRING HARBOR LABORATORY.

imaginations, Marconi was credited with the invention of wireless and was awarded the 1909 Nobel Prize in Physics for his work. Wireless transmission towers were known as "Marconi stations" and the first one on Long Island was built in Sagaponack to receive transmissions from ships.

But Marconi's claim to the invention was hotly contested by Nikola Tesla (1856-1943), a Croatian electrical engineer who emigrated to the United States to work with Thomas Edison in 1884. In contradiction to Edison's direct current, Tesla developed a system of alternating current that, after he left Edison, was bought by George Westinghouse and successfully used to light the World Columbian Exposition in 1893, the same year he was able to publicly demonstrate the transmission of radio signals.

After working in Colorado, Tesla returned to New York in 1900 and began construction of Wardenclyffe, on Long Island Sound in the Rocky Point-Shoreham area. With $150,000 capital from J.P. Morgan, the site was planned as a laboratory, transmission system, and manufacturing center. Wardenclyffe was abandoned because of a financial panic and Morgan's withdrawal of support. Although Tesla's tower was dismantled and sold for scrap, his laboratory still stands.

In all, Nikola Tesla held more than 700 patents and numbered among his friends Mark Twain and architect Stanford White, designer of Wardenclyffe. Just a few months after his death, Tesla was officially vindicated when the United States Supreme Court found in his favor that Marconi had violated Tesla's patent in his work on the wireless.

(continued)

COLD SPRING HARBOR LABORATORY IS ACKNOWLEDGED AS ONE OF THE OUTSTANDING BASIC SCIENCE RESEARCH CENTERS IN THE WORLD. MORE THAN 260 SCIENTISTS CONDUCT GROUNDBREAKING RESEARCH IN CANCER, NEUROBIOLOGY, PLANT GENETICS AND BIOINFORMATICS. PHOTO BY SCOTT LEVY, BRUCE BENNETT STUDIOS.

Brookhaven National Laboratory

As World War II was ending, the possibilities for a world in which science led the way to a better life for all seemed limitless. Penicillin was new and the atomic bomb had ended the war at Hiroshima. The scientists involved in the Manhattan Project that developed the bomb were very interested in learning what the atom could achieve in peacetime.

Toward this end, nine universities—Columbia, Cornell, Harvard, Johns Hopkins, Princeton, Pennsylvania, Yale, Rochester, and MIT—collaborated under the name "Associated Universities, Inc.," and set out to establish a nuclear laboratory in the Northeast. As the Army base at Camp Upton on Long Island was unused, it became the chosen site. Under the auspices of the Atomic Energy Commission, Brookhaven National Laboratory was established on March 21, 1947.

Today, BNL is a multipurpose research establishment under the auspices of the Department of Energy and operated by Brookhaven Science

(continued)

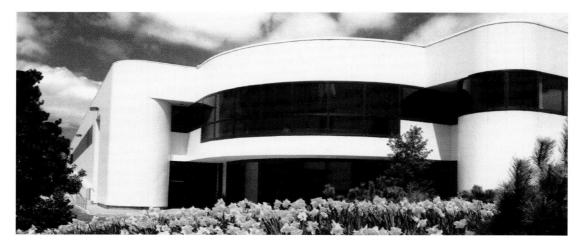

MATERIALS AS DIVERSE AS MOON ROCKS AND THE AIDS VIRUS ARE STUDIED AT THE BROOKHAVEN NATIONAL LABORATORY'S NATIONAL SYNCHROTRON LIGHT SOURCE EACH YEAR BY MORE THAN 2,500 SCIENTISTS FROM AROUND THE WORLD. PHOTO COURTESY OF BROOKHAVEN NATIONAL LABORATORY.

Associates. The Lab employs 3,000 scientists, engineers, technicians and support staff, along with more than 4,000 guest researchers from all over the world who visit each year.

Four Nobel Prizes in Physics have been won for work done at Brookhaven. Among the landmark achievements is the discovery of the drug for Parkinson's disease, L-dopa; the invention of Maglev (magnetically-levitated) trains; a quiet jack-hammer; and groundbreaking studies of addiction, mental illness, and aging, as well as the application of nuclear technology to medicine.

Brookhaven researchers and visiting scientists have at their disposal the newest and largest parti-cle accelerator for nuclear physics, the Relativistic Heavy Ion Collider; the National Synchrotron Light Source, where researchers probe materials using x-rays, ultraviolet radiation, and infrared radiation; the only heavy-ion accelerator for radiation-biology research in the United States, the Alternating Gradient Synchrotron; and the Accelerator Test Facility, a proving ground for new concepts in particle physics.

The Lab provides opportunities for students to study alongside staff scientists and provides community education programs.

Today, Brookhaven is putting a new emphasis on community involvement to deal with the legacy of environmental contamination from past practices. The Laboratory is cleaning up its site and its man-agement expresses strong commitment to keeping it clean.

The University at Stony Brook

Although nineteenth century historian Nathaniel Prime said that Long Island was not an appropriate location for a university, opportunities for higher education did exist on Long Island.

A 1963 state commission studying higher education recommended the establishment of an academic medical center on Long Island to educate physicians and other healthcare professionals. Along with the college that had moved from Oyster Bay, the Health Sciences Center was to be located at the State University at Stony Brook.

Stony Brook grew rapidly along with the Health Sciences Center. Today, the campus boasts 123 buildings on almost 1,200 acres. There are 1,682 faculty members teaching more than 18,500 stu-dents. In 1980, University Hospital at Stony Brook opened, eventually growing to a 504-bed hospital, the only public hospital in the county and the only one offering tertiary care and level one trauma.

The budget for the university grew from $3 million when it opened to more than $600 million today.

With 12,000 people, the University at Stony Brook is Long Island's largest single-site employer.

Stony Brook is one of the most successful pub-lic research universities in the nation, renowned for a range of scientific achievement.

These include a close collaboration with scientists at Brookhaven Laboratory and a Center for Excellence in Learning and Teaching. In a changing world that levies new demands on stu-dents, Stony Brook is one of ten research-intensive universities in the United States to be selected for a National Science Foundation Recognition Award for its "Integration of Research and Education in Sciences, Math and Engineering" graduate and undergraduate programs.

The Departments of Radiology, Electrical Engineering, and Computer Science are collaborating on new techniques in medical imaging. Through the Microscopy Imaging Center at the Health Sciences Center, scientists are provided resources to conduct research projects requiring advanced light and electron microscopy techniques.

The Centers for Molecular Medicine and Biology Learning Laboratories research the genet-ics of cancer, infectious diseases, and structural biology. The General Clinical Research Center, funded by the National Institutes of Health (NIH), is one of seventy-seven such centers funded nationwide. It is designed to provide investigators with the resources they need to conduct clinical research under controlled circumstances, and to encourage collaboration among basic and clinical scientists through studies that may translate into new or improved patient care methods.

Significant advances are counted among the achievements of Stony Brook faculty members. These include the drugs ReoPro, used routinely in treating cardiac patients, that was the first drug developed by the State University of New York that received Food and Drug Administration approval and Periostat, the leading drug used in the treatment of gum disease.

Moreover, a Stony Brook researcher found a new species of lemur in Madagascar. Stony Brook astronomers identified the closest neutron star ever seen and farthest galaxies ever observed.

Like Brookhaven National Laboratory and Cold Spring Harbor Laboratory, the State University of New York at Stony Brook has had an ever-growing economic impact on Long Island and has made lasting contributions to science and medicine.

In its wake, LLILCO went out of business, completing the transfer of its assets to the Long Island Power Authority (LIPA) in 1998. Still, negotiated "golden parachutes" that were in the tens of millions of dollars for LILCO's top management created a furor. Today, however, the question of who will pay for LILCO's errors is still unanswered and is a matter of ongoing litigation.

The death knell for LILCO actually began to ring in earnest in 1985 when Hurricane Gloria blew over Long Island leaving devastation in her wake. Since the 1938 hurricane there was an improved hurricane warning system and better construction laws in place than ever before on Long Island. Nevertheless, at best unprepared, at worst unapologetic, LILCO's management did not

NORA VOLKOW, MD (LEFT) AND JOANNA FOWLER, PH.D., REVIEW IMAGES OF THE BRAIN TAKEN WITH A POSITRON EMISSION TOMOGRAPHY (PET) SCANNER AT THE CENTER FOR IMAGING AND NEUROSCIENCE AT BROOKHAVEN NATIONAL LABORATORY. CENTER RESEARCHERS HAVE MADE IMPORTANT CONTRIBUTIONS TO UNDERSTANDING ADDICTION, AGING, AND NEUROPSYCHIATRIC DISEASES. PHOTO COURTESY OF BROOKHAVEN NATIONAL LABORATORY.

respond quickly to the storm. In fact, LILCO chair William Catacosinos incited great anger when he did not cut short his European vacation to personally oversee hurricane damage repair.

Some homes were without electricity for more than eleven days after the September 27 storm. Crews came from utilities all over the Eastern seaboard to help out, but LILCO seemed powerless to improve the situation. The sound of chainsaws pervaded the air for weeks as damaged trees were cut down and hauled away.

Adding to the insult, LILCO announced that ratepayers must bear the burden of the clean-up costs and repairs. Soundly denounced by ratepayers and power brokers—including Nassau County Executive Fran Purcell, his Suffolk counterpart Peter F. Cohalan, and Cuomo—the Hurricane Gloria experience convinced Long Islanders that LILCO had to go.

Thus, the activist group Citizens to Replace LILCO was born. Between that time and the time LIPA was formed, a host of Democratic candidates for local and state office ran on an independent line originated by then-Suffolk County Legislator Steven Englebright that was called "Ratepayers Against LILCO." The line garnered many votes and in the next election cycle the Republican candidates created their own anti-LILCO line. The lines were used until the utility was out of business.

Long Island made national news when a couple told doctors at University Hospital at Stony Brook not to perform surgery on their newborn child who had been born with *spina bifida.* In this disorder, there is incomplete development of the brain and spinal cord, and these organs may be left exposed. *Spina bifida* is caused by the failure of the baby's spine to properly close during the first month of pregnancy. In the Stony Brook case, doctors told the parents that their baby would suffer numerous medical problems, including severe retardation.

The hospital was following the wishes of the parents until Birthright, a pro-life group, filed suit to force the surgery. The court battle that ensued over the child known as "Baby Jane Doe" made national headlines. After a state Appellate Court sided with the parents, the Reagan Administration became involved, suing the hospital on the grounds that the child's rights were violated. In the end, Birthright's representatives were ruled to have no standing in the matter and the courts decided the child's rights were not violated.

"Baby Jane Doe" survived; today, the teenager lives on Long Island with her family.

With deep cuts in the national budget, Long Island's traditional defense-based economy would crumble by the end of the 1980s, causing a region-wide recession. Fairchild-Republic closed in 1987, and two years later, Grumman would lose its profitable F-14 franchise. Sperry became part of the new Unisys Corporation. The United States was entering a new era in which the Iron Curtain was opened, the Berlin Wall was knocked down, and the Soviet Union would be no more.

BROOKHAVEN NATIONAL LABORATORY RESEARCHERS, PAULA BENNETT (LEFT) AND BETSY SUTHERLAND.
PH.D., ANALYZE DNA FRAGMENTS RESULTING FROM RADIATION DAMAGE. DR. SUTHERLAND AND HER TEAM
DEVELOPED A METHOD TO DETECT AND QUANTIFY RADIATION DAMAGE. PHOTO COURTESY OF BROOKHAVEN
NATIONAL LABORATORY.

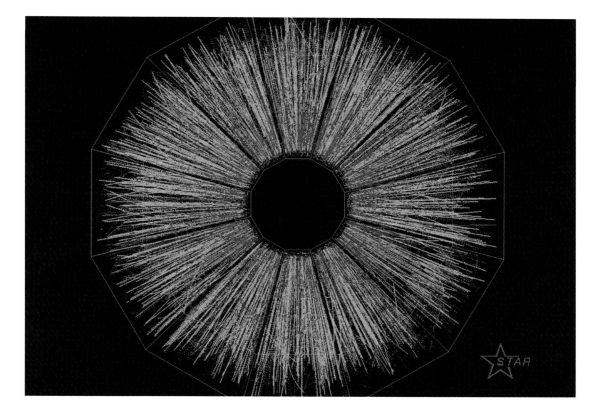

WHAT HAPPENS WHEN TWO 30-BILLION-ELECTRON VOLT GOLD BEAMS TRAVEL IN OPPOSITE DIRECTIONS AT
NEARLY THE SPEED OF LIGHT IN THE STAR DETECTOR OF BROOKHAVEN NATIONAL LABORATORY'S
RELATIVISTIC HEAVY ION COLLIDER? THEY COLLIDE AND LOOK LIKE THIS. PHOTO COURTESY OF
BROOKHAVEN NATIONAL LABORATORY.

ARIE KAUFMAN, PH.D., WHO, ALONG WITH FELLOW UNIVERSITY AT STONY BROOK SCIENTISTS JEROME LIANG, PH.D., AND MARK WAX, MD, INVENTED THE NON-INVASIVE VIRTUAL COLONOSCOPY, LOOKS AT A PATIENT'S TEST RESULTS. THE VIRTUAL TECHNOLOGY TAKES AN IMAGE OF THE COLON GAINED FROM A CAT SCAN OF BODY, AND RENDERS IT IN THREE DIMENSIONS TO BE EVALUATED. PHOTO COURTESY OF STATE UNIVERSITY OF NEW YORK AT STONY BROOK.

THEORETICAL PHYSICIST C.N. YANG, PH.D., SHOWN HERE TEACHING, MADE HIS FIRST MARK IN PHYSICS IN 1956, WHEN HE CO-AUTHORED A PAPER WITH T.D. LEE THAT OVERTURNED ONE OF THE CENTRAL DOGMAS OF PHYSICS. JUST ONE YEAR LATER THEY WON THE NOBEL PRIZE FOR THEIR WORK. YANG BEGAN TEACHING AT STONY BROOK IN 1966 AND TAUGHT THERE FOR 33 YEARS. IT WAS C.N. YANG WHO LED THE STONY BROOK'S PHYSICS DEPARTMENT TO THE FRONT RANK OF AMERICAN ACADEMIA. PHOTO COURTESY OF STATE UNIVERSITY OF NEW YORK AT STONY BROOK.

Tens of thousands of defense jobs would be lost between the mid-80s and mid-90s. In 1994, Grumman was bought by Northrup and suffered drastic downsizing.

Fortunately, local entrepreneurs would bring a new economy to Long Island in the 1990s. Companies like Computer Associates International, Inc., which was founded in 1979 and moved to Garden City in 1985, would shape the region's future.

Though the economy was suffering, there were things to celebrate at this time on Long Island.

As the result of a massive educational campaign by environmentalists, Suffolk County began to actively work to protect the Pine Barrens so essential to the region's water supply. While some money was spent for land acquisition, it was not until 1987, when Suffolk voters approved a dedicated quarter-cent increase in the sales tax to be used to purchase Pine Barrens land, that preservation was even somewhat assured.

Looking at a real paucity of space, developers continued to press local governments in the Pine Barrens towns of Brookhaven, Riverhead, and Southampton for permits to build on these sensitive lands. With individual towns granting the requested permits, at the end of 1989, the Pine Barrens Society sued to stop more than 200 pending projects until an appropriate study of the impact of all this development could be done. The developers and towns counter sued; it took three years for the case to be decided.

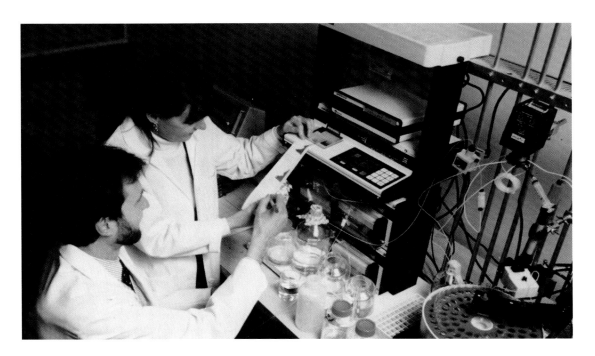

BARBARA SHERRY, PH.D., AND RICHARD BUCALA, M.D., PH.D., OF THE PICOWER INSTITUTE FOR MEDICAL RESEARCH, A PRIVATELY ENDOWED RESEARCH CENTER IN MANHASSET, REVIEW THE RESULTS OF A PROTEIN PURIFICATION EXPERIMENT. PHOTO COURTESY OF PICOWER INSTITUTE FOR MEDICAL RESEARCH.

Finally, the New York State Court of Appeals, noting the risk of environmental harm, decided against the Pine Barrens Society. The developers, however, had come to believe that negotiation with the environmentalists would serve their interests more than fighting over every foot of open space proposed for use in every development.

They began to meet with the Pine Barrens Society and negotiated the 1993 Pine Barrens Preservation Act that created a safe buffer zone and set the stage for a master plan to be drawn. That plan was signed two years later. The predicted death of the local construction industry did not come to pass.

But questions about land use and the environmental ravages brought by local development were raised on a national level in 1987 as Long Island's penchant for claiming national attention with odd news stories was once again demonstrated.

Development anywhere means garbage, generally lots of it. For a while, landfills were the solution: clear a big piece of land and start dumping. While that approach might work in places where the source of drinking water is a reservoir, Long Island gets its water from an underground aquifer. When the landfills were deemed a major source of groundwater pollution, the State Legislature passed a law in 1983 mandating the closure of all landfills by 1990.

With limited space and few usable garbage incinerators, some towns began trucking their garbage upstate. In 1987 almost 80 percent of Long Island's garbage was still being landfilled and the issues around garbage disposal were taking on crisis proportions. The economics of sending garbage off the Island were prohibitive,

costing double the amount it cost to dump trash in a local landfill. And towns were running out of time and space. The Town of Islip was especially hard hit.

Then, as if in answer to a dream, came Alabama businessman Lowell Harrelson, sailing into Long Island waters with a proposed solution. Harrelson told Islip officials that he would take their garbage by boat to willing recipients in the South. The town was agreeable and put together a group of carters and other businessmen to form United Marine Transport, the garbage barge company. The investors envisioned a profit of one million dollars a week.

Thus, on March 22, 1987, the tugboat *Break of Dawn*, with Captain Duffy St. Pierre at the helm, left New York hauling 3,186 tons of Islip's garbage on a barge as large as a football field.

The problem was, no one wanted this garbage. When the barge docked in North Carolina to offload the trash, the governor forbade the boat from docking anywhere in the state. What followed was a two-month journey to nowhere and back. Islip's garbage became the butt of national jokes. One Islip resident told a reporter, "I don't think it's fair. My garbage has done more traveling than I have."

In May, the barge returned to New York, docking in Brooklyn where it sat until the first load of garbage was taken off the barge and burned there on September 1.

The good that came out of the episode was the attention it focused on the problems of garbage. Today, better recycling and incineration programs make trash almost a non-issue.

Even in difficult times, there were things to celebrate. Prominent among these was the growth of the arts.

Facing a real paucity of space, developers continued to press local governments in the Pine Barrens towns of Brookhaven, Riverhead, and Southampton for permits to build on these sensitive lands. With individual towns granting the requested permits, at the end of 1989, the Pine Barrens Society sued to stop more than 200 pending projects until an appropriate study of the impact of all this development could be done. Photo by Deborah Ross, Bruce Bennett Studios.

In 1993, the Pine Barrens Preservation Act created a safe buffer zone between construction and the environment. Photo by Deborah Ross, Bruce Bennett Studios.

WHEN A FLOOD RUINED THE CONCERT GRAND PIANO AT THE STALLER CENTER FOR THE ARTS AT STONY BROOK, LONG ISLANDER BILLY JOEL CONTRIBUTED A NEW PIANO. HE HAS ALSO APPEARED IN CONCERT AT THE UNIVERSITY, WHERE CAMPUS PRESIDENT SHIRLEY STRUM KENNY THANKED HIM FOR HIS GENEROSITY. PHOTO ABOVE COURTESY OF THE STALLER CENTER FOR THE ARTS. PHOTO BELOW BY SCOTT FOX, BRUCE BENNETT STUDIOS.

In 1978, the Fine Arts Center opened at the University at Stony Brook. With five theaters—the largest of which seated 1,049 people—and an art gallery, the center was poised to become a cultural magnet in Suffolk County.

Today, the renamed Staller Center for the Arts hosts a year-round schedule of concerts, theater, and film. Student recitals take place there, as do performances by such as the Dance Theater of Harlem, Harry Belafonte, the New York City Ballet, Penn and Teller, Gregory Hines, and Billy Joel.

The annual Stony Brook Film Festival, begun in 1994, draws talent from around the world competing in five categories. Major sponsors include HBO.

In 1980, the Tilles Center for the Performing Arts opened at Long Island University's C.W. Post College in Brookville. Their main auditorium seats 2,200 people,

(ABOVE) ELLIOTT SROKA (RIGHT), EXECUTIVE DIRECTOR OF THE TILLES CENTER FOR THE PERFORMING ARTS AT C.W. POST COLLEGE OF LONG ISLAND UNIVERSITY, BRINGS LONG ISLANDERS CLASSICAL ARTISTS OF THE STATURE OF VAN CLIBURN (LEFT). PHOTO COURTESY OF THE TILLES CENTER FOR THE PERFORMING ARTS. (BELOW) THE STALLER CENTER FOR THE ARTS BRINGS A VARIETY OF PROGRAMS TO THE UNIVERSITY AT STONY BROOK. AMONG THESE IS A CLASSIC FILM SERIES THAT FEATURES KEY CREATIVE PEOPLE TALKING ABOUT THEIR FILMS. HERE, STALLER CENTER DIRECTOR ALAN INKLES MEETS WITH PATRICIA NEAL AT A SHOWING OF *A FACE IN THE CROWD*. PHOTO COURTESY OF THE STALLER CENTER FOR THE ARTS.

close the 20th century on a note of growth in new directions, innovation, and success.

THE UNIVERSITY HOSPITAL AND MEDICAL CENTER AT STONY BROOK

A center for scientific discovery. An institution of higher learning. A hallmark of outstanding medical care, and a beacon for broad-reaching community service programs. University Hospital and Medical Center at Stony Brook shares daily in shaping the vision of a Long Island health care system network designed to provide all Long Island residents with easy access to the services they need.

UNIVERSITY HOSPITAL AND MEDICAL CENTER IS A WINNER OF THE PRESTIGIOUS *100 TOP HOSPITALS* NATIONAL AWARD JUDGED BY HCIA, THE NATION'S LEADING HEALTH CARE BENCHMARKING FIRM.

University Hospital and Medical Center is recognized as an outstanding health care and education resource for the entire Long Island community. Through innovative partnerships with health professionals, managed care companies, and other hospitals, Stony Brook offers compassionate and highly specialized medical services to all who seek them.

Situated within the Health Sciences Center complex, the twin towers of University Hospital offer a faculty and staff sharply focused on delivering excellent health care in a demanding and challenging health care environment.

Health Sciences Center

Established in 1972 to address the shortage of health care professionals and improve access to the most sophisticated types of medical care for residents of Nassau and Suffolk counties, the Health Sciences Center at Stony Brook functions as Long Island's only comprehensive academic health center, pursuing a mission of excellence in education, patient care, research, and community service.

The center's five schools (Dental Medicine, Health Technology and Management, Medicine, Nursing, and Social Welfare) offer degree-granting programs to more than 2,000 students, and the School of Medicine's 48 approved specialty programs serve approximately 500 residents each year. The schools are directly linked to University Hospital, which serves as the chief clinical resource for students and residents.

The School of Medicine: Pacesetter for Academic Research Institutions

The School of Medicine at Stony Brook is the flagship biomedical research institution of the State University of New York system and a pacesetter for academic research institutions around the world.

The curriculum provides training through seven basic science and 18 clinical departments. The school's strong thematic research programs offer students the experience of working with world-class researchers on the cutting edge of scientific discovery, while Stony Brook's ultramodern University Hospital provides them with exposure to the broad range of clinical care and management issues that physicians encounter in their practice.

Basic science instruction at Stony Brook equals that of the most excellent medical programs in the nation. Mentored by faculty engaged in uncovering the newest biomedical information, Stony Brook students learn to understand medicine as a scientific discipline. Faculty help students grasp the complexities of modern clinical methods, which require an understanding of science at the molecular level. The academic program centers on a systems approach that presents all aspects of a study area on a continuum from the cellular level to clinical therapy. Since Stony Brook is strongly committed to primary medicine, it is not surprising that the school was recently ranked number one in New York State and 18 nationally by *U.S. News & World Report*'s survey of primary care programs.

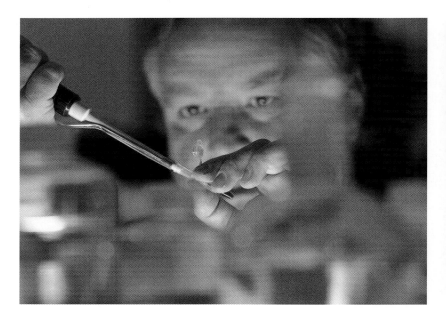

STONY BROOK HAS FOSTERED AN ENVIRONMENT IN WHICH LAB SCIENTISTS, CLINICAL INVESTIGATORS, AND PHYSICIANS WORK TOGETHER AS A TEAM, IN AN EFFORT TO SPEED BASIC RESEARCH INTO BETTER PATIENT CARE.

Stony Brook: Translating Research into Patient Care

The School of Medicine's Strategic Plan for Research stresses the collaborative and interdisciplinary approaches that have become the hallmark of biomedical research. The school's strong thematic research programs emphasize interdepartmental, interdisciplinary, and interinstitutional collaborations. They build on existing strengths by filling crucial gaps in the science base, providing an infrastructure and core facilities that will facilitate biomedical research, and strengthening translational research programs that apply advances in basic science to clinical problems.

School of Medicine faculty engaged in biomedical research represent a major asset to the university and contribute significantly to its outstanding productivity. The school takes advantage of the exceptional regional concentration of biomedical research institutions on Long Island, including Cold Spring Harbor, Brookhaven National Laboratory, Plum Island Laboratory, and the Picower Institute.

Stony Brook investigators pursue clinical research, new diagnostic methods, and patient therapies, as well as basic research into the causes and mechanisms of disease at the cellular and molecular levels. The School of Medicine is developing major research programs in human genetics and structural biology.

Stony Brook faculty members contributed significantly to the development of magnetic resonance imaging (MRI) technology, anticlotting factors to halt coronary blockages, and developing what is now the standard protocol for colon cancer treatment. Stony Brook researchers helped identify the bacterium that causes Lyme disease and isolated a new strain of Hantavirus Pulmonary Syndrome.

Many of Stony Brook's clinical researchers serve as principal investigators for nationwide research studies and Stony Brook is the regional center for numerous clinical trials in cancer and other areas. Recently, the medical center was one of 24 centers nationwide designated by the National Institutes of Health to conduct the Women's Health Initiative. This series of clinical studies seeks to determine the influence of environmental, genetic, and lifestyle factors on health and disease in women.

University Hospital and Medical Center

Conceived 25 years ago as an academic medical center that could provide the highest level of tertiary health care to Suffolk County's then-1.3 million residents, Stony Brook's University Hospital and Medical Center has since grown into a diverse, forward-looking institution that succeeds at delivering a broad range of tertiary, urgent, and primary care services to its diverse patient population.

Now serving the varied needs of young, old, rich, poor, critically ill, and healthy patients, University Hospital is a front runner in delivering a wide array of excellent preventive, diagnostic, and treatment services to the 2.7 million residents across all of Long Island. Committed to ensuring accessible health care to a wide range of patients, the medical center has developed a network of community-based outpatient and primary care centers.

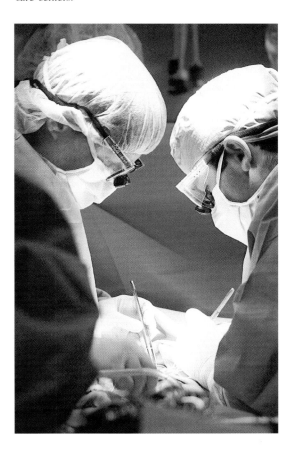

IN 2000, MD'S WERE GRANTED TO **97** GRADUATES OF STONY BROOK'S MEDICAL SCHOOL, BRINGING THE TOTAL NUMBR OF NEW PHYSICIANS TRAINED THERE TO **2,270**.

When University Hospital admitted its first patients in 1980, it sought to provide Long Island with a regional center for advanced patient care, education, research, and community service. Today, University Hospital cares for approximately 28,000 inpatients and treats more than 56,000 people in its emergency department each year. Close to 3,600 babies are born here each year, and nearly 560,000 patients visit the medical center for physician care, ambulatory diagnostic, and treatment services. With extensive laboratory services including diagnostic radiology imaging, magnetic resonance imaging, stereotactic core breast biopsy, interventional radiology, and nuclear medicine, as well as sophisticated instrumentation and computerized physiological monitoring systems, Stony Brook offers the most highly specialized diagnostic and treatment programs available.

Helicopter and ground transports deliver Suffolk County's most seriously injured and ill patients to University Hospital, the region's only designated Level I Trauma Center and the county referral center for all psychiatric emergencies. The emergency department's seven-bed shock trauma room is specifically designed to handle the most critical patients with problems ranging from multiple traumas to cardiogenic shock.

With 504 beds, the hospital operates six intensive care units dedicated to cardiovascular, coronary, pediatric, medical, neonatal, and surgical patients, plus special care units for burn injury and anesthesia recovery. Through coordinated clinical care that guarantees their patients the specialized attention they need, highly skilled teams of physicians, nurses, nutritionists, physical therapists, laboratory technicians, social workers, and chaplains care for adults and children with a variety of chronic conditions, such as diabetes, cystic fibrosis, Lyme disease, and multiple sclerosis.

University Hospital's comprehensive cardiovascular program offers the most advanced detection and treatment equipment available. With its bi-plane swing cardiac catheterization laboratory and its sophisticated cardiovascular intensive care unit, Stony Brook is positioned on the leading edge when moments count and expertise makes the critical difference. Stony Brook cardiologists pioneered enhanced external counterpulsation, a truly innovative, noninvasive, and remarkably successful treatment for patients suffering from coronary artery disease. Whether patients need high-risk open heart surgery or preventive care, Stony Brook is available as a resource for all Long Island residents.

Stony Brook's neonatal intensive care unit provides tertiary/quaternary care for premature and newborn infants in Suffolk County, babies who require careful observation and monitoring. Stony Brook's neonatologists and specially trained nurses work closely with cardiologists, surgeons, and other specialists to guide these and other seriously ill babies along the path to a speedy and full recovery.

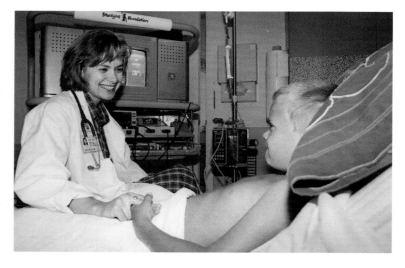

A WIDE VARIETY OF INTERDISCIPLINARY CARE ENSURES THAT STONY BROOK PATIENTS RECEIVE ALL THE SPECIALIZED ATTENTION THEY NEED.

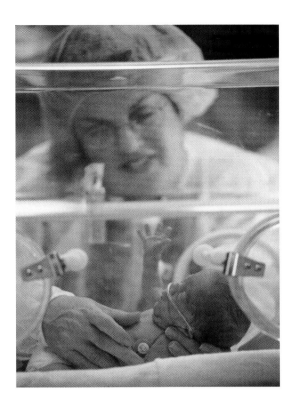

SUFFOLK COUNTY'S NEONATAL INTENSIVE CARE
UNIT IS AT STONY BROOK.

A Leader in Cancer Research and Treatment

With the resources of a major academic medical center, the physicians and researchers of the Cancer Institute of Long Island at Stony Brook provide great leadership in the field of cancer research and clinical care and play a prominent role in evaluating and developing the treatment methods that eventually become standard protocols for treating patients with cancer. Stony Brook researchers led the world in developing biochemical modulation, a technique that uses drug combinations to enhance the effectiveness of chemotherapy. Stony Brook's medical oncologists are currently testing the next generation of biochemical modulation therapies while frontline research initiatives push forward in gene therapy, tumor control, and immunotherapy. Research teams are studying how drugs interact with cancer cells at the molecular level, looking for ways to control the growth of cancers by turning their biological "switches" on and off. One of the few locations in the world offering intracarotid chemotherapy for brain tumors, Stony Brook continues its tradition of excellence in cancer treatment and prevention.

Advancing women's medicine, Stony Brook opened the Carol M. Baldwin Breast Care Center with diagnostic and treatment facilities, a full range of surgical services, complete counseling and referral services, and a strong research component in a community-based setting located at the Stony Brook Technology Center in East Setauket. The breast center's interdisciplinary focus allows patients to consult with oncology and reconstructive surgeons, medical oncologists, and counselors all in the same day.

Long Island's Resource for Community Service

Stony Brook's Health Initiative for Underserved Communities plays a key role in improving access to medical and dental care in localities that have been underserved by health professionals. And Stony Brook's community service mission brings health education programs, as well as breast cancer, prostate cancer, cholesterol, blood pressure, and other screening programs to communities throughout Suffolk County.

The Department of Preventive Medicine's Division of Occupational and Environmental Medicine provides an innovative community health service for Long Island. The division's highly specialized staff serves individual workers, unions, and industries throughout Long Island. The division has achieved national recognition and provides expert consultation throughout the country. The service is the most comprehensive in the region, providing clinical and diagnostic occupational and environmental medicine, referral, and treatment services, as well as industrial hygiene and safety training, and education to those in the public and private sectors.

The medical center's outreach program includes the region's first Cancer Helpline staffed by professional oncology nurses (1-800-UMC-2215). Stony Brook's Healthcare Teleservices Department provides community physicians and prospective patients with a direct link to physicians and medical services at Stony Brook. Callers wishing information about medical services, physician referrals, or appointment scheduling may call HealthConnect, the medical center's consumer helpline, at 1-(631)-444-4393. The address of its website is www.uhmc.sunysb.edu. ∎

Also, see related section on Stony Brook University,
pages 268-271.

MORE THAN 3,600 BABIES ARE BORN AT STONY
BROOK EACH YEAR.

LONG ISLAND POWER AUTHORITY

When state legislation gave birth to the Long Island Power Authority (LIPA) in 1986, its primary mission was to seek ways to cut electric rates for Long Island. In 1997, Governor George E. Pataki made a promise that LIPA would cut electric rates on Long Island by at least 12 percent. Good to his word, the Governor announced in May 1998 that rates for all customers on Long Island had been reduced by an average of 20 percent Island-wide.

The long-fought battle against some of the highest electric rates in the country had finally been won. The victory was particularly satisfying to LIPA in light of the fact that it had also managed to decommission the Shoreham Nuclear Power Plant in 1992, another of its stated goals. But the war against the exodus of young people and businesses from the region—the so-called "brain drain"—was far from over.

That exodus had fueled an economic downturn that seemed irreversible. But LIPA's 15-member board of trustees believed that it could be done. They set off on a mission to accomplish more than just a rate cut. They made a commitment to introduce retail electric competition, to implement an energy conservation program, and to explore new technologies for delivering power to the region.

Those were lofty goals. Some, such as the rate cut and the decommissioning of Shoreham, have been achieved. Others, including the development of new technologies, are ongoing. Nevertheless, LIPA has accomplished what few people thought possible: it has restored the public trust and contributed to Long Island's renewed economic vitality.

"We made a commitment to the people of Long Island," said LIPA Chairman Richard M. Kessel. "The obstacles that stood in our way only meant that we had to work harder to ensure that Long Island could offer consumers and businesses competitive electric rates and superior service. That is what kept us going throughout the process."

The Birth of LIPA

The environment into which LIPA was born in 1986 was one in which economic development was being stifled. Electric rates were so high that businesses were relocating off the Island, a trend that contributed to an overall economic downturn. Faced with fewer jobs and a high cost of living, increasing numbers of young people were choosing to raise their families elsewhere.

In an effort to reverse this downward spiral, the New York State Legislature passed legislation forming LIPA and authorizing it to acquire all or any part of the securities and assets of the Long Island Lighting Company (LILCO), and to issue lower cost, tax-exempt debt to finance the acquisition. Put simply, LIPA would use municipal bonds to purchase LILCO's electric transmission distribution system. In return, LIPA had to assure lawmakers that rates after the acquisition would be no higher than they would have been had LILCO remained in business.

(LEFT) AS PART OF ITS CLEAN ENERGY INITIATIVE, LIPA FIELD-TESTED SIX ALPHA FUEL CELLS. FUEL CELLS REPRESENT A CLEAN ENERGY TECHNOLOGY WHOSE MAIN BY PRODUCTS ARE WATER, USEABLE HEAT, LOW LEVELS OF CARBON DIOXIDE, AND NEGLIGIBLE AMOUNTS OF POLLUTANTS. THE SYSTEMS WERE FIELD TESTED BY LIPA TO GAIN FIRST-HAND KNOWLEDGE OF HOW FUEL CELLS WILL OPERATE IN PARALLEL WITH LIPA'S GRID WHILE ALSO ALLOWING FOR THE REFINEMENT OF THE SYSTEMS FOR COMMERCIAL AVAILABILITY. LIPA CHAIRMAN AND CEO RICHARD M. KESSEL AND HOFSTRA UNIVERSITY PRESIDENT JAMES SHUART ARE SHOWN IN FRONT OF AN ALPHA FUEL CELLS TESTED AT THE COLLEGE IN EARLY 2000. (RIGHT) LIPA CHAIRMAN AND CEO RICHARD M. KESSEL (CENTER) AT THE DEDICATION OF THE NEW SOUTH FORK TRANSMISSION LINE. THE LONGEST (22.5 MILES) SOLID DIELECTRIC, UNDERGROUND 138 KILOVOLT (KV) LINE IN THE WORLD. THE LINE'S INSTALLATION WAS COMPLETED IN RECORD TIME. THE ENTIRE INSTALLATION WAS COMPLETED IN JUST 106 DAYS, A FULL TWO WEEKS AHEAD OF SCHEDULE. THE TRANSMISSION LINE IS CURRENTLY IN FULL SERVICE AT 69 KV, AND IS CAPABLE OF OPERATING AT 138 KV IN THE FUTURE.

(LEFT) LONG ISLAND'S OSPREY POPULATION IS FLOURISHING THANKS TO THE HARD WORK OF LIPA'S POLE-SETTING CREWS. POLES LIKE THIS ONE, WHICH HAS A NESTING PLATFORM AFFIXED TO THE TOP, HAVE HELPED TO BOOST LONG ISLAND'S OSPREY POPULATION. LIPA HAS BEEN PROVIDING THE POLES, THE NESTING TOPS AND THE MANPOWER TO SETUP HUNDREDS OF NESTING SITES THROUGHOUT LONG ISLAND. LIPA IS PROUD TO BE A PART OF THE RESURGENCE OF THE OSPREY ON LONG ISLAND. (RIGHT) SEEKING WAYS TO HELP REDUCE CAR AND TRUCK EMISSIONS ON LONG ISLAND, LIPA HAS DEVELOPED A PROGRAM TO ENCOURAGE GREATER USE OF ELECTRIC VEHICLES (EVS). LIPA'S PROGRAM WILL LEND EVS, FOR UP TO THREE MONTHS, TO BUSINESSES AND GOVERNMENTS ON LONG ISLAND TO DEMONSTRATE THE ENVIRONMENTAL AND ECONOMIC BENEFITS OF INCLUDING ELECTRIC POWERED CARS, TRUCKS, AND UTILITY VEHICLES IN THEIR RESPECTIVE FLEETS.

The process was a lengthy one. It wasn't until 1996, 10 years after LIPA was created, that the Authority entered into negotiations with LILCO to acquire the utility's assets. In May 1998, LIPA acquired LILCO's stock for slightly less than book value, after LILCO transferred its on-Island generation and gas system to subsidiaries of KeySpan. LIPA emerged from the negotiations as the owner of LILCO's transmission and distribution system, its interest in the Nine Mile Point 2 facility, and its Shoreham regulatory asset. Its primary responsibility was to deliver service to electric customers in its region.

Cutting Rates

In February 1992, LIPA acquired the title to Shoreham, as well as Shoreham's Nuclear Regulatory Commission (NRC) "possession-only license." The following July, LIPA began decommissioning the controversial plant, which cost billions of dollars to build—a burden borne largely by taxpayers—but was never utilized.

By October 1994, LIPA completed the physical decommissioning of the nuclear power plant—under budget and ahead of schedule. It submitted its final report to the NRC, asking for termination of Shoreham's NRC license and the release of the site for unrestricted use. The NRC granted those requests on May 2, 1995.

"Decommissioning Shoreham was unquestionably one of our greatest accomplishments," said Kessel. "The nuclear power plant had been such an albatross around the neck of LILCO and public officials, not to mention a costly burden to taxpayers. Bringing a conclusion to that saga helped set a positive tone for the LIPA takeover."

Relieving taxpayers of the monetary burden of Shoreham was another matter. Because LILCO had built the cost of the plant into electric rates, those costs could not be decreased immediately. First, LIPA had to refinance the costs of Shoreham and other high costs associated with the transmission and distribution system. By refinancing those costs at much lower rates through municipal bonds, LIPA was finally able to begin lowering consumer and business electric rates in 1998. It helped, of course, that unlike LILCO, the municipally owned power authority does not pay federal taxes. Lower costs on the operational side also translated into lower costs for LIPA customers. LIPA is committed to holding those costs for at least five years—barring an oil shortage or some other unforeseen event out of its control.

Fostering Competition

Beyond basic rate cuts, deregulation of the electric industry has given LIPA the opportunity to explore new ways to save customers money. Deregulation, which began in the 1990s, allowed new electricity providers to enter the marketplace and compete with established utilities. Consumers can now shop around for lower rates from online providers and buying pools, which negotiate group rates. New York State has approved legislation authorizing deregulation, and LIPA has committed to facilitating customer choice through a program called Long Island Choice.

"This is something that we're doing voluntarily," said Kessel. "Even though deregulation is going forward in other parts of the country and it is being introduced in

New York State, as a municipal electric utility we're not subject to those requirements. But we are moving ahead and introducing retail electric competition anyway. That is our choice."

LIPA could have denied independent providers access to its transportation and distribution system. But that wouldn't have served its customers well, nor would it have fostered any goodwill among them. Not only that, but introducing electric competition is one of LIPA's self-proclaimed goals.

Long Island Choice is a key element of the plan that Governor Pataki and LIPA put together to lower electric rates through retail competition. The initial 400 megawatts LIPA allocated to the program is enough electricity to supply approximately 100,000 residential and commercial customers. The ultimate goal is to give all Long Islanders electric choice by 2003. Applications for the first of three implementation phases began on April 15, 1999. Delivery occurred in August 1999. Phase 2 began in May 2000 with a commitment to make an additional 400 megawatts available. Phase 3, which will make Long Island Choice available to all Long Island consumers and businesses, will be completed by January 2003.

Conserving Energy

Cutting rates went a long way toward restoring the public trust in utilities. Now LIPA wants to take that restoration one step further through energy conservation. At a cost of $32 million per year for five years—a total of $160 million—LIPA is implementing various energy conservation and efficiency programs.

Under that banner, the organization is conducting research and development on various alternative energy sources such as solar energy, wind, and fuel cell technology. Known as "clean" energy, these technologies can reduce the need to burn fossil fuels to generate electricity. While helping to reduce emissions, some alternative energy technologies can even generate income for consumers.

"There is a family in Bridgehampton who made a significant investment in solar panels for their home," said Kessel. "They're generating enough electricity for their needs and selling some back to us." Other innovative forms of energy technology include geothermal systems, which use the temperature of the earth's water table to cool and heat homes and buildings.

LIPA also helps consumers conserve energy through its toll-free EnergyWise Infoline, which provides customers

(LEFT) JIM AND VIRGINIA SAUL OF MELVILLE, ARE PROUD SOLAR PIONEERS. 31 QUALIFIED LIPA SOLAR PIONEERS HAD SOLAR ENERGY SYSTEMS, VALUED AT BETWEEN $4,000 AND $6,000, INSTALLED BY LIPA FREE OF CHARGE. THESE SYSTEMS WILL PRODUCE BETWEEN 500 AND 600 WATTS OF ELECTRICITY, WHICH IS ENOUGH ENERGY TO RUN A MEDIUM- OR LARGE-SIZED ENERGY EFFICIENT REFRIGERATOR. LIPA ESTIMATES THAT THESE PV SYSTEMS WILL SAVE ABOUT $100 ANNUALLY FOR ITS LUCKY PIONEERS WHO WERE SELECTED AT RANDOM VIA A LOTTERY. LIPA HAS MADE A LONG-TERM COMMITMENT TO SOLAR ENERGY BY JOINING THE U.S. DEPARTMENT OF ENERGY'S "MILLION SOLAR ROOFS" SOLAR PROJECT. (RIGHT) STUDENTS FROM HOLY FAMILY SCHOOL IN HICKSVILLE LEARN FIRST HAND WHAT IT TAKES TO BE SAFE AROUND ELECTRICITY. THE LONG ISLAND POWER AUTHORITY STAGED A DRAMATIC CONTACT DEMONSTRATION TO CONVEY A STRONG MESSAGE TO BOTH CHILDREN AND ADULTS REGARDING THE DANGERS OF HIGH-VOLTAGE ELECTRIC LINES. THE SIXTH GRADERS WERE SHOWN WHAT CAN HAPPEN WHEN TREE LIMBS, MYLAR BALLOONS, LADDERS, AND OTHER ITEMS, COME IN CONTACT WITH ELECTRIC POWER LINES. THE STUDENTS ALSO RECEIVED SOME HANDS-ON TRAINING FROM LIPA'S LINEMEN. EACH MAY LIPA SPONSORS SEVERAL EDUCATIONAL EVENTS AS PART OF ITS MONTH-LONG NATIONAL ELECTRIC SAFETY MONTH CAMPAIGN, WHICH INCLUDES A POSTER CONTEST AND ELECTRIC SCIENCE COMPETITION.

with information about energy efficiency. The EnergyWise Catalog lists a plethora of energy-efficient ideas, from fixtures that use compact fluorescent bulbs to CFLs themselves and other energy-saving devices. The Energy Star label program identifies energy-efficient appliances, and a variety of rebate programs offers cash back for use of energy-efficient air conditioning, heating, and ventilation systems, as well as for washing machines that use TumbleWash, front-loading technology, and geothermal heat pumps.

LIPA also offers a free home energy audit that residential customers can complete at home or via LIPA's Web site at www.lipower.org. After answering questions about appliance use, heating and cooling systems, weatherization and the like, consumers return the completed survey for a report detailing their energy costs and usage, and recommending ways of reducing consumption and cutting costs. Through independent contractors, LIPA's Home Performance Service provides a complete analysis of homes for problems such as air leaks, moisture damage, and carbon monoxide.

Educating the Public

Developing new energy-saving technologies is only half the battle. Educating the public about those technologies is the other half of the equation. So, LIPA

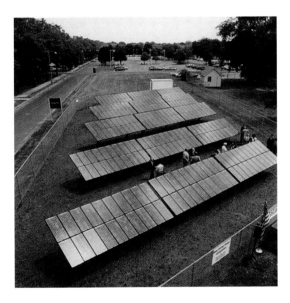

LIPA AND SUNY FARMINGDALE OPENED A SOLAR ENERGY CENTER AT THE PHOTOVOLTAIC DEMONSTRATION SITE ON CAMPUS IN MARCH 2000. AS A PARTNER IN LIPA'S LONG ISLAND SOLAR ROOFS INITIATIVE (LISRI), THE SUNY FARMINGDALE SCHOOL OF ENGINEERING TECHNOLOGIES WILL CONDUCT APPLIED RESEARCH IN THE FIELD OF SOLAR ENERGY AND PROVIDE TRAINING IN THE MAINTENANCE AND INSTALLATION OF PHOTOVOLTAIC UNITS. THE CENTER WILL USE THE EXISTING PHOTOVOLTAIC SYSTEM AS A DEMONSTRATION SITE FOR COMMUNITY, INDUSTRY, AND THOSE INTERESTED IN SOLAR ENERGY PRODUCTS.

AS PART OF LIPA'S $160 MILLION CLEAN ENERGY INITIATIVE, THE AUTHORITY DONATED A GEOTHERMAL AND PHOTOVOLTAIC ROOF SYSTEMS TO THE THEODORE ROOSEVELT NATURE CENTER LOCATED AT JONES BEACH STATE PARK. THE SYSTEM WILL PROVIDE HEAT, AIR CONDITIONING, AND A PORTION OF THE POWER FOR THE OPERATION OF THE BUILDING. THE SYSTEMS WILL PREVENT 250 LBS. OF POLLUTANTS FROM ENTERING THE ATMOSPHERE EACH YEAR AND WILL SAVE THE STATE PARKS DEPARTMENT MORE THAN $20,000 ANNUALLY IN ENERGY COSTS.

has implemented an educational program that teaches children and adults about safety and energy conservation. LIPA conducts safety demonstrations in Nassau and Suffolk counties, which teach children in their schools about electric safety and the proper use of electricity.

Electric Universe, the kids-only section of LIPA's Web site, promotes safety with games, experiments, and interactive presentations about the science, history, and safety of electricity. There are age-appropriate sections for children in grades one through 12, as well as a Teacher's Lounge, which provides lesson plans for teachers on electricity and its safe use.

The LIPA home page also features a variety of educational information for adults. There's a page that features "57 Ways to Make Your Home a Safer Place," information about solar energy, energy saving tips, and electric energy usage forecasts.

Looking Ahead

LIPA is committed to developing new and innovative ways to serve its customers. In keeping with that commitment, the Authority is developing an array of e-commerce services. Customers may, for example, be able to pay their bills online and access their individual electricity records 24 hours a day, seven days a week. That would allow them to monitor their energy usage and develop ways of cutting back.

"Consumers and businesses can become an active participant in making choices as to how they consume energy," said Kessel. "If they use energy wisely and efficiently, they can lower their electric costs. LIPA's mission is to develop innovative technologies and services that will lower the cost of electricity so that consumers can buy, install, and conserve energy efficiently." ∎

HILTON HUNTINGTON

Mounting 7,000 functions a year seems almost impossible, but for the staff at Long Island's busiest hotel, the Hilton Huntington, this is all in a day's work…a day which may involve planning and implementing the myriad details to assure that each of 15 or more private and corporate events is a special, unique, and memorable occasion for its host.

Peter Guarneiri, the Hilton's director of Hotel Sales and Marketing, calls the award-winning Hilton "Long Island's community center." That's because the Hilton, centrally located on the bustling Route 110 corporate corridor, is the regular host hotel for so many Long Island organizations, among them the Long Island Ducks baseball team, the Long Island Roughriders soccer team, the Senior Lightpath Open Classic (once the Northville) golf tournament, and the site for the gala end-year holiday celebrations of the Press Club of Long Island and the Association for a Better Long Island. Next year, the Hilton adds the prestigious U.S. Open Golf Tournament to its roster of events. Guarneiri credits the hotel's ability to keep all of these balls in the air to his "extraordinary, experienced staff of party planners." They are part of a 300-member staff which is schooled and coached in guest satisfaction on a constant, ongoing basis. Said General Manager Marie J. Kupfer, "they are taught to take proactive measures so that they can continually exceed guest expectations time and time again." The result is that numerous Hilton staff members have been recognized with Gold Medal awards and nominations, a mark of excellence in the hotel industry.

High-tech innovations also play an important role in the Hilton's efforts to meet its guests' every need. According to Guarneiri, with the Hilton now fully wired for high-speed Internet connectivity in all meeting and sleeping rooms, "we are the leaders in cutting-edge technology." What this means is that attendees at the many business meetings, conventions, and trade fairs at the Hilton now have the ability to work productively with large-screen monitors and video conferencing, while so-called new economy high-tech businesses are able to display their electronic products and services to maximum advantage.

Each company sponsoring an event at the Hilton Huntington works with their own assigned meeting

LONG ISLAND'S PREMIER MEETING AND CONFERENCE LOCALE.

planner. This person is responsible for reviewing every aspect of the event and guiding the guest in making each choice. Said Guarneiri, "we can handle events that range from major functions to an intimate meeting for interviews where there might be only two people at a time and where food and beverage needs might be minimal." Guarneiri cited one of those major functions—an eyewear company's elaborate new product launch which required theatrical staging and preparation. "It was almost like a Broadway production," said Guarneiri. Among the many event requirements of the Long Island based eyewear concern were small meeting rooms, creatively-themed food and beverage service for a variety of meals, and the availability of sleeping accommodations for many of the event's participants. Mounting this multifaceted affair involved just about the entire staff of the Hilton.

Sometimes companies sponsor events that are more appropriate to hold at their own facility. In these instances, the Hilton Huntington brings the party to them. Everything that the hotel arranges for at its own site it will do at the host's site—from equipment for preparing and serving food, to lighting, music, décor, and tenting. Guarneiri cited a new high-tech company which recently moved into the 110 Corridor. The Hilton staff orchestrated the company's entire opening party for more than 3,000 guests with the same all-inclusive service it provides for parties at the hotel.

HILTON HUNTINGTON'S MEET WITH SUCCESS.

IT HAPPENS AT THE HILTON HUNTINGTON.

Social Soirees

These corporate functions comprise an enormous sector of business for the Hilton Huntington, but just as important are the many weddings, bar mitzvahs, and other formal black tie affairs and less formal social events which take place at the Hilton. As with business customers, each individual hosting an event at the Hilton is assigned a personal party planner, each of whom, said Guarneiri, has years of operational experience in orchestrating successful events. The planners, whose services are provided at no additional fee, walk the host through every option available, pointing out opportunities to take advantage of the full scope of the hotel's services. In fact, hosts need look no further than the Hilton for every aspect of their party—the hotel can provide music, flowers, entertainment and all types of party decorations. Seemingly unflappable, the Hilton has hosted themed parties with appropriate ethnic menus and decor to honor customs as varied as Iranian, African-American, Indian, Australian, Haitian, and Russian. Here too, as with large-scale corporate functions, flexibility on the part of the Hilton's staff is key to the success of these social events.

Ever-expanding the ways in which it serves party hosts, last year the Hilton added a facility of particular interest to bridal parties. This private indoor courtyard area complete with gardens and a waterfall assures that whatever the weather, those all-important bridal photos will have a beautiful, lush background.

Creating Home Away From Home and Office Away From Office

For some business travelers, a stay at the Hilton may be months in duration. Therefore the hotel's management is particularly vigilant in providing the amenities that will make a hotel stay as homelike as possible and as workable as one's own office. Whether the guest stays in one of the standard rooms or opts for the additional measures of comfort offered by the Executive Floor, each room offers telephones with private voice mail messaging, separate data port lines, high-speed internet access, WebTV, Sony Playstation, and well-lit work areas. Guests may access valet and concierge services, a car rental service, and also enjoy the convenience of the Hilton's business center. Rooms on the Executive, or the newly decorated Concierge level are equipped with ergonomic desks and chairs, additional lighting, two two-line telephones, and high-speed Internet access. Personal amenities for Concierge level guests include robes, candies, turndown service, hospitality calls, and the use of a private lounge.

Once work is done for the day, the Hilton's resort-like facilities are particularly tempting. Its 15-acre landscaped campus includes lighted tennis courts, indoor and outdoor swimming pools, a fully-equipped health center with massage and hydrotherapy and separate saunas for men and women, an outdoor fitness trail, and a Jacuzzi. Experience the ambiance of the new signature restaurant, Whitman's Bar & Grill, for lunch and dinner and the elaborate breakfast buffet in the garden setting of the Atrium Café.

Business travelers, the Hilton's biggest single component of business, particularly welcome the wireless high-speed connectivity that is now a feature in all of the Hilton's restaurant and lobby areas. As spacious as the sleeping rooms are, the ability to move out of one's own room and work in the hotel's public areas can, for a long-term visitor, spell the difference between "cabin fever" and a comfortable stay.

Given these guest perks, it's not surprising that the Hilton enjoys one of Long Island's highest occupancy rates—82 percent as contrasted to a regional average in the mid-70 percent—making the Hilton Huntington Long Island's busiest hotel per square foot.

Perks at the Hilton also include an unusual guest loyalty program that is a leader for the hotel industry. Hilton Honors is the only program which is designed to allow guests to "double dip." They receive points redeemable for vacations and stays at Hilton resorts and casinos as well as frequent flyer point awards for most major airline programs. And unlike many other loyalty programs, each and every guest is eligible right from the first stay. All a guest need do is sign up for the free program at the time of check in.

NEW! ATRIUM GARDEN CAFÉ IS AVAILABLE AS A UNIQUE ALTERNATIVE TO TRADITIONAL, PRIVATE SETTINGS.

INNOVATIVE AND DYNAMIC MULTIFUNCTIONAL BANQUET SPACE TO MEET YOUR EVERY DREAM.

This emphasis on relationship building is also seen in the Hilton's marketing efforts toward small businesses. These smaller business are offered special rates and full use of the Hilton's meeting facilities and other amenities along with personal and business support of the hotel staff. This welcoming approach to businesses which are not yet producing extensive visits or events each year is designed to eventually add to the great number of business people who travel to Long Island frequently and call the Hilton home when they do.

Commenting on the Hilton's continual steps up to new levels of achievement, Peter Guarneiri said: "One of the attributes that has made the hotel so successful is its sheer versatility. During the week, all meeting attendees are offered personalized services with conference center facilities, while on the weekend, the hotel turns dreams into realities for our social guests." ■

THE HILTON HUNTINGTON TURNS DREAMS INTO REALITIES FOR ITS SOCIAL GUESTS.

(ABOVE) UNIQUE SETTINGS TO ACCOMODATE THE SPECIAL MOMENTS YOU WILL REMEMBER FOREVER. (RIGHT) THE HILTON HUNTINGTON OFFERS A VARIETY OF SPECTACULAR SETTINGS AS A BACK-DROP FOR THAT PERFECT PICTURE.

NATIONAL INSTITUTE FOR WORLD TRADE

On the cutting edge of today's global economy is the National Institute for World Trade (NIWT), a not-for-profit organization which provides assistance to corporations, trade and professional associations, universities and governments in meeting the challenge of an increasingly complex and rapidly evolving global marketplace.

NIWT was founded in 1986 by Spencer Ross, whose reputation for expertise in the global trade arena is so widespread that he was recently termed "Mr. Trade on Long Island" by one of the nation's largest daily newspapers. Ross, who brought to this group decades of experience in multinational corporations, continues to head NIWT. From its base in Cold Spring Harbor, NIWT has served clients as diverse as the United Nations Development Program; the U.S. Departments of Commerce, State, and Energy; New York State; several foreign governments; universities; and numerous corporations.

Programs of NIWT often stress the role of educational technology. According to Ross, the advent of the Internet affords corporations and educational entities an important tool for developing global trade skills. He cited NIWT's study for the government of Turkey which established a plan for the introduction and usage of computers in the primary and secondary school levels of that country's educational system. Another program, the Global Learning Network, links companies and universities to provide universal worldwide access to education.

NIWT HAS BEEN WORKING WITH THIS TEAM AT THE BROOKHAVEN NATIONAL LABORATORY TO RETRAIN RUSSIAN WEAPONS SCIENTISTS INTO COMMERCIAL ACTIVITY, IN A PROGRAM SPONSORED BY THE U.S. DEPARTMENT OF ENERGY.

With the collapse of the former Soviet Union and its shift from a communist to a market economy, NIWT organized the US-NIS Chamber of Commerce in 1993 and has introduced hundreds of small and mid-sized U.S. companies to these markets. As Russia's move toward economic stability realizes greater success, NIWT will be standing ready to open further opportunities for U.S. companies.

A prime organizer of conferences, seminars and special events, NIWT organized the largest international conference ever held on Long Island. GloBus98, which featured an address by U.S. Secretary of Commerce William F. Daley, attracted more than 800 attendees from more than 40 states and 20 foreign countries. Other NIWT events have dealt with trade between the U.S. and India, between Long Island and Japan, investment opportunities in China, technology on the Volga, and the future of the Panama Canal, among other topics.

A current, and particularly intriguing, consulting assignment for NIWT involves strengthening the economy of Jamaica, Queens. The goal, said Ross, is to capitalize on the area's infrastructure so that Jamaica can realize its promise as a center for international trade activity. A notable strand of this multifaceted effort is the development of an Airtrain link from Jamaica to John F. Kennedy airport. Ross stated that this long-awaited rail link will become a reality during 2003. ■

BY 2003, TRAVELERS MAY CHECK THEIR BAGS AT THE NEW LONG ISLAND RAIL ROAD TERMINAL IN JAMAICA, BOARD THE AIRTRAIN AND BE WHISKED QUICKLY TO THEIR AIRCRAFT AT JFK INTERNATIONAL AIRPORT. THIS PHOTOGRAPH SHOWS ONE SECTION OF THE AIRTRAIN ELEVATED ROADWAY NOW UNDER CONSTRUCTION.

HOSPICE CARE NETWORK

Every day of life is for living. The mission of Hospice Care Network, a not-for-profit organization, is to help patients confronting an advanced illness to maintain quality of life throughout each stage of their illness. For over a decade, Hospice Care Network's medical and nursing staff has worked with physicians in the community to provide the most highly developed palliative care to patients and their families. The care provided by Hospice Care Network (HCN) focuses on the alleviation of physical symptoms, and addresses the psychosocial and spiritual needs of the patients and families it serves. This promotes comfort and appreciation for each day of life.

HCN performs a variety of services reimbursed through Medicare, Medicaid, and most private insurance, and supported through generous contributions. Social workers help patients and their families adjust to the practical and emotional ramifications of advanced illness and end-of-life issues. Home health aides tend to patients' personal-care needs, clergy help patients and families find spiritual comfort, dietitians provide nutritional guidance, and physicians and nurses ensure that treatments address the patients' symptoms.

Bereavement care for adults and children is extended to those in the community. Hospice provides group sessions specific to age and the type of loss. HCN counselors have provided crisis intervention for schools and other organizations when tragedies cause the loss of life. A special one-day camp, Camp Hidden Heart, meets annually for children to express their grief and receive comfort through games and other play activities.

Each year, HCN cares for more patients and families than any other hospice and palliative care program in the Long Island region. However, there are many people who do not know about hospice or do not fully understand what hospice can do to help. HCN devotes a great deal of time to educating the community about end-of-life issues, palliative care, and the goals and

THE HOSPICE EXPERIENCE IS MULTI-GENERATIONAL. FAMILY MEMBERS ARE ENCOURAGED TO TAKE AN ACTIVE ROLE IN THE CARE OF THE PATIENT.

services of hospice. HCN staff contributes health columns and op-ed articles to Long Island news media and speaks with many community groups.

Professional education is a major goal of this hospice program. Each year, HCN provides internships for physicians, social workers, and nurses. For several years, HCN has also conducted an educational conference for teachers, health professionals, clergy, and others.

Hospice Care Network was founded by volunteers, and volunteers remain an integral part of the organization. Promoting the HCN mission of "Enabling persons to live with peace and dignity in a caring environment during the final stages of life," hospice volunteers serve on the board of trustees, fundraise, and provide companionship and respite to patients and families. Hospice Care Network began through the efforts of the Long Island community. It continues to grow and thrive through the efforts of this wonderful, responsive citizenry. ■

HOSPICE PATIENTS ARE ALL AGES. PROVIDING COMFORT FOR THE PATIENT, THROUGH PAIN AND SYMPTOM MANAGEMENT, IS THE PRIMARY GOAL.

TILLES CENTER FOR THE PERFORMING ARTS

Tilles Center for the Performing Arts, part of the C.W. Post Campus of Long Island University, is the region's premier concert hall. It offers highly diverse programming for adults and children and serves as the theatrical home for many of Long Island's leading cultural organizations. Described by *Newsday* as

ACTRESS/SINGER ANDREA MARCOVICCI IS ONE OF THE NUMEROUS ENTERTAINERS OF NATIONAL AND INTERNATIONAL RENOWN WHO REGULARLY RETURN TO PLAY BEFORE ENTHUSIASTIC AUDIENCES AT TILLES CENTER FOR THE PERFORMING ARTS.

"the Lincoln Center of Long Island," Tilles Center has achieved a nationwide reputation and is regarded as a model for campus-based performing arts institutions.

The world's most honored musical ensembles and soloists have performed at Tilles, as have popular artists from Broadway, Hollywood, and the worlds of jazz and cabaret, plus leading dance and opera companies representing the United States and cultures around the world. A subsidiary, Tilles Center Productions, has brought programs produced for Tilles Center to such important New York City venues as Lincoln Center, Carnegie Hall, and Symphony Space. Musica Sacra's annual New York City "Messiah" performances, a long-time holiday tradition, are co-produced by Tilles Center Productions.

Young audiences are a priority at Tilles Center: two family series introduce young people to live performances by highly acclaimed dance, music, and theater artists. Arts education, a major growth area in recent years, has been enhanced through a partnership with the prestigious Lincoln Center Institute for Arts in Education and collaborative activities with the C.W. Post Institute for Arts & Culture. These initiatives have enabled Tilles Center to

provide Long Island University students and Long Island school districts with high-caliber daytime performances that support their curricula. Study guides, in-school workshops and teacher training enrich the activities. Through these outreach activities and its public programming, Tilles Center nurtures both the audiences and the visual and performing artists of tomorrow.

Tilles Center is named for the late Long Island developer and philanthropist, Gilbert Tilles, and his wife, Rose. Mr. Tilles was founding chairman of Tilles Center's governing body, the Council of Overseers, a group which has been headed by Frank Castagna of Castagna Realty and currently is led by Jack Bransfield of Roslyn Savings Bank. The Tilles Family maintains a strong involvement, with Rose Tilles as the Council's honorary chairman, Roger Tilles as the Council's former senior vice-chairman, and Peter Tilles as founding chairman of "Swing for Kids," the highly successful annual golf and tennis tournament inaugurated to help fund Tilles Center's arts education. Tilles Center thrives through widespread support from Long Island's corporate community. Its championship helps make sure that both the adults and children of Long Island are delighted and moved by world-class entertainment. ■

Also, see related sections on Long Island University, pages 218-221, and Long Island University Public Radio Network on page 434.

MARKING ITS 20TH YEAR IN 2001, TILLES CENTER, ON THE C.W. POST CAMPUS OF LONG ISLAND UNIVERSITY, HAS BECOME LONG ISLAND'S PREMIER HALL FOR CLASSICAL AND POPULAR ENTERTAINMENT.

LONG ISLAND CONVENTION & VISITORS BUREAU AND SPORTS COMMISSION

The Long Island Convention & Visitors Bureau and Sports Commission (LICVB&SC) is the Hauppauge-based non-profit membership corporation that was designed to contribute to the economic development and the quality of life on Long Island by promoting the Nassau/Suffolk region as a world-class destination for visitors, tours, meetings and conventions, trade expositions, and sporting events as well as other related activities.

Formed in 1978, the 400-member-strong organization includes segments of the travel and tourism industry on Long Island such as accommodations, attractions, restaurants, transportation services, historic sites, and other firms and organizations which benefit from development and promotion of Long Island as a destination for the business and leisure traveler. The LICVB&SC also enjoys the membership of many allied members whose businesses are not directly related to tourism but whose products or services support the visitor/hospitality industry such as banks, accounting firms, law offices, printers, wholesalers, advertising agencies, and other professional services.

RECALLING LONG ISLAND'S GREAT GATSBY ERA, WESTBURY HOUSE, THE FORMER HOME OF THE PHIPPS FAMILY, IS ONE OF THE FINEST EXAMPLES OF GOLD COAST ARCHITECTURE ALONG LONG ISLAND'S NORTH SHORE. PHOTO BY ROBERT LIPPER, ISLAND-METRO PUBLICATIONS.

Many chambers of commerce, community organizations, arts/historic groups, and municipal agencies have joined the LICVB&SC in recognition of the importance of a strong visitor industry and its contribution to the quality of life in the region.

Tourism has been determined to be by far the largest industry on Long Island. With an economic impact of over $4.8 billion and supporting a total of close to 200,000 jobs, tourism on Long Island has no off-season and drives the region's economy. Much of this is due to an ever-expanding selection of tourist attractions that in 2000 alone saw the debut of the area's first professional baseball team, the Long Island Ducks, in brand new EAB Park in Central Islip, and the grand opening of a new, world-class aquarium, Atlantis Marine World, in Riverhead, which expects to welcome close to 800,000 visitors in its first year alone.

The LICVB&SC is designated as the official Tourism Promotion Agency by both Nassau and Suffolk counties to assist with tourism-related economic development and visitor services for the bi-county region. The LICVB&SC operates information centers on the Southern State Parkway in Nassau County and the Long Island Expressway in Suffolk County as well as on the East End at the Tanger Factory Outlet in Riverhead.

With the recent use of television commercials and the power of the Internet, where two million cyber surfers experienced the bounty and beauty of Long Island by logging on to www.licvb.com in 1999, the impact of the LICVB&SC has never been greater. In addition, with the proliferation of more hotel banquet rooms, ballroom space, and meeting and convention facilities, as well as non-traditional business meeting sites such as paddlewheel boats, airplane hangars, and water-theme and amusement parks, Long Island has never been more popular as a unique place to visit, conduct business, or host special events. ■

LONG ISLAND'S HUNDRED OF MILES OF BEACHFRONT ARE CONSTANTLY RANKED AMONG THE FINEST BEACHES TO BE FOUND IN THE WORLD.

CURATIVE HEALTH SERVICES

Hauppauge's Curative Health Services is a nationwide health services management provider dedicated to the treatment of chronic nonhealing wounds. A public company trading on the NASDAQ as CURE, it was organized more than a decade ago to offer hospitals management of outpatient treatment in an underserved healthcare sector, one which afflicts millions of people in the United States, especially those with diabetes, circulatory disorders, the elderly or immobilized, and those with various metabolic and circulatory disorders. Because of Curative Health Service's 34-state network of almost 130 hospital-based state-of-the-art Wound Care Centers®, John Prior, the company's Executive Vice President, said that "no other organization is nearly as well-suited as Curative to fulfill the large and expanding unmet needs in the area of chronic wound care."

Curative's leadership in wound care is based on the performance of its clinical pathways. Before the advent of Curative Health Services, the medical profession offered patients with chronic wounds little beyond passive treatment measures such as wound cleaning, dressing changes, and wound protection. During the decade of the 1980s, Curative pioneered the Wound Management ProgramSM, a highly focused clinical pathway that integrates all the components of care necessary to effectively diagnose and treat chronic wounds. At the same time, Curative developed effective methods for delivering wound care products and services through its growing network of wound care centers.

Curative Health Services' clinical pathway offers patients a tightly coordinated, interdisciplinary mix of clinical services. Prior explained that in this disease

JOHN PRIOR, EXECUTIVE VICE PRESIDENT, CURATIVE HEALTH SERVICES.

management model, clinicians with complementary specialties collaborate closely on each patient's therapeutic regimen. As a result, patients are afforded a single source of services and management of their condition rather than having to consult with different practitioners for each aspect of their care.

All services offered by Curative are geared toward enhancing the quality of a patient's experience, with staff members focusing on optimizing each person's ability to achieve a rapid, successful, and enduring healing outcome. This focused patient orientation has resulted in Curative having earned an overwhelming 93 percent patient satisfaction rating.

Through its research and clinical programs, Curative Health Services has served to advance the science of wound healing. Where once this serious disease was merely managed, Curative's innovative Wound Care Program has achieved a healing rate in excess of 80 percent for patients completing treatment and has spared many patients the trauma of amputation of a leg or foot. As one diabetes patient who developed a foot wound exulted: "I tried all the traditional approaches, but nothing worked until I started treatment at the Wound Care Center. My wound began healing right away, and remains completely healed. It's a terrific program." ■

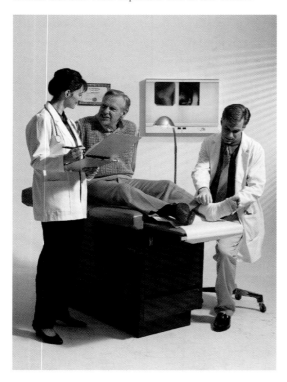

PATIENTS RECEIVE INDIVIDUALIZED TREATMENT IN STATE-OF-THE-ART WOUND CARE CENTERS.

PHOTO BY LISA MEYER, BRUCE BENNETT STUDIOS.

CHAPTER NINE

1989 AND BEYOND

9

Long Island boasts a thriving wine industry, with wineries scattered throughout the East End and their produce winning more and more praise as years pass. Photo by Scott Levy, Bruce Bennett Studios.

As it did when Long Island was first settled, the environment of the region again played an enormous role in the recovery from the crumbling of a strong defense economy.

Located so close to the business center of Manhattan, with its own full range of services to support business, and a highly educated workforce, Long Island's assets enabled the region's recovery from the recession and thrust it into a leadership role in science and technology.

The region's economic renaissance is all about the marriage of entrepreneurship and technology. For example, Computer Associates International, Inc., which moved to new headquarters in Islandia in 1992, is today the third largest software company in the world.

Cold Spring Harbor Laboratory, Brookhaven National Laboratory, and the University at Stony Brook have experienced great success in the 1990s. These large institutions are joined on Long Island by smaller research centers like the Picower Institute for Medical Research, founded in Manhasset in 1991 to do basic science research in various diseases. Together, they are the nucleus of a regional research engine.

Researchers here are finding success in their ventures. For example, in 1999, the University at Stony Brook generated $12.9 million in royalties from inventions licensed to industry, ranking it twelfth among universities in the United States. In comparison, the entire State University of New York system generated $13.5 million; Johns Hopkins generated $10.3 million; and Harvard $9.8 million.

DURING THE 1990S *AMERICAN DEMOGRAPHICS* MAGAZINE DESCRIBED LONG ISLAND AND ITS RESIDENTS IN STATISTICAL TERMS BASED ON 1992 AND 1993 CONSUMER EXPENDITURE SURVEYS FROM THE BUREAU OF LABOR STATISTICS. IN ITS ARTICLES, THE MAGAZINE POINTED OUT THAT THERE ARE 2,220 PEOPLE PER SQUARE MILE IN NASSAU AND SUFFOLK COUNTIES, RANKING THEM THE FOURTEENTH MOST DENSELY POPULATED PLACE IN THE NATION. PHOTO BY ROB AMATO, BRUCE BENNETT STUDIOS.

In the 1990s, Long Island took on a new *persona*, that of "Tech Island," a center for innovations employing new technologies in every field. Recognizing the burgeoning importance of technology, the Long Island Software and Technology Network—LISTnet—was founded in September 1997. Peter Goldsmith, founding chairman of LISTnet said, "The goals are to see Long Island recognized as a high-tech region and to help local software and technology companies grow here."

The Long Island High Technology Incubator, established at the University at Stony Brook in 1987, came into its own in the 1990s. In the years since it opened, the Incubator has successfully graduated more than twenty-five companies that, together, generate more than $100 million in annual sales revenue and provide employment to more than seven hundred people in New York State.

One of the most notable early successes for the Incubator is Renaissance Technologies. Specializing in the development of mathematical algorithms that are used in the trading of stock and commodities, Renaissance was founded by Dr. James Simons with fifteen employees. Today more than 150 are employed there and Renaissance now manages assets of over $1 billion, ranking thirty-sixth out of all privately owned companies in New York City.

THE REGION'S ECONOMIC RENAISSANCE IS ALL ABOUT THE MARRIAGE OF ENTREPRENEURSHIP AND TECHNOLOGY. PHOTO BY SCOTT LEVY, BRUCE BENNETT STUDIOS.

LOCATED SO CLOSE TO THE BUSINESS CENTER OF MANHATTAN, WITH ITS OWN FULL RANGE OF SERVICES TO SUPPORT BUSINESS AND A HIGHLY EDUCATED WORKFORCE, LONG ISLAND'S ASSETS ENABLED THE REGION'S RECOVERY FROM THE RECESSION AND THRUST IT INTO A LEADERSHIP ROLE IN SCIENCE AND TECHNOLOGY. ALONG WITH THIS UPWARD TREND CAME THE DEVELOPMENT OF NEW CORPORATE HEADQUARTERS AND NEW BUSINESS PARKS, SUCH AS JERICHO PLAZA. PHOTO BY JIM MCISAAC, BRUCE BENNETT STUDIOS.

Recently, researchers at the Incubator developed a rapid blood test that can be used to diagnose Lyme disease in a matter of minutes, rather than the several days it previously took to test for Lyme.

The plan for the University at Stony Brook to put a business incubator in the former Grumman property in Calverton, announced at the end of 2000, is considered by planners to be a giant step in the economic development of the Island's East End.

And, the young people on Long Island appear to be attuned to the future and prepared for success. Regularly named as finalists in the nation's most prestigious science competition—today sponsored by Intel; formerly sponsored by Westinghouse—in 2001, Long Island students led the country in the number of finalists.

The technology explosion has revitalized Long Island's economy, resulting in the year 2000 posting the lowest unemployment rate in twenty-six years.

And, in addition to technology, today Long Island boasts a thriving wine industry, with wineries scattered throughout the East End and their produce winning more and more praise as years pass.

The growth of Long Island is more than economic. The Island has grown, too, as a separate region, with an identity very distinct from New York City. This identity results in a sense of community that was evidenced in the 1990s, when the people of Long Island were called upon to work together to cope with some shocking events.

COLD SPRING HARBOR LABORATORY, BROOKHAVEN NATIONAL LABORATORY (PICTURED ABOVE), AND THE STATE UNIVERSITY AT STONY BROOK HAVE EXPERIENCED GREAT SUCCESS IN THE 1990S. THESE LARGE INSTITUTIONS ARE JOINED ON LONG ISLAND BY SMALLER RESEARCH CENTERS LIKE THE PICOWER INSTITUTE FOR MEDICAL RESEARCH, FOUNDED IN MANHASSET IN 1991 TO CONDUCT BASIC SCIENTIFIC RESEARCH OF VARIOUS DISEASES. TOGETHER, THEY ARE THE NUCLEUS OF A REGIONAL RESEARCH ENGINE. PHOTO BY SCOTT LEVY, BRUCE BENNETT STUDIOS.

THE IMPORTANCE OF BIOTECHNOLOGY ON LONG ISLAND IS MANIFESTED IN LEARNING CENTERS FOR CHILDREN, SUCH AS THE DNA CENTER, WHERE YOUNG PEOPLE LEARN ABOUT THE MOST FUNDAMENTAL ELEMENTS OF THE HUMAN SPECIES. PHOTOS BY BRUCE BENNETT, BRUCE BENNETT STUDIOS.

The sense of community was demonstrated for the first time on January 25, 1990, when Avianca Airlines Flight 52 ran out of fuel and crashed in Cove Neck on its way from Colombia to Kennedy Airport.

Seventy-three people died in the crash. Many of the eighty-five survivors were badly injured. Adding to the misery was the fact that Tennis Court Road, where the jet went down, was wooded and relatively isolated, with only a narrow two-lane road providing access.

Nonetheless, fire, emergency, and medical workers from across Long Island together worked to rescue the survivors and remove those who perished. Long Islanders rallied to help people alone in a strange country, many of whom were mourning the loss of loved ones.

Sadly, Long Islanders were again called upon to deal with a plane crash when TWA Flight 800, bound from JFK to Paris, went down in the bay off Center Moriches on Suffolk's South Shore. The loss of life was staggering. All 230 people on board perished. Recovery was unspeakably difficult. Since the plane had exploded over water, salvage of passengers and plane continued for months.

Long Islanders once again rallied. In a time when the questions would go unanswered for months, residents were there on the beach to comfort, to search, to help in any way they could.

Occasions like plane crashes are, thankfully, very rare. It isn't often that terror falls out of the sky onto the heads of people on Long Island. We don't expect it. Nor did we expect what happened on December 7, 1993.

That night, the 5:33 Long Island Rail Road train to Hicksville pulled out of Penn Station crowded with commuters heading home. As the train neared the Merrillon Avenue station in Garden City, a man named Colin Ferguson pulled out a gun and shot twenty-five people, six of whom died. Ferguson was eventually tried and sentenced to two hundred years in prison.

Even while mourning the loss of life, this incident gave Long Islanders another opportunity—as unwanted as it may have been—to learn about courage and self-lessness. Carolyn McCarthy, a former nurse from Garden City became a symbol of that courage. On the 5:33 to Hicksville, her husband died and her son was badly wounded. She became the spokesperson for the families of the victims. After her congressman voted against gun control, she ran successfully for his seat on a gun-control platform.

When an August 24, 1996 Pine Barrens brush fire—not an unusual event when the trees are dry in summer—could not be contained, firefighters and support services from across Long Island came to help. The fire burned for two weeks, destroying five thousand acres of Pine Barrens. But the Village of Westhampton Beach—seriously threatened by the blaze—emerged intact.

During the 1990s *American Demographics* magazine described Long Island and its residents in statistical terms based on 1992 and 1993 Consumer Expenditure Surveys from the Bureau of Labor Statistics.

The magazine looked at a 1990 population in Nassau County of 1,287,348 and in Suffolk of 1,321,977, continuing the trend of the previous decade that showed Nassau's population falling and Suffolk's growing.

In their articles, *American Demographics* pointed out the there are 2,220 people per square mile in Nassau and Suffolk Counties, ranking them the fourteenth most densely populated place in the nation. In 1993, the average Long Islander spent $5,400 to own a home. The figure included mortgage, interest, taxes, insurance, home equity loans, and lawn maintenance.

When the national average for personal insurance—excluding health insurance—was $3,510 in 1993, Long Islanders were spending an estimated $5,600. The statistics said Long Island was one of the best places in the nation to own a grocery store, an insurance agency, or any business that might appeal to middle-aged home-owners. Long Islanders spent a greater percentage of their incomes than anyone in the country for food—both at home and away from home.

Long Islanders also gave the most money to charity and spent the most on education and recreation.

No one discussing Long Island can ignore the real estate market, one of the most active in the nation. In fact, the very first recorded newspaper advertisement of real estate for sale was for local land. That ad, appearing in the *Boston News-Letter* on May 8, 1704 read:

> *"Mill, to be Let or Sold, as also a Plantation,*
> *having on it a large new Brick house, and another*
> *good house by it for a Kitchin & work house, with a*
> *Barn, Stable, etc. a young Orchard, and 20 Acres*
> *clear Land. The Mill is to be Let with or without the*
> *Plantation: Enquire of Mr. William Bradford*
> *Printer in N. York, and know further."*

At the end of 2000, the Multiple Listing Service of Long Island reported that the median price for a home on Long Island is $250,500 Nassau and $189,600 Suffolk. In the 1990s, real estate was a growth industry.

The 1990s brought a real change in the way Long Islanders are governed. In 1996, for the first time, a Nassau County Charter Revision Commission did away with the Board of Supervisors and put a County Legislature in its place. In coming years, other municipalities in both counties may be forced by the courts, as the Town of Hempstead was in 1999, to institute a councilmanic district system instead of using an at-large system to elect town board members.

But, until now, the people of Long Island have risen to all challenges, showing an ability to solve problems that began as unsolvable. It is a people who accept change, ultimately finding strength in the diversity that is Long Island.

For example, when it became obvious that the breast cancer rate on Long Island was higher than elsewhere in the nation, citizen-activists rose up and began to speak out. They lobbied government at all levels and finally won funding for a National Cancer Institute Long Island Breast Cancer Study Project, designed to conduct epidemiologic research on the role of environment plays in the occurrence of breast cancer in women who live in Nassau and Suffolk counties They formed coalitions to provide support services for people with breast cancer and other groups to raise money for research.

The decennial census of 2000 showed a combined Long Island population of 2,753,913 people, with 1,334,544 in Nassau and 1,419,369 in Suffolk. The area with the greatest growth lies east of Route 112, the

STUDENTS LEARN THE PRINCIPLES OF GENETICS AT THE DNA LEARNING CENTER. PHOTO BY BRUCE BENNETT, BRUCE BENNETT STUDIOS.

THE AGRICULTURE AND FISHING INDUSTRIES ARE STILL A VITAL PART OF LONG ISLAND'S ECONOMIC MAKEUP,
DESPITE THE ISLAND'S GROWING PREVALENCE OF THE TECHNOLOGY AND BIOTECHNOLOGY INDUSTRIES.
PHOTOS BY BRUCE BENNETT STUDIOS (ABOVE), DEBORAH ROSS (OPPOSITE, BELOW), AND SCOTT LEVY
(OPPOSITE, TOP), BRUCE BENNETT STUDIOS.

north-south road running from Port Jefferson south to Patchogue. The communities with the greatest growth were Manorville, Hampton Bays, Wading River and Middle Island in Suffolk, and New Cassel in Nassau. While New York City and the downstate areas immediately surrounding the five boroughs showed healthy growth, upstate did not. As a result, New York will lose two Congressional seats.

In the future Long Islanders will continue to deal with the weighty economic and social questions that confront us today and with new ones that will certainly arise. These issues are as diverse as the local population and include access to healthcare, balancing environmental concerns with growth, and devising new ways to finance education.

That said, however, it's worth pointing out that in several studies reported on between 1997 and 2000, *American Demographics* repeatedly predicted a rosy future for Long Island. In almost every study of income today—and in projections of future income up to the year 2017—Nassau and Suffolk Counties are in the top ten in the United States.

With such a bright forecast for the future, Long Islanders in the newest millennium seem to have the best of all worlds—prosperity in every aspect of their lives. Without having to leave Long Island, they can enjoy outstanding education, recreation and work. Like the Europeans who first settled on *'T Lange Eilandt,'* today's Long Islanders are fulfilling the destiny inherent in their environment. ■

LONG ISLANDERS LOOK INTO THE FUTURE

Asked to look ahead and speculate on what's ahead for Long Island, people at the forefront of their fields responded.

Education on Long Island, from pre-school to graduate school, will become increasingly research oriented. A national transformation of education will focus students at ever-younger ages on asking the right questions, not just providing the right answers. On Long Island, where biotechnology and software industries are thriving and shaping the economy, the educational system should provide national leadership on this new process of learning by inquiry.

At Stony Brook University, with its close alliances with Brookhaven National Laboratory and Cold Spring Harbor, undergraduate research as well as graduate research will be the bedrock of education. No longer will faculty merely pour predigested information into students; faculty and students will work together to discover new knowledge.

—Dr. Shirley Strum Kenny
President, Stony Brook University

I got into this to bring affordable baseball to my home of Long Island and this is a dream come true.

We had a spectacular first season, operating at 102 percent of capacity. More than 340,000 people attended Ducks games this year. I think that as long as the family unit is strong, the game of baseball will be strong. Our future is bright because people need affordable entertainment here. People get a lot of value for their money at our games. We bring them major league amenities in a minor league setting.

—Frank Boulton
CEO and Principal Owner, Long Island Ducks

We on Long Island are blessed with the presence of four major research institutions—Brookhaven National Laboratory, Cold Spring Harbor Laboratory, the North Shore-Long Island Jewish Health System, and the Stony Brook University—that are very actively working with the business community on Long Island and across the nation. Their basic scientific research work is complemented by their technology transfer operations. In addition, a number of economic development programs including incubators, the Small Business Development Center, and the very successful Strategic Partnership for Industrial Resurgence Program at the Stony Brook University are flourishing here. I believe that the future development of high technology will be greatly influenced by the convergence of the engineering and software fields with the life sciences. Thus, new companies and products will come about as a result of applying advances in the engineering fields to problems in other areas.

It is this convergence of technologies that has led to the establishment of the Millennium Centers for the Convergence of Technologies, being led by the four research institutions and the Long Island Association that will ensure a bright future for science, technology, and business here.

—Yakov Shamash, Ph.D.
Dean of the College of Engineering and Applied Sciences and the
Harriman School for Management and Policy at Stony Brook University

If Long Island were a freestanding state, it would be the tenth largest in the nation. It needs to cherish and enhance its universities and colleges, because these are the institutions which must educate future generations to think intelligently and appreciate beauty; to provide culture and enrichment for its residents; to create the labor force required to compete in an increasingly interconnected and competitive economic environment; and to push out the frontiers of knowledge in order to provide a healthier, more gratifying, and longer life for its many citizens. Long Island already has superb institutions of the highest quality. It needs to appreciate them more and to respect their vital importance.

—Dr. David Steinberg
President, Long Island University

IN LONG ISLAND, LIFESTYLES REMAIN CONNECTED TO THE SEA. PHOTOS BY LISA MEYER (OPPOSITE TOP),
DEBORAH ROSS (OPPOSITE BOTTOM) AND J. MCISAAC, BRUCE BENNETT STUDIOS.

LONG ISLANDERS LOOK INTO THE FUTURE

If the past can foretell the future, then the next few decades will be momentous ones in healthcare. The pace of medical discovery and technical progress which has brought astonishing progress in our ability to diagnose and treat diseases in the last two decades will be maintained or quickened. New medications and devices will be discovered. Our understanding of the mysteries of the human body and the diseases that plague it will continue to expand. Genetic knowledge will begin to tame heretofore-unconquerable diseases. Electronic communications will make it easier for health professionals and patients to stay in touch and exchange information. Health networks will develop "seamless" systems of care so patients can move easily between hospital, home ,and community resources, getting care where it is most effective and convenient. Within the North Shore-Long Island Jewish Health system, we will continue our efforts to develop high-quality programs and set new standards in healthcare.

—John S.T. Gallagher
   Chief Executive Officer, North Shore-Long Island Jewish Health System

There is a natural gravity to Long Island's high-technology industry. We have superb educational institutions, a wealth of entrepreneurial talent, and close proximity to the world's financial center. It's no coincidence that almost one-quarter of Long Island's manufacturing jobs in 1997 were in the computer and electronics industries, compared to only 11 percent of manufacturing employment statewide. And as long as we continue to welcome and nurture young, hi-tech companies, Long Island's leadership in technology will continue.

—Tomo Razmilovic
   CEO Symbol Technologies

LONG ISLANDERS LOOK INTO THE FUTURE

The future has never been brighter. Technology has opened up brave new worlds of opportunity and wealth, and transformed millions of lives, in positive, wonderful, and powerful ways. Our journey ahead will be limited only by our imagination.

—Charles B. Wang
Chairman, Computer Associates International

The cosmic question facing all healthcare today and hospitals specifically is: "How much is too much to spend on healthcare in an affluent society?" In a sense, we are victims of our success. Continued dramatic advances in healthcare technology will continue to drive the changes in hospitals. In the 20th century, treatments were developed for many of the episodic, usually contagious, often fatal diseases. As we enter the 21st century, the principal threats to public health are chronic illnesses—respiratory and circulatory diseases, for example. They generally have a relatively slow onset, are often affected by lifestyle, and require an entirely different system of healthcare delivery. Future technological changes will flow from a growing understanding of how the human body functions as we explore the extraordinary field of genomics and biogenetical science. Hospitals will continue to increase outpatient and ambulatory care on the one hand and home- and long-term care on the other.

The net result will be a continuing increase in the average severity of illness of the patients who remain in acute care hospital beds. The result will be longer life spans, an aging population, and continued upward pressure on the cost of healthcare and a concurrent growth in the need for skilled personnel able to utilize the technological advances.

—Peter Sullivan
Executive Director, Nassau-Suffolk Hospital Council

Long Island science began the new millennium with a (small) bang when Brookhaven National Laboratory's Relativistic Heavy Ion Collider went into operation in June 2000. Now the world's most powerful facility for studying the densest, hottest forms of matter, RHIC will continue to lead this exciting new branch of science well into the 21st century. What this means for Long Island is a major customer for regional technical services, a magnet for talented technical personnel, and a partner for universities, businesses, and regional hospitals.

The Laboratory's National Synchrotron Light Source, the most productive high-brightness X-ray source in the world, attracts more than 2,500 industrial, university, and government users to Long Island annually for applications that range from high-resolution cancer imaging to unraveling the mysteries of high-temperature superconductors. From biotechnology to particle physics, Brookhaven National Laboratory will maintain Long Island's science leadership in the new millennium.

—John Marburger, Ph.D.
Director, Brookhaven National Laboratory

LONG ISLANDERS IN THE NEWEST MILLENNIUM SEEM TO HAVE THE BEST OF ALL WORLDS—PROSPERITY IN
EVERY ASPECT OF THEIR LIVES. WITHOUT HAVING TO LEAVE LONG ISLAND, THEY CAN ENJOY OUTSTANDING
EDUCATION, RECREATION, AND WORK. PHOTOS BY BRUCE BENNETT (OPPOSITE TOP) AND ROB AMATO
(OPPOSITE BOTTOM AND ABOVE).

LONG ISLANDERS LOOK INTO THE FUTURE

Long Island has an outstanding cluster of academic research institutions that focus on biological and biomedical research. Coupled with an increase of state funding, an influx of biotechnology companies into our area should ensure a bright future for biotechnology on Long Island. In the next decades, Long Island will assume its place among the nation's biotechnology leaders, rivaling Silicon Valley and the Research Triangle Park in terms of discovery, revenue, and national recognition.

—Bruce Stillman, Ph.D.
   Director and CEO, Cold Spring Harbor Laboratory

I see a very bright future for Long Island. I see the quality of life maintained and enhanced. There's preservation of groundwater, acquisition of open space and, at the same time, strong attention is being paid to the enhancement of the Long Island economy. The strategic economic planning developed by the Long Island Regional Planning Board and the Long Island Association have borne rich rewards, especially in the expansion of the software industry, which has been a most suitable replacement for Long Island's prior emphasis on the defense industry.

—Lee Koppelman
   Executive Director Long Island Regional Planning Board
   Director Center for Regional Policy Studies at SUSB

IN A STUDY PUBLISHED BY *AMERICAN DEMOGRAPHICS* MAGAZINE IN THE MID-1990S, STATISTICS SAID LONG ISLAND WAS ONE OF THE BEST PLACES IN THE NATION TO OWN A GROCERY STORE, AN INSURANCE AGENCY, OR ANY BUSINESS THAT MIGHT APPEAL TO MIDDLE-AGED HOMEOWNERS, AND REPORTED THAT LONG ISLANDERS SPENT A GREATER PERCENTAGE OF THEIR INCOMES THAN ANYONE IN THE COUNTRY FOR FOOD— BOTH AT HOME AND AWAY FROM HOME. THE WEALTH OF SHOPPING OPPORTUNITIES ON THE ISLAND ATTEST TO THIS HEALTHY RETAIL ECONOMY. PHOTOS (CLOCKWISE FROM TOP LEFT) BY SCOTT LEVY, M. LEIDER, AND ROB AMATO, BRUCE BENNETT STUDIOS.

LITERARY LONG ISLAND: 1990S STYLE

As it was from the earliest days of European settlement, the riches of Long Island have attracted writers. In fact, modern fiction was born on the Long Island of F. Scott Fitzgerald.

While today's fictional Long Islanders may not look at East Egg with the longing of Jay Gatsby, the entire region still provides a rich backdrop for all sorts of novels.

Nelson DeMille, author of *The Gold Coast*, *Plum Island*, and *The Lion's Game*, among others, set several of his books either totally or partially on Long Island. He says:

> *"I find Long Island to be a rich source of material, historically, geographically, culturally, and socially. For a small area, there is an amazing amount of diversity, from tract housing to the Hamptons, from the Gold Coast to the wineries and potato farms on the North Fork. For a writer living and working on Long Island, the raw materials for a novel are all around."*

Proving his point, in his 1990 novel *The Gold Coast* DeMille described Nassau County's north shore home of his protagonist with wit and understanding:

> *"It is an area of old money, old families, old social graces, and old ideas about who should be allowed to vote, not to mention who should be allowed to own land. The Gold Coast is not a pastoral Jeffersonian democracy. The nouveau riche, who need new housing and who comprehend what this place is all about, are understandably cowed when in the presence of a great mansion that has come on the market as a result of unfortunate financial difficulties."*

A few years later, writer John Westermann looked at the same landscape as F. Scott Fitzgerald and found it still alluring. But, in Gatsby's East Egg, Westermann placed a fictional estate and mansion now used as a lock-up for police who misbehave. It is *The Honor Farm* of his book's title:

> *"Directly to the north lay marshlands, the beach, the Long Island Sound; in all other directions, the peaks of other Gold Coast hills, the roofs of other mansions, most more happily employed. A two-hole golf course was tucked away in a corner of the property, first a dog-leg right, then a dog-leg left, nine laps to make an eighteen-hole match."*

Perhaps, then, Long Island's literary landscape hasn't changed in the last decades. The change is in the perspective.

NOVELIST NELSON DEMILLE, A NATIVE, OFTEN USES LONG ISLAND AS THE SETTING FOR HIS STORIES.
IN HIS 1990 NOVEL *THE GOLD COAST* DEMILLE DESCRIBED NASSAU COUNTY'S NORTH SHORE HOME OF
HIS PROTAGONIST WITH WIT AND UNDERSTANDING: *"IT IS AN AREA OF OLD MONEY, OLD FAMILIES, OLD
SOCIAL GRACES, AND OLD IDEAS ABOUT WHO SHOULD BE ALLOWED TO VOTE, NOT TO MENTION WHO
SHOULD BE ALLOWED TO OWN LAND. THE GOLD COAST IS NOT A PASTORAL JEFFERSONIAN DEMOCRACY.
THE NOUVEAU RICHE, WHO NEED NEW HOUSING AND WHO COMPREHEND WHAT THIS PLACE IS ALL ABOUT,
ARE UNDERSTANDABLY COWED WHEN IN THE PRESENCE OF A GREAT MANSION THAT HAS COME ON THE
MARKET AS A RESULT OF UNFORTUNATE FINANCIAL DIFFICULTIES."* PICTURED OPPOSITE, A WEDDING IS HELD
AT PLANTING FIELDS, THE FORMER PRIVATE ESTATE OF WILLIAM ROBERTSON COE, WHICH NOW IS OPEN TO
THE PUBLIC WITH GARDENS AND AN ARBORETUM. PHOTO OPPOSITE BY ROB AMATO, BRUCE BENNETT
STUDIOS. PHOTO ABOVE BY GINNY DEMILLE, COURTESY NELSON DEMILLE.

LONG ISLAND OFFERS A DIVERSE RANGE OF ARTS AND ENTERTAINMENT OPPORTUNITIES. PICTURED HERE, A PUPPETEER PRESERVES AN ENTERTAINMENT ART DATING TO THE 18TH CENTURY, THE LONG ISLAND SYMPHONY ORCHESTRA PERFORMS, AND A YOUNGSTER ENJOYS A CAROUSEL RIDE AT ADVENTURELAND. PHOTOS THIS PAGE BY ROB AMATO, BRUCE BENNETT STUDIOS. PHOTO OPPOSITE, TOP BY BRIAN WINKLER, BRUCE BENNETT STUDIOS, AND BOTTOM BY BRUCE BENNETT, BRUCE BENNETT STUDIOS.

PHOTO BY BRUCE BENNETT, BRUCE BENNETT STUDIOS.

THE YOUNG PEOPLE ON LONG ISLAND APPEAR TO BE ATTUNED TO THE FUTURE AND PREPARED FOR SUCCESS. REGULARLY NAMED AS FINALISTS IN THE NATION'S MOST PRESTIGIOUS SCIENCE COMPETITION—TODAY SPONSORED BY INTEL, FORMERLY SPONSORED BY WESTINGHOUSE—IN 2001, LONG ISLAND STUDENTS LED THE COUNTRY IN THE NUMBER OF FINALISTS. YOUNG PEOPLE ON LONG ISLAND TAKE ADVANTAGE OF UNIQUE EDUCATIONAL OPPORTUNITIES IN THE OUTDOORS AS WELL, EXPLORING THE SEA THAT SURROUNDS THEM, AS WELL AS VISITING PRESERVATION AREAS SUCH AS THE ROOSEVELT BIRD SANCTUARY. PHOTOS BY M. LEIDER (OPPOSITE TOP), J. GIAMUNDO (OPPOSITE BOTTOM) AND ROB AMATO, BRUCE BENNETT STUDIOS.

LONG ISLANDERS LOOK INTO THE FUTURE

Long Island's future is one of great promise and potential. But that promise will be realized only if we commit ourselves to solving the problems that drive away so many of our young, talented people—high property taxes, the lack of affordable housing, insufficient mass transportation.

With its strong high-tech base, our economy is ready to take advantage of the continuing advances in computer technology, communications, and related fields. Our colleges and high-tech incubator programs enhance and support the research and developmental efforts of business.

While we must take advantage of growth opportunities, we must also strive to preserve our island's natural resources and ensure that all residents benefit from our prosperity.

As we prepared to enter this young century, Newsday ran a yearlong series, Long Island: Our Future. *It helped to remind us just how wondrous and resilient Long Island is and that, if we work together, there is no limit to what we can achieve*

—Raymond A. Jansen
  President, Publisher and CEO, Newsday

The internet will change the nature of doing business on Long Island. Given the diversity, talent, and entrepreneurial drive of our Long Island small businesses, I expect that long Island companies will be a global force in the future.

—Roz Goldmacher
  President and CEO, Long Island Development Corporation

I see the continuation of a healthy residential resale market for Long Island. However, I do not expect to see the same level of emotion in the marketplace. There will be a better balance of buyer and seller expectations with more inventory available and a slowing of price increases.

—Joseph E. Mottola
  CEO, Long Island Board of Realtors®

People's circumstances have changed so that they don't have as much opportunity to volunteer as they used to. It's understandable. When you look at the complexity of the jobs available for volunteers, they can seem like another job in addition to a person's "real" job and family responsibilities. Thus, in the future, not-for-profits will pay attention to this and do a better job of giving recognition to volunteers.

—Willie B. Edlow, Jr.
  President, Long Island United Way

The 21st century on Long Island will see a continuation of political trends that began in the later part of the 20th. The most notable of these will be the continuing breakup of the long-held monopoly of political power by a single party. Three factors will accelerate that trend. The first will be Long Island's increasingly heterogeneous population. A second will be New York State's continuing loss of Congressional seats after each decennial census. In 2002, we will see 31 Congressional districts reduced to 29. This will result in Suffolk residents increasingly sharing representation with residents of Nassau who, in turn, will increasingly share representation with residents of New York City. The third factor will be the change to councilmanic districts in Long Island's towns. Finally, reflecting these changes, Long Island's reputation as the last stronghold of powerful "political machines" will become an historical footnote.

—Howard Scarrow, Ph.D.
  Professor, Department of Political Science
  Stony Brook University

PHOTOS BY ROB AMATO, BRUCE BENNETT STUDIOS.

PHOTOS BY GARY FOX (ABOVE) AND LISA MEYER (BELOW), BRUCE BENNETT STUDIOS.

LONG ISLANDERS LOOK INTO THE FUTURE

The role of the educational system is to empower every child to reach his or her full potential. As people involved in education, this is our mission, our charge, our responsibility. As a society, this is our life and our future. To accomplish this, we must aggressively forge partnerships between the school communities and our local business and higher education communities. After all, we live on "tech island," so these are natural and sensible partnerships to ensure a prosperous future. Thus, all interested parties—and that should include everyone—must begin to aggressively forge these partnerships.

—Ronald C. Manning, J.D.
 President, Longwood Central School District Board of Education

Long Island is a great place to conduct business. People recognize that our Long Island community has a talented workforce and an attractive environment. I believe the future of Long Island Business is a bright one.

—Brian Cullen
Co-President, King Kullen Grocery Co., Inc.

PHOTO BY ROB AMATO, BRUCE BENNETT STUDIOS.

TOURISM IS STILL AN IMPORTANT PART OF THE ECONOMY OF LONG ISLAND, WITH BEACHES AND BEAUTIFUL HABITATS BRINGING TOURISTS TO ENJOY SUMMER'S WARM SUNSHINE NEXT TO THE OCEAN. PHOTOS BY LISA MEYER (OPPOSITE TOP), BRUCE BENNETT (OPPOSITE BOTTOM), AND ROB AMATO, BRUCE BENNETT STUDIOS.

LONG ISLANDERS LOOK INTO THE FUTURE

The Long Island public is uniquely aware of the arts. With the increasing desire to have the best in the arts close to home and more available, I anticipate the future of the performing arts on Long Island is extremely strong. I see an increasing diversity of our programs at Tilles Center and I also expect to see a proliferation of performing arts centers to better serve the whole public.

—Elliott Sroka
Executive Director, Tilles Center for the Performing Arts

Long Island has a wonderful future that's guaranteed because it has wonderful resources. First, its people, who are generally well educated, worldly, and ambitious. The people here place great value on education, so this will always be a terrific place to settle and raise children. Added to that the physical environment that is so beautiful and has quiet corners that replenish people. This is, after all, the place that is called "Bootstrap Island," with more than 84,000 companies started by residents. Long Island has proven that its spirit is entrepreneurial and flexible and, therefore, can weather any economic conditions.

—Leah S. Duane
Publisher, *Times Beacon Record* Newspapers

THOSE WHO LIVE ON LONG ISLAND ENJOY FOUR DISTINCT SEASONS. AUTUMN ANNOUNCES ITSELF WITH BRIGHT COLORS AND CRISP BREEZES, WHILE WINTER OFTEN ELANKETS THE AREA WITH SPARKLING SNOW JUST RIGHT FOR SLEDDING AND OTHER FUN ACTIVITIES. PHOTOS BY ROB AMATO (OPPOSITE) AND BRUCE BENNETT, BRUCE BENNETT STUDIOS.

PHOTO BY ROB AMATO, BRUCE BENNETT STUDIOS.

PHOTO BY BRUCE BENNETT, BRUCE BENNETT STUDIOS.

EDO CORPORATION

All the economics gurus assure us that Long Island has lost its once-mighty defense industry and must replace this economic engine of the past with newer industries. Trouble is that none of the pundits let the folks at EDO Corporation know that their day is past. So, while other defense contractors may have departed, EDO continues to grow, prosper, and innovate.

With corporate offices in Manhattan, EDO's subsidiaries are located not only on Long Island, but also in Virginia, Pennsylvania, Utah, California, and Louisiana. Over 60 percent of EDO's business serves the nation's defense industry, the remainder being divided between space and communication products and engineered materials. Here on Long Island, with business units located in North Amityville and Deer Park, fully 80 percent of the company's business focuses on national defense.

EDO has three business groups: Systems and Analysis, Electronic Systems, and Integrated Systems and Structures. Electronic Systems is located in Deer Park, and Marine and Aircraft Systems, a business unit of the Integrated Systems and Structures Group, is located in New Horizons Business Center in North Amityville.

The Electronic Systems Group along with some California business units were formerly AIL Technologies, Inc. In early 2000, EDO merged with AIL to become a major supplier of highly engineered products for governments and industry worldwide. Today, EDO's advanced electronic, electromechanical, and information systems, together with their engineered materials are products that are critical to the mission success of EDO's defense and commercial customers.

EDO DESIGNED, DEVELOPED AND IS CURRENTLY PRODUCING THE PNEUMATICALLY ACTUATED AMRAAM VERTICAL EJECT LAUNCHER FOR THE LOCKHEED MARTIN F-22 RAPTOR.

The EDO Story: A Long and Proud History Begins at the Dawn of Flight

Founded in 1925, EDO was one of the first aircraft companies in the U.S. and stands today as the second oldest aerospace company in the nation under the same continuous management. Its founder, Earl Dodge Osborn, was one of the most pivotal figures in the nation's history of aviation. His passion for flying developed in the years immediately following his service in World War I. Among Osborn's early colleagues in the fledging aviation industry were Sikorsky, Trippe, deSeversky, and Grumman. Yet, despite Osborn's critical role in the development of the new field of flight, he is among its least known pioneers.

EDO was originally formed on the shores of Flushing Bay, an area that had become a hub for the new aerospace industry. Its first product was a seaplane; however, Osborn quickly identified a new and important market in all-metal seaplane floats and began manufacturing them during the 1920s. Seaplanes supported by technologically superior EDO floats became a common sight in the years before runway areas were cleared for landings and takeoffs.

It was early in the company's history that EDO-built floats figured importantly in feats such as exploration, the beginning of transoceanic flight, and the establishment of the Great Circle Route to China. In 1930, Captain Lewis A. Yancy made the first non-stop flight from New York to Bermuda; in 1933, Admiral Richard Byrd explored the Antarctic, and Charles A. and Anne M. Lindbergh flew more than 29,000 miles surveying air routes for Pan American Airways; and, in 1935, Lincoln Ellsworth flew exploratory missions over Antarctica.

IN 1925, THE FIRST EDO BUILDING WAS LOCATED ON THE SHORE OF FLUSHING BAY IN COLLEGE POINT, N.Y. AND WAS PART OF THE EDO FACILITY UNTIL THE COMPANY MOVED TO NORTH AMITYVILLE IN 1998.

EDO also played a prominent role in World War II providing floats for the Navy's Vought OS2U Kingfisher airplane, which was catapulted from the decks of battleships and cruisers on scout and rescue missions. The Kingfisher accounted for many rescues during the war including a daring rescue of Captain Eddie Richenbacker and two other flyers who had drifted for three weeks in a life raft. With all on board the Kingfisher, the plane was too heavy for takeoff. So it taxied 40 miles on EDO floats through rough seas to complete the rescue.

Postwar Recovery and Growth

Following World War II, EDO, like many other companies, was forced to regroup and diversify. With the expansion of the passenger airline industry, the increasing availability of airports and the use of helicopters for search and rescue, the demand for seaplanes quickly diminished. To counteract this decline in business, which saw the workforce dwindle from 2,400 to less than 400, EDO formed the Electronics Division for the development, design and manufacture of underwater detecting systems and equipment. Between 1950 and 1960, EDO produced 36 different sonar systems, each answering a specific need. In 1958, the atomic submarine USS Skate was guided by EDO depth sounding sonar under the Arctic ice to surface at the North Pole. The depth sounder transducer was mounted upside down to detect holes in the ice. Following this successful mission, EDO pioneered and produced underwater ice navigation sonar for U.S. submarines.

CHARLES AND ANN LINDBERGH STAND BY THEIR LOCKHEED SIRUS EQUIPPED WITH EDO FLOATS AFTER COMPLETING THEIR 29,000-MILE FLIGHT OVER AMERICA, EUROPE, AFRICA, SOUTH AMERICA AND THE CARIBBEAN ISLANDS. THE NEWSPAPER HEADLINES THAT DAY READ, "LINDYS LAND OFF COLLEGE POINT; ENDS 29,000-MILE WORLD FLIGHT." THE PLANE NOW HANGS IN THE SMITHSONIAN MUSEUM IN WASHINGTON, D.C.

AFTER NOSING HIS WAY THROUGH THE ICE FLOWS AFTER A SURVEY FLIGHT, REAR ADMIRAL RICHARD F. BYRD'S CURTISS CONDOR SPORTING 32-FOOT EDO FLOATS IS ALONGSIDE HIS SHIP OFF LITTLE AMERICA, A U.S. BASE FOR EXPLORATION ON THE ROSS ISLAND SHELF IN ANTARCTICA.

A VOUGHT SIKORSKY OS2U KINGFISHER WITH
EDO FLOATS IS LAUNCHED FROM A SHIP'S STAR-
BOARD CATAPULT DURING WORLD WAR II WHERE
THE KINGFISHER WAS USED FOR SCOUTING AND
RESCUE MISSIONS. IN 1942, THE KINGFISHER
HELPED RESCUE 22 MEN WHO HAD BAILED OUT OR
CRASHED IN THE WATERS OFF TRUK ISLAND.

EDO continued to maintain its presence in the aircraft industry. In the mid 1950s, the company began
producing LORAN (long-range navigation) receivers
for use on ocean-going ships and later expanded this
product line to include aircraft systems that were used
by every international airline to navigate the globe.

The '50s and '60s were indeed a time of restructuring
and growth for the company. During this period, EDO
acquired a Utah-based ceramic manufacturing company
to guarantee the availability of ceramic transducers
for their sonar equipment. They established EDO
Commercial Corporation to continue the marketing of
seaplane floats and aircraft loran systems. In late 1969,
EDO also acquired Fiber Science, a then California-based
company that was later moved to Utah. One of the core
products of Fiber Science was and still is composite water
and waste tanks that are used by commercial airlines.

EDO also played a critical role in the success of the
first Apollo moon landing when EDO probes, attached
to the landing pads of NASA's lunar excursion module,
were the first objects to actually touch the surface of
the moon. The company has come full circle from its
involvement in the development of that first lunar module with the appointment last year of Neil A. Armstrong
as chairman of the board. Armstrong, of course, is the
astronaut who participated in the first moon landing,
and has since become a businessman prominent on the
national scene. He held the chairman's post at AIL prior
to being named EDO's board chairman.

In the 1970s and 1980s, EDO established two new
product lines that today are core businesses for the
company: airborne mine countermeasure systems, and
aircraft stores suspension and release equipment.
In 1971, the Chief of Naval Operations Admiral
Zumwalt ordered that future mine clearance operations
would be performed by helicopter-towed systems and
not by minesweeping ships. EDO's MK 105 minesweeping system was first used to clear mines in Vietnam's
Haiphong Harbor in 1973. Since that time, the MK 105
has been successfully employed in every U.S. mine
clearing operation including Desert Storm.

The design and production of aircraft suspension
and release mechanisms fittingly began with a contract
from Long Island's Grumman Aerospace for the MX-611
Jettison Release Mechanism for the Navy's F-14 Tomcat.
In the late 1970s, EDO won a worldwide competition to
develop and produce bomb rack units for the Tornado
fighter/bomber, which is the primary military airplane for
Germany and Italy. In the 1980s, the company received
a large contract from McDonnell Douglas for the
BRU-46/47 bomb rack units for the F-15E Eagle. Both
the Tornado and the F-15E flew many missions in
Desert Storm and in Kosovo conflict. And in the
1990s, EDO began the development of the LAU-142/A
AMRAAM Vertical Eject Launcher for the F-22 Raptor
for Lockheed Martin, which is in production today.

EDO SENSING PROBES CAN BE SEEN PROTRUDING
FROM THE LANDING PODS OF THE LUNAR
EXCURSION MODULE OR LEM AS IT APPROACHES
THE MOON IN 1969. THE PROBES CONTACT WITH
THE MOON'S SURFACE WERE THE FIRST INDICATION
OF THE ARRIVAL OF THE ASTRONAUTS. THE SENSING
PROBE WAS THE LAST LEM SUBCONTRACT AWARDED
BY GRUMMAN.

The AIL Story: One of Long Island's Anchor Companies Merges With EDO

The roots of AIL lay in meeting the nation's urgent needs during World War II. To combat German submarines, the federal government commissioned a group of scientists to develop a system for detecting U-Boats. The group met this challenge with a breakthrough system called the Magnetic Airborne Detector (MAD). The system went into production in 1942 and helped to turn the tide of the battle of the North Atlantic. The World War II organization that accomplished this was called Airborne Instruments Laboratory (AIL); it was the predecessor of AIL Technologies, Inc. and MAD was its first product.

Rapid response in times of national need has always been a proud part of AIL's corporate culture. In 1944, the Germans had brought into action two types of radio-guided missiles, and there was ample evidence that they were working on other weapons of this type. In mid April of that year the U.S. Navy placed an order with AIL for a high-power jammer to counter these missiles. A prototype of the new system was delivered to the Navy in just over two weeks. That commitment to rapid response continues to the present day. Shortly before the onset of Desert Storm, the U.S. Navy requested that AIL provide a new jamming capability for its EA-6B prowler aircraft. The AIL team developed, tested, and shipped new equipment to the Persian Gulf in time to support the air operations. More recently, AIL played a critical

AIL PROVIDED, AND CONTINUES TO SUPPORT AND UPGRADE, THE DEFENSIVE AVIONICS SYSTEMS ON BOARD THE B-1B BOMBER.

role in the Kosovo conflict when the company's B-IB (ALQ-161) electronic countermeasures were first deployed in combat, providing 100 percent protection for the B-IB bombers.

Diversity and creativity comprise essential aspects of AIL. Following World War II, AIL moved rapidly into peacetime scientific areas that were able to draw on the company's storehouse of defense technology. The new areas included medical instrumentation and satellite pay-loads. In the late 1950s AIL developed the Cytoanalyzer, used to analyze PAP test samples for the presence of uterine cancer. The Phonocardiotachometer, another AIL medical device, recorded fetal cardiograms and analyzed them 100 times faster than previous methods. AIL pay-loads for making atmospheric and earth measurements were aboard the NASA Topside Sounder and Skylab satellites in the 1960s and 1970s, and AIL's water vapor radiometer system has been aboard the U.S. Navy's Geosat satellite since 1998 as part of a system to pre-cisely measure subtle differences in sea surface height.

In 1993 AIL was among the first companies to receive federal government grants to assist in transitioning defense technology into the commercial marketplace. The award to AIL was for a unique gamma ray imaging product that would be employed to detect nuclear leaks.

This diversification has been built on a foundation of technology developed for the defense systems that continue to be the mainstay of the company's business. These include the Army's standard portable ground sur-veillance radar system, the electronic intelligence system that flew 3,500 missions aboard the Air Force's SR-71 Blackbird aircraft, the defensive avionics system on board the Air Force's B-1B bomber, and the tactical jamming systems on board the Navy's EA-6B Prowler and the Air Force's EF-111A Raven aircraft. Ravens equipped with AIL's tactical jamming system were the first American aircraft to penetrate Iraqi airspace during Desert Storm.

IN 1973, EDO ENGINEERS AND TECHNICIANS ASSISTED IN THE HAIPHONG HARBOR MINE CLEARING OPERATION USING THE EDO HELICOPTER-TOWED MK 105 MINESWEEPING SYSTEM. THIS PICTURE SHOWS THE DETONATION OF THE ONLY MINE FOUND TO BE STILL ACTIVE. THE INSET SHOWS THE CURRENT VERSION MK 105 BEING TOWED BY THE SIKORSKY MH-53 HELICOPTER.

KNOWN AS "THE VOICE OF THE PROWLER", AIL'S UNIVERSAL EXCITER UPGRADE PROVIDES THE RADAR AND COMMUNICATION JAMMING WAVEFORMS TO THE WORLDS PREMIER SUPPORT JAMMING PLATFORM, THE U.S. NAVY'S EA-6B.

In 1998, AIL built on its 50-year plus antenna experience with the acquisition of Dorne & Margolin, a producer of customer and value-added antenna applications. AIL's antenna product line now exceeds 1,400 designs.

Change has been a constant for AIL. Beginning with its founding by Dr. Hector R. Skifter in September of 1945 as a private corporation, AIL was acquired by Cutler Hammer in 1958, and the company became a part of Eaton Corporation when Eaton acquired Cutler Hammer in 1979. In 1988, Eaton restructured AIL as a subsidiary with its own board of directors, chaired by Neil A. Armstrong.

EDO Today

The merger of EDO and AIL has changed the face of the corporation by expanding its product base and capitalizing on the continuing and trusted relationship that the two companies have with the defense community. Additionally, EDO will expand its presence in the international market for defense as well as commercial products.

James M. Smith, a well-known and respected executive in defense and aerospace is now president and CEO of EDO. "We believe that this merger is a major step toward achieving the size necessary to compete effectively in today's business environment," Smith says. "We believe that this merger creates a company that is far

THE ADVANCED **ELINT** (ELECTRONIC INTELLIGENCE) SYSTEM ON THE **SR-71** BLACKBIRD COMPLETED OVER 3,500 MISSIONS.

AIL's L-Band Radiometer enables Skylab to measure the Earth's temperature and brightness from space.

more than the sum of its parts. Both of our companies supply high-technology, mission-critical products to strong niche markets. This creates excellent opportunities for cross marketing and should improve the productivity of our combined sales."

So, for the new, larger, EDO Corporation, it will be business as usual with some very important differences. Said Smith, "With our larger size, we expect our opportunities to participate in customers' larger programs also to increase." He offered as an example combining EDO's strengths in marine command and control and undersea sonar systems, airborne mine countermeasures, aircraft stores suspension and release equipment, and related

GammaCam™ is AIL's Portable Gamma Ray Imaging System used to detect potential and/or radiation leaks.

technologies with AIL's strengths in the design and manufacture of RF sensors and systems for defense and aerospace applications. He predicted that combining these strengths would position EDO to "address a broader range of markets and customers than ever before," and also noted that the two companies share a dedication "to the aggressive pursuit of customer satisfaction."

EDO is poised to pursue and build on its expertise while forging out in new directions. The company will continue to invest in new technologies applicable to the defense and space industries, and provide critical aircraft and ship platforms for both the domestic and international defense communities. EDO will remain dedicated to future growth through both internal research and development investments, and external acquisitions of companies with complementary product lines.

The future is bright for EDO. With a major role in programs like the Joint Strike Fighter (JSF), the next generation, multi-service, multi-national fighter/bomber, the EA-6B upgrade program and new mine countermeasures programs, the potential for bringing new business to Long Island is greater than ever. EDO remains dedicated to the defense and aerospace industries while actively seeking new commercial markets. And, while pursuing these avenues, EDO will remain on Long Island. Four of their major divisions are located here: Marine and Aircraft Systems, Defense Systems, Space and Communications, and Antenna Products. As EDO grows, the facilities here will also continue to grow, maintaining the presence of a major defense supplier on Long Island. ■

LONG ISLAND COMMERCIAL BANK

Swimming against the tide of giant megamergered banking institutions, Long Island Commercial Bank evokes a bygone era; a time when people actually knew their bankers personally and when urgent financial decision making wasn't delayed by layers of home-office corporate bureaucracy. Long Island Commercial Bank is headquartered on Long Island, in Islandia, and is among Long Island's youngest financial institutions. It was chartered by the state of New York in November of 1989 and opened its doors in January of 1990.

THE HEADQUARTERS OF LONG ISLAND COMMERCIAL BANK ARE IN ISLANDIA.

The independent bank's founding chairman is Perry B. Duryea, Jr., the well-respected former speaker of the New York State Assembly. Known throughout the state, Duryea's reputation and widespread contacts served as a springboard for the new institution's success. Among the other 14 founding directors were professionals and entrepreneurs with expertise in the diverse arenas of insurance, real estate development, law, medicine, retail, and several other private sector fields. Douglas Manditch, the bank's founding president and chief executive officer, also served to position the new bank solidly within the local business and financial community. A veteran of many years in the banking industry, Manditch said, "I didn't want to work for a big bureaucratic company. I prefer to work where I can see the results of my efforts." By 2000, under Manditch's leadership, the bank had grown its assets to $333 million.

From its very beginnings, the corporate mission for Long Island Commercial Bank has been to provide superior levels of service and response to the niche market that it had set out to serve. Said Manditch: "We serve primarily privately-owned businesses and professional practices, and also accommodate the businesspeople we work with by handling their private banking needs. The bank seeks to treat every request we receive with a sense of urgency and to provide superior personal service to our customers."

Treating every customer's request with a sense of urgency is everyday business at Long Island Commercial Bank, an institution which prides itself on its ability to quickly meet a wide variety of individualized needs. Manditch explained that because of the bank's small size, "we can customize products even for smaller companies where larger banks may only be able to offer them products 'off the shelf'." Small businesses also look to Long Island Commercial Bank for lock box and currency services that their size may deny at larger banking institutions. Among the other traditional commercial lending services available to Long Island Commercial Bank customers are lines of credit, revolving credit, term loans, commercial mortgages, construction loans, and letters of credit. The bank has been particularly active in the housing sector, spurring much of Long Island's economic growth in that area through home construction loans.

DOUGLAS C. MANDITCH (LEFT), PRESIDENT AND CEO AND PERRY B. DURYEA, JR.(RIGHT), CHAIRMAN OF THE BOARD.

Responding to customer inquiries, "with a sense of urgency," is ingrained in the bank's corporate culture. Manditch personally believes that a quick "no" may be almost as valuable to a businessperson as a "yes." With superior service and urgency established company bywords, Manditch said, "we're best known for our ability to provide quick decisions to our customers."

Often that answer is yes. Manditch said that the bank's guiding philosophy is that "we will do everything we can to make a loan possible." At Long Island Commercial Bank, what this means is that loan evaluation will encompass many factors, with collateral being just one among them. The bank's officers also assess cash flow, the company history, and the character of the individual requesting the loan. Visits to the customer's business site are a typical part of the review process because, as Manditch explained, the bank "seeks to build relationships, not do single transactions."

Chartered as an independent bank, Long Island Commercial Bank plans to retain that increasingly rare status. Growth has been realized through an expansion of services and locations. In recent years the bank has expanded its branch network and now boasts six branches serving Nassau and Suffolk counties. Three new branches are scheduled to open in 2001. Other growth initiatives have arisen from the new electronic marketplace. Long Island Commercial Bank now has in place a full array of Internet-based electronic products and also offers many services through its interactive web site (www.licb.com).

While serving its customers through facilities expansion and by offering new ways in which to access

IN ADDITION TO THE BRANCH AT LI COMMERCIAL BANK'S ISLANDIA HEADQUARTERS, ADDITIONAL BRANCHES THROUGHOUT NASSAU AND SUFFOLK COUNTIES IN (CLOCKWISE FROM TOP LEFT) BABYLON, JERICHO, SHIRLEY, SMITHTOWN, AND WESTBURY (BELOW).

banking functions, Long Island Commercial Bank also explores ways in which it can serve the communities in which it does business. The bank shares its resources with institutions that serve the Long Island community. Among the many organizations which have benefited from Long Island Commercial Bank's dedication to community are YMCA; Child Council of Suffolk; the United Way; Transitional Services of New York for Long Island, Inc.; Suffolk County Coalition Against Domestic Violence; Boy Scouts; Girl Scouts, and the Christian Nursing Hospice. ∎

KOCH International LLC

KOCH International started importing classical music in a small warehouse in West Babylon, Long Island, just 14 years ago with a staff of three. Today it employs over 230 employees across North America, is headquartered in a 70,000-square-foot facility in the Harbor Industrial Park in Port Washington and is one of Long Island's Top 50 Private Companies (and has been for four years running), with regional offices in New York City, Boston, Detroit, Minneapolis, Austin, Los Angeles, San Francisco, Montreal, and Toronto.

Michael Koch, who emigrated from his native Austria to scout out opportunities for the family business (which had been started by Michael's father Franz in Austria in 1975) in America in 1987, founded the company. He decided to locate the company on Long Island, because his first employee Fred Hoefer (who lived on Long Island) recommended it.

KOCH's 70,000 square-foot North American headquarters is located in Port Washington, New York.

Koch has not regretted this decision, because in his words, "Long Island offers a great environment to live and work in, high-quality labor and skilled workers as well as easy access to New York City, the music capital of the world." He also values the proximity to the major airports— allowing his company to distribute millions of CDs every year from its Long Island distribution center.

KOCH International brings almost 1,000 new recordings to market every year, ranging from the popular to the esoteric, catering to virtually every musical taste. Its catalog showcases the Grammy-award winning Leonard Bernstein's "Arias and Barcarolles" side by side with the WWF's entrance themes; Pokemon, the biggest children's album of 1999; Broadway's *Kiss Me Kate* and cabaret star Barbara Cook; the latest Webster Hall dance compilation or DJ Mix by Keoki or Carl Cox; Loretta Lynn's first recording in over 10 years and Ricky Van Shelton; Woody Guthrie's famous Folkways recordings and punk-folk heroine Ani Difranco; Jerry Garcia and David Grisman and a host of other great artists and timeless music— grossing over $100 million in America and in excess of $200 million worldwide.

KOCH International now ranks as one of the world's three largest independent music companies with operations in eight countries—two in North America (USA and Canada) and six in Europe (Austria, Germany, Switzerland, the Netherlands, Poland, and United Kingdom). Its American recording arm, KOCH Entertainment, was ranked number two by Billboard in its 2000 mid-year industry statistics. KOCH Entertainment was formed in 1999 to house its own record labels, KOCH Records, KOCH International Classics, KOCH Jazz, and its urban imprint In the Paint. Its partnerships include the Nashville-based Audium Entertainment for country music; LA-based Moonshine Music, America's front-runner for electronica; NYC-based DRG Records, a prominent theater music imprint; as well as Shanachie and Razor & Tie Entertainment. Its diverse artist and label roster covers all genres of music—"there is nothing we don't have now—you name name it, we have it."

KOCH International's management team, seated from left to right; Tom Donovan, VP Distribution; Michael Rosenberg, President; Nick Phillips, CFO; Elizabeth Jones, Executive Vice President, standing from left to right; Nancy Young, Senior VP Human Resources & Administration; Rich Waters, Controller; Brenda Place, Director Marketing; Michael Koch, CEO; John Toney, VP Sales; Vincent Luciani, VP Information Technology; Cheryl Milman, Director Operations.

KOCH International has strategically positioned itself to close the gap between the major multinationals and the small, but vibrant independent record labels which spring up almost every day and blaze the trail for new music. KOCH International had revolutionized independent music distribution when it became America's first national independent distributor in 1991, replacing the previous system of regional distribution. The company was also the first to adopt a central fulfillment model, servicing the entire North American continent from its Long Island distribution center from inception to this day. The resulting efficiencies contributed to the company's rapid ascent. Subsequently, *Inc.* magazine named KOCH International one of America's 500 fastest-growing private companies and Michael Koch was named Entrepreneur of the Year by the Long Island chapter in 1995.

Steady growth, permanent service improvement, and expanding business fields may have changed the face of KOCH International. However, the company has stayed true to its philosophy. "Our development would never have been imaginable without entrepreneurial spirit, creativity, innovation, and the steady strive for musical and technological excellence on behalf of our artists, labels, and customers," Michael Koch remarks. As the company enters the new millennium, it will continue to thrive and expand by employing its founding principles.

KOCH International is proud of its link to Long Island and is active in community and organizational activities. In 2000, Michael Koch was honored with the American Heart Association's District Leadership Award.

"AMADEUS," KOCH'S PATENTED ROBOT PICKING MACHINE, AT WORK IN THE KOCH WAREHOUSE.

Additionally, the company has made major contributions to the Holocaust Museum in Glen Cove, sponsors the music for the annual Port Washington Harbor Festival and has received recognition from various schools and organizations for its proactive hiring practices. KOCH International continues to be one of the fastest-growing private companies and remains committed to beautiful Long Island as a great place to work and live. ∎

MICHAEL KOCH, THE CEO OF KOCH AMERICA, AT WORK IN HIS LONG ISLAND OFFICE.

GENERAL SEMICONDUCTOR, INC.

General Semiconductor, Inc., may not be a household name, but it plays a major role in the lives of consumers on Long Island and throughout the world. As a leading manufacturer of discrete semiconductor components, General Semiconductor's products help power a wide range of consumer products, from televisions, dishwashers, and camcorders, to automobiles, alarm systems, and exercise equipment.

"We're fond of saying that we power the products that empower your life," says Ronald A. Ostertag, chairman, president, and CEO of General Semiconductor. "Without the rectification or the management of raw power as supplied by power generating plants, it's not really in usable form. We produce the components that make it usable."

The General Semiconductor components that power consumer products include power rectifiers, transient voltage suppressors, small signal transistors, diodes, MOSFETs, and analog devices. By applying these products in the automotive, computer, telecommunications, lighting, and consumer electronics markets, General Semiconductor has grown its revenues substantially since it went public in 1997. Net sales for the year ending December 31, 2000 were $493.7 million, up from $380.0 million in 1997.

Ostertag attributes much of the company's success to its commitment to quality throughout the organization, from corporate headquarters in Melville, New York, to its manufacturing facilities in Taiwan, China, France, Germany, Ireland, and Westbury, New York.

RONALD A. OSTERTAG, CHAIRMAN AND CEO
CORPORATE HEADQUARTERS, MELVILLE.

Strong Beginnings

General Semiconductor traces its roots to 1955 and a company named General Transistor. The business was subsequently acquired by General Instrument, and in 1960, operations were relocated to Hicksville. At this site, the company was renamed Power Semiconductor Division (PSD) and manufactured rectifiers that were used in the automotive, computer/power supply, consumer, military, and telecommunications markets.

Several early moves in the division's history helped establish it as a global company. In the early 1960s, for example, General Instrument established a manufacturing facility in Taiwan, a move to which Ostertag attributes much of the company's success. "We have established significant relationships with the computer and computer peripheral industry," he says. "The consumer goods industry has seen tremendous growth in Asia, and we have been supplying these companies since they were just starting out. So we've grown in direct relation to their success."

In 1997, General Instrument restructured the company and spun off its three divisions—semiconductor, broadband communications, and cable. The move transformed PSD into General Semiconductor, Inc. and gave the company control over its own cash flow and business strategy, including the opportunity to develop new product lines.

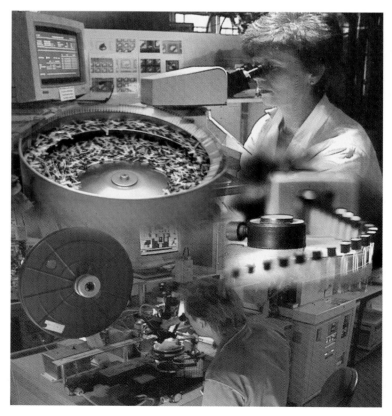

AUTOMATED REEL TO REEL ASSEMBLY AND
ELECTRICAL TESTING OF TRANSISTOR PRODUCTS.

EPITAXIAL REACTOR, WESTBURY FACILITY.

Global Reach

General Semiconductor's facilities span continents, time zones, and languages. The company has developed a sophisticated communications network that connects all six manufacturing facilities, its multitude of sales offices around the world, and the corporate office in Melville. In addition to maintaining that network, corporate head-quarters is responsible for treasury activities, taxes, risk management, human resources, new business development, corporate counsel, and investor relations/corporate communications. A new e-business division is developing the company's online capabilities, which now include automatic invoicing and data delivery.

The Westbury manufacturing facility produces the epitaxial wafers utilized in manufacturing processes overseas. The factory is ISO 9001 certified and employs more than 50 researchers, technicians, managers, and operators. A 360,000-square-foot manufacturing facility in Taipei, Taiwan, employs more than 2,000 people. It is ISO 9001 and QS-9000 certified, and has received numerous quality awards.

In 1997, General Semiconductor acquired the ITT Intermetall Discretes business in Freiburg, Germany and Colmar, France. More than 220 people work in Freiburg, in three buildings spread out over 16,854 square feet and the 72,178-square-foot factory in Colmar, France, now employs more than 400 General Semiconductor employees. The company's Macroom, Ireland plant employs approximately 800 workers in a 112,000-square-foot facility that achieved ISO 9001 certification two years ahead of schedule. The Ireland, Germany, and France facilities were also recently awarded ISO 14001 certification.

General Semiconductor's newest facility is in Tianjin, China. The company chose to follow many of its clients to the mainland by building a wholly foreign-owned 100,000-square-foot facility. The location gives General Semiconductor proximity to those customers and impor-tant cost savings due to the region's low operating costs. Today, the company employs over 1,100 people in its China factory.

Pointing to Success

The power of General Semiconductor's global reach is obvious. What is not immediately apparent is the cor-porate philosophy that drives the company's success. When Ostertag took over as president in 1990, he and members of senior management developed a set of principles to guide the company.

"We put together a list of what I like to call 'culture points'," says Ostertag. "These points make up the phi-losophy by which we manage the business, and which will, in turn, determine our success."

Ostertag believes that integrity is fundamental and permeates every aspect of the company. It involves the commitments General Semiconductor makes to its customers, shareholders, and employees. All General Semiconductor employees exhibit a passion for customer service, which includes the best quality at the lowest cost. The company is also committed to technological innova-tion, continual improvement, and teamwork. Internally there is a sense of job satisfaction and a commitment to creating an environment that fosters respect for, responsiveness to, and empowerment of employees.

Finally, a winning, competitive spirit helps ensure that General Semiconductor will remain a strong industry player for years to come. "You've got to like to win," says Ostertag. "To say that you played the game well but didn't win doesn't cut it. You've got to win and play extremely well." ■

VISITORS LOBBY, TAIWAN FACILITY.

NORTH SHORE-LONG ISLAND JEWISH HEALTH SYSTEM

The North Shore-Long Island Jewish Health System (North Shore-LIJ) is the region's powerhouse in the development of medical technology, in research initiatives, and in the delivery of patient care. Ranking as one of the largest hospital and health care systems on the East Coast, it is the result of the union of two of Long Island's major health care systems—North Shore Health System and Long Island Jewish Medical Center. North Shore-LIJ is now an 18-hospital, 5,700-bed network boasting a professional staff which includes 8,000 physicians and 6,000 nurses.

The cornerstone of North Shore-LIJ is excellence in clinical care, medical education, and research. With components ranging from community hospitals and ambulatory facilities to highly sophisticated speciality centers, North Shore-LIJ patients can remain in one system for all of their lifelong health care needs. Within the organization are three tertiary hospitals, two specialty hospitals, 13 community hospitals, three long-term care facilities, three regional trauma centers, a hospice, and a vast network of ambulatory facilities. North Shore-LIJ's specialty centers, each of which exercises leadership within its given sector, include Hillside Hospital, a pioneer in behavioral health; and Schneider Children's Hospital which draws pediatric patients from all over the world for specialized services in cancer, heart disease, digestive disorders, neurological problems, and surgery. Other specialty centers within the North Shore-LIJ system provide regional leadership in radiation oncology, cardiology, rehabilitation, high-risk pregnancy, ob/gyn services, orthopaedics, vascular disease, stroke, pain management, neurology, sleep disorders, bone marrow transplantation, urology, hearing and speech, neonatology, and the surgical, medical, and

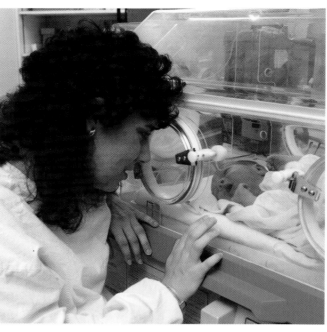

TINIEST PATIENTS ARE ASSURED THE BEST CARE THROUGH NORTH SHORE-LONG ISLAND JEWISH HEALTH SYSTEM'S STATE-OF-THE-ART TECHNOLOGY.

clinical care needs of cancer patients. The Hospice Care Network provides palliative care and bereavement services to families throughout Queens, Nassau, and Suffolk counties. The far-flung North Shore-LIJ network of hospitals includes:

• *North Shore University Hospital in Manhasset*—A tertiary care, academic, and clinical hub. Level 1 Trauma Center. Don Monti Cancer Center. Research Center, HIV/AIDS Center. Cardiology and Cardiac Surgery Center. Ambulatory Care Center. Orthopedic Center. High-risk obstetrics.

• *Long Island Jewish Medical Center*—A tertiary care center and clinical and academic hub. Joel Finkelstein Cancer Foundation Radiation Oncology Institute. Vascular Institute. Stroke and epilepsy programs.

• *Schneider Children's Hospital*—Tertiary hospital committed to comprehensive care of children. Teaching and research facility. Pediatric Urgicenter provides extended-hour pediatric care.

• *North Shore University Hospital at Syosset*—Acute care community hospital specializing in eye surgery, pain management, and laparoscopic surgery. Inpatient services and Emergency Department.

• *North Shore University Hospital at Plainview*—An acute care community hospital with same-day surgery program, full obstetrics program, and emergency department with Level 11 Trauma Center and Chest Pain Emergency Room.

• *North Shore University Hospital at Glen Cove*—Community hospital with advanced services in spinal surgery, joint replacement, and comprehensive physical rehabilitation. Oncology, obstetrics with LDRPs, general surgery, vascular surgery.

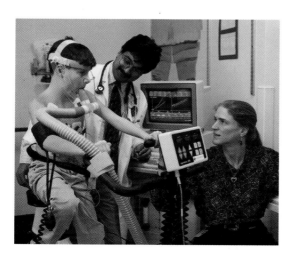

AT NS-LIJ, EARLY DIAGNOSIS AND TREATMENT FOR CHRONIC AND ACUTE MEDICAL CONDITIONS IS ACHIEVED BY THE USE OF THE MOST ADVANCED TECHNOLOGIES AVAILABLE TODAY.

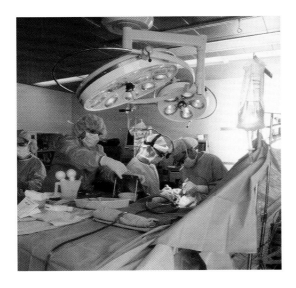

SURGEONS WITHIN THE NORTH SHORE-LONG ISLAND JEWISH HEALTH SYSTEM INCLUDE THE LATEST MINIMALLY-INVASIVE METHODS AMONG THEIR TECHNOLOGICALLY ADVANCED SURGICAL PROCEDURES.

• *North Shore University Hospital at Forest Hills*—Completely modernized. Participates in New York City 911 emergency response program. Special orthopedic, men's and women's health programs. Renovated maternity facilities.

• *Southside Hospital*—Regional Center for Physical Medicine and Rehabilitation, state-designed Brain Injury Rehabilitation Center. Advanced bloodless medicine, radiation therapy, wound, vascular, pain, and new maternity center.

• *Franklin Hospital Medical Center*—Includes a dedicated skilled nursing and short-term rehabilitation center and Adult Day Health Care program. Pediatric, women's, and family care. Certified Home Health Agency.

• *Hillside Hospital*—Psychiatric facility known for pioneering work in diagnosis, treatment, and research in mental illness. Designated by the National Institute of Mental Health as a schizophrenia study center.

• *Huntington Hospital*—Acute care facility. Specialized centers for spine surgery, pain management, and elderly and stroke patients. Don Monti Cancer Center. Women's Health Center. Cardiac Catheterization Laboratory.

• *Staten Island University Hospitals, North and South*—International reputation in treating body and brain tumors and blood vessel malformation through stereotactic radiosurgery. Regional Burn Center, Trauma Center, Nalitt Cancer Institute, and Heart Institute.

• *Peconic Health Corporation*—A group of three community hospitals with a wide range of programs serving eastern Long Island. Includes Southampton Hospital, Eastern Long Island Hospital, and Central Suffolk Hospital.

• *Peninsula Hospital Center*—Acute-care, teaching hospital with outstanding emergency services and hospital-based skilled nursing facility; sophisticated diagnostic imaging and specialty care, pediatrics, radiation oncology, cardiology, and traumatic brain injury rehabilitation.

Predominant also as a teaching facility, North Shore-LIJ maintains full academic partnerships with the New York University School of Medicine and the Albert Einstein College of Medicine. On-site education is provided for 1,300 medical students and 1,200 nursing students, along with ongoing continuing professional education for physicians and nurses.

While the focus at all units of North Shore-LIJ is patient-centered care, the system has also established its position at the forefront of high-technology medical services and clinical research. The Research Institute was recently established to integrate major research initiatives in the coming years. Groundbreaking research is currently underway in many areas such as cancer, Parkinson's disease, arthritis, and gene therapy. The medical staff also collaborates regularly in major federally-sponsored national clinical trials, and with major pharmaceutical houses and medical device manufacturers.

The North Shore-Long Island Jewish Health system is committed to quality in medical care and service to its neighbors in local communities. This commitment is reflected in unique programs that reach tens of thousands of individuals each year. Through the Department of Professional and Public Health Education, health screenings, health fairs, lectures, and workshops provide the most up-to-date information to the public.

As a leader, the North Shore-Long Island Jewish Health System is setting new standards in health care. As the century brings new challenges, the system will meet them, turning today's inspiration into tomorrow's good medicine. ■

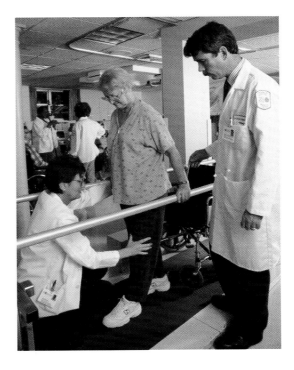

NS-LIJ's GERIATRIC PROGRAMS, AMONG THEM PHYSICAL REHABILITATION, CREATE OPPORTUNITIES FOR SENIORS TO MAINTAIN A HIGH QUALITY OF LIFE THROUGHOUT THEIR LATER YEARS.

LONG ISLAND PARTNERSHIP

Long Island's educated workforce and enviable quality of life make for a highly desirable business environment, but nobody will dispute that it's costly to do business on Long Island. Companies often need help to develop and thrive in this region, which is why the Long Island Partnership was established in 1992.

Most of Long Island's economic development agencies participate in the Partnership. The Partnership works closely with the region's utilities and governmental bodies to provide a variety of services to businesses and to help develop successful strategies for companies that are

LONG ISLAND'S CAPACITY FOR DEVELOPMENT IS AIDED BY A HOST OF PROMINENT ARCHITECTS AND CONSTRUCTION FIRMS CREATING FIRST CLASS FACILITIES. PHOTO BY ROBERT LIPPER © ISLAND METRO PUBLICATIONS.

in the process of relocation to Long Island and/or expansion on Long Island. Hundreds of local businesses have already been assisted by the Partnership in their efforts to relocate to, remain, or expand on Long Island. Whether it's assisting in applications for tax abatements, negotiating reduced utility costs, or seeking financial assistance, the goal of the Partnership is to work with Long Island's businesses to boost their competitiveness.

The result has been that Long Island's industrial sector is now better positioned to successfully compete in the increasingly global marketplace.

The Partnership functions as a regional entity, ensuring that all clients are routinely informed of any and all resources available in the region to serve their needs. Given the organization's region-wide focus and its fundamental awareness that any development impacts the total economy of the region, no preferences are made in referrals to any one jurisdiction or location. Thus, the activities and services offered by the Long Island Partnership have proved pivotal to the region's successful transition over the past decade from a nationally-known defense-related business sector to an important player in the new high-tech arena.

Some of the agencies participating in the Partnership are:

Town of Brookhaven Industrial Development Agency

One of Long Island's largest townships, the 326-square mile Town of Brookhaven is actively charting its growth as a primary site for business expansion within the region. Brookhaven is home to such high technology giants as the internationally-renowned Brookhaven National Laboratory and the State University of New York at Stony Brook, the state's flagship science and technology campus. Brookhaven has its own municipal airport (Calabro Airport), and is home to the Dowling College National Aviation and Transportation Center. Companies also have convenient access to Long Island MacArthur Airport in nearby Islip Town. An Empire Development Zone also spurs the town's enormous growth potential. Utilizing the services of the Long Island Partnership, along with its own local commission and advisory council, the Town of Brookhaven has positioned itself to fulfill its economic potential for its present residents and for generations yet to come. Call 631-451-6563.

Town of Islip Economic Development Agency

The Town of Islip is widely regarded as a business-friendly government. This is due, in large part, to the services provided by its Office of Economic Development. The Islip Industrial Development Agency provides companies with access to low cost financing and significant tax advantages.

Islip is also home to Long Island's first ever State-designated Empire Zone in Central Islip, where companies can operate in a virtually tax free environment. Islip Town is the proud owner and operator of Long Island MacArthur Airport, the gateway to the Long Island region. MacArthur services such national carriers

CORPORATE OFFICE PARKS OFFER CAMPUS LIKE SETTINGS FOR LONG ISLAND'S DIVERSE INDUSTRIAL BASE. PHOTO BY ROBERT LIPPER © ISLAND METRO PUBLICATIONS.

as Southwest, American, and Delta. Islip operates a Foreign Trade Zone at Long Island MacArthur Airport, where companies engaged in import/export trade can operate duty free. All these services, plus more, are why many nationally known companies, such as Computer Associates, Entenmann's, Tellabs, and Nortel Networks, call Islip their home. Call 631-224-5512.

Nassau County Department of Commerce and Industry/Industrial Development Agency

With a wide variety of programs designed to assist businesses, the Nassau County Department of Commerce and Industry is the central source of information for business location and development activities within the county. Additionally, it functions as the central contact for companies dealing with other agencies involved in the development process. Nassau's Industrial Development Agency serves as the primary financing conduit for major industrial projects and also is able to offer substantial incentives to qualified businesses. Call 516-571-4160.

Suffolk County Department of Economic Development

Suffolk County offers businesses proximity to regional markets and swift access to national markets, a highly skilled workforce, and access to companies and

BUSINESS DEVELOPMENT INCENTIVES HAVE CONTRIBUTED TO THE GROWTH AND EXPANSION OF LONG ISLAND INDUSTRIES CREATING A BOOMING REAL ESTATE MARKET. PHOTO BY ROBERT LIPPER © ISLAND METRO PUBLICATIONS.

institutions at the forefront in today's technology and research fields. For companies wishing to locate or expand within Suffolk County, the county's Department of Economic Development can provide access to financial assistance and incentives. The county also sponsors an Industrial Development Agency that can issue tax-exempt bonds or undertake a straight lease transaction. For company expansion projects, call 631-853-4800.

Enterprise Park-Calverton

Located in the Town of Riverhead, the Calverton Empire Zone is a 2,900-acre property that exemplifies the integration of a flexible, prestigious high-tech business environment with a world-class quality of life. It is located in close proximity to the tourist magnets of the Tanger Outlet Center, Splish Splash Water Park, and Atlantis Marine World Aquarium, and is the gateway to the many physical and cultural attractions of the East End of Long Island. The remarkable renaissance of the Riverhead region will be further stimulated by the planned development at EPCAL, including an agriculture/aqua-culture incubator for new businesses to be run by Stony Brook University. Call 631-208-0570. ∎

ENTERPRISE PARK-CALVERTON (EPCAL), A FORMER NAVAL WEAPONS INDUSTRIAL PLANT, BOASTS A COMPLETE SUPPORT INFRASTRUCTURE READY FOR MULTI-PURPOSE DEVELOPMENT.

LIGHTPATH—VOICE. DATA. INTERNET.

Lightpath, a service of Cablevision Systems Corporation, provides superior communications over a state-of-the-art fiber-optic network to businesses in New York, Connecticut, and northern New Jersey. Lightpath's advanced network technologies deliver faster transmission speeds, clearer sound quality, greater route diversity, and higher dependability—so customers can rely on one provider for all their voice, data, Internet, and video services needs. And, along with the most sophisticated communications available today, every customer gets care and attention from personal account and service representatives.

With Lightpath as the communications backbone, businesses experience a whole new level of reliable technology and customer service. Our state-of-the-art, Synchronous Optical Network (SONET)-based, all digital fiber-optic network allows companies to take advantage of the most advanced communications applications available now and in the future.

Lightpath customers can choose from a full suite of services, including: Local Dial Tone, Toll and Long Distance Calling, CENTREX, Voice Mail, Calling Cards, and Operator Services; DS1/DS3, Private Lines, Frame Relay/ATM, and Ethernet Connections; Lightpath.net Services and Business Optimum Online-Internet services for the enterprise and small/home office market, respectively.

THE HIGHLY RELIABLE, COST-EFFECTIVE SERVICE IS AVAILABLE IMMEDIATELY FROM LIGHTPATH.

And as technology changes, Lightpath is ready and able to help integrate new advances as soon as they reach the market. So wherever the future takes business, Lightpath is prepared to provide better service to Long Island companies and their customers, partners, employees, and suppliers.

Lightpath's client roster includes a diverse range of businesses from financial and academic institutions to government and healthcare organizations. Second only to Lightpath's unsurpassed growth and success has been its commitment to the Long Island community. As title sponsor of the Lightpath Long Island Classic Senior PGA Tour event, the "Classic" has raised nearly $2 million to benefit the Schneider Children's Hospital. The hospital, which opened in 1983 as the New York metropolitan area's only hospital designed exclusively for children, is a resource that provides comprehensive medical, surgical, dental, and psychiatric care for the Long Island community.

Managed Solutions. Managed Costs

Everything connecting our advanced fiber-optic network to your facilities is owned, installed, and maintained by Lightpath. Not only will you gain all the advantages of state-of-the-art services and support, but you will not experience the headaches and costs associated with creating and maintaining your own private network or working with multiple providers. Your phone bills alone may drop by as much as 30 percent.

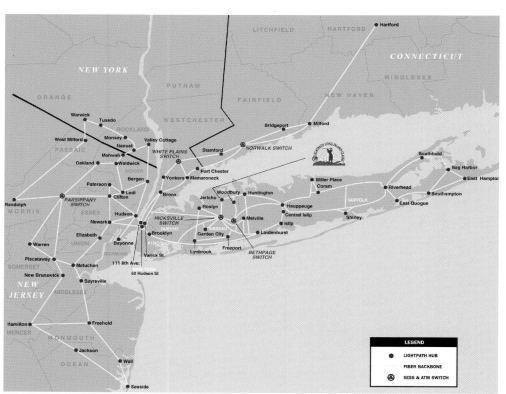

SERVING THE TRI-STATE AREA. THE LIGHTPATH INTELLIGENT NETWORK EXTENDS THROUGHOUT LONG ISLAND, NEW YORK CITY, WESTCHESTER COUNTY, NEW YORK, NORHTERN NEW JERSEY AND SOUTHERN CONNECTICUT.

One Network. One Contact. One Bill.

Lightpath's highly-trained, experienced customer service staff is available at all times, every day of the year, to help see that you get the most from your communications network. If you have a question or problem, you can make a local call to a single individual who has the experience and expertise to handle the situation. If needed, they will immediately dispatch a Lightpath technician to your location in a Lightpath truck! Issues are resolved in minutes, not days. You get one invoice for all our services, so account reconciliation is fast and easy.

The Power of Cablevision

Backed by leading management, state-of-the-art technology, and Cablevision Systems Corporation—one of the nation's leading telecommunications and entertainment companies and one of Long Island's leading businesses—Lightpath is committed to being the New York metropolitan area's premier provider of business telecommunications and community leader. To learn more about Lightpath and the communications solutions and services we provide, visit us at www.lightpath.net.

History of Lightpath

1988: Began deploying fiber optics in the marketplace.
1990: Filed with New York State Public Service Commission to provide local service.

BRUCE FLEISHER AT SCHNEIDER
CHILDREN'S HOSPITAL.

LIGHTPATH'S HEADQUARTERS IN
JERICHO, NEW YORK.

1993: Officially changed name to LIGHTPATH.
1994: Deployed initial Lucent 5ESS switch on Long Island.
1996: The Telecommunications Act signed into Law. Certified to provide local service in Connecticut.
1997: First $1 million revenue month.
1998: Certified to provide local service in New Jersey.
1999: Celebrated the direct fiber-optic connection to our network of the 500th commercial building. Became the official sponsor of the Lightpath Long Island Classic Senior PGA Golf Tournament.
2000: Westchester County awards metropolitan area voice and data network to Lightpath. Lightpath exceeds $100 million in annual revenues.

Lightpath Advantages

• The Lightpath network has over 200 SONET (Synchronous Optical Network) rings.
• Since 1999, they added nearly 200 new network elements and 44 new rings. They have over 1,000 multiplexing elements in its network today.
• They have 7,300 route miles of fiber-optic cable and are connected to over 700 buildings in the New York Metropolitan Area.
• They own and operate internal backup generators to support the network in the event of a power outage. Backup 30 amp gas generators have been deployed for disaster recovery at the customer sites in the event of a customer internal network outage.
• Their technicians proactively visit customer sites at least twice a year to inspect and ensure that the equipment meets the high standards of operation.
• They have invested over $300 million in the Lightpath Intelligent Network. ■

LONG ISLAND UNIVERSITY PUBLIC RADIO NETWORK

Through its radio stations, Long Island University's Public Radio Network (a component of National Public Radio) serves audiences from Brooklyn to Montauk. Knitting the Island together with its first network providing public radio programming, the university broadcasts jazz, news, and features of regional interest through WPBX, 88.3 FM at Southampton College and WCWP, 88.1 FM at the C.W. Post Campus. Programming originates anywhere from the Brooklyn Campus to Long Island's East End.

Wally Smith, the network director and general manager of WPBX, said that the two FM stations are operated by professional broadcasters but that students—especially those seriously pursuing careers in broadcasting—"work alongside the professional staff, assisting us in the programming, production, and operation of the stations."

The two stations simulcast, airing locally produced programming as well as offerings of the larger NPR network. Taking advantage of the university's far-flung facilities, the network has broadcast live the prestigious annual Polk Awards in journalism (which the university administers) and events like a full day of music and interviews marking the appointment of

LEGENDARY JAZZ FIGURES ARE REGULAR VISITORS TO THE **WPBX-FM** AND **WCWP-FM** STUDIOS. SHOWN IS BASSIST PERCY HEATH OF THE MODERN JAZZ QUARTET, TALKING WITH MUSIC DIRECTOR HENRY MAXWELL.

THE STATIONS OF LONG ISLAND UNIVERSITY'S PUBLIC RADIO NETWORK PRODUCE PROGRAMS FOR NATIONAL DISTRIBUTION FROM STATE-OF-THE-ART BROADCAST FACILITIES. BONNIE GRICE, HOST OF "THE ECLECTIC CAFÉ," IS SHOWN DURING A RECENT BROADCAST.

the legendary jazz pianist Dr. Billy Taylor as a University Professor. Programming from Southampton often includes discussions with writers of national and international renown who are associated with the school's graduate and undergraduate programs in writing.

More than half of the network's programming is locally produced, but some is finding a national audience. Said Smith: "We expect that originating programs and features to the national network will become an ever larger sector of what we're doing." He cited as an example Jazzworks, a syndicated hookup that the Long Island University network both receives from and contributes to. The network also serves to enhance public understanding of the university's offerings. Its evolution came about, said Smith, because of the vision of University President David J. Steinberg, who "has understood the role these stations can play in outreach from the university to the communities it serves."

Underlying all programming decisions is the goal of creating and serving an Island-wide village also served by the university's other programs, a population ranging from the urban to the suburban to the rural. "In a world that is increasingly global," said Smith, "we're connecting these varied presences and people." ∎

Also, see related sections on Long Island University, pages 218-221, and Tilles Center for the Performing Arts on page 380.

ISLAND ASSOCIATES REAL ESTATE INC.

O ne of the top ranked Long Island commercial real estate brokers, Island Associates Real Estate is a full-service firm that provides professional brokerage, leasing, tenant representation, and management services for institutions, investors, developers, and retailers of commercial, retail, industrial, and multi-family properties.

A clear industry leader, Island Associates has established a singular track record, one that has the company recognized for the quality of its brokerage projects, as well as its property management and leasing services. That's because Island Associates approaches each property from the owner's perspective, providing hands-on, detail-oriented performance. The company has expertise in all aspects of commercial real estate, specializing in retail investments, leasing, and tenant representation.

As one of the region's leading real estate firms, Island Associates represents many of the country's most prestigious retailers and developers, with a concentration on properties ranging from freestanding single tenant buildings to multi-tenant anchored developments spanning community, neighborhood, power center, and downtown locations.

Island Associates actively manages more than 2.1 million square feet of commercial space throughout the New York metropolitan area and services more than 800 retail, office, and residential tenants.

Recent Long Island projects for Island Associates have included the $7.5 million sale of the former Brent City Shopping Center in Brentwood and the $9 million sale of a shopping center property in Middle Island; the establishment of a Tutor Time Child Care Learning Center into almost 11,000 square feet of space in Middle Island and Smithtown, and the representation of Adelphi University in the $4 million plus brokering of their off-campus apartments to a local investor, a transaction in which Island Associates represented both the tenant and the landlord. The company was also responsible for the

THIS **140,000**-SQOARE-FOOT SHOPPING CENTER IS A RECENT PROJECT BROKERED BY **ISLAND ASSOCIATES.**

relocation of Happiness Express, Inc., an organization that *Business Week* called the country's fastest growing small company, from Port Washington to an expanded 65,000 square foot facility in Hauppauge.

Island Associates has been particularly associated with the CVS Drug store chain and serves as that large chain's preferred broker, assisting as CVS adds new locations on the Island. Island Associates brokered locations for CVS in Franklin Square, North Babylon, Bellmore, Lindenhurst, Central Islip, Miller Place, and Holbrook, among others. Taco Bell, KFC, Checker's, and Walgreen's are among the other national corporations that access the expertise of Island Associates as they consider new or expanded locations on Long Island.

Island Associates is guided by an approach in which real estate is practiced as both an art and a science; it is through this comprehension that the company is able to create innovative and practical solutions to the objectives of each client. ∎

ONE OF THE MANY **CVS** LOCATIONS THAT **ISLAND ASSOCIATES** BROKERED THROUGHOUT THE LONG ISLAND MARKET.

ENTERPRISE INDEX

Cold Spring Harbor Laboratory
One Bungtown Road
Cold Spring Harbor, New York 11724
Phone: 516-367-8455
Fax: 516-367-8496
E-mail: pubaff@cshl.org
www.cshl.org
Founding Date: 1890
Research Institution
Pages 190-191

Computer Associates (CA)
One Computer Associates Plaza
Islandia, New York 11749
Phone: 631-342-6000
Fax: 631-342-6800
E-mail: info@ca.com
http://ca.com
Founding Date: 1976
Software for eBusiness
Pages 316-319

Contemporary Computer Services, Inc.
200 Knickerbocker Avenue
Bohemia, New York 11716
Phone: 631-563-8880
Fax: 631-563-5185
E-mail: info@ccsinet.com
www.ccsinet.com
Founding Date: 1974
High Technology
Page 345

Creative Bath Products, Inc.
250 Creative Drive
Central Islip, New York 11722
Phone: 631-582-8000
Fax: 631-582-2020
E-mail: talk2mat@aol.com
www.creativebath.com
Founding Date: 1974
Manufacturing & Distribution
Pages 308-311

Curative Health Services
150 Motor Parkway
Hauppauge, New York 11788
Phone: 631-232-7000
Fax: 631-232-9322
www.curative.com
Founding Date: 1987
Health Care
Page 382

The DeMatteis Organizations
102 E.A.B. Plaza
West Tower, 15th Floor
Uniondale, New York 11556-0102
Phone: 516-357-9000
Fax: 516-794-2448
E-mail: dematteisdevelop@aol.com
Founding Date: 1918
Real Estate, Development & Construction
Pages 182-183

DiCarlo Distributors, Inc.
1630 North Ocean Drive
Holtsville, New York 11742
Phone: 631-758-6000
Fax: 631-758-6096
E-mail: sales@dicarlofood.com
www.dicarlofood.com
Founding Date: 1963
Manufacturing & Distribution
Page 344

Dowling College
Idle Hour Boulevard
Oakdale, New York 11769-1999
Phone: 800-DOWLING
Fax: 631-589-7551
E-mail: info@dowling.edu
www.dowling.edu
Founding Date: 1955
Education
Pages 284-285

DuPont Pharmaceuticals Company
1000 Stewart Avenue
Garden City, New York 11530
Phone: 516-832-2250
Fax: 516-832-2015
Founding Date: 1969
Pharmaceutical Manufacturing
Page 346

EAB
1 EAB Plaza
Uniondale, New York 11555
Phone: 516-296-5149
Fax: 516-296-6504
www.eab.com
Founding Date: 1968
Business & Finance
Pages 322-323

EDO Corporation
1500 New Horizons Boulevard
North Amityville, New York 11701
Phone: 631-630-4000
Fax: 631-630-4182
E-mail: ggraf@edony.com
www.edocorp.com
Founding Date: 2000
High Technology
Pages 416-421

E.W. Howell Co., Inc.
113 Crossways Park Drive
Woodbury, New York 11797
Phone: 516-921-7100
Fax: 516-921-0119
www.ewhowell.com
Founding Date: 1891
Real Estate, Development & Construction
Pages 178-179

The Fala DM Group
70 Marcus Drive
Melville, New York 11747
Phone: 631-694-1919
Fax: 631-391-0680
E-mail: marketingdirector@fala.com
www.fala.com
Founding Date: 1916
Direct Mail Communications
Pages 186-187

Forest Laboratories, Inc.
500 Commack Road
Commack, New York 11725
Phone: 631-858-6030
Fax: 631-462-2794
E-mail: jodi.drubin@frx.com
www.frx.com
Founding Date: 1975
Pharmaceutical Manufacturing
Pages 334-335

The Garden City Hotel
45 Seventh Street
Garden City, New York 11530
Phone: 516-747-3000
Fax: 516-747-1414
E-mail: psmalley@gchotel.com
www.gchotel.com
Founding Date: 1874
The Marketplace
Pages 114-115

General Semiconductor, Inc.
10 Melville Park Road
Melville, New York 11747
Phone: 631-847-3000
Fax: 631-847-3236
www.gensemi.com
Founding Date: 1990s
High Technology
Pages 426-427

Godsell Construction Corp.
351 Duffy Avenue
Hicksville, New York 11801
Phone: 516-939-0280
Fax: 516-939-0288
E-mail: agodsell@optonline.net
Founding Date: 1968
Construction
Pages 336-337

Hilton Huntington
On Route 110 at 598 Broad Hollow Road
Melville, New York 11745
Phone: 631-845-1000
Fax: 631-845-1223
E-mail: bconnaghan@hiltonhuntington.com
www.hiltonhuntington.com
Founding Date: 1988
The Marketplace
Pages 374-377

Hofstra University
Bernon Hall
Hempstead, New York 11549
Phone: 516-463-6700
Fax: 516-463-5100
www.hofstra.edu
Founding Date: 1935
Education
Pages 240-241

Hospice Care Network
900 Merchants Concourse
Westbury, New York 11590
Phone: 516-832-7100
Fax: 516-832-7160
E-mail: home@hospicecarenetwork.org
www.hospicecarenetwork.org
Founding Date: 1988
Health Care
Page 379

HSBC Bank USA
452 Fifth Avenue
New York, New York 10018
Phone: 800-975-4722
us.hsbc.com
Founding Date: 1850
Business & Finance
Pages 108-109

Island Associates Real Estate Inc.
455 Sunrise Highway
West Islip, New York 11795
Hauppauge, New York 11788
Phone: 631-587-5050
Fax: 631-587-0230
E-mail: roger@islandassociates.com
www.islandassociates.com
Founding Date: 1990
Commercial Real Estate, Brokerage
    & Management (Retail, Industrial, Office)
Page 435

KeySpan Corporation
175 East Old Country Road
Hicksville, New York 11801
Phone: 631-755-6650
www.keyspanenergy.com
Founding Date: 1910
Networks
Pages 172-175

Koch International LLC
2 Tri-Harbor Court
Port Washington, New York 11050
Phone: 516-484-1000
Fax: 516-484-4746
www.kochint.com
Founding Date: 1990
Music Distribution
Pages 424-425

Lackmann Culinary Services
303 Crossways Park Drive
Woodbury, New York 11797
Phone: 516-364-2300
Fax: 516-364-9788
E-mail: mpearl@lackmann.com
www.lackmann.com
Founding Date: 1965
Food Services
Pages 340-341

Lightpath—Voice.Data.Internet
200 Jericho Quadrangle
Jericho, New York 11753
Phone: 516-803-5600
Fax: 516-803-5661
www.lightpath.net
Founding Date: 1990
Business Communications
Pages 432-433

Lloyd Staffing
445 Broadhollow Road
Melville, New York 11747
Phone: 631-777-7600
Fax: 631-777-7626
E-mail: info@lloydstaffing.com
www.lloydstaffing.com
Founding Date: 1971
Staffing/Employment Resources
Pages 338-339

Long Beach Medical Center
455 East Bay Drive
Long Beach, New York 11561
Phone: 516-897-1000
Fax: 516-897-1214
E-mail: info@lbmc.org
www.lbmc.org
Founding Date: 1922
Health Care
Page 244

Long Island Association
80 Hauppauge Road
Commack, New York 11725
Phone: 631-493-3000
Fax: 631-499-2194
E-mail: info@longislandassociation.org
www.longislandassociation.org
www.thesmallbusinessstore.com
Founding Date: 1926
Business & Finance
Pages 228-229

Long Island Commercial Bank
One Suffolk Square
Islandia, New York 11749
Phone: 631-348-0888
Fax: 631-348-0830
www.licb.com
Founding Date: 1990
Business & Finance
Pages 422-423

Long Island Convention & Visitors
Bureau and Sports Commission
330 Motor Parkway, Suite 203
Hauppauge, New York 11788
Phone: 631-951-3900
Fax: 631-951-3439
E-mail: tourism@licvb.com
www.licvb.com
Founding Date: 1979
Tourism
Page 381

Long Island MacArthur Airport
100 Arrival Avenue
Ronkonkoma, New York 11779
Phone: 631-467-3210
Founding Date: 1943
Transportation
Pages 242-243

Long Island Partnership
c/o Suffolk County Economic Development
100 Veterans Highway
Hauppauge, New York 11788
Phone: 631-853-4800
Fax: 631-853-4888
www.co.suffolk.ny.us
Founding Date: 1991
Business Development
Pages 430-431

Long Island Power Authority
333 Earle Ovington Boulevard
Uniondale, New York 11553
Phone: 516-222-7700
Fax: 516-222-9137
www.lipower.org
Founding Date: 1986
Electric Utilities
Pages 370-373

Long Island Rail Road
Jamaica Station
Jamaica, New York 11435
Phone: 718-558-8228
Fax: 718-558-8212
www.mta.nyc.ny.us
Founding Date: 1834
Transportation
Pages 116-117

Long Island University
University Center
700 Northern Boulevard
Brookville, New York 11548-1327
Phone: 516-299-2501
Fax: 516-299-2072
E-mail: Brooklyn: attend@liu.edu
        C.W. Post: enroll@cwpost.liu.edu
        Southampton: info@southampton.liu.edu
www.liu.edu
Founding Date: 1926
Education
Pages 218-221

Long Island University Public Radio Network
239 Montauk Highway
Southampton, New York 11968-4198
Phone: 631-591-7000
Fax: 631-591-7080
E-mail: wpbx@southampton.liu.edu
www.liu.edu
Founding Date: 1990s
Entertainment
Page 434

Molloy College
1000 Hempstead Avenue
Rockville Centre, New York 11571
Phone: 516-678-5000
Fax: 516-678-7295
E-mail: mharrison@molloy.edu
www.molloy.edu
Founding Date: 1955
Education
Page 288

MSC Industrial Direct
75 Maxess Road
Melville, New York 11747-3151
Phone: 516-812-2000
Fax: 516-812-1710
E-mail: robinsov@mscdirect.com
www.mscdirect.com
Founding Date: 1965
Industrial Distribution
Pages 324-325

National Institute for World Trade
PO Box 55
Cold Spring Harbor, New York 11724
Phone: 631-367-4608
Fax: 631-367-3602
E-mail: ross@niwt.org
Founding Date: 1986
Global Trade
Page 378

Newsday
235 Pinelawn Road
Melville, New York 11747-4250
Phone: 631-843-2306
Fax: 631-843-5424
E-mail: vincent@newsday.com
www.newsday.com
Founding Date: 1940
Networks
Pages 230-231

New York Institute of Technology
PO Box 8000
Old Westbury, New York 11568
Phone: 800-345-NYIT
www.nyit.edu
Founding Date: 1955
Education
Pages 272-275

North Shore-Long Island Jewish
Health System
145 Community Drive
Great Neck, New York 11021
Phone: 516-465-8000
www.northshorelij.com
Founding Date: 1997
Health Care
Pages 428-429

Northrop Grumman
South Oyster Bay Road
Bethpage, New York 11714
Phone: 516-575-5119
Fax: 516-575-2164
E-mail: onewebmaster@mail.northgrum.com
www.northrop-grumman.com
Founding Date: 1929
High Technology
Pages 232-233

Palanker Chevrolet
670 Montauk Highway
West Babylon, New York 11704
Phone: 631-422-3700
Fax: 631-422-8621
E-mail: billadkins@aol.com
www.palankerchevy.com
Founding Date: 1960
The Marketplace
Pages 326-329

P.C. Richard & Son
150 Price Parkway
Farmingdale, New York 11735
Phone: 631-843-4300
Fax: 631-843-4309
www.pcrichard.com
Founding Date: 1909
Retail
Pages 192-193

Polytechnic University
6 MetroTech Center
Brooklyn, New York 11201
Phone: 718-260-3100
Fax: 718-260-3446
E-mail: admitme@poly.edu
www.poly.edu
Founding Date: 1854
Education
Pages 110-111

Roslyn Savings Bank
One Jericho Plaza
Jericho, New York 11753
Phone: 516-942-6950
Fax: 516-942-6955
E-mail: wmullins@roslyn.com
www.roslyn.com
Founding Date: 1875
Business & Finance
Pages 112-113

Ruttura & Sons Construction Co., Inc.
165 Sherwood Avenue
Farmingdale, New York 11735
Phone: 631-454-0291
Fax: 631-454-8804
E-mail: ruttura@ruttura.com
www.ruttura.com
Founding Date: 1918
Real Estate, Development & Construction
Pages 176-177

Sbarro, Inc.
401 Broadhollow Road
Melville, New York 11747
Phone: 631-715-4100
www.sbarro.com
Founding Date: 1959
The Marketplace
Pages 276-279

Slant/Fin Corp.
100 Forest Drive
Greenvale, New York 11548
Phone: 516-484-2600
Fax: 516-484-5921
E-mail: info@slantfin.com
www.slantfin.com
Founding Date: 1949
Manufacturing
Pages 282-283

South Nassau Communities Hospital
One Healthy Way
Oceanside, New York 11572
Phone: 516-632-3000
Fax: 516-632-3799
E-mail: info@southnassau.org
www.southnassau.org
Founding Date: 1928
Health Care
Pages 222-223

Southside Hospital
301 East Main Street
Bay Shore, New York 11706
Phone: 631-968-3477
Fax: 631-968-7322
E-mail: mjsacca@aol.com
www.northshorelij.com
Founding Date: 1911
Health Care
Page 194

St. Joseph's College
Brooklyn Campus:
245 Clinton Avenue
Brooklyn, New York 11205
Phone: 718-636-6800
        866-AT-ST-JOE
Fax: 718-636-7242
E-mail: asinfob@sjcny.edu
Suffolk Campus:
155 West Roe Boulevard
Patchogue, New York 11772
Phone: 631-447-3200
        866-AT-ST-JOE
Fax: 631-447-1782
E-mail: admissions_patchogue@sjcny.edu
www.sjcny.edu
Founding Date: 1916
Education
Pages 180-181

Standard Microsystems Corporation
80 Arkay Drive
PO Box 18047
Hauppauge, New York 11788
Phone: 631-435-6000
Fax: 631-273-3123
E-mail: chipinfo@smsc.com
www.smsc.com
Founding Date: 1971
High Technology
Pages 342-343

State University of New York at Farmingdale
2350 Broadhollow Road, Route 110
Farmingdale, New York 11735
Phone: 631-420-2000
Fax: 631-420-2693
E-mail: coleyks@farmingdale.edu
www.farmingdale.edu
Founding Date: 1912
Education
Pages 184-185

Stony Brook University
Stony Brook, New York 11794
Phone: 631-689-6000
www.stonybrook.edu
Founding Date: 1957
Education
Pages 268-271

Sulzer Metco (US), Inc.
1101 Prospect Avenue
Westbury, New York 11590
Phone: 516-334-1300
Fax: 516-338-2414
E-mail: info@sulzermetco.com
www.sulzermetco.com
Founding Date: 1933
High Technology
Page 245

Sutton & Edwards Inc.
1981 Marcus Avenue, Suite E104
Lake Success, New York 11042
Phone: 516-328-6500
Fax: 516-328-6749
E-mail: info@suttonandedwards.com
www.suttonandedwards.com
Founding Date: 1969
Real Estate, Development & Construction
Pages 312-315

Symbol Technologies, Inc.
One Symbol Plaza
Holtsville, New York 11742-1300
Phone: 631-738-2400
        800-722-6234
Fax: 631-738-5990
E-mail: webmaster@symbol.com
www.symbol.com
Founding Date: 1975
High Technology
Pages 330-331

Telephonics Corporation
815 Broad Hollow Road
Farmingdale, New York 11735
Phone: 631-755-7000
www.telephonics.com
Founding Date: 1933
High Technology
Pages 234-235

Tilles Center for the Performing Arts
PO Box 570
Greenvale, New York 11548
Phone: 516-299-2752
Fax: 516-299-2520
www.tillescenter.org
Founding Date: 1980s
Entertainment
Page 380

Tilles Companies
7600 Jericho Turnpike
Woodbury, New York 11797
Phone: 516-364-1200
Fax: 516-364-1973
Founding Date: 1925
Real Estate, Development & Construction
Pages 236-237

The University Hospital and Medical Center at Stony Brook
State University of New York at Stony Brook
Stony Brook, New York 11794
Phone: 631-689-8333
www.uhmc.sunysb.edu
Founding Date: 1980
Health Care
Pages 366-369

Verizon Communications
741 Zeckendorf Boulevard, 2nd Floor
Garden City, New York 11530
Phone: 516-542-7880
        212-395-0013
E-mail: frances.l.mcdonald@verizon.com
www.verizon.com
Founding Date: 1896
Telecommunications
Pages 168-171

Wiedersum Associates, P.C. Architects
200 Motor Parkway, Suite C-14
Hauppauge, New York 11788
Phone: 631-434-7900
Fax: 631-434-7906
E-mail: wapc@i2000.com
Founding Date: 1926
Professions
Pages 224-225

BIBLIOGRAPHY

Bailey, Paul. *The Thirteen Tribes of Long Island*. West Islip, NY. Carl A. Starace. 1959.

Denton, Daniel. *A Brief Description of New-York: Formerly Called New-Netherlands*. London: Printed for John Hancock and William Bradley 1670; New York: Gowans, 1845.

Berbrich, Joan D. *Three Voices from Paumanok*. Port Washington, NY. Ira J. Friedman, Inc.1969.

Braunlein, John H. *Colonial Long Island Folklife*. Stony Brook, Long Island. The Museums at Stony Brook. 1976.

Flint, Martha Rockée. *Long Island Before the Revolution: A Colonial Study*. (originally published 1895 as *Early Long Island*). Port Washington, NY. Ira J. Friedman, Inc. 1967.

McKay, Robert A, Rossano, Geoffrey L., Traynor, Carol A, Eds. *Between Ocean and Empire: An Illustrated History of Long Island*. Northridge, CA, Windsor Publications. 1985.

Marhoefer, Barbara. *Witches, Whales, Petticoats, & Sails*. Port Washington, NY. Ira J. Friedman, Inc. 1971.

Murphy, Robert Cushman. *Fish Shape Paumanok: Nature and Man on Long Island*. Philadelphia. The American Philosophical Society. 1964.

Naylor, Natalie, ed. *Exploring African-American History*. Hempstead, NY. Long Island Studies Institute. Hofstra University. 1991.

Overton, Jacqueline B. *Long Island's Story*. Port Washington, NY. Ira J. Friedman, Inc., 1963.

Prime, Nathaniel S. *A History of Long Island: From Its First Settlement by Europeans to 1845*. New York. Robert Carter. 1845.

Sachs, Charles L. *The Blessed Isle: Hal B. Fullerton and His Image of Long Island 1897-1927*. Interlaken, New York. Heart of the Lakes Publishing. 1991.

Smits, Edward J. *Nassau: Suburbia, U.S.A.*. Syosset, NY. Friends of the Nassau County Museum. 1974.

Strong, John A. *The Algonquian Peoples of Long Island from Earliest Times to 1700*. Interlaken, N.Y.Empire State Books. 1997.

ACKNOWLEDGEMENTS

Assemblyman Steven C. Englebright

Peter Lambert, Long Island Regional Planning Board

Gaynel Stone Levine, Ph.D., Museum Director, Suffolk County Archeological Society

Peter Lambert, Suffolk County Planning Department

Patrick Calabria, Stony Brook University

Stu Vincent, *Newsday*

Gerald J. Stanonis, Librarian, Suffolk County Historical Society

The Reference Staff at Emma S. Clark Memorial Library, Setauket, New York

And most especially to:

Barbara M. Kelly, Ph.D., Director, Long Island Studies Institute at Hofstra University

Walter Broege, Executive Director, Suffolk County Historical Society

INDEX

Printed in Canada.